THE EFFECTIVE
MANAGER

This reader is part of an integrated teaching system; the selection is therefore related to other material available to students and is designed to evoke critical understanding. Opinions expressed are not necessarily those of the course team or of the University.

If you would like to study the course to which this reader relates or receive further information about Open University Business School courses, please write to:

The Customer Service Centre,
The Open University,
PO Box 222,
Walton Hall,
Milton Keynes MK7 6YY

Or telephone on 01908 653449 or 01908 652226.

THE EFFECTIVE MANAGER

Perspectives and Illustrations

edited by
Jon Billsberry

SAGE Publications
London • Thousand Oaks • New Delhi

in association with

The Open
University

SAGE Publications Ltd
6 Bonhill Street
London EC2A 4PU

SAGE Publications Inc
2455 Teller Road
Thousand Oaks, California 91320

SAGE Publications India Pvt Ltd
32, M-Block Market
Greater Kailash – I
New Delhi 110 048

British Library Cataloguing in Publication data

A catalogue record for this book is available
from the British Library.

ISBN: 978-0-7619-5111-7

Library of Congress catalog record available

Typeset by Mayhew Typesetting,Rhayader, Powys

Contents

Acknowledgements

The editor and publishers wish to thank the following for permission to use material.

Academy of Management for material from D.E. Bowen, G.E. Ledford and B.R. Nathan (1991) 'Hiring for the organization, not the job', *Academy of Management Executive*, 5.

Blackwell Publishers for material from Iain L. Mangham (1986) *Power and Performance in Organizations: An Exploration of Executive Process*, pp. 1–9.

Butterworth-Heinemann Ltd for material from R. Meredith Belbin (1981) *Why They Succeed or Fail*, pp. 1–2, 77–8, 154–8.

Cambridge University Press for material from Nigel Nicholson and Michael West (1988) *Managerial Job Change: Men and Women in Transition*, pp. 1–5.

The Economist for (1995) 'The trouble with teams', *The Economist*, 14.1.95. Copyright © 1995 The Economist.

The Free Press, an imprint of Simon & Schuster for material from Irving L. Janis and Leon Mann (1977) *Decision Making: A Psychological Analysis of Conflict, Choice and Commitment*, pp. 25–7. Copyright © 1977 The Free Press; and James G. March (1994) *A Primer on Decision Making: How Decisions Happen*, pp. 8–15. Copyright © 1994 by James G. March.

Adrian Furnham for (1993) 'Reaping the benefits of teamwork', *Financial Times*, 19.5.93.

The Controller of Her Majesty's Stationery Office for Peter Warr (1992) 'Job Features and Excessive Stress; from *Prevention of Mental Ill Health at Work*.

IPD Enterprises Ltd for material from A. Mumford (1993) *Management Development: Strategies for Action*, 2nd edition, pp. 178–91.

Judith Knelman for (1984) 'How Can I Win If You Don't Lose?', University of Toronto *Graduate*, Jan/Feb 1984.

Lexington Books, an imprint of Simon & Schuster, for material from Lawrence R. Murphy (1991) 'Prevention and Management of Work Stress; in John W. Jones, Brian D. Steffy and Douglas Bray, eds.,

Applying Psychology in Business: The Handbook for Managers and Human Resource Professionals, pp. 715–21. Copyright © 1991 by Lexington Books.

MCB University Press for S. Maddock and D. Parkin (1993) 'Gender Cultures: Women's Choices and Strategies at Work', *Women in Management Review*, 8 (2); and N.S. Rashford and D. Coghlan (1989) 'Phases and Levels of Organisational Change', *Journal of Management Psychology*, 4 (3).

John Murray (Publishers) Ltd for material from C. Northcote Parkinson (1957) *Parkinson's Law*, pp. 26–33.

Newsweek, Inc for table 'How Others See Americans', *Newsweek*, 11.7.83, p. 50. Copyright © 1981 by Newsweek, Inc.

Open University for R.J. Thompson (1992) 'Actions speak louder than words' in B784 *The Effective Manager, Resource Book: Communication*, Open University.

Penguin UK and Addison-Wesley Publishing Company, Inc for material from T.E. Deal and A.A. Kennedy (1982) *Corporate Cultures*, (Penguin Books, 1988) pp. 107–9, 112–23. Copyright © 1982 Addison-Wesley Publishing Company, Inc.

Personnel Publications Ltd for A. Mumford (1993) 'How managers can become developers', *Personnel Management*, June; C. Fletcher (1993) 'Appraisal: An idea whose time is gone?', *Personnel Management*, Sept.; Jerry Hawkins (1994) 'Taking action on harassment', *Personnel Management*, March; R. Kandola and J. Fullerton (1994) 'Diversity: more than just an empty slogan', *Personnel Management*, Nov.; Peter Herriot and Carole Pemberton (1995) 'A new deal for middle managers', *People Management*, 13.6.95; and with the author for material from Emmanuel Ogbonna (1992/3) 'Managing organisational culture: Fantasy or Reality?', *Human Resource Management Journal*, 3, 2, Winter.

Prentice-Hall for material from A.A. Huczynski and D.A. Buchanan (1991) *Organizational Behaviour: An Introductory Text*, 2nd edition, pp. 512–17.

Random House UK Ltd for material from Charles Handy (1994) *The Empty Raincoat*, Hutchinson, pp. 80–2, 104–5.

Sage Publications Ltd for material from P. Herriot and C. Pemberton (1995) *Competitive Advantage through Diversity: Organizational Learning from Difference*.

South-Western College Publishing for material from Nancy J. Adler (1991) *International Dimensions of Organizational Behavior*, 2nd edition, pp. 63–91. Copyright © 1991.

Souvenir Press Ltd for material from L.J. Peter and R. Hull (1969) *The Peter Principle: Why Things Always Go Wrong*, pp. 19–27.

Times Newspapers Ltd for Adrian Furnham (1994) 'Does Money Motivate?', *The Times*, 9.10.94. Copyright © 1994 Times Newspapers Ltd.

The University of Western Ontario for Geert Hofstede (1983) 'The Cultural Relativity of Organizational Practices and Theories', *Journal of International Business Studies*, Fall.

John Wiley & Sons, Inc for material from Stephen L. Fink (1993) 'Managing individual behavior: bringing out the best in people' in A.R. Cohen, ed., *The Portable MBA in Management*, pp. 71, 103.

Every effort has been made to trace all the copyright holders, but if any have been inadvertently overlooked the publishers will be pleased to make the necessary arrangement at the first opportunity.

Figures

Tables

1

There's nothing so practical as a good theory: how can theory help managers become more effective?

Jon Billsberry

Introduction

I remember well the first time I taught a group of managers about the motivation of staff. I was confronted by twenty very keen managers who were on the first course towards their MBA. They had received the material about a month earlier and some students had read several of the units. They had been chatting before the tutorial and did not seem happy. Steve voiced the first concerns.

'Look, I feel a bit cheated. I signed up for this course because I was told it would make me a better manager. I've read two units now and nowhere does it tell me what I should do.'

'I agree,' added John. 'It's stuffed full of theory – what use is that? I'm a manager. I've got people I have to supervise. I can't start coming out with names like Herzberg or Vroom and expect my staff to take me seriously. I'd be laughed out of the building.'

Initially, I was somewhat nonplussed by the reactions of Steve and John, although relieved that someone in the room had read the course material. In response to their comments, I stammered out something about the need to have frameworks around which to base one's decisions and about learning from the actions of others. I was rather uninspiring. However, this experience started me thinking about the role of theory for managers. Why don't we just tell managers what to do? Why does theory dominate the curricula of management courses? How can managers become better managers by studying theory? Why did Lewin (1945) say that there's nothing so practical as a good theory? In this chapter, I shall try to answer these questions.

What is theory?

I've noticed that managers tend to react in two ways to a theory. The first response is to take the theory on board unquestioningly.

'Professor So-and-So found this out, so it must be right. If I just do what he says, I'll be an excellent manager.' Alternatively, rather than embracing the theory without question, other managers disapprove of the ideas and reject it immediately. 'What a load of rubbish. It's all very well Professor So-and-So saying that, but it's all just pie in the sky. Lots of fancy ideas, but I work in the real world and these ideas aren't practical.' These positions demonstrate a misunderstanding of the purpose of theory. We use theory to generalise, to generate questions and to invite criticism. It is not meant to be a doctrine or a tenet to be followed zealously. To appreciate this better, it is important to understand what a theory is and how it is created.

Brief and Dukerich describe theory as 'a set of logically related propositions that describe and explain a range of observations' (1991: 328). This is quite a useful definition because it identifies the three key components of a theory:

- It makes a proposition or argues a point.
- It is built on a number of observations.
- It explains something.

Theories, then, are ideas that have developed over time after many observations to explain phenomena or events. This is why research is said to 'add to the body of knowledge'. Most research doesn't produce earth-shattering new ideas. Instead, it tends to examine an existing theory and produce a little bit of evidence to support or rebut it. Over time, all these research findings build up until someone is able to put all of the pieces together to develop a new theory. This illustrates another key aspect of a theory: it can never be proved to be right in all circumstances, but it can be shown to be inaccurate, inappropriate or wrong in some circumstances. Therefore, research is undertaken to test the appropriateness of particular theories across a wide range of relevant contexts. It is important to understand the difference between induction (inferring ideas from many observations) and deduction (logically valid arguments), as theories are inductive ideas that can never be proved to be universally correct. This is perhaps best illustrated with an example.

The inductivist turkey

[An] interesting if rather gruesome example of the point is an elaboration of Bertrand Russell's story of the inductivist turkey. This turkey found that, on his first morning at the turkey farm, he was fed at 9 a.m. However, being a good inductivist, he did not jump to conclusions. He waited until he had collected a large number of observations of the fact that he was fed at 9 a.m., and he made these observations under a wide variety of circumstances, on Wednesdays and Thursdays, on warm days and cold days, on rainy days and dry days. Each day he added another observation statement to his list. Finally, his inductivist conscience was satisfied and he carried out an inductive inference to conclude, 'I am always fed at 9 a.m.' Alas, this conclusion was shown to be false in no uncertain manner when, on Christmas Eve, instead of being fed, he had his throat cut. An inductive inference with true premises has led to a false conclusion. (Chalmers, 1982)

It seems that one of the turkey's mistakes was to ask the question 'what is happening?' and then to draw conclusions without understanding the context. Had the turkey asked 'why am I being fed?' or 'in what circumstances would I not be fed?', his research might have revealed his unhappy future. If another turkey were to read the inductivist turkey's theory the following January, knowing his cruel fate, how would he use the theory? His amended theory might now include the likelihood of slaughter on Christmas Eve. However, being a rather bright turkey, he first questioned how relevant the first turkey's theory was for himself. He noted that the first turkey only entered the farm in the middle of the year. He then asked the question 'why am I being fed?' His research led him to the conclusion that he was being fattened to be eaten by humans on Christmas Day. He then investigated the concept of Christmas to find that it was just one of many holidays when turkey was ritualistically consumed. His research indicated that the next such celebration was Easter. This gave him about three months to devise a plan to save himself.

He first reasoned that as the farmer feeds the turkeys daily to make them larger, only fat turkeys would be slaughtered. Therefore, he ruminated on the idea of a hunger strike. Unfortunately, he had no data to suggest that small turkeys would survive. And he couldn't conduct any long term research into the idea because he would be decorating a dining table with sage and onion between his legs before he had any results. Try as he might he could only find one way to avoid the chop. He had to escape. He waited for the cover of dark before burrowing under the wire and making a run for it. He scampered across the farmyard, over the perimeter fence, and into the wilderness. He was a free turkey.

All theories you will meet on a management course will be of an inductivist nature. Take Herzberg's two-factor theory of job satisfaction as an example (sometimes Herzberg's theory is referred to as 'motivation-hygiene' theory). Herzberg (1968) found that there tend to be two groups of factors that influence the satisfaction of workers. One set of factors, which tend to be internal or intrinsic, improves the satisfaction of people when present. He found that another set of factors, which tend to be external or extrinsic, leads to dissatisfaction. Interestingly, he found that these two sets of factors are largely independent of each other and that the removal of satisfiers doesn't cause dissatisfaction, it merely reduces satisfaction. Likewise, the removal of dissatisfiers doesn't lead to satisfaction, it merely reduces dissatisfaction. Herzberg's research added to the existing body of knowledge and it allowed him to explain the satisfaction of workers. Subsequent work by other researchers has added weight and substance to Herzberg's two-factor theory and we know that it is appropriate in very many circumstances. However, we can never prove that it is right as 'Christmas Eve' might be discovered in the next piece of research.

As Herzberg's two-factor theory is an inductive theory, how do you use it? Suppose that the second turkey had decided to examine satisfaction levels in the turkey farm, rather than the delivery of gastronomic delights. His first step would have been to apply Herzberg's theory to his own situation. He would take the satisfiers (intrinsic factors) and dissatisfiers (extrinsic factors) and try to define these factors in terms suitable for his environment. Amongst intrinsic factors he might find that his colleagues relish being first to the feeding trough when food is delivered, take pleasure from finding a quiet spot to nap in, or enjoy a good preen. These are all intrinsic factors as a third party is not involved. On the other hand, the turkey might identify that levels of dissatisfaction rise when the food is delivered late, there is not enough food, the food is of a poor quality, or fights break out. All of these are extrinsic as they involve a third party. The turkey would try to quantify the amounts and duration of satisfaction or dissatisfaction due to each factor. Finally, the turkey would write up the report to explain the satisfaction levels of turkeys on his farm, which would implicitly indicate that he had understood Herzberg's two-factor theory of job satisfaction. But what if the turkey had found a factor that ran counter to Herzberg's theory?

Imagine that the turkey had found the factors described above, but in addition had noted that the farmer's weekly washing of turkeys with water, an extrinsic factor, was a major cause of heightened levels of satisfaction. What does this mean for Herzberg's theory? Is it useless? Quite the reverse is true. Herzberg's theory gave the turkey a framework with which to analyse satisfaction levels in his own environment which has allowed the turkey to gain a good understanding of satisfaction levels, even when they contradict the theory. In writing up his research now, the turkey still demonstrates that he has understood how the theory works by describing the factors that fit with Herzberg's theory; but with his bathing caveat, he can also show an even greater understanding of how the theory can be applied in his own situation. The turkey will have shown that Herzberg's theory still applies, but that in this context – a turkey farm – the theory has to be used with caution.

The purpose of relating this fable is to illustrate how you might use a theory to demonstrate that you have understood it and to apply it to a practical situation. The first thing the turkey did was to examine the appropriateness of the theory for his own circumstances. He then used the theory to explain what might happen to him. Finally, he amended the theory to suit his own circumstances. This gave him guidance for action.

So the lessons from this discussion are as follows:

1   Theories should never be used without first considering their appropriateness to your circumstances.
2   Theories can never be proven to be correct in all situations.
3   Theories will work differently in different situations.
4   Theories should be moulded and adapted to suit your own circumstances.
5   When you reject theories, you should be able to justify why you have done so and these justifications should produce useful insights about your own circumstances and the theory.

Differences between academic and in-company research

At the start of this chapter, I related the objections of Steve and John to the use of theory in their course. The previous discussion might have helped them to understand why theory can be useful to managers. But they might counter this argument by saying, 'we don't need to explain things – that's for eccentric professors – we need skills and knowledge about how to do things.' They might mention that the course includes a section on motivation, but they are not taught what to do to actually motivate people.

These objections illustrate the difference between research carried out on behalf of organisations for business reasons, such as market research or surveys of staff attitudes to see how a new initiative will be received, and research carried out for academic reasons. As we shall see, when we look at the difference between these two types of research, it is clear that they diverge. Each one has certain characteristics because of the way in which it is used.

Imagine that a London advertising agency fears that it's losing its best staff because it's paying salaries below market rates. The Personnel Director decides to conduct some research of salaries at competitors. Through networks, she gets information on five agencies in central London and one agency in Glasgow. From these data, she sees that salary rates for top performers are about 20 per cent below the market. This prompts her to reconsider the salary structure in the organisation.

The research has several typical characteristics:

- The research was initiated in response to a particular *problem* that the organisation faced (the failure to retain high performers).
- The research was *specific* to the organisation, its location, and its staff.
- The research involved an issue that had a relatively *short time horizon*.
- And finally, the research was initiated for *practical* reasons (i.e. the Personnel Director knew how she would use the results).

Some academics might sneer at such research, but they should not. The Personnel Director used experience and common sense to determine that the data are satisfactory for her purposes and that any greater effort would be a waste of time and money (there is more on the subject of practical managerial decision making in Chapters 20 and 21).

Academic research, on the other hand, tends to have another set of characteristics:

- It tends to be initiated through *curiosity* (e.g. 'I'm interested in better understanding what satisfies people at work').
- A goal is to be able to *generalise* from the research (even when the subject is a single organisation or the analysis of an individual).
- It tends to have *long time horizons*.
- It tends to be *conceptual*.

Which of these approaches is more relevant? The answer is simple: these are two different types of research, each ideally suited to the situation in which it is being carried out. The reason for highlighting the difference is to illustrate that the research you will be reading about in your management courses is of a different nature to that which you might have experienced at work.

One of the characteristics of academic research is that much of it seeks to generalise. Herzberg's two-factor theory of motivation, for example, was carried out on a relatively small sample, but the results allowed him to generalise about the factors that satisfy or dissatisfy workers. He was able to broaden out his research to help him better understand the world in which we live and work. One of the benefits of this is, as we have seen, that Herzberg's theory is applicable and relevant to a wide range of managers in all manner of different environments – even a turkey farm.

This last sentence contains the response that perhaps I should have given to Steve and John. As an academic, I hope that the people I teach understand the world in which they live and work better and, in addition, that they develop intellectually during the course. In doing so, they will be able to adapt as the world changes, which it seems to be doing ever more quickly. In practical terms this means that when I teach motivation, I don't ask managers to individually analyse a member of their staff and dissect what motivates that person without using any theory – and then say, 'you should give Jim a pat on the back sometimes' or 'Jill needs more responsibility.' Instead, I investigate the theories and ideas underpinning motivation so that managers can understand what motivates people more generally. In this way, when they come to manage different people, they will be able to transfer the ideas and develop an understanding of the motivation of their new team.

Values

My local school has the following value statement boldly emblazoned across its front gate: 'enlightenment for all'. A noble sentiment, but one hopes that this is the goal of every school. A cynic might argue that such statements are worse than meaningless because they mask underlying problems with an aura of sublime virtue. Of course, this is not always the case, and mission, vision and value statements can be useful management tools in the right context when accompanied by congruous actions. But, one suspects, in a world characterised by soundbites and presentation skills, this is rarely the case.

There are many situations where a statement of underlying values would be genuinely enlightening. Unfortunately, in many such cases (e.g. political parties, governments, television and radio producers) where the clear exposition of the underlying values would help us put into context the message being broadcast, it is not so. The same is just as true for teaching. Many educationalists assert that their teaching is value-free. In a politically correct world, this might be thought of as a defensive declaration. But there is more to it than this, as many teachers genuinely believe that they are able to deliver a value-free curriculum. Is this possible? It might be worth looking at the Open University to illustrate the nature of the problem.

Among other goals, the Open University actively asserts that it wants both to be open to everyone who wishes to study with the university, and to treat every student equally. The goals of the university have helped to attract staff who, by and large, support these goals. The academics work in teams to produce and maintain every course and this is a further inhibition on individual values. This has an impact on the teaching material, which must not offend unduly. As a very general comment, the teaching material tends to show that different approaches might be taken to understand a particular subject. By contrasting different ideas, students can pick and choose which theories have most applicability or are most congruent with their own values. This book is a good example of the approach. It offers different perspectives on each subject covered to allow students to form their own position according to their own situation and values. Consequently, it might be argued that this book is free from the values of the course team or the editor. But this is simply not possible as there have to be choices about what subjects to cover and what perspectives to include. Furthermore, the choice of the course team or editor will always be bound by the experience, knowledge, reading and values of those making the decision.

This can cause a problem for students. If they do not appreciate the underlying value system or approach that is being adopted, it is likely that they will not fully appreciate the purpose, direction and philosophy of the course. Whereas, if they know the underlying values, they can analyse the course and adapt it to their own value systems and circumstances. So, by not coming clean about the values underpinning a course, the originators of the course can hinder students from adapting ideas and theories to their own circumstances. Clearly then, a brief description of the values used to gather together these readings should help you, the reader, determine the relevance of the ideas and theories to your own view on the world.

The original idea for this book surfaced in a course team meeting for the rewrite of *The Effective Manager*, the 'managing people' component of the Open University Business School's Professional Certificate in Management. *The Effective Manager* can be very broadly described as a course in organisational behaviour for junior and middle managers (although we know that the course has been valuable to people at all levels in organisations). The focus of the course is on managers and what they need to become more effective. It eschews strategic topics and instead concentrates on those matters which managers can influence. For example, when the course covers the topic of organisational structure it ignores the important issue of how to design an effective organisational structure. Instead, it concentrates on how an organisation's structure affects the actions of managers. The focus is specifically to help managers identify when problems they face are being caused by the organisation's structure so that they can adopt appropriate responses. The same approach is taken in this anthology: the focus is on individual managers and the ideas and theories they need to perform more effectively.

As the focus is on individual managers and how they can become more effective, an implicit value within this book is that *managers are responsible for their own actions* and have the power to control, at least to some extent, their own destiny. Managers make choices that affect both themselves and other people. One purpose of this book is to help managers to make better informed choices and to be aware of some of the possible implications and effects on others. In asserting this, another value emerges: *respect for the individual.* Being a manager does not make someone a 'better person' than someone else who is not in a managerial position. It just means that they do different jobs. Unfortunately, this point is frequently ignored by many writers and teachers. This is typified by the economic view of the organisation which has become commonplace on many MBA courses. According to this idea, the employees of organisations are referred to as 'human capital'. Implicit in such an economic approach is the impression that employees are a 'resource' or 'unit of capital' to be manipulated for the good of the organisation: they can be hired and fired so long as it can be justified as being in the best interests of the organisation. Such an approach has little respect for the concerns of individuals and possibly partly accounts for the change in psychological contracts in organisations which has resulted in greater levels of managerial anger, alienation, dissatisfaction and frustration (Herriot and Pemberton, 1995).

One reason why the articles in this book have been included is that they share an implicit respect for the individual. In addition, the articles recognise that people are different, have different needs and values, and can contribute in different ways to the organisation. This adds to the complexity of the managers' jobs because they have to think through the implications of their actions upon people holding different priorities and values. Such diversity helps the organisation in a number of ways. A diverse group of people is more likely to:

- produce innovative ideas
- understand the external market better
- avoid stagnation and decline
- avoid the dangers of 'groupthink'.

As importantly, managers open to the benefits of diversity are more likely to consider a broader range of issues and options when trying to solve problems. However, whilst this illustrates the third underlying value of this book – *diversity is a strength* – it does raise an important issue that managers must confront. With diversity can come differences of opinion, disagreements, conflict, and cliques. Consequently, unless organisations are to become factional war zones, managers need to treasure diversity and seek compromise, mutual understanding and concord. One of the most useful ways to do this is to try to put yourself in the shoes of others and to appreciate the world as they see it.

The final point that needs to be acknowledged explicitly is *the importance of assessing the contextual issues* when using management theory. As mentioned earlier, most theory is derived from empirical research. This research is set in a time and a place and additional research is undertaken to examine the extent of the generalisability of the theory. This has become increasingly important in recent years as the world has shrunk and new fads seem to circulate ever more quickly. Take the idea of quality circles. This was shown to be highly successful in Japanese car manufacturing plants, particularly in Toyota which served as the subject of countless articles. Such was the success of Toyota that the idea of quality circles (and the associated theories of total quality management, team-working, Kanban, Kaizen, continuous improvement and so on) rapidly travelled the world in the early 1980s and became the panacea for the ills of all organisations. Many organisations adopted these ideas and gained considerable success. Just as many adopted them and found them to be an unmitigated disaster. One of the problems that many organisations discovered was that what works well in one context does not automatically work well in a different context. Quality circles seem to work well in a national culture characterised by team-working and a dislike of conflict. In national cultures characterised by individualism, the introduction of quality circles often leads to heightened conflict and greater scepticism of 'newfangled' ideas. A recurring theme in the articles in this book is the need to take account of the internal and external environment and cultures before adopting new ideas.

Cultural differences in management

There were three businessmen, an American, a Frenchman and a Japanese, captured by an extremist group in Beirut. They were about to be executed when the group leader, in a final concession to Western custom, offered each man a last wish. The French manager asked if he could sing 'La Marseillaise' one final time. The Japanese manager asked if he could tape-record how he built such a successful business empire. The American asked to be shot first, 'because I don't want to have to listen to another goddamn lecture on Japanese management'. (Huczynski and Buchanan, 1991)

The selection of articles

There are two main reasons why the articles in this book have been included. The first reason for inclusion is to demonstrate that a multiplicity of *perspectives* might be taken on any particular subject. Hopefully, this will demonstrate that there are rarely any clear-cut right or wrong answers in management. In doing this, these articles highlight the need to analyse any theories that are presented to you to determine their suitability to your own circumstances. Within the debates described in this book, you should also begin to get a sense that criticism (in the sense of evaluation, appreciation and adaptation) of theories is to be encouraged.

The second reason for the inclusion of an article in the book is to *illustrate* a key idea or debate. Theories, though lively and provocative, are often discussed in the abstract or demonstrated in a specific setting. Some of the illustrative articles in this book are intended to show how the theories can be applied to, or used to explain, the jobs of managers. Theories do not simply provide managers with a course of action. Sometimes the use of a theory will give managers fresh insights into their work, or help them to see the implications of their actions. In both cases, managers become better informed about their work. As such, an idea or theory that produces this response is just as practical as an idea that gives managers clear direction for future action. Another reason for the inclusion of illustrative articles is to demonstrate that 'there is more than one way to skin a cat.' As managers, we tend to filter the world through our own experiences and knowledge. One purpose of these articles, therefore, is to broaden this experience.

Another objective of this book is to collect together short, accessible and jargon-free articles covering a wide range of subjects relevant to the jobs of managers. This book has been designed to accompany a first course in management or organisational behaviour. Consequently, the articles assume that readers have no prior knowledge of the subject. The articles are certainly not dull. Another reason for the inclusion of some of the articles is that they are provocative. A number of the articles (such as those by Maddock and Parkin, Furnham, Ogbonna, Herriot and Pemberton, and Bowen et al.) challenge commonly held theories within management theory. Not only do these articles offer a fresh perspective, but they are also likely to agitate you. They make interesting and lively reading, and I hope that they will also stimulate and enthuse you to read more broadly on management subjects.

The articles

This book is split into six parts and a postscript. Each part concentrates on a key management topic (management, motivation, organisational culture, decision making, staff development, and diversity) and some of the key debates taking place within each subject.

Part 1   Management, leadership and conflict

The first article in the main body of the book, which is entitled 'Men and women in transition' (Chapter 2), formed the introduction of Nicholson and West's book *Managerial Job Change*. In that book, the authors examine the job changes and role transitions of managers. One of their most interesting findings was that more than half of the job changes of managers were to newly created jobs. This suggests that change is widespread in the business environment and that the job of manager is continually evolving. In the piece selected here, the authors argue that change is pervasive and that stability is the exception. They also argue that this change is not just a positive opportunity for challenge, there is also a darker side. It can lead to greater uncertainty and danger, meaning that managers are under increasing pressure to update their skills and knowledge.

Whereas the article by Nicholson and West places managers' roles within the context of change, the piece by Mangham (Chapter 3) places managers' roles within the context of increasing internationalisation and globalisation. An interesting debate revolves around the issue of whether management practice is becoming similar around the world as ideas circulate. One perspective in this argument is that national cultures will always ensure that management theory is interpreted differently in different societies. The other side of the coin is that the jobs of managers are becoming increasingly alike around the globe. Whatever the case, managers are now having to deal with an increasingly diverse working environment. The internal environment is generally characterised by employees from a wider range of cultures and societies, and the external environment is similarly more diverse. This has an impact on the jobs of managers, and provides the perspective for Mangham's article, entitled 'Chocolate eggs and Chester Barnard'. The following chapter by Handy, called 'The Chinese contract' (Chapter 4), illustrates the sort of issues that might be confronted by managers when operating across cultures and societies.

In many management texts, you will often find the words 'manager' and 'leader' used as synonyms. However, when one consults the literatures on management (e.g. Fayol, Mintzberg, Drucker, Stewart) and leadership (e.g. Tannenbaum and Schmidt, Fiedler, Blake and Mouton) it is clear that these people are researching into distinctly different subjects. It seems that research into 'management' is concerned with what people with responsibility for others actually do. By contrast, research into 'leadership' is concerned with the ability of people to influence others toward the achievement of goals. Mintzberg (1973) has described this as the difference between what people actually do and what they should do. The difference between the two appears small, but it is an important difference as the term 'leadership' assumes a particular way of getting things done based around the ascendancy and inspiration of managers. This idea originates in the United States and is typically found in American texts. However, this view of the virtue of leadership might not be appropriate in all circumstances. For example, in cultures where team-working has become the accepted way of organising (e.g. Scandinavia and the Far East) some of the connotations of leadership, such as the ascendancy of certain individuals in organisations, might cut across other, more important, ways of working. Leadership, though, remains an important issue which is relevant in many organisations and cultures. Currently, one of the main perspectives on leadership is termed 'contingency theory'. This states that leaders should adapt their leadership style to meet the needs of the situation. But, is this possible? Can people change their style of leadership? This is the question addressed in the article 'Can leaders change their styles?' (Chapter 5) by Huczynski and Buchanan.

Chapter 6, entitled 'How can I win if you don't lose? Games where the winner doesn't take all', focuses on another important feature of managers' jobs: how should they cope with conflict? One way to look at this issue is to use game theory. In its simplest form, game theory is concerned with the analysis of events where there are winners and losers. Much of the focus within game theory is to find ways to maximise the likelihood of achieving a win–win result. Unfortunately, many situations in management seem to result in lose–lose situations where all participants come off poorly. In societies where conflict and aggression are highly regarded, it can be psychologically compelling to act defensively so that your opponents or correspondents do not get the upper hand. Such a defensive attitude can be counterproductive and game theory can highlight how managers can avoid falling into this trap. The article by Knelman looks at some of the ideas underlying this approach. The following article by Handy, entitled 'The £5 auction' (Chapter 7), illustrates this problem with an example from the author's own teaching.

Part 2 Motivation and stress at work

While we can look at motivation and stress in general terms, here we are interested in the motivation and stress of employees resulting from the behaviour of managers. How do people react to the efforts and actions of managers? One cognitive perspective on motivation, commonly known as 'expectancy theory', suggests that people will put in extra effort if they believe it will result in greater performance and that the greater performance will lead to desirable outcomes, such as bonuses, promotion, a feeling of satisfaction, or simply someone saying 'thank you'. This is a cognitive perspective because the most important factor resulting in people exerting more effort is their perception of the strength of the links between their own effort, performance and rewards. Where the links are strong, so the argument goes, people will put in more effort; where the links are weak, people will do no more than they have to. I should very much like to win £20 million on the national lottery, but I have never bought a lottery ticket. Why not? It's not because I don't value the outcome, but because I don't believe that the purchase of a ticket will lead to me winning. Others view the link between buying the ticket and the outcome differently and consequently buy the tickets every week.

To the uninitiated, it might be thought that money is an important motivator of people. Similarly, linking part of employees' pay to company profits might help to link the actions of employees to organisational goals. Hence, the extravagant salaries, pay rises and share option schemes given to many senior executives. But do they actually motivate? And, if they do, are they also applicable to other employees? In the article by Clark, entitled 'Profit-related pay: a retrospective' (Chapter 8), which was specially written for this book, the author looks at the introduction of profit-related pay in Great Britain and whether it has resulted in employees exerting greater effort. The following chapter by Furnham, 'Does money motivate?' (Chapter 9), looks at the same issue from a different perspective.

Work stress

Across North America, the majority of large companies are reducing staff. Those employees who survive these layoffs are being expected to absorb the increased workload. The result is increased stress levels. A recent sample of 600 US workers found that 46 percent said their jobs were highly stressful and 34 percent reported the stress was so bad they were thinking of quitting. The Japanese call it *karoshi*. It means sudden death by a heart attack or stroke triggered by overwork. In a land where 16-hour workdays are not uncommon, experts estimate that 10,000 Japanese die each year from *karoshi*. (Robbins, 1996)

It seems, therefore, that high levels of stress are a widespread problem. The issue of stress raises several difficult questions. As some amount of stress seems to improve productivity, should managers create environments which put employees under stress? To answer this question of ethics, it is useful to examine the causes of stress in workers. After all, it might be that employees create stress themselves. There are three articles on stress in this part. The first article, entitled 'Job features and excessive stress' (Chapter 10), starts by looking at the causes of stress. In this article Warr notes that 'stress is inevitable in any job . . . That is not necessarily bad. But when job stress is extreme or extended over a long period, then [managers] should be concerned.' He then examines the characteristics of jobs that cause stress. The following article, entitled 'Prevention and management of work stress' (Chapter 11) by Murphy, looks at ways that managers can help to reduce occupational stress. The final article in this part was specifically written for this book by Daniels. 'Stressed?' (Chapter 12) links the chapters by Warr and Murphy and shows the manager how to develop an appropriate stress management strategy. In the article, Daniels notes that he and Murphy adopt different perspectives on the subject of stress management interventions. Murphy appears to favour secondary stress management interventions (i.e. strategies to help individuals cope with the symptoms of stress), whereas Daniels advocates primary interventions which remove the cause of stress.

Part 3   Organisational culture and the changing nature of organisational entry

Organisational culture is one of the 'hot' topics in the management literature. So much so that it is almost impossible to read any book on any management subject without coming across references to an organisation's culture. Is it just that organisational culture is the latest fad, or is there something more to it? Perhaps the best way to answer this question is to think about what organisational culture actually is. You will find countless definitions of the term 'organisational culture' in the literature. However, within the myriad explanations of the term there is something of a consensus that allows us to make sense of it. Most would agree that organisational culture constitutes a collection of beliefs, values, norms, customs, policies, attitudes and so on that are held by most employees in an organisation. These items may or may not be openly shared and discussed; the important factor is that employees agree about the nature of the culture. In short, you might view an organisation's culture as its personality. This is relevant for other management subjects that you will study because organisational culture is the pervasive context for everything that is thought and done in organisations. Appreciating what constitutes the organisation's culture is important to managers, therefore, so that they can better understand and predict the implications of their actions.

Just as every person is different, so is every organisation. To make sense of these differences researchers have tried to categorise the differences they find within organisations.

Popper's lecture

Popper . . . argued that observation was not as objective as it seemed, but was actually rather theory driven. His famous lecture demonstration was to tell people in the audience: 'Observe!', to which the obvious and immediate retort was, 'Observe what?' This demonstration makes the point that no one ever observes without some idea of what it is they are looking for. In other words, scientific observation is always driven by hypotheses and theories, and what you observe depends in part on what you expect to see. (Eysenck and Keane, 1990)

The first two articles in this part demonstrate this point very sharply. When Deal and Kennedy analysed organisational cultures they focused on improving the profits of commercial organisations. They found that the two most important factors that emerged when they analysed organisations were the amount of risk in the organisation and the speed of feedback. In the section of their book included here, 'Corporate tribes: identifying the cultures' (Chapter 13), the authors explore the four types of culture they elicit. Once you have identified your own culture by analysing it for risk and the speed of feedback, this article will help you to see what is required to succeed or survive in the culture.

Maddock and Parkin analysed organisational cultures from a very different perspective to Deal and Kennedy, for they focused on equality between men and women in organisations. Just like Deal and Kennedy, they were able to identify four types of culture. But the factors underlying these cultures are male and female attitudes towards women. For many people, women as well as men, the article entitled 'Gender cultures: women's choices and strategies at work' (Chapter 14) will be both shocking and provocative. It illustrates most forcibly the point that different people view the same situations in very different ways. To be effective, managers need to be able to put themselves in other people's shoes. This helps managers to understand the views of other people so that they can adapt their behaviour and actions for best advantage.

'Managing organisational culture: fantasy or reality?' (Chapter 15) discusses two important questions. Firstly, is organisational culture something an organisation *is*, or is it something an organisation *has*? This might appear a subtle difference, but as Ogbonna points out, it is an important difference. Secondly, Ogbonna asks if an organisation's culture can be managed. He uses the first question to inform his discussion. If organisational culture is something an organisation has, then the implication is that it can be managed and changed. If it is something an organisation is, then to all intents and purposes the management of culture is impractical. Given the ubiquity of organisational culture change strategies in organisations in many parts of the world, these are important questions that must be addressed by managers considering such drastic policies that will inevitably affect the lives of everyone connected with the organisation.

The article by Nicholson and West (Chapter 2) highlighted the way that the environment in which managers work is rapidly changing. Indeed, this is a recurring theme in many of the articles in the book. Much of this change is initiated by managers, often in response to pressures for change in the external environment. Some writers view this change as all-pervasive and hence define the role of the manager as that of managing change. Whilst you might not agree with this perspective, it does highlight the need for the manager to be able to manage change. There is a vast literature on the management of change and it is not possible to do justice to it here. Instead, one article has been included, entitled 'Phases and levels of organisational change' (Chapter 16) by Rashford and Coghlan, which uses the metaphor of death and dying to explain how organisations, groups, teams and individuals respond to change.

The article by Parkinson entitled 'The short list, or principles of selection' (Chapter 17) offers a tongue-in-cheek and humorous historical perspective of recruitment and selection. Despite the wicked black comedy, this article contains some very serious messages for managers. Amongst these are the importance of advertising jobs appropriately so that only a small (or manageable) number of suitably qualified candidates apply, and of using tests that measure job-related qualities; the article also illustrates how easily unfair bias can creep into the process.

Whilst the article by Parkinson reviews historical approaches to recruitment and selection, the article by Bowen, Ledford and Nathan entitled 'Hiring for the organization, not the job' (Chapter 18) illustrates the very latest thinking on the subject. In short, this involves an assessment of applicants against the organisation's culture as well as an assessment of applicants against the actual job. The idea behind this approach is that employees must 'fit in', share the values of the organisation, and be able to thrive in the organis-ation's culture, if they are to maximise their contribution. The danger with this perspective is, of course, that assessments of applicants' fit might be subjective and not based on any objective or justifiable evidence. The authors of this article illustrate the lengths that managers have to go to in order to assess fit and to avoid unfair discrimination.

'When does the recruitment and selection process end? The organisational entry cycle and a horticultural metaphor' (Chapter 19) was written by me specially for this book. In this short article, I wanted to put an alternative perspective to the traditional view that recruitment and selection are discrete processes which can be managed separately from future events. This perspective is commonly found in the recruitment and selection literature where the prime event is the decision about whom to offer the job to. The alternative perspective that I wanted to highlight is that recruitment and selection are simply subprocesses within a much larger process of organisational entry. This larger process only terminates once a new recruit is performing effectively. I have illustrated this perspective with a horticultural metaphor which, I hope, spotlights the analysis and induction (adjustment) stages of the organisational entry process.

Part 4   Decision making and teams

Earlier in this chapter, I compared academic research with research conducted for business purposes and tentatively suggested some characteristics that set the two types of research apart. One of the issues that emerged was that managers conduct research to help them to make better business decisions. In doing so, managers are under pressure not to waste time and money in needless extra research (the 80/20 rule in action). Should managers expend extra effort in order to make even better decisions? Janis and Mann explore this question in the article entitled 'Satisficing' (Chapter 20). Is satisficing a superficial form of decision making, or is it a natural and advisable way of coping with the mass of information available?

The article by March, entitled 'Limited rationality' (Chapter 21), looks at another key factor that affects the decision making of managers: namely, the problem that everyone is limited in their ability to make precision decisions by their own experiences and knowledge. The inductivist turkey failed to predict his demise because he did not know about Christmas Eve, i.e. he was unable to make a strong prediction because he had limited awareness. March first notes that decision makers have serious limitations in attention, memory, comprehension and communication before examining the implications of these limitations. In particular, the author concentrates on the ways in which decision makers simplify the decision-making process.

'Groupthink' (Chapter 22) is an analysis by Janis of the decision making of 'one of the greatest arrays of intellectual talent in the history of American Government'. Despite having such excellent talents to draw upon, this group blundered into the ill-fated Bay of Pigs incident. Janis uses this example to understand better some of the problems that can occur within groups when decisions have to be made. Amongst the problems he surfaces are included the following: members of an 'in-group' share an illusion of invulnerability which leads them to ignore clear warnings of danger; collective rationalisms are constructed that cause negative feedback to be ignored; groups feel morally justified in their actions; opposition is stereotyped and this can lead to the group only forming a partial understanding of its adversaries; doubting voices within the group are pressured into silence; group members avoid deviating from the group consensus; there is an illusion of unanimity; and some people within the group act as 'mindguards' to protect the group. These features of group-think can be seen reasonably easily on the football terraces where people take pride in belonging to a particular clan. But the strength of Janis's analysis is that it reveals some of the possible dynamics in supposedly rational decision-making groups such as management teams, autonomous working groups, and the like. In doing so, it cautions managers to listen actively to dissent and to constantly question the basis on which they make their decisions.

The second article by Furnham, 'Reaping the benefits of team-work' (Chapter 23), looks at teamwork in the context of the national culture into which it is being foisted. He sees teamwork as just the latest management fad with a simplistic message: 'the power of the waterfall is nothing but a lot of drips working together.' He argues that teamwork will only be useful in cultures where people are collectivistic by nature.

What induces team behaviour in people? Furnham would clearly argue that it is personal dispositions that incline them, or not, toward behaviour likely to foster teamwork. This is also the perspective taken by Belbin. He argues that people have predispositions to particular roles within teams. In the article entitled 'Team roles and a self-perception inventory' (Chapter 24), which was specially constructed for this volume, you can use Belbin's self-perception inventory to ascertain your own preferred team role, rather than the one that others might incorrectly ascribe to you. Be careful, though: Belbin's view that people have a predisposition to team roles is just one perspective. An alternative perspective is advanced by Herriot and Pemberton in 'Teams: old myths and a new model' (Chapter 25). They argue that, rather than people having a predisposition for particular team roles, the situations in which people find themselves largely determine the behaviour they exhibit in teams.

The final article in this part, 'The trouble with teams' (Chapter 26) from *The Economist*, looks at some of the problems that team-working can cause if implemented inadvisedly. These include: the additional expense of training; increased conflict and stress; more meetings on superfluous issues; the difficulty in giving teams clear objectives; a reduction of managerial control over business processes; groupthink; and the stifling of individual talent. This is a cautionary tale, rather than a pronouncement against team-working. And it is a tale that reminds us of Furnham's message: you need to understand the context before you can introduce team-working. Furthermore, an appreciation of the likely pluses and minuses of introducing teams also needs to be acquired before you take action. Few decisions in management are clear-cut, are without a downside as well as an upside. If team-working were a solution to every organisation's problems, then it would surely have been identified long ago.

Part 5   Developing staff

Despite managers' best attempts to recruit people who have the knowledge, skills and abilities to be effective, it is rarely the case that they find the 'perfect' employee. There is almost always some training or coaching necessary and it is the line manager who is usually the first port of call for help. Perhaps more importantly, we have already noted how change is a characteristic in the organisational milieu. How can people cope with this change? One method is through training and development, and much of this takes place at the workplace under the guidance of the line manager.

Help me, but don't help the hell out of me

How can you capture the best of what [. . . an overly helpful] boss has to offer without being obligated to take all the advice and 'guidance' that comes your way? The key . . . is to show such a boss that too much 'help' hurts his or her own interests. Being swamped with more advice than you wanted will reduce the challenge in your job and thus reduce your ownership of the problems and your responsibility for solving them. If your boss rides the bike for you instead of just giving you instructions, support, and a gentle push, you'll soon have to call her every time you want to get anywhere. (Cohen and Bradford, 1989)

'The Peter principle' (Chapter 27) states that 'in a hierarchy every employee tends to rise to his level of incompetence.' Look around at work: can you identify people who seem to have been promoted once too often? If you are in a typical organisation, or one which hasn't yet been 'rightsized', it is likely that you will be able to identify several such people. Although the Peter principle might be thought of as a light-hearted piece of frippery, it contains some very serious messages. You could use the principle to analyse the career drive of workers, or you might use it as evidence to demonstrate how poorly selection is carried out in organisations. Alternatively, you can use the principle to highlight the inadequacies of training and development in many organisations. The authors, Peter and Hull, themselves admit that many of the people they have spotted exhibiting the principle's symptoms have previously been very effective in similar jobs, which is the reason they were promoted in the first place. If newcomers fail to perform, what might be the cause? As we saw in an earlier article (Chapter 19), one reason might be that they were poorly inducted into the job and were not given the training and development needed to become effective.

The two articles by Mumford, 'How managers can become developers' (Chapter 28) and 'Special needs, different solutions' (Chapter 29), focus on two different aspects of staff development. In the first of the articles, he looks at work-based learning, commonly known as 'sitting next to Nellie', which is a powerful development tool for managers when used properly. Mumford argues that much valuable learning on the job happens as a result of unplanned experiences and that managers should be helped to appreciate when such opportunities arise and to take advantage of them when they do. In the second of the articles, Mumford looks at whether female managers have different training needs to male managers and at the training needs of graduates. In addition, he considers how management development in multinational organisations differs from management development in organisations with a single national base.

Whereas Mumford focuses on the *ad hoc* opportunities for staff development in Chapter 28, Fletcher concentrates his attention on the more formal and planned appraisal interview as a method of staff development. 'Appraisal: an idea whose time has gone?' (Chapter 30) looks at the links between staff development, performance management and appraisal interviews. He notes that the traditional appraisal interview has changed much in recent years and is now more usefully employed as a development tool rather than a tool to appraise the performance of workers. He says, 'Among other things, [Deming (1986)] argues that appraisal does harm because managers cannot effectively differentiate between individual staff and organisational systems as the cause in performance variation and that the latter rather than the former are the major factor.' The short article by Fink, entitled 'Managing individual behavior: bringing out the best in people' (Chapter 31), describes Deming's well-known experiment that illustrates this point.

Part 6   Diversity in organisations

One of the themes of this book is diversity. Whether it be the need to try to see things from others' perspectives, or the difficulty in adopting similar policies in different organisations or different cultures, the issue of diversity keeps rearing its head. Take motivation as an example: is an American worker motivated by the same things that motivate a Greek or a Swedish manager?

Motivation theories are culture bound

Maslow's need hierarchy argues that people start at the physiological level and then move progressively up the hierarchy in this order: physiological, safety, social, esteem, and self-actualisation. This hierarchy, if it has any application at all, aligns with American culture. In countries like Japan, Greece, and Mexico, where uncertainty avoidance characteristics are strong, security need would be top of the need hierarchy. Countries that score high on quality-of-life characteristics – Denmark, Sweden, Norway, the Netherlands, and Finland – would have social needs on top. We would predict, for instance, that group work will motivate employees more when the country's culture scores high on the quality criterion. Another motivation concept that clearly has an American bias is the achievement need. The view that a high achievement need acts as an internal motivator presupposes two cultural characteristics – a willingness to accept a moderate degree of risk (which excludes countries with strong uncertainty avoidance characteristics) and a concern with performance (which applies almost singularly to countries with strong quality-of-life characteristics). This combination is found in Anglo-American countries like the United States, Canada, and Great Britain. On the other hand, these characteristics are relatively absent in countries such as Chile and Portugal. But don't assume there aren't any cross-cultural consistencies. For instance, the desire for interesting work seems important to almost all workers, regardless of national culture . . . Similarly, in a study comparing job preference outcomes among graduate students in the United States, Canada, Australia, and Singapore, growth, achievement, and responsibility were rated the top three and had identical rankings. Both of these studies suggest some universality to the importance of intrinsic factors in motivation-hygiene theory. (Robbins, 1996)

How we as managers can make sense of this diversity is the subject of the articles in this part of the book. Not only do we look at national differences, but we also look at sexual diversity within organisations.

Hofstede has been a pioneer in the field of understanding national differences. He surveyed the staff of one global organisation, IBM, to determine the characteristics of national cultures. Hofstede found that he was able to 'map' the cultures of nations onto four dimensions: individualism versus collectivism; power distance; uncertainty avoidance; and masculinity versus femininity. In the article 'The cultural relativity of organizational practices and theories' (Chapter 32), Hofstede explains these dimensions and maps the nations of the world. He suggests that the culture we grow up in deeply affects us. He concludes by looking at the consequences of this for the application of management theory in different parts of the world.

One of the issues that confronts managers who have to operate across national cultures is the seemingly straightforward task of communication. This is the subject of the article entitled 'Communicating across cultural barriers' (Chapter 33) by Adler. She illustrates many of the problems that managers face. In particular, she draws attention to the ease with which misunderstandings can arise through misinterpretation. An interesting debate within this article concerns the nature of stereotypes. We might feel that stereotypes are not 'politically correct' as holding them fails to acknowledge that people are different from each other and that everyone needs to be understood individually. But how could we possibly cope with collecting, processing and analysing the information required to understand everyone we meet? Adler argues that stereotyping is a useful tool for coping with this problem when the stereotypes are: consciously held; descriptive rather than evaluative; accurate; the first best guess before actual information is received; and modified to reflect experience with actual people and situations. One aspect of cross-cultural communication is examined by Thomson in the article entitled 'Actions speak louder than words' (Chapter 34). In this article, she illustrates the importance of non-verbal communication in a variety of managerial situations.

The article by Kandola and Fullerton switches attention from the external environment to the internal environment. 'Diversity: more than just an empty slogan' (Chapter 35) begins by defining diversity. 'The basic concept of managing diversity accepts that the workforce consists of a diverse population of people. The diversity consists of visible and non-visible differences which will include factors such as sex, age, background, race, disability, personality, work style. It is founded on the premise that harnessing these differences will create a productive environment in which everybody feels valued, where their talents are being fully utilised and in which organisational goals are met.' Within this definition is the idea that not all differences are apparent. This is important because it illustrates one important issue in the diversity debate: it is not necessarily about helping minorities or the disadvantaged, but instead focuses the attention of managers on the need to treat everyone with equal respect. As the authors say, 'if managing diversity is truly about creating an environment where everyone feels valued and their talents are being fully utilised, then actions ought to be targeted on any individual who has a particular development need and not restricted to those who are members of a particular group.'

Sims, Fineman and Gabriel say the following in Chapter 36: 'Looking at organizations purely as places of work is almost as naive as looking at sex purely as sexual intercourse. Men and women are sexual beings. Our sexuality is a central part of our personality. We all have sexual desires, anxieties and fantasies and we spend some of our working time talking, joking and thinking about sex.' In the article, entitled 'Sex', the authors examine how sex exhibits itself in organisations and the implications for employees. They see sex as an implicit part of the workplace with both lighter and darker sides.

The article by Shallenberger encapsulates many of the underlying messages of this book. Entitled 'Professional and openly gay: a narrative study of the experience' (Chapter 37), this article can be read on a number of different levels. It can be read simply as an illustrative piece that describes a gay view of careers, jobs and organisations. On this level, 'straight' readers experience a perspective that might be quite new and shocking. By seeing the world through someone else's eyes, readers are challenged to think about how they relate to gay people in the workplace. On another level, the article illustrates that stereotypes, in this case about gay men, can be misleading if you fail to adapt them in the light of evidence that you receive. This reinforces Adler's point (in Chapter 33) that stereotypes are only useful when the subject is beyond your experience. On yet another level, the article illustrates that twelve managers – regardless of their sexual orientation – have different aspirations, different goals, different values, different reasons for coming to work and so on. It reinforces the point that you cannot take people for granted. Everyone is different, and if you are to perform effectively as a manager you need to adjust your actions to suit the circumstances.

'Taking action on harassment' (Chapter 38) by Hawkins is the last article in this part of this book. The focus of this article is on sexual harassment, which seems to be a problem in almost all national cultures, and ways to combat it. It ends with some 'dos and don'ts for managers' which, if followed, can help you reduce or eliminate sexual harassment by you and your staff.

Postscript

The final article in this book, 'A New Deal for Middle Managers' (Chapter 39), brings our discussion full circle. The book draws a distinction between what managers actually do and what they should do, and looks at how managers manage in times of great change and across cultural barriers. The article by Herriot and Pemberton, which is an overview of their book *New Deals*, looks at how all this change is affecting managers. In particular, the authors focus on the changing nature of managers' psychological contracts (the unspoken agreement between managers and their employers about what each party expects of the other).

Herriot and Pemberton argue that, far from creating greater profitability, the increased attention to efficiency and cost-competitiveness is forcing organisations to break their long-standing psychological contracts with managers. In the traditional notion of the psychological contract, managers offered loyalty, conformity, commitment and trust. In return, the organisation offered security, promotion opportunities, training and development, and care when in trouble. But gone are the days of a job for life.

The new psychological contract is very different. Managers must work long hours, hold more responsibility, have more skills, and tolerate increasing change and ambiguity in their jobs. In return, organisations offer a job. And, if managers are lucky (and the market forces organisations to do so), they will also get rewards for high performance. Gone are the days of managers putting in that little bit extra effort.

The authors argue that managers are no longer treated as people. Instead, organisations view them as resources to be used up and exhausted in pursuit of the organisation's mission. In times of recession, many organisations are abusing their position of power in the employer–employee relationship and 'exploiting' those that work for them. The violation of the traditional psychological contract and the unilateral replacement with the new one by organisations has affected managers to the root of their being. First, managers perceive inequity both in the change and in how it has happened. Second, the violation of the previous contract has led to managers losing all the trust that they once had in their employers. Third, the imposition of the new contract has made them feel powerless. Fourth, they feel worthless and at risk from the whim of senior executives and the 'flavour of the month'. But managers cannot complain: market forces see to that. If they don't like it, all they can do is leave the organisation and hope that they can find a less abusive employer. In a deep recession, this is simply not realistic. The authors end by looking to the future and a new model for psychological contracts which suggests that managers will have to think about their employers and their jobs in a new way.

A note on the editing of articles

Most of the articles in this book have been heavily edited down from longer pieces to extract the key messages for readers. The sections that have been cut out fall into several categories:

- links to other parts of the original text that were not included in this book
- examples that would not transfer well across cultures
- debates within debates that would distract the reader from the key message in the article
- material covered in other articles in this book
- sections that required specialist knowledge.

Some cuts have been made simply to reduce length.

Many of the articles in this book are extracts from books. Two, the articles by Belbin and Fink, were created from separate parts of their books. By editing down the original, I may, on occasion, have accidentally distorted the author's intentions. I have tried to obtain the author's permission to edit the material in the way that I have, but this has not always been possible. So, if you intend to quote from edited articles (my deletions are marked with square brackets), please refer to the original article or book. You will find the original sources on the chapter title pages.

References

Brief, A.P. and Dukerich, J.M. (1991) 'Theory in organizational behavior: can it be useful?', in L.L. Cummings and B.M. Straw (eds), *Research in Organizational Behavior*, vol. 13. Greenwich, CT: JAI Press. pp. 327–52.

Chalmers, A.F. (1982) *What is this Thing Called Science?*, 2nd edn. Milton Keynes: Open University Press.

Cohen, A.R. and Bradford, D.L. (1989) *Influence without Authority*. New York: Wiley.

Deming, W.E. (1986) *Out of the Crisis*. Cambridge, MA: MIT Institute for Advanced Engineering Study.

Eysenck, M.W. and Keane, M.T. (1990) *Cognitive Psychology: a Student's Handbook*. Hove: Lawrence Erlbaum.

Herriot, P. and Pemberton, C. (1995) *New Deals: the Revolution in Managerial Careers*. Chichester: Wiley.

Herzberg, F. (1968) 'One more time: how do you motivate employees?', *Harvard Business Review*, January–February: 53–62.

Huczynski, A.A. and Buchanan, D.A. (1991) *Organizational Behaviour: an Introductory Text*, 2nd edn. Hemel Hempstead: Prentice-Hall.

Lewin, K. (1945) 'The research center for group dynamics at Massachusetts Institute of Technology', *Sociometry*, 8: 126–136.

Mintzberg, H. (1973) *The Nature of Managerial Work*. New York: Harper and Row.

Nicholson, N. and West, M.A. (1988) *Managerial Job Change: Men and Women in Transition*. Cambridge: Cambridge University Press.

Robbins, S.P. (1996) *Organizational Behavior: Concepts, Controversies, Applications*, 7th edn. Englewood Cliffs, NJ: Prentice-Hall.

PART 1

MANAGEMENT, LEADERSHIP AND CONFLICT

2

Men and women in transition

Nigel Nicholson and Michael West

We live in times of change – rapid and radical change – and much of it centres on our working lives. Even if we lived in times of tranquil stability we would still be confronted with the task of adjusting to transitions, compelled by the perpetual motion of the life cycle. People would still have to undergo training and socialization to acquire occupational competence at the start of the life/ career cycle, have to maintain and reform skills in the middle years to be able to fill the slots vacated by departing seniors, and eventually move on into retirement, renewing the cycle by passing on their positions to junior successors. Transitions are, to this degree, inevitable, but [. . .] such orderly and measured change is not the normal experience of most managers.

What do we know about how people adjust to the demands of change? Within the various literatures on people at work, change is too often treated as a troublesome aberration – an external force that disturbs the stable patterns of daily life. The snapshots of survey designs and case studies are often used to deduce and uncover these patterns, for example, in the search for law-like relationships between such factors as job characteristics, personality, work satisfaction, and performance. Social scientists seem to be more comfortable studying the world with an assumption of stability than they do in confronting the problem of how such patterns may be disturbed or reformed by change. Indeed, given the pervasiveness of change perhaps it would be better to assume that change is the constant and stability the exception. One might even argue, like some post-Freudian and

Abridged from N. Nicholson and M.A. West, *Managerial Job Change*, Cambridge: Cambridge University Press, 1988, pp. 1–5.

existentialist writers, that one of the main functions of culture is to cushion and protect us from our fundamental insecurities about change (Fromm, 1942). The most anxiety-inducing questions about the meaning of our existence, the uncertainty of the future, and the nature of identity, are solved for us, partially at least, by the mechanisms of cultural transmission – the socialization of values, beliefs and behaviours and the institutionalization of social relationships.

Change and constancy are bound together through various dynamics, and their interaction can often appear paradoxical. In many spheres of life we engineer changes in order to reinforce the status quo, for example, changing jobs to maintain our professional status and skills. Conversely we can see how stability is a cause of radical change, for example, where rigidity in the face of environmental challenges leads individuals and organizations to experience breakdown or revolution. These dynamics can be looked at from various perspectives within the social sciences: from the macro level of social strata, economic systems and cultural forces, through to the micro level of individual growth, adaptation and decline. [. . .]

Change and the manager

In many ways the society we live in today is almost unrecognizable as a product of the society of our recent forebears. In other respects there is a remarkable continuity from former to present times (Halsey, 1978). Our experiences in organizations play a considerable part in providing us with a sense of continuity, and at the same time prepare us for the bewildering range of major changes we are witnessing in almost every area of our lives in industrialized society. The primary social institution of the family has a different appearance and some changed functions: family size has fallen, divorce and remarriage have risen, and forms of childcare have altered (*Social Trends*, 1985). The content and extent of education have changed: syllabi are more varied, training is more pragmatically oriented to a widening range of occupations and professions, and people are spending longer in educational institutions. There have been revolutionary advances in transportation and communications, and major shifts in the form of both product and labour markets. There have been parallel changes in how we use our leisure time and spend our money. Household technology and entertainments, the growth of the superstore, and the increasing use of private transport have all contributed to ways of living that are simultaneously more privatized and mobile (Fothergill and Vincent, 1985). All this has been accompanied by huge shifts in patterns of industrialization and social structure. Rapid advances in industrial and information technology, declining demand for the traditional products of manufacturing, coupled with increasing demands for a widening range of services, have led to a major redistribution of employment from the primary and secondary (extractive and manufacturing) sectors to the tertiary (service and support) sector of the economy (Payne and Payne, 1983). At the same time organizational forms have changed. Increasingly, the equity of companies is owned by large institutions rather than private individuals (*Britain 1986*). The size of enterprises has grown, to exceed in some cases the wealth of national economies, whilst there has been a continuing proliferation of small businesses, creating and filling more and more new market niches. The state and the law, despite whatever attempts are made to curb them, have had to evolve ever more complex and extensive systems to regulate these activities.

Although inequalities in wealth and power are little different in scale from those of half a century ago, standards of living have risen, and the identities of class and status groups have altered. The industrial proletariat and agricultural working class have declined in number, as has the size of the landowning plutocracy, whilst there has been great growth in [salary] at all levels. Menial white-collar jobs, service and technical functions, supervisory and managerial roles, and professional and executive jobs have all proliferated dramatically (Institute of Manpower Studies, 1986).

One of the most radical changes of recent years [. . .] is the changed role of women. Many of the changes [. . .] have meant that women have different opportunities for time use and a changing sense of their own identity and motives. By virtue of reduced family demands, new technical aids to domestic labour, and more flexible work schedules and demands, women now have time to seek other forms of occupation (Martin and Roberts, 1984). The dramatic increase in the number of employed women, together with other changes in social behaviour and values, has initiated a far reaching revolution in the social identity of women. This is an area of considerable current ferment. Traditional gender roles and stereotypes are still pervasive in the family, the workplace and communications media, but large numbers of women are actively producing changes in each of these areas, consciously and unconsciously challenging traditional ways and assumptions, often with a new sense of their own purposes and needs (Alban-Metcalfe, 1985).

So we can see that the forces of change converge on human experience by altering the social structure, shaping social needs and values, and reordering the means by which needs are fulfilled by social structures. Here our interest is in management, since it is managers who are charged with coordinating and focussing responses to change while at the same time functioning as some of the most influential agents for change within organizations. Management itself has been fundamentally affected in three major ways by the social and economic developments we have described.

First, the number of people who are managers has been growing rapidly in this century (Parker et al., 1981). But what is a manager? A simple definition might be: one who is required to facilitate and coordinate the efforts of others to achieve organizational objectives. Adopting such a definition, we can see how the shift from basic industrial processes to complex and varied information-based activities means that increasing numbers of people are managers: charged with the task of supervising, coordinating, integrating and interacting to fulfil organizations' goals. Managers are no longer a small minority in the community of occupations. They are the executors of many of our most valued and significant social processes.

Second, a corollary of the first point, the scope and variety of what managers are required to do has been continually expanding. The French writer, Henri Fayol, laid the foundations at the start of the century for management as a discipline by portraying managerial work as following the rationality of planning, organizing and controlling, but modern empirical studies by scholars such as Mintzberg (1973) and Stewart (1967) offer a different image. Any measured rationality in managerial work has to be forged out of a hectic and apparent chaos of unscheduled demands, fragmented interactions, and *ad hoc* decisions. Moreover, the boundary between the general or supervisory managerial functions and those of the technical or professional specialist is becoming increasingly blurred (Cullen, 1983). To be able to perform effectively general managers need to have greater specialist knowledge than ever before about their organizations, markets and technology. Technical specialists, for their part, have increasingly to manage subordinates or coordinate their work within teams to cope with the expanding scope and complexity of their tasks and goals. No longer can technical managers so easily function within the splendid isolation afforded by their expertise. They are having to improve their ability to communicate, or to sell their knowledge to non-specialists and to manage relationships with client populations. The complexity of the modern organization and its multiple interdependencies with external groups, interests, and institutions has also meant that boundary-spanning roles have been growing in number and significance (Drucker, 1973). All of this amounts to a widening of challenge and opportunity for managers and professionals. The managerial career may have once looked like a clear and reasonably straight track towards a visible horizon, but now the paths have multiplied. Their courses are increasingly devious, with numerous lateral intersections, and the horizons they lead to are obscured by cloud. Managers today have more reason than their forebears to doubt whether they will get to a valued destination more quickly by staying on the main path than by taking some new diversion to the side.

The third manifestation of change is just this – uncertainty and danger constitute the darker opposite side to challenge and opportunity. Managers can no longer feel secure in the knowledge that their psychological safety and well-being will be provided for by life-long attachment to a single employer. Organizations and careers are increasingly precarious, and the bleak landscape of unemployment is no more inhabited solely by the underclass: managerial redundancy has been increasing dramatically (Kaufman, 1982; Fineman, 1983). The rate of environmental change places imperative demands on organizations to adapt if they are to survive and prosper, reflected in the increasing numbers of mergers, business failures and new starts. For individual managers there is a constant pressure to update skills and knowledge, and to retain their status in organizational systems and the labour market. The galloping pace of the information technology revolution is a harbinger of profound uncertainty. How sure can one be that one's lifetime-accumulated skills will be needed tomorrow as they are today? To protect one's future it may be wisest to try to keep ahead of the game by making career choices that will enhance one's repertoire of marketable attributes.

References

Alban-Metcalfe, B.M. (1985) 'The effects of socialization on women's management careers: a review', *Management Bibliographies and Reviews*, 3.

Britain 1986: An Official Handbook. London: HMSO.

Cullen, J.B. (1983) 'An occupational taxonomy by professional characteristics: implications for research', *Journal of Vocational Behaviour*, 22: 256–67.

Drucker, P. (1973) *Management*. London: Heinemann.

Fineman, S. (1983) *White Collar Unemployment: Impact and Stress*. Chichester: Wiley.

Fothergill, S. and Vincent, J. (1985) *The State of the Nation*. London: Pan.

Fromm, E. (1942) *Fear of Freedom*. London: Routledge and Kegan Paul.

Halsey, R.H. (1978) *Change in British Society*. Milton Keynes: Open University Press.

Institute of Manpower Studies (1986) *UK Occupation and Employment Trends to the 1990s*. Brighton: IMS.

Kaufman, H.G. (1982) *Obsolescence and Professional Career Development*. New York: AMACOM.

Martin, J. and Roberts, C. (1984) *Women in Employment: a Lifetime Perspective*. London: HMSO.

Mintzberg, H. (1973) *The Nature of Managerial Work*. New York: Harper and Row.

Parker, S.R., Brown, R.K., Child, J. and Smith, M.A. (1981) *The Sociology of Industry*, 4th edn. London: George Allen and Unwin.

Payne, G. and Payne, J. (1983) 'Occupational and industrial transition in social mobility', *British Journal of Sociology*, 34: 72–92.

Social Trends (1985). London: HMSO.

Stewart, R. (1967) *Managers and their Jobs*. London: Macmillan.

3

Chocolate eggs and Chester Barnard

Iain Mangham

I have in front of me a chocolate egg, designed in Italy, manufactured in Germany and sold throughout Europe. It is wrapped in foil and secured within an attractive (5 x 2 inch) box proclaiming in several languages the virtue of the product: 'Confiserie recouverte de chocolat au lait contenant une surprise dans une capsule plastique.' When opened, not without difficulty, the packaging is seen to hold the egg (in its protective yet decorative covering) and the egg contains – in this case – a set of miniature plastic tools for the collection of refuse: pan, brush, cart and bin. It also holds a set of instructions for assembling the toys, in a fine print appropriate to the size of the implements. It is worth reflecting for a moment upon this product. Since it is supplied throughout Western Europe in quantity, it implies an organization of some size and, given issues of language and customs barriers, an enterprise of some complexity. The principles that inform it – someone with an idea and the structure and process to translate that idea into a product through the coordination of the efforts of others – are no different to the principles that guide and direct the activities of other larger concerns. What is bizarre is the thought of grown men and women coming together in a multi-national enterprise to sit around a table and deliberate about chocolate eggs. One can imagine what Bob Newhart would have made of it all:

> Conference phone New York/Rome:
> 'Chocolate eggs, Luigi. OK. OK. I'll buy that. What you gonna put in them, Fritz? Toffee? Not toffee. Cream? . . . I like it – cream eggs . . . not cream eggs? . . . jelly beans, Pierre, that's what's gonna be in them! . . . You're gonna put *what* in them? You're gonna put miniature plastic refuse implements in them? You mean . . . uh, huh . . . shovels? Brushes and plastic dustcarts? With wheels that spin? Really . . . well, that's just great, Luigi, just great. Wonderful . . .'

This [article] is not about chocolate eggs, nor is it at all concerned with a particular product. It is, however, about executives like Luigi, Fritz and Pierre; about how they relate to each other in their

Abridged from I.L. Mangham, *Power and Performance in Organizations*, Oxford: Blackwell Publishers, 1986, pp. 1–9.

attempts to bring off the development, manufacturing and marketing of their product. About, that is, the executive function.

What is taken to be executive work is outlined in Chester Barnard's classic book *The Functions of the Executive*, first published in 1938 and never superseded in its informed description and analysis. Barnard argues that an organization comes into being when certain conditions obtain: (1) there are people able and willing to communicate with each other (2) who are also willing to do something – 'to contribute action' as he puts it – in order (3) to accomplish a common purpose. These elements, he asserts, are necessary and sufficient for organization to occur. The vitality of organizations consists in (a) the willingness of individuals to cooperate, which is dependent upon their belief that the purpose can be determined and achieved, 'a faith that diminishes to vanishing point as it appears that it is not, in fact, in the process of being attained'; and (b) the satisfaction that individuals derive from carrying out the process. When an organization becomes ineffective – is unable to accomplish its specific objectives, be this manufacturing chocolate eggs or putting a man on the moon – willingness disappears and the enterprise disintegrates.

A manager, according to Barnard, operates in two areas simultaneously: he performs a set of functions that relate directly to the technical aspects of his job, such as commissioning a piece of equipment or developing a part for a product. Such activities are, in Barnard's terminology, non-executive. He or she also performs a set of functions relating to the maintenance of the organization as a cooperative activity; such functions, and only such functions, may be taken to be executive: 'Executive work is not that *of* the organization, but the specialized work of *maintaining* the organization in operation.' The specialized work of the executive is 'maintaining systems of cooperative effort'.

The executive function is not only to maintain cooperation but to achieve it and, presumably, change its nature through persuasion and debate. 'Organization results from the modification of the actions of the individual through control and influence upon . . . purposes, desires and impulses of the moment.' Indeed, 'deliberate, conscious and specialized control' is the 'essence of the executive function.' Cooperation and organization consist of 'concrete syntheses of opposed facts, and of opposed thought and emotions of human beings'. Neither cooperation nor organization just happen, neither is a spontaneous natural phenomenon. The establishment of either is a delicate, a precarious matter, their maintenance an issue of skills and dedication and it is 'precisely the function of the Executive to facilitate the synthesis in concrete action of contradictory forces, to reconcile conflicting forces, instincts, interests, conditions, positions and ideals'.

The microsituational perspective

[. . .] I have argued elsewhere (as have others) that organizations and collectivities do not behave, individuals do, and thus I make no apology for the focus upon a small group of individuals rather than upon the organization, or upon organizations in general.

Microsociology is the detailed analysis of how people 'cheat, favour, teach . . . hold meetings'; the minute by minute concern with what individuals apparently feel, think, say and do as they go about their business. Strictly speaking, there is no such thing as, say, an 'economy', a 'culture' or a 'social class'. Terms such as 'organization', 'group' and 'state' may be capable of legal distinction but remain, for all that, nothing more than collections of individuals acting in particular kinds of settings. Such notions cannot be grounded in any real sense other than by talking about the actual activities of those who constitute the collectivities. It is these individuals who act, not the ideas so beloved of sociologists and philosophers. Terms such as 'group' and 'organization' are simply abstractions from the behaviour of individuals, summaries of scores of pieces of individual behaviour distributed in a particular time and space. Thus Fritz's chocolate factory is an organization, but *what* it is, how it functions, is a product of thousands of pieces of individual behaviour. [. . .]

I propose that executives, no less than other human beings, are born psychologists. Indeed, those lacking the skill to handle themselves and others are unlikely to *be* successful executives, however outstanding their technical, non-executive abilities. The good executives – they who would excel in the maintenance of cooperative effort – are better able than their fellows to anticipate and influence the behaviour of those same fellows. Making and selling chocolate eggs is a matter of considerable interest to those of us who would understand more about executive activity. Who persuades whom to do what and how does he or she do it? Who is manipulated, exploited, cajoled, reassured, cared for, put down, humoured, ridiculed, tolerated or ignored?

It is possible to argue that one's success as an executive is dependent upon one's ability to conduct oneself in the complexity of the organization as a subtle, insightful, incisive performer. Successful executives appear to have a natural and/or a highly developed ability to read the actual and potential behaviour of others around them and to construct their own conduct in accordance with that reading. Not that this ability is peculiar to them – we all read behaviour and react – just that the more successful amongst us appear to do social life with a higher degree of skill than the rest of us manage.

Fritz, Luigi, Pierre and their colleagues may have initially shared the technical tasks for the creation of chocolate eggs; a simple division of labour: you do the eggs, you the wrapping, I'll do the boxes. Very quickly, however, a need to coordinate and organize cooperation is recognized and different, higher order skills are demanded: that of understanding, being sensitive to mood and style and bringing the effort of all together with the minimum of friction and trauma; that of rendering the nascent organization effective. He who survives in this role is the person with the most highly developed ability to 'read' his fellows. On a grander scale, those who are successful in the community or on the even more prominent stages of social life, national and international endeavours, may be seen to have a highly developed ability to do psychology on others and on themselves.

And on themselves. Part of [my] argument [. . .] is that the ability to do executive work is highly dependent upon one's awareness of one's self. To explain why this should be so, let me take you back for a moment or two to Fritz, Luigi and Pierre. Assume, if you will, that it is early days in the development of their enterprise. Fritz, Luigi and Pierre have (as I shall argue we all have) a marked degree of self interest in any activity undertaken: what's in it for me and how can I maximize my returns (economic, social or whatever)? Fritz, Luigi and Pierre are *calculating* beings, capable of assessing a situation and spotting the opportunities it presents for themselves. They are also capable of recognizing that they need each other if they are to derive individual benefits. No one of them can realize the enterprise alone. Given this, each of them has to have a level of understanding of his fellows, for without it, the enterprise could founder without benefit to any one of them. It is no longer a matter of can Luigi make the eggs, can Fritz manufacture the wrapping, but more, much more a matter of can each of us accommodate each of the others at a level which ensures survival? Each needs a rudimentary skill in reading behaviour. Each does it by reference to his own behaviour. Fritz, no less than Luigi and Pierre, arrives at his knowledge of others by reference to his knowledge of himself. Fritz is able to put himself in Luigi's shoes because he is able to put himself in his own shoes. Uniquely a human being, every human being, has the ability to look in on his own behaviour; to observe it, inspect it, monitor it, speculate about it, rehearse it.

Now, this ability is the key to an understanding of conduct in organizations. Executives, no less than the rest of us, infer what is going on in others from ideas and feelings they have about themselves. Given the ability to reflect upon aspects of our selves, a consciousness of consciousness, we use it to derive guides to our actions with and towards others. Executive skill, from this perspective, is a matter of working effectively and efficiently with others and, equally clearly, a matter of awareness of self and others. Fritz engaged in some solitary enterprise has no cause to develop any skill other than the technical; once dependent upon Luigi and Pierre, his survival becomes linked to his ability to control himself and them. His ability to control their actions (and, to an extent, his own) depends in turn upon his ability to anticipate them. In a real sense, what he knows of the likely actions of his fellows is determined by what he knows about himself. Simultaneously, Luigi and Pierre are seeking to relate Fritz's action to themselves; add a dozen more executives around the table of Chocolate Enterprise Ltd and you have considerable complexity. [. . .]

One difficulty in adopting an approach to conduct in organizations such as that implied above – the study of a small group of people interacting – is that very little is known about how people *do* social or organizational life. Most social scientists, whether sociologists or psychologists, choose not to consider notions such as self, self-awareness, role taking (putting oneself in the shoes of others) and the like. Instead, they focus upon behaviour; what it is that subjects 'do', what is the output; the 'black box' of what goes on in the head of a person is ignored. There are, of course, exceptions to this rule [. . .] but considering that each of us, every day, does social life, it is remarkable that on a formal level we know so little about it. [. . .] If we are to understand the conduct of people in organizations better, we must address what it is they appear to think about themselves and others, what it is they feel and what it is they say and do – simple to declare, but difficult to deliver. [. . .]

Familiarity and complexity

To comprehend some of the [. . .] difficulties, I must return to the nature of the executive process which, as I have shown, is a part or an aspect of the process of organization as a whole. For Barnard, the essential aspect, the key element of executive activity is 'the sensing of the organization as a whole and the total situation relevant to it'. It is, as Barnard notes, a matter of art rather than science, aesthetics rather than logic; terms such as 'feel', judgement', 'balance' and 'appropriateness' are its currency. Such features are 'recognized rather than described' and known by their effects 'rather than by analysis'. So the core of the executive process (at least as seen by Barnard) consists of a series of activities which are beyond description, let alone analysis. How does one depict 'sensing' and 'feel'?

The assertion that is repeatedly made in *The Functions of the Executive* is that the essence of the executive process is synthesis – the 'art of sensing the whole' and acting in accordance with this 'judgement'. Not that 'judgement' is always sound: some companies and organizations stress one aspect of their activity at the expense of others and lurch from crisis to crisis, a vague sense of the whole only becoming more distinct in the reasons for taking this or that corrective action. Occasionally, however, the art of sensing the whole is present in 'a few men of executive genius, or a few executive organizations, the personnel of which is comprehensively sensitive and well integrated'. [. . .]

A related difficulty is that of complexity. To illustrate, I can return to the case of the manufacturer of chocolate eggs. Assuming, for the moment, that I can become relatively familiar with the company and the four or five senior managers who exercise the executive function, what is it that I observe? As good students of Chester Barnard, I observe them 'maintaining an equilibrium of organization activities through the satisfaction of the motives of individuals sufficient to induce these activities' – a neat phrase packaging a lifetime's work and masking the dynamic of interaction. It is likely that each executive [. . .] has different 'motives', but it is equally likely that motives will arise in the process of interaction, that those held at the outset will diminish or grow; that some will be known and disclosed, others known and not disclosed. In other words, any chart of what is going on in any specific encounter can, at best, be little more than a snapshot, a picture postcard. To secure a moving picture, even in black and white, is a very large undertaking indeed.

References

Barnard, C.I. (1938) *The Functions of the Executive.* Cambridge, MA: Harvard University Press.

4

The Chinese contract

Charles Handy

I remember my first exposure to the 'Chinese contract'. I was the manager in South Malaysia for an oil company, responsible amongst other things for negotiating agency agreements with our Chinese dealers. I was young, enthusiastic and, I suppose, naïve. After the conclusion of one such negotiation, the dealer and I shook hands, drank the ritual cups of tea, and were, I felt, the best of friends. I took the official company agency agreement out of my case and started to fill in the figures, preparatory to signing it. 'Why are you doing that?' asked the dealer in some alarm. 'If you think that I am going to sign that you are much mistaken.' 'But I am only writing in the figures which we agreed.' 'If we agreed them, why do you want a legal document? It makes me suspect that you have got more out of this agreement than I have, and are going to use the weight of the law to enforce your terms. In my culture,' he went on, ' a good agreement is self-enforcing because both parties go away smiling and are happy to see that each of us is smiling. If one smiles and the other scowls, the agreement will not stick, lawyers or no lawyers.'

I think that I persuaded him that it was just a piece of company ritual and of no significance, but the episode sent me away thinking. I had grown up in a culture which believed that a good negotiation was one in which only one of us, myself, came away smiling, but concealed that smile lest the other guess that one had got the better of him or her. Negotiation was about winning at the expense of the other party. You then had to enforce your side of the deal, using the law or the threat of the law. I had met a culture where negotiation was about finding the best way forward for both parties. No wonder we needed so many more lawyers in our culture.

The Chinese contract, I later realised, embodied a principle which went far beyond the making of lasting commercial deals. It was about the importance of compromise as a prerequisite of progress. Both sides have to concede for both to win. It was about the need for trust and a belief in the future. Writ large, it was about sacrifice, the willingness to forgo some present good to ward off future evil,

---

Abridged from C. Handy, *The Empty Raincoat*, London: Hutchinson, 1994, pp. 80–2.

or, more positively, it was about investment – spending now in order to gain later.

We have no chance of managing the paradoxes if we are not prepared to give up something, if we are not willing to bet on the future and if we cannot find it in ourselves to take a risk with people. These are our Pathways through the Paradoxes, if we have the will. The pursuit of our own short-term advantage, and the desire to win everything we can, will only perpetuate animosities, destroy alliances and partnerships, frustrate progress, and breed lawyers and the bureaucracy of enforcement.

The Chinese contract, as I discovered to my chagrin, involves a major rethink of our cultural habits, even in China, where they may not appreciate my magnification of their trading habits into a principle of life. The pursuit of self-interest has to be balanced, as Adam Smith's two books remind us, by 'sympathy', a fellow feeling for others which is, he argues, the real basis of moral behaviour. Only if we are conditioned by this 'sympathy' will we want to take any risks with our fellow men and women, will we trust them farther than we can count them, or want to make life better for those we never meet. As Arthur Okun put it: the 'invisible hand' needs to be accompanied by an 'invisible handshake'. Self-interest, unbalanced, can only lead to a jungle in which any victory will mean destroying those on whom our own survival will ultimately depend. That would be the paradox to end all paradoxes. The tragedy of the commons, it was labelled, when the individual farmers maximised their own short-term use of the common land only to find that, when everyone did the same, the land deteriorated until all the grazing failed.

There are those who think that 'sympathy' will remain a very weak force, always yielding to self-interest. The evidence, however, is against them. Jean Piaget studied young children playing, and observed an inherent sense of fairness, particularly in older children who had longer time horizons. 'It makes her happy' or 'I don't want to see him cry' were the common explanations for gifts of generosity, and there was more generosity than there was hoarding. The Chinese will be relieved. Their policy of one child per family means that all young children spend their early years without siblings. The Chinese have, therefore, started courses in 'sharing' in the primary schools – to help them learn the principle of the Chinese contract! Adults don't always lose the habit. Most people don't put up the price of candles in a power strike or shovels in a snowstorm. There is sympathy in humankind as well as greed and cruelty.

5

Can leaders change their styles?

Andrzej Huczynski and David Buchanan

Contemporary theories of leadership are mainly contingency theories which argue that the most effective style for the leader to adopt depends on the context. Organizations, the abilities of their managers, the characteristics of their employees, the nature of their tasks and their structures are unique. No particular style of leadership can be said to be better than any other.

There is, however, a good deal of research that indicates that a participative style of leadership in organizations is generally (if not always) more effective. There are two main reasons for this.

First, the development of participative management is part of a wider social and political movement which has encouraged increased public participation in all spheres of social life. Participation thus reflects changing social and political values.

Rising levels of affluence and educational standards in Western industrial countries have developed expectations about personal freedom and the quality of working life. Education may also be expected to raise ability to participate in the first place. There is a widespread recognition of the rights of the individual to develop intellectual and emotional maturity. These values encourage resistance to manipulation by mindless, impersonal bureaucracies and challenge the legitimacy of management decisions. This trend has affected local and national government as well as private industry and is well established. The trend appears to be a universal one, and is not restricted to Britain or America. European and Scandinavian countries have legislated on the rights of employees to information about and participation in the activities of their employers.

Second, participative management has been encouraged by research which has demonstrated that this style is generally more effective, although an autocratic style can be more effective in some cases.

A participative management style can improve organizational effectiveness by tapping the ideas of people with knowledge and

Abridged from A. Huczynski and D. Buchanan, *Organizational Behaviour*, 2nd edn, Hemel Hempstead: Prentice-Hall, 1991, pp. 513–17.

experience, and by involving them in a decision-making process to which they then become committed. This style can thus lead to better quality decisions which are then more effectively implemented.

People who are involved in setting standards or establishing methods are thus more likely to:

- Accept the legitimacy of decisions reached with their help.
- Accept change based on those decisions.
- Trust managers who actually make and implement decisions.
- Volunteer new and creative ideas and solutions.

Autocratic management may stifle creativity, not use available expertise, and fail to establish motivation and commitment. Autocratic management can, however, be more effective when time is short, when the leader is the most knowledgeable person, and where those who would participate will never reach a decision with which they all agree.

Participative management leads to better decisions . . .

Many managers reject the concept of participative management because they do not want to lose control over 'management' decisions. Participation thus depends on the attitudes of managers towards this aspect of their job. There is a lot of research demonstrating the advantages of such attitude change.

William Pasmore and Frank Friedlander were asked to study work injuries which were reducing productivity in an American electronics company. About a third of the company's 335 employees had complained about pains in their wrists, arms and shoulders, some had undergone surgery to relieve their symptoms, and one woman had permanently lost the use of her right hand. A series of medical and technical investigations had failed to find the cause of the injuries.

But the company management had never thought of asking the employees themselves about the possible causes of their injuries. So the researchers suggested that a 'Studies and Communications Group' be set up drawing workers' representatives from each area of the factory. The group members discussed their own work experiences and injuries, designed a questionnaire, surveyed over 300 other employees and produced sixty recommendations for solving the injury problem.

Management at first rejected the Group's recommendations because management practices were identified as the main cause of the problem. The Group had found that injuries were related to:

- Inadequate training.
- Rapid, repetitive arm movements.
- Badly adjusted machines.
- Frustration at machine breakdowns.
- Stress from supervisors' behaviour (such as favouritism).
- Pressure from management for more output.

The first attempts by management to solve the problem had in fact made it worse. When workers were injured, production fell, management increased the pressure for more output, which increased workers' stress, which in turn led to more injuries.

The researchers conclude that a permanent change in the relationships between workers and management is necessary to create a climate of effective participation. The managers in this company felt that they had lost control over the situation. But as the workers' recommendations were gradually implemented the number of injuries fell and the overall performance of the factory rose.

Based on William Pasmore and Frank Friedlander (1982), 'An action research programme to increase employee involvement in problem solving', *Administrative Science Quarterly*, 27 (3): 343–62.

Research and theory thus suggest that organizational leaders should adopt a contingency approach and choose the most appropriate style for each occasion. There are however three reasons why an organizational leader may not be able to change style and still be effective.

First, personality may not be flexible enough. One of the theories of personality [. . .] argues that personality is inherited and fairly static. This would create problems for the manager who wished to be participative in some circumstances and dictatorial in others. The manager who is motivated by affiliation and who values the friendship of others may find it hard to treat subordinates in a harsh and autocratic way.

Second, the demands of the task and of other managers constrain what is acceptable for an individual manager to do. If a manager's own superior believes in the effectiveness of an autocratic leadership style then it may be hard for subordinate managers to behave in a way that could block their own promotion chances.

Third, there may be advantages in honesty and consistency. Subordinates may not accept the fickle behaviour of the participative manager who adopts an autocratic style when that appears to be necessary. Subordinates may see through the act of the autocrat who tries to act in a participative way. The leader who changes style from

Organizational demands constrain the manager ...

On the shop floor it's said, about a couple of Riverside managers in particular, that 'They aren't bad blokes. Given that they're managers, that is. They'd do anything for you *personally.*' '*Personally*' means letting a bloke borrow your car spraying equipment, or talking to him about what it would be like for his son to do O-level chemistry, or, providing things aren't too tight, helping him to get time off. It also means not driving it home unnecessarily that you are a manager. But 'personally' or not, these men are still managers. The theories of psycho-sociology notwithstanding, they've had to learn the hard way about 'man-management' and how to defend their 'right to manage'. And this means that 'in this game you can either be a bastard or a bad bastard'. ('Bad bastards' are managers who behave like bastards because they are bastards. Common or garden 'bastards' are men who find that, as managers, there are unpleasant things they have to do.)

From Theo Nichols and Huw Beynon (1977), *Living With Capitalism: Class Relations and the Modern Factory*. London: Routledge and Kegan Paul. p. 34.

one situation to another may not inspire confidence and trust in subordinates.

There are on the other hand three reasons why an organizational leader should be able to change style to suit the circumstances in order to be more effective.

First, theorists disagree about the rigidity of human personality. Many theorists have argued that it is possible for individuals to alter their personality and to incorporate new behaviours as a result of their experiences. So the autocrat who finds that a task-orientated style does not always work well could adopt a participative approach at least in some circumstances.

Second, organizations themselves are not rigid social arrangements with fixed tasks and structures. The tasks of an organization and the people who perform them are constantly changing. Organizational leaders thus need to be able to change as organizational circumstances change. As demands for improved quality of working life and more worker participation develop, managers who fail to respond appropriately will find themselves in difficulty.

Third, the manager who is able to adapt in a flexible way to changes in circumstances may be seen as more competent than one who sticks rigidly to traditional routines or who fails to adapt to the expectations of another culture.

Management styles vary around the world . . .

André Laurent, from Insead in France, asked nationals from twelve countries whether they agreed with the statement, 'It is important for a manager to have at hand precise answers to most of the questions that his subordinates may raise about their work.' The percentages agreeing with this were:

Japan	78
Indonesia	73
Italy	66
France	53
Germany	46
Belgium	44
Switzerland	38
Britain	27
Denmark	23
United States	18
Holland	17
Sweden	10

Managers in France and Indonesia, for example, are seen as experts who are expected to have the answers. Managers in America and Holland are regarded as participative problem-solvers. Differences like this explain some of the problems that, for instance, Japanese managers might have when working in Denmark, or that Swedish managers might have in relationships with colleagues and subordinates in Italy.

Based on André Laurent (1989), 'The cultural diversity of Western conceptions of management', *International Studies of Management and Organization*, 13 (1–2): 75–96.

Leadership style is not a problem that an organization manager can approach in a mechanical way. The factors that have to be taken into account are many and complex, and include:

- The manager's own personality.
- The needs of subordinates.
- The demands of the task.
- Organizational constraints.
- Cultural values and expectations.

There is, therefore, no simple recipe for the manager looking for the most effective style. Management style probably can be changed, but only if management values change too. Any attempt to change deep rooted values is ambitious, but this may be necessary in the interests of organizational effectiveness.

6

How can I win if you don't lose? Games where the winner doesn't take all

Judith Knelman

It's commonly believed so-called zero-sum games like Monopoly, poker and bridge, in which what one player wins represents the loss to his opponents, are an imitation of life. Success means someone else's failure, a feast someone else's famine. Survival of the fittest means it's you or the other guy: to keep on top of the competition, you have to deprive others of what you all want.

Anatol Rapoport, professor emeritus at University of Toronto, director of the Institute for Advanced Studies in Vienna [. . .] demonstrates, among other things, the folly of this notion [. . .] in a statistical analysis of how people tend to resolve conflict.

By means of a program of strategy he has worked out for a simple game called the Prisoner's Dilemma, which looks something like tick-tack-toe and takes even less time to play, he is able to show that life is not a zero-sum game at all. Not only is it not necessary for the winner to take all: it is impossible. The winner does best by sharing and never attempting to put one over on the opponent. To win, you quietly follow the other person's lead, never trying to outmanoeuvre him except in immediate retaliation.

Life, says Rapoport, is a mixed motive game in which the interests of people partly coincide and partly conflict. To get what they want, they have to co-operate. They must trust each other consistently and be prepared to share the rewards available.

The game, which was discovered and circulated in the early 1950s, has aroused a tremendous amount of interest in academic circles, he says, because it demonstrates an important moral lesson: that the meek shall inherit the earth. When it is played in a situation that simulates society or evolution – a tournament environment wherein every player used his own peculiar strategy consistently against every other player and then against himself – those who co-operate do much better than those who try to trick their opponents.

Abridged from J. Knelman, 'How can I win if you don't lose?, in G. Morgan (ed.), *Creative Organization Theory*, Newbury Park: Sage, 1989, pp. 84–6; originally from University of Toronto *Graduate*, January/February 1984.

'Think of two scorpions in a bottle', he suggests. 'If neither attacks, both will survive. If one attacks, the other retaliates, and both die. An even worse situation for the scorpions develops when one has to plot its strategy for survival on the assumption that the other may attack at any time.'

The game worked out to represent the Prisoner's Dilemma mathematically gives each prisoner two alternatives. Each is told that if both keep quiet they will both get a sentence of two years, but if one rats he will get off free while the accomplice will get five years. The catch is that if they rat on one another, both will get four years. If each is sure that the other will keep quiet as well, that is the best course for both. But can they trust each other?

The dilemma of the game is in the circumstance that it is in the best interest of each prisoner to implicate the other whether or not the other co-operates. If the other keeps quiet, he will still get a two-year sentence, while telling on the other gets him off free. As betrayal by both results in a four-year sentence, while keeping quiet could result in a five-year sentence, it's best to rat no matter what the other does. However, if neither rats, both get only two years.

Robert Axelrod decided to extend this problem to a tournament using computers to find the best consistent strategy for this sort of dilemma, which regularly confronts individuals and governments, in the form of potential rewards rather than punishments. The goal is to do as well as possible in your dealings with others over the long term. Rapoport won over all the other experts with the shortest and simplest program submitted, TIT FOR TAT, which shows that you do not have to deprive others in order to succeed yourself. His strategy is to co-operate or defect according to the lead of the other player. Even the most successful of the rival programs came to grief when they had to play against themselves, but TIT FOR TAT did nothing to hurt itself. It demonstrates the golden rule, do unto others as you would have them do unto you.

You play the game over and over again with the same partner, so that what happens in one game influences what happens in the next. You also play it over and over again with other people, just as you interact more than once with a large group of people in your everyday life. The idea is to accumulate the highest overall score. It is not necessary to vanquish individual rivals in order to do this. [. . .]

The research has obvious implications in many areas from domestic to international. Rapoport uses it to plead publicly for nuclear disarmament. [. . .] He thinks that like two scorpions in a bottle we are doomed if we do not trust our rivals. And even if our trust is not justified, he points out – if the other side does not disarm and we do – we may actually be safer than if we remained armed, since once we are no longer a threat they would have no need to attack us.

'I have no use for either superpower', says Rapoport. 'I very much admire the small democratic countries that are not powerful.' Canada, he says, is 'sensible'. It has the advantages of the US without succumbing to the excesses. [. . .] As in the game, the secret of success lies in the correct definition of the problem. 'You make your choice by asking not "How do I do better"', says Rapoport, 'but "How do we do better?" You have to trust each other to co-operate. Then the answer is obvious.'

References

Hofstadter, D.H.R. (1983) 'Metamagical themas', *Scientific American*, May: 16–26.
Rapoport, Anatol (1960) *Fights, Games and Debates*. Ann Arbor: University of Michigan Press.

7

The £5 auction

Charles Handy

I used to play a simple game with executives on training exercises. It
was a variety of what logicians call the Prisoner's Dilemma, except
that in this game I offered to auction three £5 notes between two
participants. I would place two volunteers in chairs facing away
from each other so that they could not see the other's face. I asked
them to bid in turn for the first note. Invariably the first person bid
£1, the second upped it, and so it went on, by alternate bids,
sometimes going up by £1, sometimes jumping by £2, sometimes by
parts of a pound, until one of them reached £5 at which point the
other normally, but not always, stopped bidding. In one case,
someone actually bid £23 for the first £5 note! The auction for the
second note gave first bid to the other side but the outcome was the
same – £5 or more bid for my £5 note. So it was for the third note,
although there was often overbidding for this note, too, so that one
side could claim a sort of pyrrhic victory – more notes won, and to
hell with the cost!

The rest of the group would be watching, amazed by the apparent
idiocy of the bidding. There would be a rush of volunteers for the
next round, eager to try their theory of pre-emptive bidding or
whatever. The result would be the same, as long as I was careful to
pick them from different sides of the room. Finally, I would choose
a couple who had been sitting and whispering together and who
volunteered in unison. When they started the bidding, the first
person would bid 10 pence and the second would say 'no bid'. The
note had been sold for 10p. The same happened the other way round
with the second note. The third note was more tense. Usually their
agreement held. The first person bid the now-standard 10p and the
other passed. At the end, they took the three £5 notes, paid me 30p
and shared the proceeds. Occasionally, however, competition flared
up again for this final note and the second bidder would come in
with a pre-emptive £5 bid. They would then have to make do with
£4.90p profit and live with a sense of betrayal.

What was going on? I would ask the group. Logical, sensible,

Abridged from C. Handy, *The Empty Raincoat*, London: Hutchinson, 1994, pp.
104–5.

mature individuals were competing to the point of lunacy because I had kept them apart. By not allowing them to communicate, I had also prevented them from establishing an alliance, an agreed objective and a means of proceeding. Only when I picked people who had had a chance to talk together were they able to achieve a common goal which benefited them both, although even that broke down on occasion. A common cause, the willingness to deny oneself in the interests of that common cause, and the trust that the other party will do the same – these are the essentials of sensible organisation behaviour. Much of the time this sensible behaviour does not happen because people do not talk, do not trust and have no common cause. To put it more crisply, there is no sense of a second citizenship, and therefore no possibility of sensible compromise, of a proper balance between the whole and the parts.

The depressing thing was that the experiment never failed. It always worked the way I knew it would. We instinctively work for our own immediate advantage unless there is an obvious common cause with people whom we can trust so that an initial sacrifice turns out in the end to be to our mutual advantage. We can, today, see the £5-auction game being played for real around the world.

PART 2
MOTIVATION AND STRESS AT WORK

8

Profit-related pay: a retrospective

Greg Clark

Since the mid 1980s, the British government has been eager for employees to be paid according to the profitability of the companies that employ them. Profit-related pay (PRP) has attracted tax relief in Britain since the 1986 budget. The Government's enthusiasm seems to be having some effect: by 1995 over 2 million employees were covered by PRP schemes. Ten years after PRP first received government sanction, it is opportune to step back and review how far PRP has achieved its aims.

Even without tax relief, paying people in ways which differ from the conventional fixed wage system has found favour in continental Europe. German organisations have been the focus of much research attention (Cable and Wilson, 1988) which has sought to evaluate the success of payment systems involving profit-sharing.

In this chapter we explain the arguments which have been advanced to justify the decision by companies to introduce profit-related pay schemes, and offer a set of critical perspectives with the aim of encouraging a more questioning approach to the benefits of PRP.

Arguments for PRP

Three main arguments have been made to justify the introduction of profit-related pay. These are that:

- PRP provides an incentive for employees to be more productive.
- PRP reduces the need to dismiss employees during recessions.
- PRP brings about increased identification of employees with their employer.

PRP as an incentive

Tying people's pay to company profits means that if the company becomes more prosperous, so do employees.[1] If we assume that employees can influence the prosperity of the company through their behaviour, for example by putting in more effort, or taking care to avoid waste, then, the argument runs, a system of profit-related pay will provide them with an incentive to behave in ways which are productive for the company.

The view of PRP as an incentive places profit-related pay in the field of *performance*-related pay more generally. Performance-related pay systems, whilst they have attained some recent popularity, have a long pedigree: the very earliest systems of pay (such as share-cropping) rewarded workers by giving them a share of their output. More recently, theoretical models have been built which seek to explain *how* incentives cause people to supply more effort. Most prominent among these is *expectancy theory*.

Expectancy theory suggests that cognitive links between people's effort, performance and outcomes determine behaviour at work. In particular, for PRP to motivate people to work harder, three conditions must be met:

1 People must feel that changing their behaviour will affect the profitability of the company (expectancy).
2 They must be convinced that an improved performance by the company will bring them reward in the form of a higher PRP payout (instrumentality).
3 Employees must value the reward on offer (valence).

This means to say that if people see it as clear that by supplying more effort they will improve company profitability, and that this will lead to them receiving a valuable payout from a PRP scheme, then they are more likely to work harder than if they believe any of these relationships are slight or uncertain.

PRP to promote employment stability

The argument that PRP can reduce the need for companies to make their workers redundant during slack times is straightforward. Companies are subject to turbulent conditions in their environment, including the business cycle of recession and recovery. During recessions companies inevitably come under pressure to cut costs. Since labour accounts for an average of 75% of firms' total costs, employees cannot avoid bearing a share of the need to adjust. Faced with the need to moderate labour costs, companies can introduce flexibility into their wage bills in two ways: they can either maintain a stable wage for those employed and vary the number of employees during the cycle; or they can maintain a relatively stable workforce and allow pay to fluctuate.

.On the assumption that company profits fall during recessions, introducing PRP can help lower the wage bill without recourse to redundancies. This is better for companies, it is argued, because they can avoid incurring redundancy costs, and losing the investment which they have made in training their employees. Moreover, when trading conditions improve, they do not have to engage in large-scale programmes of recruitment and selection, which can be both costly and disruptive.

It was the employment stability argument which persuaded the government to offer tax relief for companies practising PRP. In his 1986 Budget Speech, the Chancellor Nigel Lawson told the House of Commons: 'The problem we face in this country . . . is the rigidity of the pay system. If the only element of flexibility is in the number of people employed, then redundancies are inevitably more likely to occur.'

PRP to promote co-operation at work

The third argument made to promote PRP is that it can serve as a means to unite the interests of owners and employees, and so encourage a climate of co-operation and common purpose at work. This arises from the idea that all parties will share an interest in the profitability of the firm, so that they will put aside purely sectional interests. In the words of Cable and FitzRoy (1980), who made a detailed study of PRP in German organisations, 'participatory firms . . . will produce better outcomes than traditional firms if the negative collusion to maximise one party's share . . . can be replaced by positive collusion to maximise joint wealth.'

Such effects are argued to be good for both employees and the firm: a greater interest in the company, and a reduction in 'us and them' attitudes between owners, managers and workers, improves the quality of working life for everyone at work. A more harmonious culture will reflect itself in the firm becoming more productive and competitive as it changes from being 'us against them (the managers)' to 'us against them (the competition)'.

The problems with PRP

When PRP enjoyed its renaissance during the mid 1980s, some commentators had high hopes for what it could achieve. One of the most influential proponents, Professor Martin Weitzman, of the Massachusetts Institute of Technology, went so far as to argue that PRP could permanently cure the Western economies of the problem of stagflation – low growth co-existing with high inflation. Today, even the strongest advocates of PRP do not regard it as a panacea for the ills either of companies or of the economy. Each of the arguments in favour of PRP has been subject to robust criticism.

PRP as an incentive

Expectancy theory has been used by critics of PRP, as well as its advocates, as the primary framework for analysing the viability of PRP as an incentive for employees to work harder.

Expectancy theory predicts that only if the three conditions of high expectancy, instrumentality and valence are met in a profit-related pay contract will PRP have the power to boost employee effort. But the effect an individual employee can have on the performance of the company as a whole is likely to be vanishingly small, implying a low level of expectancy. Also the profitability of a company may well be determined by a multitude of other factors, including the actions of competitors and the state of the economy, tending to suggest that the instrumentality between superior employee performance and profits will be low.

Related to this is a third point: profits are not as objectively verifiable as may first appear to be the case. In practice, firms enjoy considerable discretion over how much profit they report in a particular year. This may be achieved, for example, by varying depreciation policies. Another problem is that, since the average proportion of salary paid as a profit-share is less than 3%, the rewards offered by PRP are likely to be insufficient to motivate employees to alter their behaviour: in other words its valence is low. Taken together, these problems can lead to the conclusion that in most cases the policy of PRP cannot be relied on to increase effort.

There are other reasons why PRP may not succeed in spurring the workforce. One is that some people may not be especially motivated by money as a reward; this hypothesis is discussed by Adrian Furnham in the next chapter. Another is that not everyone may *think* in the kind of individualistic, calculative way which expectancy theory implies: rather than determine their actions by weighing up the rewards on offer, they may be happy to conform to group norms almost irrespective of the outcome. Etzioni (1988) has argued that in practice people behave according to their values, rather than as the rational calculating machine which underlies expectancy theory.

PRP to promote employment stability

If a company enters a recession from which it expects to recover, it may be reasonable to encourage all employees to share a dose of financial austerity, rather than have to resort to redundancies, followed by a new round of recruitment and training when conditions recover. A problem arises, however, in that it may be difficult for the firm to see at the time whether trading difficulties it faces are cyclical or long term. That is to say, will the same number of employees be needed in the future as in the past? If not, retaining all workers by paying them less may simply put off the day when redundancies have to be made.

An example of this problem can be found in the experience of some financial institutions in the City of London during the early 1990s. Having invested large sums of money in recruiting brokers in the aftermath of the market deregulation of October 1986 (the so-called 'Big Bang'), the financial markets experienced much less business than anticipated. It was argued that the low volume levels were a temporary phenomenon and would recover. The fact that much of employees' pay was profit-related allowed firms to retain their staff in spite of the contraction in business. Yet it gradually became clear that the downturn in volume was not a short-term aberration, and in 1989, over two years later, substantial redundancies were made in many City firms.

Even if a company expects to recover from a downturn, and is minded to retain its workforce intact, it may be thwarted by investors. The economic journalist Robert Chote has argued that financial institutions have come to regard redundancy programmes as a signal that the management of a recession-hit company is making serious attempts to restore profitability. So for short-term reasons, companies may be under pressure to make redundancies to avoid criticism or a takeover attempt in the stock market.

In circumstances in which good employees are relatively footloose – they can leave to join other firms – a profit-sharing company experiencing hard times, reflected in reduced pay for employees, may find itself unable to retain a high-quality workforce. This is especially true if there is any suspicion among employees that firms might seek to massage profit to damp down profit-related bonuses when recovery comes. During downturns, firms who pay the market wage may be in a position to poach the top employees of profit-sharing firms, since their pay will have been hit by the contraction in their PRP element. As a result, the ability of the firm to recover from recession may be undermined, as competitive advantage is ceded to the competition.

PRP to promote co-operation at work

The case against the argument that profit-related pay can bring about an improvement in relationships at work has much in common with the expectancy theory critique of PRP. That is to say, most PRP schemes provide for such a small proportion of employees' income being tied to profits that any fundamental conflict of interest which exists between workers and managers will be largely unaffected.

Trade unions in Britain have generally opposed the introduction of PRP. It is not difficult to see why: PRP represents an erosion of the principle of collective bargaining with unions over pay, and thereby threatens one of the traditional *raisons d'être* of the union movement. This may be the key to the actual intention of PRP regarding industrial relations. Rather than fundamentally altering the interests of employees and employers, PRP may be a catalyst which enables managers to communicate directly with employees, rather than via trade union representatives. Much recent practitioner-oriented writing in management has emphasised the desirability of building networks of direct communication in organisations: PRP may be seen as a means to this end.

Whether this is in the interests of employees, as well as owners, is a matter of debate. Some argue that the blurring of traditional boundaries and policies results in employees misperceiving an essential conflict of interest with their employers; others contend that a profitable firm is a prerequisite for employee prosperity whatever the size of the payback in terms of a profit-related bonus.

Does PRP work?

Despite increasing use of profit-related pay by companies, most research studies conclude that there is only patchy evidence that PRP is achieving any of the aims put forward in the three arguments outlined above.

Poole and Jenkins (1988), in a survey of 2,000 employees covered by profit-sharing schemes, found that 67% said that having PRP had made no difference to the effort they put into their work (although a significant minority, 32%, said it had made them supply more effort). Addressing the employment stability argument, Luther (1992) found that employers were reluctant to retain workers who would otherwise have been made redundant during recessions: 'employment decisions are perceived to be taken on the basis of the work that will need to be done in the future, and are not affected by the way in which surpluses or deficits may be shared with employees.' Among researchers investigating the industrial relations case for PRP, Estrin and Wilson (1989) noted that profit-sharing firms enjoyed more harmonious records of employee relations, but questioned whether this was a result of PRP being favoured by companies already disposed to participation.

Conclusion

Almost ten years after profit-related pay received government encouragement, the case for introducing PRP is far from proven. In fact the terrain has become more complex, with widely different arguments both for and against the policy, and an ambiguous set of empirical findings. Companies considering introducing PRP must address this complexity by being clear as to which of the various possible aims they have, and monitoring performance against them. It cannot be taken for granted that PRP will achieve the desired results in every organisation.

Notes

1 Although profit-related pay is, by definition, limited to for-profit companies, the incentive argument applies to performance-related pay more generally, which is common in the public and not-for-profit sectors as well as in the private sector.

References

Cable, J. and FitzRoy, F. (1980) 'Cooperation and productivity: some evidence from West German experience', *Economic Analysis and Workers Management*, 14 (2).
Cable, J. and Wilson, N. (1988) 'Profit sharing and productivity: an international comparison'. Research paper, University of Warwick.
Estrin, S. and Wilson, N. (1989) 'Profit sharing: the marginal cost of labour and employment variability'. Discussion paper, London School of Economics.
Etzioni, A. (1988) *The Moral Dimension*. New York: Free Press.
Luther, R. (1992) *Profit-Related Pay: Practice and Theory*. London: Institute of Chartered Accountants.
Poole, M. and Jenkins, G. (1988) 'How employees respond to profit sharing', *Personnel Management*, July.

9

Does money motivate?

Adrian Furnham

Academics, management gurus and front-line managers do not always agree. Often they don't like or respect each other, and occasionally the people at the coalface simply disagree with those in the ivory tower.

One topic that never goes away is money – or, more importantly, its ability to motivate the average worker. Middle managers believe money is the most powerful motivator. Paradoxically, it is nearly always those who do not have it in their power to motivate with money who believe this to be the case. By contrast, the people who have control over the purse strings may not regard money as very relevant.

Is money a consistent and powerful motivator? Or should companies look to job satisfaction and career advancement? What other motivators are there?

Classical organisation theorists assumed that workers had to be driven by the carrot and the stick, which may often have been true during the industrial revolution.

Occupational psychologists reacted very strongly to these views and in some books failed to discuss economic incentives at all. The psychologists cite support from surveys in which workers were asked which factors were most important in making a job good or bad. Pay commonly came sixth or seventh after security, co-workers, interesting work and welfare arrangements. Recent surveys have rated pensions and other benefits as more important than the level of wages.

The basic psychology of incentives is that behaviour can be influenced if it is linked to some desired reward. Speed of work is an example. There is little doubt that people work harder when paid by results than by time put in.

Other studies have shown the effects of an incentive plan for reducing absenteeism, which fell at once as soon as the plan was introduced and which rose again when it was discontinued. Money may also act as an incentive for people to stay with their organisation.

From A. Furnham, 'Does money motivate?', *The Sunday Times*, 9 October 1994.

In a performance-related pay system, performance may be measured by piecework, group piecework, measured day work or merit appraisal, and pay may include profit sharing. But the competitiveness that characterises these systems can often cause problems.

The simple fact is that money is but one motivator. Job security, a pleasant environment and a considerate boss are all motivators as well. Consider the following: would you prefer £1,000 (tax free) or a week's extra holiday? £1,000 or a new job title? £5,000 or a job guarantee for life? Put like that, as a choice between money alone and other motivators, the power of money declines.

If money *is* a powerful motivator or satisfier at work, why has research consistently shown that there is no relationship between wealth and happiness? There are four good reasons why this is so:

- *Adaptation*   Although everybody feels 'happier' after a pay rise, windfall or pools win, one soon adapts to this and the effect disappears rapidly.
- *Comparison*   People define themselves as wealthy by comparison against others. However, on moving into more upmarket circles they find there is always somebody who is wealthier.
- *Alternatives*   As economists say, the declining marginal utility of money means that as one has more of the stuff, other things such as freedom and true friendship seem much more valuable.
- *Worry*   Increased income is associated with a shifting of concern from money issues to the more uncontrollable elements of life (such as self-development), perhaps because money is associated with a sense of control over one's fate.

Money does not always bring happiness. People with £10m are no happier than people with only £9m. Yes, everyone wants more money. Economists, the dismal scientists, are right: money does act as a work motivator, but to a large extent *in the short term*, for some workers more than others, and at a cost often to the morale of the organisation.

We live in a world in which money is overestimated. It does not buy friends, merely a better class of enemy. The accumulation of money does not end people's troubles, it merely changes them.

The power of money as a motivator is shortlived. Furthermore, it has less effect the more comfortable the people are. Albert Camus, the author, was right when he said it was a kind of spiritual snobbery to believe people could be happy without money. But given or earning a modest amount, the value of other work benefits become greater.

10

Job features and excessive stress

Peter Warr

Good mental health at work can be promoted by two means: assisting and counselling individual people, or the effective design of jobs. [. . .] The former approach is of great value (see also Firth and Shapiro, 1986), but if job conditions remain unchanged we have not usually altered the source of the problem. Organizations should therefore start their investigations into mental ill-health by examining the nature of their jobs.

Focusing upon the content of work is also valuable in enhancing the acceptability of mental health issues to managers and other employees. It is often difficult to gain company interest in [stress . . .], because people prefer to give the impression that mental ill-health is a problem for someone else rather than for them. However, discussions about the effective design of jobs have clearly practical objectives, focusing upon improved work performance as well as procedures to reduce excessive employee stress.

I start from the position that some stress is inevitable in any job, as indeed in any aspect of life. That is not necessarily bad. But when job stress is extreme or extended over a long period, then we should be concerned. Our concern may be because of the harm that is being done to an employee and his or her family; or it may be because of the fact that excessive stress impairs work effectiveness, reduces productivity, and costs the organization money.

Research on the causes of excessive stress at work

Research findings in this area are based on two kinds of study. First, one can look at the people employed in different kinds of work, and ask them about their job-related anxiety, tension, distress, dissatisfaction, depression and so on, investigating how those stress reactions differ between jobs (e.g. Loher et al., 1985). Second, an investigator

Abridged from P. Warr, 'Job features and excessive stress', in R. Jenkins and N. Coney (eds), *Prevention of Mental Ill-health at Work*, London: HMSO, 1992, pp. 40–9.

might carry out an experiment, arranging for changes to be made in a stressful job, and recording the effects of the changes in terms of employee mental health (e.g. Wall and Clegg, 1981). From both kinds of study, the picture is now becoming clear; there are certain features of jobs that are particularly implicated in causing excessive stress.

I will summarize those characteristics in terms of nine general features, which are present at some level in every job (Warr, 1987). First, however, I should emphasize that at most levels those job features are not particularly problematic. Across a wide range of, say, working conditions, employees are not especially stressed. But at certain *extreme* levels, we can expect problems.

The characteristics of jobs which influence stress

The nine key job characteristics can be listed as follows. In most cases, I have identified one end of the continuum for particular consideration in the present context.

1   Low job discretion
2   Low use of skills
3   Low or high work demands
4   Low task variety
5   High uncertainty
6   Low pay
7   Poor working conditions
8   Low interpersonal support
9   Low value in society.

The first feature, *low job discretion*, is particularly likely to cause excessive stress in a job. Job discretion is the most important single characteristic of work. It is absolutely essential that employees should have an area of freedom, in which they (rather than their boss or the equipment) are empowered to make decisions, to plan their work, and to tackle problems as they arise. Research has repeatedly shown that people whose jobs are excessively constraining in this respect are likely to experience undesirable levels of stress, in terms of anxiety, depression, apathy, low self-esteem and low self-confidence (e.g. Ganster and Fusilier, 1989).

To many readers that may sound like common sense, but in practice most organizations arrange things so that many lower-level employees have only a little opportunity to control what goes on in their work-place. People are often constrained by fixed procedures and routines, by unchangeable pacing, or by the requirements of computers or other machines.

There are a number of reasons for that, including a general wish within organizations for standardized procedures and for strong managerial control over what goes on. Yet increasing employee job discretion has the obvious benefit of permitting work problems to be tackled effectively at their source, rather than passing requests up and down a chain of command. For that pragmatic reason alone, you would expect it to be attractive to many companies.

A second feature that can give rise to excessive job stress is the *low use of skills*. It is repeatedly found that workers who have greater opportunity for skill use are mentally more healthy than colleagues with little opportunity. That relationship is found across manual jobs themselves, as well as between white- and blue-collar workers. For example, among production workers in a car factory, a particularly strong predictor of low mental health was the extent to which people felt unable to use their skills (Kornhauser, 1965).

This job characteristic is associated with the fact that employees in *lower-level* jobs are often the ones under particular stress. Research has repeatedly indicated that the poorest mental health, in terms of greater depression and lower active involvement in life, is found among workers at the bottom of an organization, not among the supposedly overstressed executives; the latter are however more likely to report job-related anxiety (e.g. Warr, 1990).

The harmful effect of under-use of skills means that when considering the third job feature, *work demands*, we should be concerned about very low levels as well as very high levels of demand. Particularly important are *intellectual*, as well as physical, demands. It is certain that long periods of repeated deadlines, intense concentration, and relentless pressure can cause excessive stress. There is nothing surprising about that. But it should be emphasized that very *low* work demands also impair mental health, and there are a lot of jobs that are deficient in that respect (e.g. Warr, 1987).

Jobs that make very few intellectual demands on a person are also those that are low in terms of the first two features in the list: job discretion, and the use of skills. Those three features are of course overlapping in practice, and I will return to that fact later.

A fourth feature that can impair mental health is the marked absence of *task variety* in a job. Repetitive, monotonous work is soul-destroying and alienating; workers in that kind of job do not learn anything new and they have no challenges to draw them out and give them a sense of achievement. Poor mental health is common in those unchanging circumstances. That is seen both in low-level jobs and also among mid-career people at all levels who have become locked into fixed and over-familiar activities. Such people experience little active involvement in their work, and they contribute to their employer much less than they could.

A fifth potential stressor is *high uncertainty*, especially when that extends across a long period of time. There are two main forms of uncertainty at work. First is an absence of knowledge or feedback about how well you are doing, and about what kinds of behaviour are considered desirable. Second is a lack of information about the future: how likely is the company to survive, how secure is your job, or how will your career develop?

Everyone has those concerns at some time, and of course they can have an unavoidable basis in reality. Sometimes these uncertainties can be reduced, but in many cases one has to live with them. In general, however, surveys have indicated that many people believe that their employer does not take seriously enough the requirements of effective communication.

Low pay, the sixth feature, is also unavoidable in some cases. Nevertheless, it is undoubtedly true that people living in very difficult financial circumstances exhibit considerable mental ill-health of the kind discussed here. As a major job stressor, I take it that we should concentrate on those low levels of income that are clearly harmful. People will always grumble about their pay and its comparability with others, and I certainly would not count those quite normal grumbles as evidence of excessive stress.

Seventh in the list are *poor working conditions*. In a sense, several of the previous features represent poor conditions of a psychological and social kind; the focus in item 7 is on poor *physical* conditions. Particularly noisy, hot, wet, or dangerous environments, from which a person cannot escape, are known to be associated with employee stress. Of course, poor physical conditions in a job are often accompanied by other stressful features of the kind I have already mentioned.

Low interpersonal support at work has been found to be associated with high anxiety, emotional exhaustion, job tension, and low job and life satisfaction. I would emphasize again that it is only when support is extremely low that we are justified in seeing that as a cause of excessive job stress.

Finally, research has pointed to the negative impact of being employed in a job which is viewed as being of *low value in society*. People see their jobs as important or unimportant to them in various ways, one of which is their contribution to society. Many jobs, in medicine for instance, can be very satisfying in those terms. Most other jobs are broadly neutral in this respect, but some are clearly viewed as 'the dregs'. Given that such low-value work has to be done by someone, it is not clear how that evaluation can be changed, and I include this theme mainly for completeness.

The distribution of these job characteristics

What can be said about the pattern of these nine job features in work as a whole? It seems to be the case that *lower-level positions* in

British industry and commerce are constrained in such a way that often there are only low levels of the first four features. Of course, that does not necessarily lead to mental ill-health, but it certainly makes it more likely in the extreme cases I have been considering. For *managers*, high work demands and high uncertainty (features 3 and 5) are perhaps more prevalent, so that their stresses (if any) are likely to have a different source.

In many cases, it is the *combination* of job features that we need to consider. For instance, very low use of skills is in practice likely to be accompanied by low job discretion. However, less obvious combinations may arise from seemingly sound management motives. In one company that was introducing new computer-based equipment, operators were now required to attend very closely to their equipment for long periods. The job was altered in ways which demanded careful and continuous monitoring. Those greater attentional demands increased operator stress levels, but arguably to a still acceptable level.

However, the company thought it appropriate to transfer to the new machines their most expensive products, so that the employees were now responsible for material that was worth many thousand pounds. That material could be lost by a mistake on their part; and the additional cost responsibility *in conjunction with* the raised attentional demands proved to be particularly stressful (Martin and Wall, 1989). Such a high level of stress could quite easily have been avoided, by rescheduling the work, but of course the problem had to be recognized in the first place.

One combination that is especially harmful is found in jobs that have both very high work demands and very low employee discretion. Many investigations have shown that this particular combination (high demands and low discretion) gives rise to lowered mental health and a range of physical symptoms, including an increased risk of heart attacks and other cardiac problems (e.g. Karasek and Theorell, 1990). If the *combination* of the two potential stressors can be avoided, then high work demands can often be handled well. Hard work alone is not necessarily an excessive stressor, but sustained hard work in the absence of personal discretion is definitely harmful.

That leads on to the general, over-riding, importance of employee job discretion. An absence of the opportunity to make decisions about how to get the work done is the primary source of unacceptable stress. From a lack of discretion flow the restricted use of skills, low job variety, and other problems within the nine features I have listed previously. Conversely, if a job is designed to permit employees to control some important aspects of their work, it will be necessary for them to possess and use relevant skills, and they will have the ability to introduce some variation into what they do. In addition, raised job discretion allows people to tackle unavoidable demands at times and in ways that are most satisfactory to them.

How may unacceptable job stress be reduced?

It follows from the section above that the primary way to reduce unacceptable job stress is to enhance employee job discretion. However, there are several other actions that need to be considered. I think that there are four main steps in redesigning jobs.

First, it is obvious that we have to think seriously about possible sources of stress: which job features in our organization are likely to be particularly harmful? We should review work in terms of the nine characteristics I have described, and particularly look out for combinations of those features which might be *unexpectedly* stressful.

Assuming that we identify some jobs that appear to be problematic, we have to be realistic. The second step is to decide what can, and what cannot, be changed. In some cases, there is not much that can be done without enormous expenditure. In those cases, the situation will probably have to remain as it is, but we can achieve a lot by rotating people between roles, so that any one worker is not exposed to the same stressors continuously and for long periods.

Third, we must try to tackle isolated problems one by one. For instance, if our enquiries reveal that the level of experienced uncertainty is so great that action is warranted, we might develop and implement new communication and feedback procedures. Or it might be possible and desirable to change some aspects of the physical working conditions.

The fourth step is the one with widest applicability and importance. Management should recognize the value of introducing into jobs greater freedom of action by lower-level employees. For the reasons I have outlined, that one step can have the greatest impact on excessively high levels of stress.

The downwards delegation of decision-making can also be very effective in increasing productivity. When employees are required, and trusted, to understand how their equipment functions, to think ahead to anticipate problems, and to take action to meet current targets, then their performance will be better than if they merely respond retrospectively to problems by calling on someone else to sort out the difficulty.

One important research finding is that the productivity benefits of downwards delegation are especially great in relatively unpredictable situations, when machine errors are likely to occur, or when materials are especially variable (Wall et al., 1990). That is especially notable, since in those unpredictable settings management is liable to move in the opposite direction – centralizing rather than devolving the authority for action.

Conclusions

Many British companies are now moving towards greater discretion for lower-level employees, and it has been commonplace for a long time in some other countries. In practice, the downward delegation of decision-making often creates the need for increased training, so that people can acquire the required knowledge and skills. It may also be helpful to permit *groups* of workers to decide among themselves how things should be done. That in turn requires more flexibility of procedures so that people can undertake a range of different activities.

Trade unions have often resisted developments of that kind, although they are increasingly seeing their value, especially when increased responsibility is accompanied by increased wages. However, greater discretion for low-level workers means that the jobs of chargehands or supervisors may need to be changed; there can be resistance from that quarter. Associated with that is the fact that financial savings can flow from a reduced need for supervisory staff, to counterbalance the increased responsibility and pay for lower-level employees.

Although I am recommending increased job discretion as a general approach to the reduction of excessive stress, it is clear that changes of that kind can themselves initially generate *more* stress. In terms of the job features I described previously, the new stress is mainly in terms of increased uncertainty: people initially have inadequate skills and knowledge, they do not know what to do, there may be conflicts between groups, and the future is unclear.

There is thus a paradox. In order to reduce the excessive stress arising from low discretion, low skill use and low work demands, it is often necessary to move through a period of enhanced stress, albeit of a different kind. Employees have to live with increased uncertainty, initially at a high level. For that period of change there is a need for careful planning, increased training and support for people to learn new things, and a willingness to amend decisions if they do not work out well. In a sense, then, we may sometimes have to make matters worse before they become better.

However, the important point here is that the *interim* stresses which are increased in a programme of downward delegation have the potential for developing employee skills and increasing personal competence, self-confidence, and job involvement. If the necessary changes can be worked through, both employees and the organization can become more confident and more effective.

The focus [here is on] excessive stress and improved mental health, and positive changes in those terms are of course inherently desirable. But, in addition to that inherent value, I am forcefully struck by the findings from research of several kinds, that excessive stress is bad for business. Managers are sometimes unimpressed by recommendations about stress-reduction, partly because it is not always clear when normal stress reaches a level that is unacceptable. However, procedures to manage stress are often the same as those which increase productivity. In many organizations, the procedures I have outlined can pay off in both respects: reducing stress and also increasing productivity.

References

Firth, J. and Shapiro, D.A. (1986) 'An evaluation of psychotherapy for job-related distress', *Journal of Occupational Psychology*, 59: 111–119.

Ganster, D.C. and Fusilier, M.R. (1989) 'Control in the workplace', in C.L. Cooper and I.T. Robertson (eds), *International Review of Industrial and Organizational Psychology*. Chichester: Wiley. pp. 235–80.

Karasek, R. and Theorell, T. (1990) *Healthy Work: Stress, Productivity, and the Reconstruction of Working Life*. New York: Basic Books.

Kornhauser, A.W. (1965) *Mental Health of the Industrial Worker*. New York: Wiley.

Loher, B.T., Noe, R.A., Moeller, N.L. and Fitzgerald, M.P. (1985) 'A meta-analysis of the relation of job characteristics to job satisfaction', *Journal of Applied Psychology*, 70: 280–9.

Martin, R. and Wall, T.D. (1989) 'Attentional demand and cost responsibility as stressors in shop-floor jobs', *Academy of Management Journal*, 32: 69–86.

Wall, T.D. and Clegg, C.W. (1981) 'A longitudinal field study of group work design', *Journal of Occupational Behaviour*, 2: 31–49.

Wall, T.D., Corbett, J.M., Martin, R., Clegg, C.W. and Jackson, P.R. (1990) 'Advanced manufacturing technology, work design, and performance: a change study', *Journal of Applied Psychology*, 75: 691–7.

Warr, P.B. (1987) *Work, Unemployment, and Mental Health*. Oxford: Oxford University Press.

Warr, P.B. (1990). 'The measurement of well-being and other aspects of mental health', *Journal of Occupational Psychology*, 63: 193–210.

11

Prevention and management of work stress

Lawrence R. Murphy

Occupational stress continues to be a topic of concern for employees and employers alike. The nature and complexity of the problem of occupational stress has been addressed in numerous published articles (e.g., Caplan et al., 1975; Cooper and Marshall, 1976; Ivancevich and Ganster, 1987) [. . .]. It has become clear that (1) stress occurs in all aspects of life, including work, and can lead to ill health; (2) stress is a highly individual experience that is determined by personal appraisals of work environment factors (one person's meat is another person's poison); and (3) stress is costing companies increasingly large amounts of money in terms of health care, productivity losses, and worker compensation claims (DeCarlo, 1987; National Institute for Occupational Safety and Health, 1987; Rosch and Pelletier, 1987). This state of affairs has prompted more and more companies to seek ways to deal with occupational stress.

Three distinct approaches to the problem of occupational stress are evident in organizational settings, each reflecting a different perspective on the problem. The most common approach is to provide treatment services to 'troubled' workers, usually in the form of employee assistance programs. This is a reactive approach (a problem already exists) that considers stress a personal problem. It typically does not involve efforts to identify stressful work factors. A second approach seeks to identify and change workplace factors that produce employee stress. This approach can be reactive or proactive (to prevent stress from becoming a problem). The approach acknowledges that work factors can contribute to employee stress and deals with the sources of stress, not employee distress. Unfortunately, scientific evaluations of this type of intervention are extremely rare in the published literature.

A third approach (and the topic of this chapter) is to offer health promotion or wellness programs to employees. Commonly labeled

Abridged from L.R. Murphy, 'Prevention and management of work stress', in J.W. Jones, B.D. Steffy and D.W. Bray (eds) *Applying Psychology in Business*, New York: Lexington Books, 1991, pp. 715–21.

stress management, these programs have become popular in work settings and have been the subject of a growing number of scientific evaluation studies. By and large, these programs have been pro-active; they are offered to all employees (not just those with evident problems), and the aim is stress prevention, not treatment. As a reactive measure to employee stress problems, these programs are clearly inappropriate.

Stress management techniques

Many of the techniques commonly used in stress management were borrowed from clinical psychology where they have demonstrated success in the treatment of anxiety and psychosomatic disorders (Pomerleau and Brady, 1979). Examples include biofeedback, progressive muscle relaxation, meditation, and cognitive (appraisal) restructuring (Murphy, 1984a).

In *biofeedback*, the individual is provided with information or feedback about the status of a biological function and, over time, can learn to control that function. For example, the electrical activity produced when muscles contract (tense) can be recorded and transformed into a tone whose pitch rises as the muscle tenses and falls as the muscle relaxes. By 'listening' to their muscle tension levels over a period of daily trials, individuals learn how to create a state of deep muscle relaxation. Through biofeedback, individuals have learned to control a range of biological functions, including heart rate, blood pressure, blood flow, stomach contractions, and muscle tension (Birk, 1973).

Progressive muscle relaxation (PMR) involves a series of tensing and relaxing exercises designed to foster awareness of muscle activity and heightened control over muscle activity (Jacobson, 1938). This is accomplished by first creating tension in a muscle group (e.g. making a tight fist), studying the feelings of tenseness, and then allowing the muscles to relax, noticing differences between the two states. By systematically moving through the major muscle groups of the body, individuals become proficient at recognizing tension in a muscle and relieving that tension. Exercises are continually abbreviated in length and scope to the point where a state of muscle relaxation can be self-induced in a matter of minutes. A number of audiocassette tapes containing PMR exercises are commercially available (e.g., Budzynski, 1974).

Various forms of *meditation* exist ranging from transcendental meditation (TM) to a nonreligious method developed by Benson (Benson, 1976). In Benson's method, one finds a quiet place and sits comfortably for 20 minutes twice a day. While maintaining a passive attitude toward intruding thoughts, the word *one* is repeated with each exhalation. Benson argues that such meditation invokes a relaxation response, the opposite of the stress response. With practice, individuals learn to invoke the relaxation response at will.

Finally, *cognitive strategies* focus on modifying perceptual or appraisal processes, which determine the stressfulness of situations. Such training involves examination of thinking patterns to modify irrational thoughts (e.g., 'everybody must like me all the time', 'everything I do must be perfect'), substitution of positive self-talk for the more common negative self-talk, and development of flexible problem-solving skills (Meichenbaum, 1977).

Stress management in work settings

In clinical settings, these techniques are taught to patients over an extended period of time (at least 12 weeks), during individualized, weekly sessions in the therapist's office. This format was modified extensively for application in work settings as follows. Program emphasis was on prevention, not treatment, training was compressed into six consecutive days, sessions were conducted with small groups and using taped instructions, and sessions were held at the worksite. These modifications were deemed necessary because the intended participants (workers) were not clinical patients with evident stress problems and the program needed to be cost-effective for organizations to implement.

As applied in work settings, stress management is usually offered as a prevention activity designed to educate workers about the nature and sources of stress and to provide basic relaxation skills that are useful in everyday life. Programs typically contain brief training sessions and range from one-day programs to several-week-long programs. These programs are not designed for treatment of troubled workers or those with manifest clinical problems.

The research questions asked in the first two case studies were: Can 'normal' workers learn stress management skills in a short period of time in small groups at the worksite? and Will the modified training format be effective in helping workers reduce tension levels and feelings of distress?

Case study 1: hospital setting

The first study (Murphy, 1983) was performed at a local hospital in Cincinnati, Ohio. Its purpose was to evaluate the feasibility and effectiveness of stress management as applied in a work setting. Since the program sought to foster well-being and not to treat stress problems, the assistance of the hospital training department (not medical department) was sought. The director of training at the hospital was contacted to explain the nature and intent of the study. The program included stress education and training in biofeedback, progressive muscle relaxation, or self-relaxation (comparison group).

Training was conducted on-site during normal working hours and involved daily 1-hour sessions over two consecutive work weeks. The hospital supplied a room to conduct training and allowed nurses to receive training without loss of pay. During the first two days of the program, participants were given information on the nature and sources of stress, with specific attention to stressors at work, and common reactions to stress. Training took place on days 3–8. During each session, participants were instructed to listen to taped muscle relaxation exercises or try to lower the biofeedback tone. On the last two days, participants were asked to apply what they had learned and become as relaxed as possible during the session.

Physiological recordings were taken of muscle activity and hand temperature at the start and end of each session, and detailed questionnaires were administered at various times during the study. (The detailed data collection procedures were necessary given the experimental nature of the study; in practice, inexpensive instruments can be used to assess training effectiveness. See Stainbrook and Green, 1987.)

The results indicated significant benefits for the trained groups compared to the comparison group: for the muscle relaxation group: lower muscle tension and reduced anxiety; for the biofeedback group: higher hand temperature (indicative of relaxation) and lower anxiety. Three months later, follow-up questionnaires were administered to all participants. Between the end of training and the follow-up period, nurses in both trained groups reported increases in stress coping. Nurses in the self-relaxation group, on the other hand, reported more job dissatisfaction at follow-up relative to the trained groups. All groups reported improvements in sleep behavior at follow-up.

The study demonstrated that stress management was feasible in work settings and that nurses could learn relaxation skills in a matter of four or five days. It showed that relaxation training led to significant changes in subjective and physiological measures associated with stress. Finally, it showed that even nurses in the self-relaxation group felt that they benefited from the study, though they did not receive stress management training.

Some negative features of the program are also noteworthy. For example, physiological measures were not taken at the follow-up to corroborate the self-report results. Also, there was no mechanism developed to continue the program once the experiment was finished. These shortcomings were rectified in the second case study, described next.

Case study 2: highway maintenance workers

The second case study (Murphy, 1984b) was conducted in a municipal public works department and used the same experimental design as the first study. Its purpose was to replicate and extend the findings of the prior study using a blue-collar work group. Again, since the program focused on prevention, not treatment, the program was offered through the training department of one division (highway maintenance). The division agreed to provide a quiet room in which to conduct the study and permitted employees to participate during normal working hours without loss of pay.

Significant changes were made to the program based upon experience gained from the first case study. First, the stress education materials were expanded and group discussions were held with participants during the first two days of the program (baseline recording days). Second, on each training day (days 3–8) and each application practice day (days 9–10), participants were given feedback on their muscle tension and hand temperature levels after each session. This feedback was in the form of a graph showing daily pre- and post-session levels. Participants could thus track their progress at the end of each day. Third, physiological recordings were taken at the three-month follow-up in addition to questionnaire assessments. These were used to determine whether changes on physiological measures were durable over time. Finally, an attempt was made to involve an employee assistance program in the study. The director of the city's public employees assistance program (PEAP) was invited to attend training sessions for the purpose of continuing the program after the experiment was completed. I also conducted seminars for PEAP staff on the use of biofeedback equipment.

The results indicated that biofeedback (but not muscle relaxation) training led to significant reductions in muscle tension levels. The lack of effects in the muscle relaxation group was thought to be due to providing too much learning material to participants. The cassette tape series used in this study (Budzynski, 1974) included instruction in differential relaxation, conditioned relaxation, and autogenics in addition to progressive muscle relaxation. The manual associated with the cassette tapes suggested that the listener master each relaxation exercise before attempting others. The abbreviated training format used in the study precluded this type of mastery. It was concluded that either fewer relaxation techniques be taught in a short training program or the length of the program be extended to counter the negative effects of overtraining.

At the three-month follow-up, muscle tension levels increased in all groups compared to day 10 levels but were still significantly lower than day 1 levels for the two trained groups.

This case study had a second component: to assess program impact on organization variables of absenteeism, performance ratings, and worker accidents. Although these programs are not designed to influence such variables directly, indirect effects might be predicted. For example, Kohn (1981) has shown that workers trained in progressive muscle relaxation made fewer performance errors under conditions of high noise stress compared to controls. Thus, beyond health-related benefits, relaxation training may directly improve work performance under conditions of elevated stress.

To assess organizational effects of stress management, a quasi-experiment was designed in which data on employee absenteeism, performance ratings, equipment accidents, and work injuries for two and a half years before training were compared with those one and a half years after training (Murphy and Sorenson, 1988). A group of eighty workers who did not participate in the program were selected randomly from the division personnel roster to serve as a comparison group.

The results indicated that workers in the muscle relaxation group had fewer absence periods in the year following training compared to controls. (An absence period was a consecutive period of absence regardless of the number of days absent.) The reductions were small, amounting to -1.23 absence periods per worker per year, but statistically significant. Biofeedback-trained workers also had lower absenteeism after training and fewer work injuries, but the changes were not statistically significant. Neither trained group showed reductions on performance ratings or equipment accidents after training.

It was apparent from this study that the primary effects of stress management were on worker physiology and feelings of distress. The results confirmed other reports in the research literature supporting the feasibility and effectiveness of worksite stress management programs (Murphy, 1984a). [. . .]

Discussion

The results of these case studies and other reports in the literature indicate that stress management programs are feasible in work settings and that many techniques can be effective in helping workers to recognize stressors and to reduce physiological arousal levels and psychological manifestations of stress. Such programs have potential for improving worker well-being and partially offsetting the costs of stress arising from productivity losses and stress-related disorders. In the light of the fact that excess stress can promote cigarette smoking and alcohol use, stress management also may be a useful adjunct to other worksite health promotion effects.

Rising worker compensation claims for stress-related disability and the knowledge that behavioral factors play a significant role in seven of the ten leading causes of death will likely prompt a significant growth in worksite stress management programs. Despite the benefits to workers, it is not recommended that such programs be established in a cavalier fashion. For example, stress management can be used to complement organizational change and job redesign efforts to deal with stressors that cannot be designed out of the job (Ganster et al., 1982). As a prevention activity, organizations could offer stress management to employees on a periodic basis much like other training programs (e.g., safety, materials handling) or on a continuous basis through employee assistance-type programs. In this way, training would emphasize health promotion and disease prevention goals and parallel the preventive focus employed in research studies.

There is a danger, however, of organizations offering brief stress management workshops to workers while making no attempt to alter work factors that may be generating stress. The choice of a primary intervention strategy for reducing occupational stress should be based upon a careful evaluation of the sources of stress in the work environment (i.e., organizational, ergonomic, and psychosocial) and the most promising, realistic, and cost-effective strategies for reducing stress. While stressors cannot be designed out of some jobs, in many cases, work environment and organizational factors can be modified to improve worker health and well-being.

References

Benson, H. (1976) *The Relaxation Response*. William Morrow & Co.

Birk, L. (1973) *Biofeedback: Behavioral Medicine*. New York: Grune & Stratton.

Budzynski, T.H. (1974) *Progressive Relaxation Training*. New York: BMA Audio Cassette Programs.

Caplan, R.D., Cobb, S., French, J.R.P., Jr, Harrison, R.V. and Pinneau, S.R. (1975) *Job Demands and Worker Health*. DHHS (NIOSH) Publication no. 75–160. Washington, DC: US Government Printing Office.

Cooper, C.L. and Marshall, J. (1976) 'Occupational sources of stress: a review of the literature relating to coronary heart disease and mental ill health', *Journal of Occupational Psychology*, 49: 11–28.

DeCarlo, D.T. (1987) 'New legal rights related to emotional stress in the workplace', *Journal of Business and Psychology*, 1: 313–25.

Ganster, D.C., Mayes, B.T., Sime, W.E. and Tharp, G.D. (1982) 'Managing occupational stress: a field experiment', *Journal of Applied Psychology*, 67: 533–42.

Ivancevich, J.M. and Ganster, D.C. (1987) *Job Stress: from Theory to Suggestion*. New York: Haworth Press.

Jacobson, E. (1938) *Progressive Relaxation*. Chicago: University of Chicago Press.

Kohn, J.P. (1981) 'Stress modification using progressive muscle relaxation', *Professional Safety*, 26: 15–19.

Meichenbaum, D. (1977) *Cognitive-Behavior Modification.* New York: Plenum Press.

Murphy, L.R. (1983) 'A comparison of relaxation methods for reducing stress in nursing personnel', *Human Factors,* 25: 431–40.

Murphy, L.R. (1984a) 'Occupational stress management: a review and appraisal', *Journal of Occupational Psychology,* 57: 1–15.

Murphy, L.R. (1984b) 'Stress management in highway maintenance workers', *Journal of Occupational Medicine,* 26: 436–42.

Murphy, L.R. and Sorenson, S. (1988) 'Employee behaviors after stress management training', *Journal of Occupational Behavior,* 173–82.

National Institute for Occupational Safety and Health (1987) *National Strategy for the Prevention of Work-related Psychological Disorders.* Cincinnati, Ohio: NIOSH.

Pomerleau, D.F. and Brady, J.P. (1979) *Behavioral Medicine: Theory and Practice.* Baltimore, MD: Williams & Wilkins Company.

Rosch, P. and Pelletier, K. (1987) 'Worksite stress management programs', in L.R. Murphy and T.F. Schoenborn (eds), *Stress Management in Work Settings.* DHHS (NIOSH) Publication no. 87-111. Washington, DC: US Government Printing Office.

Stainbrook, G. and Green, L.W. (1987) 'Evaluating stress management programs', in L.R. Murphy and T.F. Schoenborn (eds), *Stress Management in Work Settings.* DHHS (NIOSH) Publication no. 87-111. Washington, DC: US Government Printing Office.

of the problems of stress, in themselves
an affect both the individual and the
literature on work stress indicates that
ionships between stress and coronary
rtension, susceptibility to infectious
aints such as back pains, the onset of
rs, drug/alcohol dependence, anxiety,
ob dissatisfaction, low commitment,
upational accidents and poor per-
, stress is something that should be
to explain the nature of stress and
is, the chapter will begin with an
and the sources of stress at work.
ope with stress at work. Finally,
n, the chapter will outline some

l
c
d
de
ab
for
mai
how
expl
Then
buildi
strateg

What does it come from?

The common sense view of stress is that too much stress is bad for
our health, but that a little stress is actually good for us. To state that
a little stress is good for us is unhelpful because it confuses stress with
stimulation: most people need a bit of excitement and interest, but
too much stimulation, such as very loud noise at work, is unhealthy.
This illustrates the problems of defining stress and the many ways in
which the term is commonly used. Some people think stress is the
same as stimulation or work load; others think that stress is the same
as anxiety or anger. For stress to be a useful concept, we need a
much clearer definition.

One commonly agreed definition is that stress is 'a psychological
process that occurs when an individual's perception of the environment or him/herself is noticeably different from what the individual
desires' (Daniels, 1992). Stress arising from perceptions of the
environment may occur when an individual isn't given the resources

he or she believes necessary to do an important piece of work. Stress arising from self-perceptions may occur when a manager agrees to take on responsibilities and duties that are not consistent with longer term career goals. This difference between perception and desire leads to some psychological discomfort; this is usually experienced, at least initially, as anxiety, anger or sadness, but if prolonged can lead to the problems listed earlier.

This definition implies that stress is related to individual perceptions and desires. Therefore, it is not surprising to discover that there is a huge range of events that can be stressful. However, some researchers have attempted to categorise these events to help identify those jobs that are particularly stressful. Warr (1992) has listed nine features of jobs that are related to stress (see Chapter 10). Although these nine features do not cover all sources of stress at work, they do cover most sources. The nine features are:

1   Low job discretion.
2   Low use of skills.
3   Little variety at work.
4   Low or high work demands.
5   High uncertainty.
6   Low pay.
7   Poor working conditions.
8   Low interpersonal support.
9   Valued social position.

Stressful jobs are ones in which one or more of these nine features are present in excessive amounts. Blue collar jobs are more likely to be characterised by the first three job features. In contrast managerial jobs are more likely to be characterised by the fourth and fifth job features. Nevertheless, management style, organisational culture and structure can also influence the degree to which each feature is present in a job. For example, a senior management consultant may not allow junior consultants to use their full range of skills. Junior consultants may then experience low use of skills and low variety. Cooper and Marshall (1976) have provided a model of how different organisational and work factors can produce the job features listed by Warr. According to Cooper and Marshall, stressful work events can come from six sources:

1   *Factors intrinsic to the job*   Some jobs, by their very nature, contain many stressful elements. For instance, fire-fighters and police officers are often exposed to physical risk in their jobs in the course of carrying out their duties.
2   *The role of the individual in the organisation*   Whilst the former

category refers to the nature of the job itself, this category is concerned with how the job fits into the wider organisation. To illustrate: whilst nursing involves dealing with dying patients, exposure to disease and working unsociable hours – which are potentially stressful factors intrinsic to the job – in some hospitals, management, in defining the role of nurses, may make conflicting demands and give unclear information, both of which can create stress through increased uncertainty.

3   *Relationships and interpersonal demands*   Whilst this category clearly overlaps with Warr's idea of low interpersonal support, it is also wider. This category also takes into account arguments, conflicts and demanding and insensitive colleagues. For example, an incompetent colleague may create higher work demands for everybody else, as well as providing little interpersonal support.

4   *Career development factors*   This refers specifically to under- or over-promotion. Under-promotion can lead to problems such as little variety, low use of skills, low work demands, low pay and a social position that is not valued. Over-promotion can lead to problems of too much work and work that is too difficult.

5   *Organisational structure and climate*   A number of organisational issues can influence the experience of job stress. If the senior management of a company is doing a poor job, this can have stress-related effects throughout the organisation in terms of poor job security and increased job demands as people try to make up for poor organisational performance.

6   *Home – work interface*   It is often the case that problems at work can influence home life, and problems at home can influence work life. For example, problems such as divorce or anxiety can lead to problems with concentration associated with depression and anxiety – which may then lead to an increase in work demands, as the work appears to become more difficult.

Coping with stress

Whilst there are many types of stressful events, and many origins of such events, not everybody that performs a stressful job develops mental or physical health problems. If we are able to cope well, then we can tolerate moderate and brief periods of stress without too many consequences. Therefore, although Warr's and Cooper and Marshall's models provide a useful starting point, it is important to understand how people cope for a full explanation of work stress. Figure 12.1 shows a model of the process through which people cope with stress. This model is based upon the work of several researchers (e.g. Lazarus and Folkman, 1984; Cox, 1987; Daniels and Guppy, 1994). There are five major stages in the model: occurrence of an event, appraisal of that event, coping choices, immediate impact upon well-being and reappraisal, and longer term consequences. Individual characteristics influence all five stages and characteristics of the organisational and social environment influence three stages.

At the first stage, a potentially stressful event happens. As noted above, most of these events will belong to one of the categories identified by Warr, although other events such as family problems may get carried over to the work place – as noted by Cooper and Marshall. Cooper and Marshall's model also informs us that organisational characteristics may influence this event. For instance under-performing organisations may require that employees work very long hours, or managerial communications may be conflicting and/or ambiguous. Also, individual characteristics can influence the event; for instance where two people have incompatible working styles, arguments may occur. However, it is possible that other factors may also cause the event; government legislation, the moves of competitors and chance events can all influence the occurrence of potentially stressful events.

At the second stage, the individual appraises the event. Appraisal is very important, since this is when the individual decides whether the event is stressful or not. This implies that different individuals find different events stressful. This is indeed the case. However people do have enough in common that some events are almost universally stressful. An event becomes stressful when it brings or threatens consequences that the individual does not desire. The most stressful events are those with more severe consequences, those that are personally relevant, those that occur frequently and those that endure.

If the individual appraises the event as stressful, then at the next stage, the individual decides how he or she will cope with the event. Broadly, there are two forms of coping: *problem focused coping* directed at changing the event and *emotion focused coping* directed at regulating individual responses to the event. Typically, people use a mixture of both approaches. Emotion focused coping can be useful in the short term, although exclusive long term reliance on emotion focused coping can be harmful, since the stressful event is allowed to continue. In this respect, problem focused coping is more successful. Two factors influence how the individual decides to cope: the coping resources available in the social and organisational environment, and individual characteristics. The most useful social and organisational resources are:

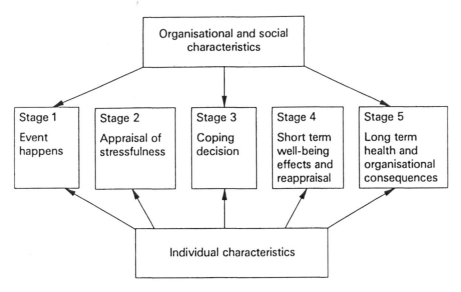

Figure 12.1 *A model of stress and coping*

1   Control over the job. This can allow the individual to change those aspects of the working environment that he or she finds stressful.
2   Support obtained from colleagues at work and from outside work. Support can take many forms: helping the individual to reappraise the event as less stressful than originally thought, supplying tangible help with the problem or simply conveying feelings of care and esteem to the individual.

If there is sufficient job control and/or social support, then the individual may have the necessary resources to use problem focused coping. If these resources are scarce, then the individual may have to use emotion focused coping exclusively, which typically uses less coping resources. Importantly, individual characteristics ultimately influence the coping decision. People who are confident in their ability to change the environment are more likely to make effective use of job control and social support when they are available than those who are less confident.

The immediate reaction to the event occurs at the next stage. If coping is successful, the process ends and there may be few short term effects. When coping is unsuccessful, then short term effects will be more numerous. These short term effects include emotions such as anger, worry, sadness and perhaps even loss of confidence. More stressful events, especially very severe or long lasting events, are probably more likely to cause anxiety and depression. At this

---

Box 1   A case of unsuccessful coping

I met N during my research into work stress after he agreed to be interviewed on this topic. Whilst he was happy with his job when I met him, he told me about several years he had spent working for a small accountancy practice in London. N claimed that he sometimes had to work up to 20 hours a day. These long hours were a source of stress for two reasons: not only were the work demands heavy, but N also had no control over whether he could accept the work or not, for the work needed to be taken to pay the overheads. Since he worked for a small practice, there were very few other accountants to whom N could turn for support: importantly, these others were also overloaded, so did not have any time to help N with his workload. Unable to solve the problem, through lack of control and support, N, like his colleagues, coped by drinking heavily. Whilst this provided some relief, the problem did not go away. Unable to continue to work in this way, N realised that it would be better for him and his family if he removed himself from the situation. So he eventually left London for a promotion and a much less intensive job in a small practice based in a small town in the south of England.

---

stage, the event will be reappraised. The event may have ended, but if it is ongoing then the individual must decide whether it is still stressful and, if so, how to cope with the event again.

The first four stages of the stress process are likely to happen relatively quickly. However, if the event is especially severe or is ongoing, or there is a long term sequence of stressful events and coping continues to be unsuccessful, then the individual may enter the fifth stage. The fifth stage involves long term health and organisational outcomes of the stress process, such as increased absenteeism, staff turnover, poor performance, major disease and mental ill-health. Such outcomes can happen after a few hours of exposure to a stressful event or may take several years to appear. Individual characteristics can often influence this stage. Life style and hereditary factors can predispose individuals to certain diseases, whilst ability and general attitudes towards work may influence organisational outcomes.

To illustrate the process of coping with work stress, Boxes 1 and 2 describe two cases – one involving unsuccessful coping and the other successful coping.

Box 2 A case of successful coping

When I met P, she was a partner in a small accountancy practice in a city in the east of England. When I asked her about the sources of stress in her job, she replied that she found clients behaving in an unreasonable manner to be particularly irritating. However, she recounted how the other partners often provided her with support. She would often talk with the other partners to get advice on how to deal with problems. This information was often helpful. She also found that one of the partners was an especially useful source of support. P described this partner as having a calming influence that helped her to reappraise the events as perhaps less stressful than she first thought.

Stress management

Table 12.1 shows a number of symptoms of stress, grouped according to whether they are psychological or behavioural/physical, and whether they are individual or organisational. By themselves, each of these symptoms is unlikely to be caused by stress – although some investigation of likely causes would be useful. However, if a number of these symptoms occur together, then the cause is more likely to be stress related – and further investigation is clearly needed. If stress is identified as a cause, then there are a number of strategies that organisations can use to proactively manage stress by both limiting stressful events at work and helping to improve coping methods. Murphy (1988) has grouped stress management strategies under three headings: primary interventions targeted at the organisation, and secondary interventions and tertiary interventions, both targeted at the individual.

Warr's (1992) nine stressful job features indicate that certain environments and certain events are stressful for most people. Accordingly, primary interventions involve job and organisation redesign to eliminate events that could be stressful or to provide necessary coping resources. Such interventions include instituting autonomous self-managing work teams, job rotation and enlargement schemes, limiting the amount of work to be done, limiting the hours of stressful work, improving work conditions, recruitment and selection of individuals that can cope with the demands of the job, and changing communication styles.

Secondary interventions seek to enhance individuals' ability to cope with the causes and symptoms of stress. Examples of secondary interventions are relaxation training, employee fitness programmes,

Table 12.1   *Some of the symptoms of stress*

Individual	Organizational
Psychological	
Feeling irritable	Low job satisfaction
Anger	Low commitment
Anxiety	Poor motivation
Depression	
Problems relaxing	
Feeling bored	
Feeling tired	
Loss of concentration	
Loss of memory	
Behavioural/physical	
Changes in appetite	Increased absenteeism
Problems sleeping	Greater staff turnover
Frequent headaches	Lower productivity
Stomach pains	Lower quality output
Heartburn	More accidents
Frequent diarrhoea or constipation	
Muscle spasms	
Palpitations	
Back pain	
Increased alcohol/drug intake	
Increased smoking	

meditation, problem solving skills training, assertiveness training, time management, and combinations of these methods (see Chapter 11). Problem solving skills training may be particularly effective since this type of training helps problem focused coping. Also, secondary interventions that contain a number of distinct components may be most effective, since they provide a greater range of coping skills.

Tertiary stress management interventions are implemented when an individual is suffering from extreme symptoms of stress. They are concerned with counselling the employee to change his or her perception of work, to change destructive behaviours, to manage emotions or to provide him or her with a more effective coping repertoire. Most of these programmes concern non-clinical counselling, and these are referred to as employee assistance programmes (EAPs). However, in extreme cases, psychotherapy conducted by a trained clinical psychologist may be necessary.

What is the most suitable form of stress management intervention?

Although Murphy (1991) appears to favour secondary stress management interventions, it is primary stress management interventions that are potentially the most effective form of stress management, since they have the widest coverage of all the interventions, they are preventive, and job/organisation redesign is more enduring than secondary and tertiary interventions. Nevertheless, they are not appropriate in every circumstance. Primary interventions are likely to be most successful both when most of the recipients of the intervention experience common sources of stress or need similar coping resources, and when the sources of stress are easily removed or the coping resources easily provided. In jobs that are inherently stressful (e.g. emergency services), secondary interventions are more likely to provide useful prevention. Tertiary stress management interventions are most likely to be appropriate where either a very small fraction of the work force show extreme stress symptoms, or a major stressful event has already affected health, and the event is unlikely to recur. An example of the former situation would be where certain vulnerable individuals receive counselling for rehabilitative purposes. Counselling for post-traumatic stress disorder after a major disaster, such as an aeroplane crash, is an example of the latter.

Clearly, prior assessment of stress-related problems is useful for identifying the most appropriate form of intervention. In many instances, the results of an assessment of stress in an organisation will indicate that a combination of interventions can be effective. For example, Steffy et al. (1986) report a comprehensive approach to stress management that includes all three levels of intervention. Their approach involves job redesign, health education programmes and EAPs being introduced together for the whole organisation. It is important to monitor the progress of interventions: stress management interventions can be both costly and sometimes unsuccessful, so it is important to ensure that they are effective. Figure 12.2 summarises the various stages we have discussed in implementing a stress management intervention: assessment, evaluation, implementation and monitoring.

Conclusions

This chapter has indicated that there are many ways of looking at work stress and how to manage work stress. Warr's and Cooper and Marshall's models of work stress are useful starting points to understand where work stress is likely to originate. Models of coping are useful for understanding why some people can tolerate situations which others would find stressful. The three categories of stress management – primary, secondary and tertiary – illustrate different approaches to managing stress. The choice of which strategy, or combination of strategies, depends very much upon how many people are experiencing stress and the nature of the source of stress.

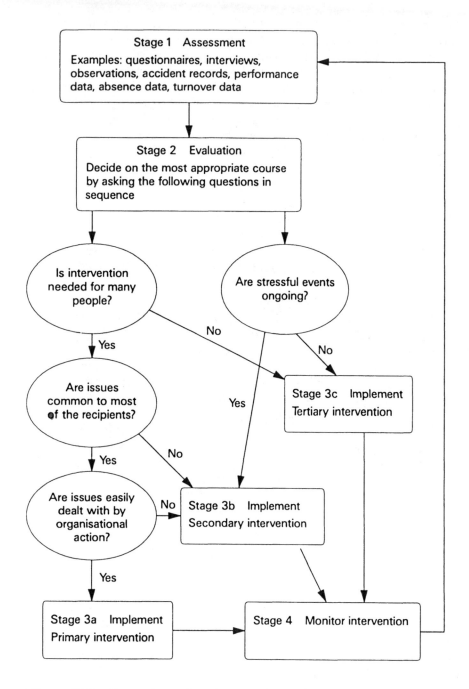

Figure 12.2 *Stages in implementing stress management*

References

Cooper, C.L. and Marshall, J. (1976) 'Occupational sources of stress: a review of the literature relating to coronary heart disease and mental ill health', *Journal of Occupational Psychology*, 49: 11–28.

Cox, T. (1987) 'Stress, coping and problem solving', *Work and Stress*, 1: 5–14.

Daniels, K. (1992) 'Occupational stress and control: implications for employee well-being'. Unpublished PhD thesis, Cranfield University.

Daniels, K. and Guppy, A. (1994) 'Occupational stress, social support, job control and psychological well-being', *Human Relations*, 47: 1523–44.

Lazarus, R.S. and Folkman, S. (1984) *Stress, Appraisal and Coping*. New York: Springer.

Murphy, L.R. (1988) 'Workplace interventions for stress reduction and prevention', in C.L. Cooper and R. Payne (eds), *Causes, Coping and Consequences of Stress at Work*. Chichester: Wiley.

Murphy, L.R. (1991) 'Prevention and management of work stress', in J.W. Jones, B.D. Steffy and D.W. Bray (eds), *Applying Psychology in Business*. Lexington Books: New York.

Steffy, B.D., Jones, J.W., Murphy, L.R. and Kunz, L. (1986) 'A demonstration of the impact of stress abatement programs on reducing employees' accidents and their costs', *American Journal of Health Promotion*, 1: 25–32.

Warr, P. (1992) 'Job features and excessive stress', in R. Jenkins and N. Cooney (eds), *Prevention of Mental Ill Health at Work*. London: HMSO.

PART 3

ORGANISATIONAL CULTURE AND THE CHANGING NATURE OF ORGANISATIONAL ENTRY

13

Corporate tribes: identifying the cultures

Terrence Deal and Allen Kennedy

The focus in this [part] of the book is on managing cultures – that is, on understanding them, analyzing them, shaping them, and retooling them when change is necessary. Most of the information here is suggestive, not prescriptive. We intend it as a different way of looking at management within an organization and we hope that it will offer a new perspective for both managers and employees.

[. . .] The biggest single influence on a company's culture is the broader social and business environment in which the company operates. A corporate culture embodies what it takes to succeed in this environment. If hard selling is required for success, the culture will be one that encourages people to sell and sell hard; if thoughtful technical decision-making is required, the culture will make sure that happens too.

After examining hundreds of corporations and their business environments, we have come to see that many companies fall into four general categories or types of cultures. These categories are determined by two factors in the marketplace: the degree of risk associated with the company's activities, and the speed at which companies – and their employees – get feedback on whether decisions or strategies are successful. From these market realities, we have distilled the four generic cultures:

Abridged from T. Deal and A. Kennedy, *Corporate Cultures*, Harmondsworth: Penguin, 1982, pp. 107–27.

The tough-guy, macho culture   A world of individualists who regularly take high risks and get quick feedback on whether their actions were right or wrong.

The work-hard/play-hard culture   Fun and action are the rule here, and employees take few risks, all with quick feedback; to succeed, the culture encourages them to maintain a high level of relatively low-risk activity.

The bet-your-company culture   Cultures with big-stakes decisions, where years pass before employees know whether decisions have paid off. A high-risk, slow-feedback environment.

The process culture   A world of little or no feedback where employees find it hard to measure what they do; instead they concentrate on how it's done. We have another name for this culture when the processes get out of control – bureaucracy!

This division of the world of business into four categories is, of course, simplistic. No company we know today precisely fits into any one of these categories. In fact, within any single real-world company, a mix of all four types of cultures will be found. Marketing departments are tough-guy cultures. Sales and manufacturing departments work hard and play hard. Research and development is a world of high risk and slow feedback. And accounting sits squarely in the upper reaches of bureaucratic life.

Moreover, companies with very strong cultures [. . .] fit this simple mold hardly at all. These companies have cultures that artfully blend the best elements of all four types – and blend them in ways that allow these companies to perform well when the environment around them changes, as it inevitably does. However, we do think that this framework can be useful in helping managers begin to identify more specifically the culture of their own companies. Let's take a look at each type of culture and how it works within an organization.

The tough-guy, macho culture

Fortunes and flops are made overnight in this world of high-risk stakes and quick feedback, the most grueling of all business cultures. Police departments are the essence of this type of culture since the stakes there are often life and death. The same is true for surgeons. But the marketplace also provides a variety of other organizations that fall in this category: construction, cosmetics, management consulting, venture capital, advertising, television, movies, publishing, sports – in fact, the entire entertainment industry.

The financial stakes are high – big advertising campaigns, expensive construction projects, the fall television season, a $32 million movie, the World Series. And the feedback is quick. A year is probably the longest it takes to get feedback; more likely, companies will know whether their products will make it or not in a single season. In extreme cases – like a Broadway show or a movie opening – feedback comes right away.

In construction, for instance, a team digging a tunnel described for us the process of exploding the last stretch, called the 'plug'. They have only one shot to 'blow the plug'. If their sense of thoroughness or anxiety leads them to be overly generous in their use of explosives, they could destroy the surrounding terrain. If, on the other hand, their sense of caution prevails, they could damage the tunnel by flooding it, making all their previous work – the engineering, the hardships, the time – disappear on one throw of the plunger. High risk, very fast feedback.

Tough-guy, macho cultures tend to be young ones with a focus on speed, not endurance. Not taking an action is as important as taking one. If the automobile executive puts off the decision on design changes and the old model doesn't sell, chances are the executive will get fired. If changes are made and the car is a hit, the executive will become a star. The financial rewards also come early; all of those twenty-eight-year-old millionaires walking around probably come from tough-guy cultures. But the intense pressure and frenetic pace of the culture often burns people out before they reach middle age.

The all-or-nothing nature of this environment encourages values of risk-taking and the belief that 'we can pull off the big deal, the best campaign' . . . whatever. Slogans of these companies reflect the value of best, biggest, and greatest. 'Make great ads' (Leo Burnett Advertising); 'The Last Smart Move' (an inventive technology company).

The survivors/the heroes

Tough is the byword in this culture. The need to make a quick decision and to accept the risk that very soon it may be proven wrong requires a tough attitude. So does the internal competition. Every meeting can become a war game where the most junior person in the room has to best the most senior person in order to win respect. If the junior person doesn't fight, he or she will be dismissed out of hand as a lightweight. A comer is the one who's aggressive whether right, wrong, or indifferent.

Survivors also must maintain a tough attitude in this culture because anyone will go after you given the right opportunity. A newcomer in one macho business asked what sorts of things needed to be learned in order to succeed. The senior staffer replied, 'Learn that you never cry in public. No matter how bad it hurts, go back to your office and cry in private.'

The junior staffer seemed mystified by this: 'But why do you have to cry?'

'Ah, because the bastards will get you when you're down.'

'Who are the bastards?'

'They're all over the place,' said the senior staffer. 'They're your colleagues, your customers. They'll get you down, especially when you're depressed. But don't cry. Cry and they'll just tear you apart.'

'Well, what else is there?' the junior staffer felt brave enough – or perhaps just scared enough – to ask.

'It's o.k. to shout, scream, and curse. It gets frustrating, and while you're not allowed to cry in public, it's all right to express emotion – particularly emotion that can forcefully affect the situation. So, if you really get upset, say some outrageous curse word and storm out of the person's office, rush back to your own office, and then cry. Just remember, don't do the crying first.'

Persons who survive this culture best are the ones who need to gamble, who can tolerate all-or-nothing risks because they *need* instant feedback. This is a world of individualists. For these people there is no reward in being part of a team; their goal is to become a star. In this culture it is very possible to become a star overnight – the genius who finances the last big deal in venture capital, the player who scores the winning point in the hockey game, the management consultant who totally reorganizes the *Fortune* 500 company, the book editor who plucks a first novel out of the slush pile and makes it a bestseller. Of course fame can fly just as quickly as it comes. When a deal sours and the star is to blame, he can be out on his ear. As the old saying goes, 'You're only as good as your last movie.'

Stars are temperamental. But the tough-guy culture tolerates them because it would be nothing without them. In fact, outlaw heroes are the norm for this culture. They may behave outrageously, but as long as they hit the success button every time they go out, they'll be heroes. Although this is called a tough-guy, macho culture, it probably discriminates the least against women of any of the four types. After all, a star is a star.

The importance of rituals

Chance plays a major part in tough-guy cultures. What worked once may not work again, so employees devise rituals that tend to 'protect' them from the vagaries of the environment. As an example, people in tough-guy cultures will wax poetic about the importance of 'problem-solving' or 'strategizing' in their work. Don't believe them. These are only security blankets used to slow the work routine down and give employees a sense of safety. Any procedure becomes a temporary haven from the fear of taking risks and making the BIG mistake. That's how surgeons work on a difficult case. When they operate, they follow a procedure, even if it's experimental. If the patient dies, surgeons say 'I've done everything I can.' To further protect themselves, doctors display degrees on their walls and bound editions of medical journals on their shelves. What they communicate is 'I'm reading all the time. I keep up with what's new. I did all the procedures right.' You will recognize that if you are dead as a result, you will not be too convinced by these arguments. But the surgeon will be.

Such rituals become superstitions in a tough-guy culture. They help individuals believe that they can, in fact, do the things they are supposed to do. In the winter of 1982, the ratings for CBS Evening News were sagging. Walter Cronkite was gone, and he was obviously a difficult act for anchorman Dan Rather to follow. ABC and NBC moved in quickly and started taking viewers away from the formerly preeminent CBS. News executives were becoming alarmed. In the dead cold of the winter, Rather started wearing a sweater under his jacket on the air because the studio was chilly. Soon after he donned the sweater, ratings began to climb. Rather quickly developed a superstition about the connection between the sweaters and success, even hinting that he might continue wearing them during the summer. [. . .]

Stars in some cultures band together so that the 'magic' won't be diluted. A group of venture capitalists who have financed a string of successful projects form a tight little cabal. They claim that it is their magic that makes their work so successful. No one else can join the group because the luck might go sour – they call it 'being in the deal stream'. It's a ploy as old as Napoleon, who insisted on taking only 'lucky men' with him to the front lines – just in case.

Strengths and weaknesses

Tough-guy cultures enable companies to do what needs to be done in high-risk, quick-return environments. Successful companies in such industries try to buffer individual stars from the agony and uncertainty of high-stakes ventures, then reward them handsomely when heart-stopping gambles pay off.

Through rituals of bonding and problem-solving, and with values that make taking sensible risks a virtue and relying on the safe and sure an unpardonable sin, star cultures move industries ahead. They promote employment for the risk-takers we need [. . .].

But their very strength is the source of real weakness. The tough-guy emphasis on quick feedback diverts resources from long-term investments; thus there is no value placed on long-term persistence. This short-term orientation has several consequences. First of all, the competition to become a star is so keen that the virtues of co-operation are forgotten. Also, because the culture is superstitious, it breeds out the ability to learn from mistakes. Tough cultures foster immaturity by tolerating tantrums; often top management encourages this attitude and delights in watching everyone trying to score points off the other guy. The result of all this is a culture that rewards individuals who are temperamental, short-sighted, and superstitious; and that devastates people whose careers might blossom over time. Because of the high turnover created by people who fail in the short term, building a strong, cohesive culture can become quite difficult in the tough-guy climate.

Work-hard/play-hard culture

This business kingdom is the benign and hyperactive world of sales organizations: real estate, computer companies, automotive distributors, any door-to-door sales operation – such as Avon, Mary Kay Cosmetics, and encyclopedia companies – mass-consumer-sales companies like McDonald's [. . .], office-equipment manufacturers such as Xerox [. . .], and all retail stores [. . .].

The employees of these companies live in a world of small risks – no one sale will make or break a sales rep – and quick, often intensive feedback – a rep either gets the order or doesn't. Activity in this world is everything. As long as employees can keep up, the work will get done. Success comes with persistence. Go back to the customer one more time. Make one more telephone call.

Of course, within any single corporate culture, the sales division fits this mold. But manufacturing also falls within the culture. Most factory workers have to keep at the job, day after day. The feedback is quick – everyone knows when something isn't working right away. But the real risks are comparatively few; the system is full of checks and balances to keep the job from becoming a big risk.

The primary values of this culture center on customers and their needs. If the tough-guy culture is built on 'find a mountain and climb it', then work-hard/play-hard rests on 'find a need and fill it.' The idea of good customer service is one that permeates most of these organizations; 'IBM means service' is probably the hallmark slogan. Digital Equipment has taken the IBM idea one step further by developing 'warm armpit marketing' – a concept where the sales representative stays in the field and gets closely involved with the customer's problems.

But also consider McDonald's – experts say the company's success does not come from better burgers, but rather a faster turnaround at the counter. The secret: volume against fixed cost. But that isn't the whole story. McDonald's creates a mystique of quality, service, cleanliness, and value – QSCV – among its employees and franchisees. This theme is repeated and repeated from the day a new franchisee first goes to Hamburger University. Employees become true believers and the culture's intensity is McDonald's secret. While all companies aren't sales driven, some of the best companies in America have gravitated some or part of the way towards an action culture. The rationale for this is simple. In a dynamic environment, the worst thing that can often happen from a performance point of view is to stand still. To protect against this natural human tendency, good managers work hard to instill an action orientation. 'Try it; fix it; do it' becomes the operative ethic of companies like Hewlett-Packard (H-P), Intel, DEC, and others. The managers of these companies are saying to their employees that the race is to the quick; and they demand a high level of activity and initiative to make sure they stay in the race.

The survivors/the heroes

The heroes of this culture are the super salespeople, the silver-tongued charmers who could sell an igloo to an Eskimo *or* a sun worshipper with equal ease. Unlike the tough-guy heroes, the work-hard heroes measure the worth of their activity in volume, not high stakes.

The best of the workers/players are friendly, carousing, hail-fellow-well-met kinds of people. They aren't worried or superstitious. While anyone who succeeds in a tough-guy culture becomes a star, here the team beats the world because no *individual* really makes a difference. The team produces the *volume*. That's why salesmen's clubs and contests are so important – everyone wants to be part of the group that goes to Hawaii.

Rites and rituals

This is the play-hard aspect of the culture; fun becomes the flip side of an intense day of selling. More than any other culture, this one revels in energetic games. Contests, meetings, promotions, conventions. Anything that will work to keep motivation up. [. . .]

Language plays a big part in the business rituals of the work-hard culture. The perfect sales pitch enjoys a special position in the folklore. But so do salesmen's jokes, sports metaphors, and, of course, exaggeration, as when salesmen tell how much damage they did to the hotel room last night. Boasting, by contrast, is a tough-guy game because it's a form of self-aggrandizement. A star will say 'That's the best goddamn project I've ever done', while the super salesperson will say, 'That customer was the worst creep in the world, but we made the sale!' They'll both be talking about the same thing.

Strengths and weaknesses

Work/play cultures get a lot done. If the objective is to make or move some quality item fast, a work/play culture can do it. The environment is ideal for active people who thrive on quick, tangible feedback. The action culture makes available the mass-produced goods the American market wants – better than anyone else can.

But action also carries great disadvantages. Volume can displace quality in the culture's pell-mell rush to produce and sell more. The worst of the culture comes out in lack of thoughtfulness or attention; the tendency is toward the kind of back-of-the-envelope calculations that can backfire. Also, work/play-hard cultures often get fooled by success, forgetting that today's successes may become tomorrow's failures. High-tech companies, especially, grow enormously overnight but often face the prospect that the growth was just a one-time spurt.

When they get in trouble, these cultures often go for quick-fix solutions. Like tough-guy cultures, they tend to have a short-term perspective. Companies with this culture can suffer dramatic turn-over when their sales forces become disillusioned and easily cynical. When their activity doesn't produce, they go somewhere else rather than search out the root of the problem. The troops don't stick to the company long enough to weather the tough times because they are often more committed to the action than to the company.

Also, high-energy enthusiasts can drift into cynicism when their quick-fix existence has lost its meaning. The work-hard/play-hard culture requires stamina that ebbs as we age. These cultures are often cultures of young people who are looking for places to prove their worth. The action's attractive. These people are young chrono-logically; by contrast, tough guys are young emotionally. And unless a company can retain older people, the culture loses some of its most important lessons.

Savvy companies spend a lot of time trying to counteract all of these tendencies. First of all, they aim to keep product quality on par with customer wants and encourage the worker/players to slow down and make more considered decisions. IBM counteracted the high-energy sales attitude by placing 'Think' signs all over the company. They were trying to find a good balance between quality and activity, identity and growth: a difficult trick.

Bet-your-company culture

Life in this culture means a dict of high risk, but slow feedback. Slow here doesn't mean less pressure; instead it means pressure that is as persistent as slow-drip water torture. It means investing millions – sometimes billions – in a project that takes years to develop, refine, and test, before you find out whether it will go or not. Mobil or Exxon considers sending a $500 million drilling rig to explore for oil off Georges Banks; Boeing Aircraft spends several billion to build the 757 and 767; NASA commits billions to the Space Shuttle Program. All very high stakes. And all with feedback years down the line.

Industries in this culture include capital-goods companies [. . .], mining and smelting companies [. . .], large-systems businesses, oil companies, investment banks [. . .], architectural firms, computer-design companies, and the actuarial end of insurance companies. We also include the Army and the Navy because they spend billions of dollars preparing for the war they might never have to fight.

Instead of putting their careers on the line – as tough guys would – corporate bettors often risk the future of the entire company. These corporate giants may not flounder on one bad investment decision; but it's possible for two bad decisions to sink a company.

The importance of making the right decisions fosters a sense of deliberateness throughout the companies. The world of bet-your-company cultures moves in months and years, not days and weeks. Once, at a meeting in a capital-goods company, someone raised a question that couldn't be answered then and there. No one batted an eyelash. The meeting was stopped while the participants went off for two weeks to find an answer, and then resumed later, answer in hand. Other cultures would have 'put that one aside for now' and moved quickly on to finish the meeting. In faster-feedback environments, managers typically have one hundred pages to review in a two-hour meeting. In the bet-your-company culture, the agenda will include ten pages for review, but the meeting will spend two hours on each page.

The primary ritual of this culture *is* the business meeting. Although people from all levels of the organization might attend, seating will be strictly prescribed by rank, and only the senior members will talk. Decision-making comes from the top down – once all the inputs are in. In a shorter-cycle business, by contrast, decisions are made more quickly because the organization is flat and less formal, and it doesn't really matter if the decision is wrong; it can always be corrected.

The values of this culture focus on the future and the importance of investing in it. [. . .] The beliefs center on the attitude that good ideas should be given the proper chance for success. [. . .]

The survivors/the heroes

People don't make it as bettors unless they have a great deal of character and confidence that can carry them through the waiting period. They are just as self-directed and tough as people in the macho culture, but they have the stamina to endure long-term ambiguity with little or no feedback.

Bettors' moves are measured and deliberate because they need the assurance that they're right. They take time to make a decision, then double check every component of it. And once they have made up their minds, bettors don't change their convictions easily.

Survivors all respect authority and technical competence. When the organization can't afford mistakes, those who have proven themselves gain great respect. The heroic figures tend to be hunker-down heroes, the people who were fired or shuffled off to the corner but who kept working on the big project until it became a reality. Heroes take on great importance because they provide psychological support during all the rough times.

Immaturity is not tolerated in this culture. Young bettors will do trivial jobs for years and still take them seriously. Evaluations of employees are made over decades. Top management says: 'He's just a young fellow, give him a chance.' Or, 'He's only been here five years; it's too early to tell.' In the work/play culture, if someone says, 'He's been here a month already and nothing's happened', they mean, 'He's on the way out.'

Sharing hard-won knowledge is another component for success, so bettors become highly dependent on one another and treat one another with infinite politeness. It's like getting married – they have to preserve links in the bettor culture. There is none of the denigration that runs rampant in the macho world but instead a reliance on respect for authority. Younger employees look to mentors, who become the backbone of the system. For example, people happily defer to their boss because they know he has likely been through the waiting period on more than one important project – and made the right decision. That experience is something they can look up to.

Strengths and weaknesses

[. . .] Bet-your-company cultures lead to high-quality inventions and major scientific breakthroughs – they help move the country's economy ahead. But they also move with awesome slowness. They do not produce on a mass scale, or perform with the speed and decisiveness of a quick-feedback environment. In addition, because of their long-term perspective, these companies are vulnerable to short-term fluctuations in the economy and cash-flow problems while they wait for major ventures to pay off.

In the end, however, these companies may be the ones our economy needs most desperately. Careers, products, and profits don't develop quickly. But when they do, they last a long time.

The process culture

This low-risk, slow-feedback corner of the world is populated by banks, insurance companies, financial-service organizations, large chunks of the government [. . .] and heavily regulated industries like pharmaceutical companies. As in the work/play culture, the financial stakes here are low: no one transaction will make or break the company – or anyone in it. But unlike worker/players, the employees here get virtually no feedback. The memos and reports that they write seem to disappear into a void. As a result, they have no idea how effective they are until someone blames them for something. In a government agency, for instance, employees may work like crazy, but the only time they get any recognition is when a legislator decides to kill their agency or indicts it for violating the public trust or for promoting inefficiency and corruption.

This lack of feedback forces employees to focus on *how* they do something, not what they do. They start developing artificial ties to elements of the world in the organization; small events take on major importance – a certain telephone call, that snippet of paper, or the section head's latest memo. People in these cultures tend to develop a 'cover your ass' mentality. The most trivial event becomes the subject for a memo. They describe the incident in minute detail, giving the best explanation for their actions. They copy the world with it. Those fellow sufferers who receive the memo don't want to acknowledge that they've missed anything. So they send an answer, often as detailed as the original. Everything goes into a file so that they can prove that they didn't make the mistake, should someone mention it five years from now.

The values in this culture center on technical perfection – figuring out the risks and pinning the solutions down to a science. In other words, getting the process and the details right. [. . .] Again, these values are particularly well suited to the business environment of the culture. What we describe may just sound like so much red-tape. But if banks, insurance companies, or governmental agencies responded to every fad or fashion, we would all suffer. Imagine a major change each year in the driver's test. Or a new procedure for income taxes. And would anyone really want a work-hard/play-hard type keeping track of his or her [bank] account?

The survivors/the heroes

Protectiveness and caution are natural responses to the absence of feedback. If process people don't know where or when they will be attacked, they try to have all of their flanks covered. But caution in this culture isn't personal, rather it becomes related to the end product. So, how neatly and completely workers do something is often more important than what they do. If the pink slip isn't filled in correctly, the world comes to a standstill. If the job application has a typographical error in it, then the job seeker is shown the door. People who are valued in this culture are those who are trying to protect the system's integrity more than their own.

The real survivors learn to live within this artificial world. They are orderly, punctual, attend to detail, and survive on their memories. They carry out the procedures as they are written down without asking whether they make sense in the real world. In fact, the real world ceases to exist, and most successful bureaucrats have trouble dealing with it when it infringes on their turf. [. . .]

Rites and rituals

Rituals center on work patterns and procedures, and there is a great deal of discussion about these matters. Long, rambling meetings focus on the way in which a decision should be made. Who is best at keeping track of milestones in resource allocation and management plans? Or which way is that reorganization going to go? Is one department going to be collapsed into another? Whose job may be threatened? Reorganization becomes a strong candidate for the most important ritual in a process culture. But there are others, like retirement ceremonies honoring those who have stuck it out the longest.

Like corporate bettors, process people also pay inordinate attention to titles and formalities. Their tightly structured hierarchies come very close to a class system. At a major insurance company, for instance, the hierarchy runs from 'class 19' for those with a high-school diploma, all the way up to 'class 49' for the highest vice-presidential level.

One of the company's managers described the system this way:

Classes 17–27	'In-tray/out-tray people.' The work is a never-ending process and there is a lot of job burnout.
Classes 27–33	'The professional/technical brunt group. They have college degrees and do the brunt of the paper work.'
Classes 34–39	'The "men in the middle", the department heads. They are a highly stressed group.'
Classes 40–49	'The group that's made it. They identify with top management. I'd say these guys work sixty-hour weeks.'

This system is so strong, he said, that 'People want a class change over a salary increase any time. They feel movement up through the class system is a better indicator of success. I've literally had people refuse a raise if it meant staying at the same class rank.'

The system is also highly visible; at this company your office furniture shows exactly where you are in the pecking order. Classes 17–25 have small steel desks and one chair with no arms. Classes 26–29 have the same chairs behind their desks but have an additional typewriter wing and one chair with arms. By contrast, classes 30–33's desks are known as 'aircraft carriers' or 'flat-tops', so much larger are they; and – hallelujah – they come complete with armchairs (two). Managerial classes 34–39 are offered wooden desks, three-quarter-length walls, a conference table, and a book-shelf. Classes 40–42, assistant vice presidents, get that same bonanza plus a choice of a sofa and chairs, or a round table and a credenza. Classes 43–49, vice presidents, have floor-to-ceiling offices. They also have a choice of upholstery from a fabric book updated and controlled by the company, so that their couches and chairs are sure to look distinct from those belonging in the offices of assistant vice presidents.

These distinctions are no small part of the company. The very day a person's promotion is placed before the board of directors for ceremonial final approval is the day the furniture men move in with the right trappings to match the new rank. As one vice president commented, 'The furniture is never a day earlier or a day later.'

Strengths and weaknesses

The process culture has become a scapegoat for much that is wrong with the modern world. [. . .] No one can say they really *like* an efficient administrator. And we all complain about how hard it is to get anything done in a world of red-tape.

Yet, these cultures did not simply spring forth full-blown. Special creations designed to fit special circumstances, they offer a perfect counterpoint to the high-risk world of the star culture or the quick, sometimes thoughtless energy of work/play. Process cultures put order into work that needs to be predictable. In many ways, good process cultures make sure the world works for the stars, worker/players, and bettors.

14

Gender cultures: women's choices and strategies at work

Su Maddock and Di Parkin

Everyone knows the atmosphere at work can be either stressful or rewarding, but what is not so apparent is how gender cultures influence both men's and women's expectations and behaviour. Women either 'go along with' or challenge gender cultures; those who have least power have little choice but to collude with cultural norms and are often resentful of other women who rebel.

Daily life at work is affected by peers, bosses and clients. But it is white middle-class men who continue to lead British companies and public institutions, so it is they who determine gender and general cultures and their significance at work. Women who lack status are not only subjected to the power of their employers, as are all employees, they are also subjected to a more personal form of treatment because of their gender. (Working class, black people and people with disabilities may also be victims of managers' stereotypes about them.)

Men's and women's attitudes towards each other and their inter-personal relations constitute a gendered culture peculiar to each work environment. Gender cultures are not as vague or imprecise as they might first appear. They may be difficult to quantify, but they are clearly recognizable and understood by every woman we have interviewed.

This article describes the gender cultures we have identified during the course of conducting equality audits, training sessions and discussions with men and women managers in British public authorities in the early 1990s.

Women tend to be more aware of gender culture at work than men, precisely because they are aware of how it restricts their behaviour and expression. Men on the other hand usually felt more comfortable with the prevailing atmosphere at work.[1,2] Women, in our experience, complain as much about the way they are treated by managers and preconceptions about them, as they do about pay.

From S. Maddock and D. Parkin, 'Gender cultures: women's choices and strategies at work', *Women in Management Review*, 8, 2 (1993), pp. 3–9.

Equality audits also reveal that it is common for male managers to believe that gender bias only exists in blue-collar or male trades, that discrimination and job segregation are remnants of a bygone age, and that equality will come naturally through the mere passage of time. The strength of this popular view was also shown in the work of Ulla Ressner in Sweden.[3] But evidence suggests the contrary is the case. When people do not challenge pre-ordained cultures they remain firmly intact. The fact that powerful gender cultures persist in the public sector even after 20 years of equal opportunities programmes illustrates the power of gender cultures[4-6]. It is therefore necessary to look at why gender cultures are so persistent, how gender cultures affect both men and women and how both concur with them, and why women find it so difficult to articulate their gendered perspective within organizations.

We have both worked for many years in local government and in developing women's organizations and have felt continually frustrated by the marginal nature of equality work and the narrow interpretation of equal opportunities which usually failed to grasp what women wanted from work. We started to analyse gender relations through equality audits to give voice to what women themselves felt about work organization and service delivery as well as what they wanted for themselves in terms of career development.

Equality audits illustrate how subtle the web of internal gender cultures is and show how all women operate strategically, to combat resistance to them as women in order to be effective. Women manage gender cultures as well as their work.

Common gender cultures are described more fully below. Each organization has its own specific variety determined by both males and females, managers and employees. Although the tone of a company is usually set by corporate management, individual departments will develop their own local cultures reflecting the gender attitudes of employees. Some have said that all the cultures mentioned here are at work within their organizations – this is more likely to be the case where the workforce is heterogeneous in character.

The gentleman's club

Women find this exclusive culture extremely difficult to challenge and many are happy within it. 'The gentleman's club' is polite and civilized, women are kept firmly in established roles by male managers who are courteous and humane; they patronize in the nicest way, the old paternalist is one of the few men who will ask after employees' welfare and remembers when a secretary's child is sick.

It's so difficult asking Mr . . . about promotion or re-grading, he's always so sweet and friendly, I think he may be upset and think I'm unhappy here. (Secretary)

The chief education officer is always very polite and is embarrassed if anyone swears in front of me – he always looks to me for moral support in meetings and I convey my feelings about a policy by looking 'prim', 'cross' or 'upset'. (Principal officer education)

My boss told me it would be dangerous for me to go out on site on my own, and there wasn't anyone to accompany me. (Trainee surveyor, aged 24 years)

This last woman was inordinately determined to be a surveyor and yet she had not wanted to bully her boss to let her go on site. She was very easy-going and waited. Yet, the whole point of her traineeship was to experience site opportunities. We discovered that the reason for not sending her out with another surveyor was that the principal officer thought she would start a relationship with her colleague once out of the office. She recognized this to be the problem and said: 'I told him I had a regular boyfriend, but this didn't seem to make any difference.'

This fear that men and women will start sexual relationships as soon as they are alone is still common in workplaces where there are very few women managers. In such an environment older men frequently say they feel it is their duty to restrict younger women in order to protect them. This attitude is very common in the construction industries, where white-collar managers are fearful and exaggerate the sexual prowess of building workers, creating a sense of sexual danger for those women who want to venture out into new areas of work.[7]

The gentlemanly culture is not hostile to women who conform

Women are valued in the jobs they do, but they are not expected to break barriers and move outside traditional women's work. Over-protected women frequently conform to type. The 'gentleman' expects women to be 'caring and moral' at work and if they behave appropriately they are rewarded by warmth and concern. Women recognize that if they become too demanding, too assertive and ask for change and promotion, they will lose the friendly 'gentlemanly' boss and instead he will become difficult and they will become outsiders. These exclusive cultures rely on women understanding what they have to lose if they seek to challenge common practice. In this way women are warned that if they seek less traditional work, or more decision-making power, men and women may become antagonistic towards them.[8]

The gentleman's club reinforces the notion that a woman's role as

mother and homemaker, and a man's role as breadwinner, are
natural and pre-ordained. This *Janet and John* land (*Janet and John*
books were a sexually stereotyped reading scheme used in British
primary schools in the 1950s and 1960s) not only affects managers in
their selection procedures but also women in their choices about
hours of work, promotion and caring for their children. It is as
difficult for women to resist such a culture as it is for men –
particularly if their peers believe in it. 'I think women like running
the home; they only want part-time work – not all women want to
be managers.'

The traditional stereotype is projected onto all women. One
manager commented: 'We have a tendency to think of all women
employees as white, middle-class, married with children.'

This perspective creates a myth about women and hides the reality
of black women, single parents and those people in need of full-time
employment irrespective of domestic arrangements. This type of
working environment clearly determines women's expectations, sense
of possibility and general confidence. Those who think that women
lack ambition should understand the source from which ambition
springs and how it can be thwarted. A survey in one authority revealed
that male managers thought women lacked ambition, while the
majority of women said they lacked encouragement and were waiting
for the 'green light' to contemplate promotion as a possibility.[9]

The barrack yard

This culture dominates in hierarchical organizations where a chain
of command exists from top to bottom. 'The barrack yard' is
associated with the military, although in reality the armed services
nowadays have more sophisticated management structures than
many other public sector organizations.

'The barrack yard' is a bullying culture where subordinates are
shouted at and rarely listened to – it leads supervisors and managers
to bawl at people when they make mistakes and to despise those
beneath them. Juniors are frequently women, manual workers or
black people for whom managers have little respect.

> He shouts at everyone, he's known as the Führer.

> We ask for training but never get it – we can't do what they want without it –
> then we make mistakes but when we try to explain they don't listen.

> It's not just the women who are scared of him, so are some of the managers –
> but he blocks women and says things such as 'no women will work above scale 5
> in this department.'

'The barrack yard' hides a real hostility towards women, black
people, manual workers and anyone 'weak' or possessing little

institutional power, but it tends to be led by a few people and most other employees are merely responding to them out of fear. 'The barrack yard' can be vicious and is basically an authoritarian culture where power delivers respect. As women rarely have senior status within organizations their interests and comments are ignored and they are rendered invisible.

The locker room

This is an exclusion culture, where men build relationships on the basis of common agreements and common assumptions, frequently talk about sport and make sexual references to confirm their hetero-sexuality. Although this tends to be a white male culture, male outsiders can join the group through sport and sexual innuendo. It is more difficult for women to join the club.

> I would learn about the sport and talk about it, then they would change the subject – they didn't want me, a woman, in the group. (Chief officer, northern authority)

It is not just junior status women who are subjected to 'locker room culture'. Women with power, but who are isolated as chief executives or directors, tell us that they have to listen to endless references to sport and sex in both formal and informal situations.

> Men still exclude women from 'drinks-in-the-pub' and evening socializing, it's difficult asking a woman because everyone assumes you must fancy her even if all you want to do is talk about work. (Male director of housing)

A man at home with 'the locker room' culture may justify 'pin-up' calendars as harmless and fun, but then he puts them in full view to intimidate younger women. Although 'girly' pictures and calendars are more rare in public sector organizations than private companies (policy statements have made it clear that they are not endorsed by management), even today some men in local government have them in filing cabinets and behind doors.[10]

Another form of masculine domination in 'the locker room' culture is exaggerated body language. Some men, when feeling in control in meetings, will lean backwards on chairs with arms outstretched, rocking backwards and forwards and drawing attention to their bodies – detracting attention from other people. A few women managers have told us that they have developed their own tactics to match this behaviour, for instance:

> I spray myself with perfumes in meetings and wear low cut dresses and generally flaunt myself. (Public relations officer)

> I've learnt to wear bright colours and generally be loud, otherwise you just disappear. (College assistant principal)

But most women say that they find this overt physical body flaunting either too threatening to challenge or too trivial to imitate. Some women, perhaps more aware of gender dynamics, feel that mirroring male behaviour is dangerous and/or inappropriate.[11]

> I think too many women managers are either taming or exaggerating their sexuality at work – and that encourages men to think of women as sex objects not as managers. (Women's officer in education)

The gender-blind

In the 1980s, one of the arguments used to persuade managers that women were capable and should be promoted at work was that there were no differences between men and women,[12] that a woman could function in exactly the same way as could any man. But, when we pretend that women live the same lives and have the same experiences as men, a 'gender blindness' develops. Although this perspective has been challenged by many feminist writers,[13] the perspective is very persistent as it allows people to ignore the significance of gender at work.

'Gender-blind' persons make no mention or reference to a colleague's home life or personal experiences. They assume, or assert, that there is a 'level playing field' at work and men and women can excel if they try. The 'gender-blind' ignore a woman's identity and experience, and they probably also deny racial differences and disabilities. Such blindness usually grows out of an illusion that everyone is white, able-bodied and male. 'Gender-blind' persons do not want to discriminate, but instead they deny reality and difference.

For instance, one manager organized 24-hour shifts for all employees in the computer pool without any reference to the difficulties that most women had with this. Women are more likely to be anxious about working late, being alone in buildings or walking to car parks at night. A gender blindness to the reality of women's lives is to ignore the fact that domestic responsibilities and social realities do affect the choices women can make.[14]

The 'gender-blind' can be sincere in their commitment to removing barriers for women, but by ignoring reality, they encourage women to aspire to superwomen status – the perfect mother, the model manager and perfect colleague. Women's magazines have also encouraged this romantic notion that women can be everything and can overcome all obstacles by sheer willpower. However this is changing, and magazines such as *She* and *Options* now stress the importance of women making priorities, relaxing and having time off. Those who deny the difference that a person's gender makes to their lives are like ostriches, hoping traditional power relationships will go away, without them having to challenge the status quo: 'I can't think of a job I wouldn't give a lady but not many apply with the right qualifications.'

Frequently this perspective hides a fear of men to ask questions and be direct with women.

Such an avoidance of women's lives is also convenient, for it creates an illusion of 'sameness' between men and women and denies the obstacles and difficulties many women face, especially when they seek to break with traditional practice.

Paying lip-service and the feminist pretenders

Some public sector organizations, which have well developed equal opportunities policies, have also developed a new breed of men: men who are well versed in feminism and think of themselves as non-sexist.

There are those who pay lip-service to equality programmes and declare themselves to be equal opportunities employers but do little to promote or develop women or black people. As equality work becomes more respectable, the number of people espousing support for equal opportunity policies grows. Those who pay lip-service produce policies and charters and then ignore them.

Then there are also those who are adept at manoeuvring around equal opportunity policies. They have learned the language and how to use it to their own advantage. Highly politicized authorities have developed highly politicized administrations and officers criticize and judge each other on the basis of their political perspectives, their 'equality' behaviour and their own identities (i.e. whether they are white, black, able-bodied, female or male).

The culture of the 'feminist pretenders' or equality 'experts' is one of moralistic tendencies where men and women will attempt to out-do each other over the 'correct way to deal with equality issues'. Hierarchies of oppression have developed where a person's status is determined by his/her position on the ladder of oppression – female, black, gay, working-class, etc.

New forms of oppression develop in such a culture. Individuals who do not conform to alternative stereotypes are belittled and patronized. Instead of men assuming women will get pregnant, there is a tendency to think all women must speak in meetings and be confident, or that all black people must have a position on black politics: 'I think Mary should be more assertive, I've suggested she read. . . .'

Such advice between colleagues, who are mere acquaintances, is often insulting and perpetuates the idea that the woman is a victim in need of male assistance and, to add salt to the wound, suggests how she might be liberated. Many older women find younger men espousing feminism more irritating than traditional bullies. The 'feminist pretenders' create a myth of 'equality' based on a form of gender or ethnic determinism, rather than an understanding of equality based on human values. This results in the idea that 'all' women make good managers. The pretenders are rather like missionaries, unable to distinguish between individuals within the oppressed group who are their pupils. Everyone represents the group and is treated not as a person, but as a representative of a class, gender or ethnic group. This creates a dangerous culture where some individuals are persuaded that, because they are victims, they have no responsibility for events and blame other people instead of developing themselves.[15]

The smart macho

The current commercial climate in the National Health Service, and elsewhere, which encourages economic efficiency at the expense of all other criteria, is a breeding ground for smart and macho managers.[16]

Managers dominated by the 'smart macho' culture feel under such pressure to reach performance and budget targets that they have no desire to block or obstruct employees who can work 80 hours a week and deliver on time. These new managers are driven by extreme competitivity, they discriminate against those who cannot work at the same pace or challenge economic criteria. If you cannot keep up, you are likely to be sacked, demoted or passed over, whoever you are. Superficially, this appears not to be a gendered culture and many women managers are known to be as ruthless as male managers, sometimes more so.

> She was known throughout the region as focused totally on objectives and meeting them within deadlines, there was no point in explaining difficulties to her, she wouldn't listen. (Woman director, NHS)

> Some of the new women unit managers have ended up sacking the old gentlemen in cardigans and replacing them with young ruthless yuppies, and most of them are male with no domestic responsibilities or interest in staff development. (Woman medical director)

But this type of management culture is actually a more ruthless form of the gender-blind. If you work hard and fast and can focus on narrow targets, your gender or ethnic origin is irrelevant. Of course, most women over 35 years of age do have 'caring' responsibilities, whether they be for parents or children. A recent audit showed that women still do over 75 per cent of housework.[17]

It has not gone unnoticed by other people in the NHS that this new breed of macho manager, men and women, is often childless and highly mobile. Although, of course, men can continue to function in the same way even when they do have children, yet again women are faced with the same choices in 1993 as they were in 1903; if you want a career you have to forgo other aspects of your life. This type of management style is being challenged by both older men and women, because both are having to adapt to fit into it. One woman said:

> The trouble is, we got a new dynamic woman unit manager and she sacked all the men in cardigans and now we've got young macho men and women managers with Gucci shoes and Armani clothes who are much worse. They never listen, they rush about competing with each other over performance targets – and seem to care little about the service.

Conclusion

Corporate managers can play a significant part in creating 'gender cultures' and gender dynamics.[18] Although there are common themes, each organization has its own brand of leadership and its own characteristic work culture, and each in turn develops its own peculiar resistance to equality proposals. The lack of attention to the spirit, informal norms and values of an organization has led to many equality programmes being sabotaged by both management and male and female staff.

The prevailing culture dominates and determines women's behaviour, as well as men's. Women may collude or fail to resist stereotypes and prejudices which undermine their own sex. Their self-esteem and survival may be so closely connected to traditional norms, that they see no advantage in changing common practice. In many county councils in the UK, for instance, women still form the backbone of the support services and administrative structures and yet very few have reached senior middle management. We have found from equality audits that the majority of women within the organization do not consider this to be odd or something to question. The lack of opportunities for women results not just from male managers' resistance to women, but also from women's own sense of place.

Those cultures which are firmly rooted in people's sense of the naturally ordained, where patriarchal relations are firmly embedded and men continue to be confident of their natural right to manage, are difficult for individual women to challenge. Therefore, they continue to collude and conform, even if they do not want to. Many women in their 30s, fed up and stagnated in middle management, do turn their attention to children, to their lifestyle or to changing careers.[19]

In all these cultures, male managers told us that they thought the main reason for women's under-representation in management was their lack of ambition and that this was due to their commitment to domestic life. Many male managers still suspected that women manager candidates might become pregnant and leave and so they rejected or ignored them.

> It's difficult you know, because women do get pregnant and if you employ a woman aged 35 years as a senior manager and she gets pregnant, we cannot afford the cover and then we are short staffed. (County council senior manager)

By contrast, the women working for the same authorities felt that while women received less encouragement and were given less training compared with their male colleagues, they still took opportunities when they were offered them. Women, who acknowledged being more ambitious, felt that they were categorized as being 'too hard working' and too competitive, were 'put under the microscope', were criticized for not spending enough time with their children if they had any, and were generally targeted for abuse.[20]

In reality, women plan their pregnancies around their work, not their work around their pregnancies. Women senior managers rarely have more than three months off even when they do have a baby.[21] It can be more common for women to stick with an employer than it is for men, who may move posts every two or three years. The possibility of pregnancy is clearly a rationalization and defence mechanism, used conveniently as an excuse for not developing women managers or women staff.

Public organizations have invested in male managers who have then promptly left for better paid posts in the private sector or other authorities. These same organizations continue to ignore management training for women.[22]

The phantom of pregnancy is one example of a social prejudice which is reinforced by a gendered culture. Equality audits reveal that some gender cultures are understood to reflect a natural order, illustrated by the 'gentleman's club', in which women feel valued if they conform to female stereotypes. The 'barrack yard' and the 'locker room' are more authoritarian versions of the 'gentleman's club', where men's and women's collusion is out of fear, as well as being based on a cultural agreement.

In organizations where there is an acceptance of women in the workplace and an acceptance that women have a right to promotion, there is lip-service to equality, which is expressed through cultures such as the 'gender-blind' and the smart macho. Corporate rather than natural agendas tend to reinforce these cultures, which are driven by the profit motive and the need for greater efficiency. Managers are not interested in sustaining patriarchal power if it conflicts with economic interest. These cultures are determined by economics as well as patriarchal relationships. If barriers to women hinder performance targets, then inequality for the new breed of macho and smart managers becomes a management issue, because 'inequalities' are understood to mean a reduction in efficiency and performance levels. However, the force of the economic argument appears to be influencing executives rather than middle managers, and it is the middle managers who are the 'gatekeepers' over women and it is they who need to change. And, while executives are looking to promote women in middle management, they still protect their exclusive male culture at board level.[23]

The 'feminist pretenders' are committed to the theory of equality but in reality are reluctant to relinquish their power over women. These men are often using women in a battle with other men. The 'feminist pretenders' push women in directions they think important, the result being that they are often more oppressive than 'the gentlemen' who leave women alone if they fulfil their traditional roles.

All these gender dynamics create barriers for women and are disastrous for organizations. Democratic organizations will only develop when the power of gender cultures is acknowledged and challenged by both men and women.

Notes

1 R.M. Kanter, *The Men and Women of the Corporation*, (Basic Books, New York, NY, 1977).

2 S.J.M. Freeman, *Managing Lives: Corporate Women and Social Change* (University of Massachusetts Press, MA, 1992).

3 U. Ressner, *The Hidden Hierarchy: Democracy and Equal Opportunities* (Gower Publishing, Avebury, 1987).

4 C. Cockburn, *In the Way of Women: Men's Resistance to Sex Equality in Organizations* (Macmillan, London, 1991).

5 Cabinet Office for the Civil Service, *A Review of Equal Opportunities for Women in the Civil Service* (HMSO, London, 1991).

6 S. Goss, and H. Brown, *Barriers to Women in the National Health Service* (The Management Foundation, 1991).

7 Corporate Management and Policy Services, *Service and Equality Audits in Direct Labour Organizations* (CMPS, Stockport, 1990–2).

8 CMPS equality audits and interviews from eight local authorities, county councils, district councils and metropolitan boroughs.

9 CMPS, *Opportunity 2000 Report* for a County Council (CMPS, Stockport, 1992).

10 CMPS equality audits and interviews.

11 S.J. Maddock, 'Women's frustration with and influence on local government management in the UK: an investigation from a woman manager's perspective', *Women in Management Review*, 8, 1 (1993), pp.3–8.

12 J. Rosener, 'The ways women lead', *Harvard Business Review*, November/December (1990), pp. 119–25.

13 C. Gilligan, *In a Different Voice: Psychological Theory and Women's Development* (Harvard University Press, Cambridge, MA, 1982).

14 CMPS, *Opportunity 2000*.

15 CMPS equality audits and interviews.

16 Health Service Management Institute, *Women Managers' Training* (University of Manchester, 1992).
17 CMPS, *Opportunity 2000*.
18 CMPS equality audits and interviews.
19 Maddock, 'Women's frustration'.
20 CMPS equality audits and interviews.
21 Ibid.
22 Ibid.
23 C. Handy, informal discussion (1991).

15

Managing organisational culture: fantasy or reality?

Emmanuel Ogbonna

Is culture manageable?

[. . .] There is no consensus on the definition of culture. Indeed, it has been noted that in organisation theory, there are as many definitions of culture as there are experts on the subject (Ogbonna, 1990). It would appear that the definition adopted is bound up with a particular researcher's view of the world and the preferred methodology (Burrell and Morgan, 1979; Smircich, 1983). Yet a definition is necessary to operationalise the concept and to distinguish it from similar organisational concepts. Culture is defined in this article as the interweaving of the individual into a community and the collective programming of the mind that distinguishes members of one known group from another. It is the values, norms, beliefs and customs that an individual holds in common with members of a social unit or group. Schein (1985) identifies three levels of the cultural phenomenon in organisations as follows:

1   on the surface are the overt behaviours and other physical manifestations (artifacts and creations);
2   below this level is a sense of what ought to be (values);
3   at the deepest level are those things that are taken for granted as 'correct' ways of coping with the environment (basic assumptions).

It is the pattern of basic assumptions which are taken for granted that Schein describes as culture. This conception of culture is important for discussions of whether culture can be managed and will be taken up later.

The debate on managing culture is characterised by two extreme arguments rooted in the very conception of the subject. Smircich (1983) identifies two distinct approaches [. . .]: culture as something an organisation *is* and culture as something an organisation *has*.

Abridged from E. Ogbonna,' Managing organisational culture: fantasy or reality?', *Human Resource Management Journal*, 3, 2 (1993), pp. 42–54.

These two stances, which appear to be mutually exclusive, have dominated not just the research on organisational culture but also explorations of the very nature of the concept. When viewed as something an organisation has, culture becomes a powerful organisational tool. It shapes behaviour, gives organisational members a sense of identity and establishes recognised and accepted premises for decision-making. For those researchers who see culture as what an organisation is, the concept is inseparable from organisations. To be sure, 'organisation is culture and culture is organisation'; hence there is little point in trying to control this socially constructed phenomenon which is embedded in the very roots of organisational existence. This point was illustrated by Weick when, in a response to an article on managing corporate culture, he was reported to have stated: 'organisations don't have cultures, they are cultures, and this is why culture is so difficult to change' (Siehl, 1985: 125).

In a similar vein, Fombrun (1983: 151) has concluded that 'managing corporate culture is . . . an awesome if not impossible task', and Uttal (1983: 72) provides a summary which captures the feeling of many on the issue:

> For all the hype, corporate culture is real and powerful. It's also hard to change and you won't find much support for doing so inside or outside your company. If you run up against the culture when trying to redirect strategy, attempt to dodge; if you must meddle with culture directly, tread carefully and with modest expectations.

Other researchers go further, arguing that culture simply exists and *cannot* be created or managed by individuals.[1] The point being made by these researchers is that no matter how managers try, they cannot change or manage the subconscious assumptions and values which guide people's behaviour. This is because, by definition, these assumptions exist without the individual's awareness. As Krefting and Frost (1985: 156) so eloquently put it:

> If organisational culture is funnelled through the unconscious and is therefore not always orderly, then it is unlikely that efforts to manage such a culture can be precisely predicted or tightly controlled.

However, it is quite plausible to argue that the extreme stance of this view is logically inconsistent as well as empirically suspect. This is because culture, like reality, is a social phenomenon which depends on human action and interaction (Berger and Luckmann, 1966). For example, what appears today to be an unquestionable way of behaving was once an alternative mode of behaviour, and once chosen, it is reinforced and passed down to new members who may come to view it as the appropriate and unquestionable response. In organisational settings, it has been argued that the entrepreneur is the creator of meaning through symbols, ideologies, rituals, beliefs and myths (Pettigrew, 1979; 1985). By implication, if the value system guiding members' behaviour is no longer appropriate, it must be replaced by that which is more appropriate by manipulating the elements identified above. That culture is a learning process capable of being 'unlearned' is a view consistent with that of Schein (1984; 1985) who is probably the most widely cited writer on the concept. Schein's conception of culture is that of adaptive agent which enables organisational participants to learn to cope with problems of survival. This line of thinking suggests that where a culture has outlived its usefulness as a means of sustaining a people's behavioural pattern, they learn (or soon develop) alternative ways of legitimising the old or new behaviours which may eventually translate into a new set of beliefs and values. There are, after all, many examples of 'cultural change' in the literature, including forced change.[2] Herein lies the major locus of the argument of researchers who see cultural change as not only possible but desirable.

The emerging theme [. . .] is that changing the 'deep fabric' of the organisation is awfully difficult; hence it is sensible to advise companies not to attempt to change their cultures without serious thought. One only has to read Tunstall's (1983) description of the obstacles to cultural transition encountered by one of the world's largest corporations, AT&T, to know the nature of the problem involved. Tunstall provides an account which indicates technological, operational and organisational obstacles. Yet changing the corporate culture may be critical to the success of the company, as Tunstall himself argues. Failure to change the culture of the organisation (AT&T) in response to environmental pressures beyond the company's control would almost certainly have led to disaster. A proposition consistent with this line of thinking is that in some cases organisations may have little choice but to attempt to manage their culture.

Robbins (1987: 368) shifted the argument from whether culture can be managed to the conditions under which it can be managed. He stressed that 'if managers cannot guide their organisations through planned cultural change, the subject [culture] has limited practical utility and may be of only academic interest.' Robbins goes on to discuss the factors that will determine the success of any attempted change in culture, including the emergence of a crisis, leadership change, the organisational life cycle, age, size, strength of the current culture and absence of subcultures. Furthermore, Kilmann (1982) observes that if culture is not controlled, organisations will spend time and money protecting their outdated assumptions about the business environment. Indeed, where assumptions are not related to the current business environment, the organisation may suffer as a result. Mercer,[3] an IBM employee for fifteen years, takes this point further. Providing an 'insider account', he demonstrates how IBM's strong culture is making it difficult for the management to manage the organisation in a changing environment. Bates (1984) has made a similar point, arguing that culture is capable of locking people into their own problems. This is because necessary cultural change may be avoided on sentimental grounds or may even be made difficult by an existing strong culture. Although this point may be held to be a vindication of the argument that culture can and should be managed, it nonetheless exposes the inherent weakness in the underlying attempts to manage culture. This point is crucial and will be taken up later.

Whatever stance researchers take on the issue of managing culture, it is clear they all agree on one thing: culture can have a pervasive effect on organisational outcomes. Krefting and Frost (1985) assert that it constructs the boundaries within which individuals interact in their everyday life and as such limits the processing of information to within human capability. Luhmann (1979) has similarly observed that it has the potential to reduce ambiguity and facilitate social interaction. Handy (1986), taking a more functional view, argues that a strong culture makes a strong organisation, and this may well be so since a strong culture can shape patterns of behaviour in the organisation which may present a competitive advantage (Scholz, 1987). This agreement implies the necessity for the cultural aspect of the organisation to be kept attuned with other organisational variables such as the environment. Often the organisational environment is dynamic and this presents a challenge to managers in managing corporate culture. [. . .]

Writers have noted that the results of managing culture are often unanticipated (Krefting and Frost, 1985; Ackroyd and Crowdy, 1990), implying that the management of culture may be fraught with unintended organisational consequences. This is because although organisational culture, rather like the culture of societies, can and does change, its direction cannot be precisely controlled. This line of reasoning appears convincing when it is considered that for anyone attempting to change culture to be taken seriously, the person needs to have a vision of what the new culture will be like. Unfortunately, many managers are often unsure of what they want to change and are unlikely to be able to formulate visions of the future, which in itself is characterised by uncertainty and ambiguity. Indeed, far from analysing and planning the future of their organisations, managers tend to be reactive, dealing with problems as they arise (Mintzberg, 1975). An important practical implication of this work is, therefore, that any manager who is seriously interested in managing culture must be certain and unambiguous about what is to be managed and what outcomes are desired. Specific policies and success levels will vary depending on the definition of culture and the changes desired.

To summarise, the literature on managing organisational culture is confusing. There are clearly two ways in which culture is treated in relation to change. There are those who treat culture as behaviour and there are those who treat it as values and taken-for-granted assumptions. The consequence of this confusion is that there is no convincing conceptual model which clearly demonstrates how change of deeper level values should be attained. This is despite the fact that much of the literature accepts such change as constituting a change of culture. Instead, what we are presented with are haphazard treatments of cultural change which either equate it to behavioural change, or simply assume that behavioural change will in the long run lead to change in culture. Attempting to change culture then becomes a journey into the unknown which may or may not achieve the desired aim. Whatever the case, it is clear that the concept of culture has lost much of its value as a tool for analysing and interpreting the behaviour of people within organisations. It would appear that many academics, like consultants and managers, have been taken in by the search for mechanisms which will generate behaviours concomitant with the strategies of organisations. Culture appears then to have been reduced to the status of yet another concept which, like many before it, has reached the decline stage of its 'life cycle'. Although it may never be completely exterminated, it is doubtful whether, as in the 1980s, three of the top management journals will devote special issues to it in the 1990s. Its value as a tool of social research may be revived only at the expense of it being treated as an expedient tool of management effectiveness. In Martin's cogent expression, the question of managing culture has 'the capacity to annoy anyone seriously interested in the topic' (1985:95).

Notes

1 See for example Martin and Siehl (1983).

2 For instance, Tichy et al. (1986) demonstrate how Honeywell Information Systems, a major American corporation, was forced by environmental pressures to change its culture. The prevailing culture was deemed inappropriate to its new strategic direction.

3 As Golzen (1987) reported in *The Sunday Times*, Mercer argues that IBM's problems are rooted in the corporate culture, the very attribute which is said to have been instrumental to the company's success. He cited an example of the company's appraisal system whereby managers spend a lot of time ensuring that their subordinates are happy with the result. He also referred to the example of IBM's unsuccessful attempt to modify its belief system to highlight the importance of being a low-cost producer. This was resisted by many because it was perceived to contradict its fundamental philosophy of being a quality-conscious company.

References

Ackroyd, S. and Crowdy, P.A. (1990) 'Can culture be managed? Working with raw material', *Personal Review*, 19(5): 3–13.

Bates, P. (1984) 'The impact of organisation culture on approaches to problem-solving',*Organisation Studies*, 5(1): 43–66.

Berger, P.L. and Luckmann, T. (1966) *The Social Construction of Reality*. New York: Doubleday.

Burrell, G. and Morgan, G. (1979) *Sociological Paradigms and Organisational Analysis*. London: Heinemann.

Fombrun, C.J. (1983) 'Corporate culture, environment and strategy', *Human Resources Management*, 22(1/2): 139–52.

Golzen, G. (1987) 'How corporate culture can be carried too far', *The Sunday Times*, 15 November.

Handy, C.B. (1986) *Understanding Organizations*. Harmondsworth: Penguin.

Kilmann, R.W. (1982) 'Getting control of the corporate culture', *Managing (USA)*, 2: 11–17.

Krefting, L.A. and Frost, P.J. (1985) 'Untangling webs, surfing waves, and wild-catting: a multiple-metaphor perspective on managing culture', in P.J. Frost et al. (eds), *Organization Culture*. Beverly Hills, CA: Sage.

Luhmann, N. (1979) *Trust and Power*. Chichester: John Wiley.

Martin, J. (1985) 'Can organization culture be managed?', in P.J. Frost et al. (eds), *Organization Culture*. Beverly Hills, CA: Sage.

Martin, J.M. and Siehl, C. (1983) 'Organization culture and counterculture: an uneasy symbiosis', *Organizational Dynamics*, 12(2): 52–64.

Mintzberg, H. (1975) 'The manager's job: folklore and fact', *Harvard Business Review*, July–August: 49–61.

Ogbonna, E. (1990) 'Organisation culture and strategy in the UK supermarket industry'. PhD thesis, Cardiff Business School.

Pettigrew, A.M. (1979), 'On studying organisational cultures', *Administrative Science Quarterly*, 24: 570–81.

Pettigrew, A.M. (1985) *The Awakening Giant*. Oxford: Basil Blackwell.

Robbins, S.P. (1987) *Organization Theory: Structure, Design and Application*. Englewood Cliffs, NJ: Prentice-Hall.

Schein, E.H. (1984) 'Coming to a new awareness of organizational culture', *Sloan Management Review*, 25, Winter: 3–16.

Schein, E.H. (1985) *Organizational Culture and Leadership*. San Francisco: Jossey-Bass.

Scholz, C. (1987) 'Corporate culture and strategy – the problem of strategic fit', *Long Range Planning (UK)*, 20(4): 78–87.

Siehl, C. (1985) 'After the founder: an opportunity to manage culture', in P.J. Frost et al. (eds), *Organization Culture*. Beverly Hills, CA: Sage.

Smircich, L. (1983) 'Concepts of culture and organisational analysis', *Administrative Science Quarterly*, 28: 339–58.

Tichy, N.M. et al. (1986) 'Cultural revitalisation at the Honeywell Information Systems', *Journal of Business Strategy*, 6(3): 70–80.

Tunstall, W.B. (1983) 'Cultural transition at AT&T', *Sloan Management Review*, 25(1): 15–26.

Uttal, B. (1983) 'The corporate culture vultures', *Fortune*, 17 October.

16

Phases and levels of organisational change

Nicholas S. Rashford and David Coghlan

In her seminal work, Elizabeth Kubler-Ross (1970) describes how individuals respond to the unexpected information that they are terminally ill. Her famous stages of denial, anger, bargaining, depression and acceptance have provided the basis for much reflection and education on the traumatic processes of coping with dying and death. It is hypothesised that these stages occur in the face of all categories of personal change, of which dying and death are the ultimate instance. What is in question in this article is how organisations as corporate systems respond to organisational change. Lippitt (1982) cites one model that articulates phases of organisational crisis: shock, defensive retreat, acknowledgement, and adaptation and change. Much of the literature on organisational change has been based on Lewin's three stages of unfreezing, moving and refreezing. What is common in most frameworks is a thematic movement that begins in a denial mode and moves to an acceptance or change mode. Critical distinguishing factors must be identified in any attempt to link organisational change models with individual therapeutic models. For instance, in the Kubler-Ross model, the outcome, death, is more often specific and certain for the individual, although in some cases bargaining may produce psychological and physical changes to facilitate arresting the disease. Such cases are rare. The movement of the stages towards that fixed outcome in organisational change is not fixed to that degree of certainty. Bargaining may result in an alternative outcome. Only in rare instances of the arrest of terminal illness is there equivalence of refreezing or sustaining change. It could be argued that the Kubler-Ross five stages are all steps in the unfreezing process. An undifferentiated transfer of Kubler-Ross' framework to the organisational context does not do justice to the complexity of either. At the same time, an indebtedness to her work as a significant source can be acknowledged.

From N.S. Rashford and D. Coghlan, 'Phases and levels of organisational change', *Journal of Managerial Psychology*, 4, 3 (1989), pp. 17–22.

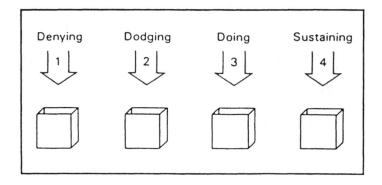

Figure 16.1   *Stages of organisational change*

This article presents a four-stage process: denying, dodging, doing and sustaining (see Figure 16.1).

Four stages of the change process

First stage: denying

Theme – This does not affect us
The denial stage begins with a presentation of the data supporting a change into an organisation. It can be a denial of the need for change in the face of others' need to change or a need for change caused by environmental forces. This phase centres on processing information, disputing its value, relevance or timeliness. The change agent may be anywhere in the organisation and will meet with denial from above and below. If the change agent is a 'change generator', either as 'key change agent' or as 'demonstrator', he/she will need the support of 'patrons' and 'defenders' to enforce the drive for change (Ottaway, 1983). For movement to occur, there has to be an acceptance of the data as valid, relevant and pertinent and place it on to others.

Second stage: dodging

Theme – Ignore this. Don't get involved
The dodging stage begins when the accumulated evidence shows that the change process is likely to take place. The data are perceived as relevant. It is agreed that a small amount of change is needed, but what is questioned is whether it is critical to change or not. There can be a searching for countervailing data. As the change is coming from outside, dodging is the equivalent of organisational anger. This anger is expressed in a passive-aggressive non-participation. Everyone else

has to do it. The effort is spent stopping the change or at least finding some way to be peripheral to it. The energy for this comes from many sources. Frustration, lack of ownership, fear of change are some possible sources. It may be grounded in the rivalry between one team and another.

At the same time, this can be a creative stage. This stage has its active components though it is characterised by hedging and not getting involved. A subordinate can confuse the issue by presenting the weakness of the approach to the change. There may be a more serious issue that needs to be dealt with first. This shifts the action to a different focus. Another method to subvert is to change the form. If the discussion is on work-flow change, change it to personnel. If it is on personnel, change it to bulk capital budget funding or to the expense budget. The mode of agreement for the subordinate is often silence, which can be, and often is, misread as opposition. The manager articulates the critical need for the change and pins the subordinate involvement on its success. This tends to have negative consequences. Failure and blame tend to be involved, proving the need for the change. The failure and blame are the positive forces for it, but become negative motivators in the team. In fact, quiet behaviour, sometimes indicating agreement, is read at this phase as disagreement and insubordination. The need for the team to adapt the process and approach is essential in this stage to make it their own. These slight changes are the price paid for ownership. Movement comes when ownership of the need for change is accepted.

Third stage: doing

Theme – This is very important. We have got to do it now
This stage occurs quickly and sometimes startles the observer in its contrast. When the opposition has been voiced, the frustration released and there is agreement in the team – not always vocal – that the change deserves a try, this 'doing' phase begins. It is earmarked by energy used in going for the change. As the specific change is worked on, more things are uncovered that require change. Minor moves, such as budgeting, restructuring, hiring, emerge. These may have to be worked on so as to facilitate the major change. For the manager, the general tendency is to let the momentum take over. The difficult part of gaining consent and involvement is over, so sit back and let it happen. This is dangerous for two reasons. If the team labour is not divided well between teams and individuals, this can warp the relationships and destroy the whole change process. Secondly, there is the danger of overloading the change process with trying too many things, in addition to the ones that began the change process. The organisation has the capability and the readiness to change. The focus moves from the 'change

generators' to the 'change implementors' (Ottaway, 1983). The tendency is to overload. There needs to be bargaining as to what can or cannot be put into the change. This is equivalent to Beckhard and Harris' (1987) notion of managing the transition state between the present and the desired future. These two pressures will cause critical judgement to arise again as it did early on in the change process.

There are two outcomes to the issues of this stage. One is death, where the whole thing collapses under its own weight. The other is a focusing of energy. What is required is an accurate drawing of the force field of the change so that the critical elements in the change are pinpointed and appropriate goals are set. This stage may be spread over several years. When the component steps are sustained, the change can move to the next stage.

Fourth stage: sustaining

Theme – We have a new way of proceeding
This stage is less well defined but is a key stage of any change process. It is the focusing of energy to follow through on programmes and projects. This is the refreezing stage and the 'change adopters' come into prominence (Ottaway, 1983). The successful completion of this stage is the integration of the change into the habitual patterns of behaviour and structure.

Four levels of organisational behaviour

The four stages of change impact on the behaviour of an organisation at four levels. The framework put forward by Rashford and Coghlan (1987) describes four levels of participation in organisations – individual, face-to-face team, group/divisional and policy/strategy (see Figure 16.2). These levels can be viewed as degrees or types of involvement, or as degrees of complexity, depending on whether one approaches the question from the point of view of the individual moving towards the organisation to participate or from the point of view of the organisation viewing the commitment of individuals. From the point of view of the individual, the least complex approach is the relationship that the individual has with the organisation. The more complex approach to participation exists in working out and solving the difficulties of a face-to-face working team.

An even more complex involvement exists in terms of the group or divisional type of interface, where teams must work together to achieve complex tasks. The most complex, from the point of view of the individual, is the relationship of the total organisation to its external environment in which other organisations are individual competitors, competing for scarce resources to produce similar

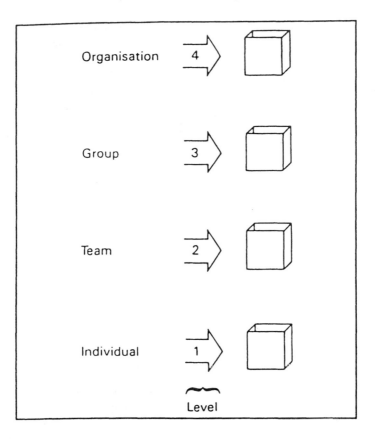

Figure 16.2 *Levels of organisational behaviour*

products or services. From the point of view of the organisation, the question is one of involvement at the group or divisional level in which complex MIS and data systems must be used to extend the knowledge and co-ordinate the functions of complex working divisions or strategic business units. Finally, the most complex of all is the unified effort of all participants in an organisation towards making the organisation profitable, growth oriented and functional in its external environment. This set of complex behaviours, then, is separated into a cognitive map – a mental construct of different types of participation and involvement – by the use of the concept of levels of participation.

Level 1: individual

Level 1 describes the individual level. The task of the individual is to be him/herself and fulfil his/her life tasks. The task of the organisation is that the individual belongs in an appropriate psychological contract. When this level is in place and operating effectively, a person will allow the organisation and its goals to be a source of personal goal motivation. The individual will still retain his/her own individuality while 'belonging' to the organisation. The key intervention on this level is the career interview in which the dynamics of the life cycle, the work cycle and the family cycle are located and placed in juxtaposition so that the individual can locate his/her career in the context of his/her life.

Level 2: face-to-face team

Level 2 describes the team level. The individual enters into working face-to-face relationships. Effectiveness on this level means that a team is capable of finding and correcting its own dysfunctions. A successful team is only perceived as successful after it has successfully corrected its own dysfunction. The individual's task is to contribute to the team's functioning while the team's task is to be a functioning unit. The organisation's task is that the team be significant in its output. The key intervention on this level is team-building.

Level 3: group/divisional

The group or divisional level is level 3. This level is made up of several face-to-face working teams that must function together to accomplish a divisional purpose, such as manufacturing, sales or marketing. It can be a collection of individual work teams that provide a strategic business unit function for an organisation. When this third level is in place, the group or division is capable of obtaining information and converting it into decision processes, enabling the implementation of complex programmes or operations. The task of this level is to map the flow of information and partially completed work from one unit to another. The organisation's task is that these units form an effective aggregate. The key intervention on this level is internal mapping, where dysfunctions in information or work flow are identified and corrected.

Level 4: organisational strategy/policy

The fourth level is the organisational policy or strategy level. It is the final fusion of these divisional groups together to form a working, whole organisation. It must be capable of reflecting on its own strengths and weaknesses, as well as being engaged in proactive relationships in determining the opportunities and threats from the external environment. It matches these two in a selection process that determines programmes, services and products aimed at accomplishing the goals of the organisation and servicing the external environment with its products and services. The key intervention is open systems planning, performed in terms of the organisation's core mission, with its internal and external constituencies that make demands on the organisation.

There is a close link between each level. For instance, an action taken on level 4 can affect a team's functioning and lead to an individual's questioning his/her sense of belonging to the organisation. So a triggering even on level 4 must be dealt with on levels 1 and 2. Effectiveness on level 2 depends on level 1 being in place; level 3 depends on levels 1 and 2, and level 4 on all three. The delineation of levels in terms of definition, tasks and key intervention provides a valuable diagnostic construct for the manager, the consultant and the trainer. The framework helps unravel the complexity of the task of understanding how people function in organisations, and provides a valuable consultation and training tool (Coghlan, 1987: Rashford and Coghlan, 1988).

Phases of organisational change

We have described the behavioural reactions to change and have discussed the levels of an organisation and what is required in human interaction on each of these levels. Figure 16.3 details how these two factors interact in a seven-phase sequence. There is a domino effect as the hierarchy of the organisation, after recognising the need for change, intervenes appropriately in the organisation, frequently through a consultant.

Phase I

Change enters the organisation through an individual. That individual as a 'generator' (Ottaway, 1983) goes through his/her own reaction to the need for change by initially denying the validity, relevance and pertinence of the change. Once that is recognised – that the change does apply – it can be dodged and applied to others. 'We do not have to move now. We still have time. Only minor adjustments are required.' This gives way to a realisation that the information is real and threatening, that the organisation is in peril if something is not done. Ownership by the key individual concludes this phase. The key individual is the person concerned with boundary maintenance. Allen (1977) describes such a role as 'technological gatekeeping', in which an individual brings to the team the special information it needs to perform its task.

Phase I	Individual	denying, dodging, doing
Phase II	Individual	doing
	Team	denying, dodging, doing
Phase III	Individual	doing
	Team	doing
	Group	denying, dodging, doing
Phase IV	Individual	doing
	Team	doing
	Group	doing
	Organisation	denying, dodging, doing
Phase V	Organisation	doing
	Group	doing
	Team	doing
	Individual	sustaining
Phase VI	Organisation	doing
	Group	doing
	Team	sustaining
	Individual	sustaining
Phase VII	All	sustaining

Figure 16.3   *Phases of organisational change*

Phase II

When the key individual has worked through denial and dodging the change, he/she moves to the doing stage and presents the change data to his/her team, emphasising the necessity for change and beginning to define the dimensions of the change. A key issue is the degree of choice and the ultimate control over the change. The team denies – 'we don't have to do it' – then it dodges – 'we don't have to do it now' – and enters into a period of vocal bargaining. The tendency to shoot the messenger who has brought the bad news must be recognised. This phase is concluded when the team recognises the issue and the need to do something. Ownership of an articulated problem ends this phase, not just as defined by an individual, but as articulated by the team.

Phase III

This phase involves the bringing together of multiple teams at the group level to confront the issue of the change. The group denies the validity, relevance and pertinence of the change. The cultural assumptions are central as history and tradition are used to block change (Schein, 1985). Dodging needs to be addressed by internal mapping processes (Beckhard, 1975; Rashford and Coghlan, 1987). The interfacings of teams – work flows, information processing – are the most relevant ones for areas of trouble. The critical aspect of evaluating the need for change, and getting ownership, is to see the problem in a new way. The work flow mapping is a means of extending the boundary of the group's search for information to solve the problem. Each functioning team must be conscious of what others do and how, and how what they do interacts with what others do. The dodging stage at this level confronts the assumption that if everyone else did their work my team would have no problems. This phase ends with agreement on the articulation of the problem and the process steps needed to introduce change. Typically, this involves correct identification of the critical people needed to make the change and description of what the new steady state looks like (Beckhard and Harris, 1987). The phase concludes with ownership of the question of what effect the change will have on the organisation's relationship with the external environment.

Phase IV

Initially in this phase, the question is about how other organisations and stakeholders perceive themselves and us if we introduce the change. The assumption that they will act if we do is discussed. At first it is denied and, when it is accepted, the question of what the least amount of change is acceptable is asked. Accurate competitive analysis leads to ownership of the interlinking of organisations in competitive markets (Porter, 1980). Successful change requires an understanding of stakeholder demands and behaviour and a pro-active stance in their regard.

Phase V

The key individual goes into a sustaining stage when energy is no longer required to initiate the change effort. The energy of the key individual is released to look for new data and new change directions. The renewed energy for this comes from the team's commitment to making the process work. This phase is concluded when the key individual can look at other data.

Phase VI

The team goes into the sustaining stage when the process regarding the terminal point of change is defined. The key team defines the end, the phases, time deadlines, who, what, when. Then it is freed as the momentum is under way and there is continuity in the entire organisation.

Phase VII

When there is a new relationship between the organisation and peer organisations and when stakeholders come to accept it and interact with it in the new way, then sustaining has occurred. At this point, there is the lowest absorption of energy. The organisation is moving and it has its own impetus. The organisation is fat and happy. Through its normative behaviour, it reinforces its culture and thereby sets up the mode for future denial (Schein, 1985).

Stress points in change phases

A break in the process anywhere can stop the change. There are some key stress points, that is, points in the process where a breakdown is likely to occur that will effectively stop the change (see Figure 16.4). Attention to these stress points can help maintain the change impetus. If denial succeeds at level 1, then the change does not get in. At level 2, the dodging stage is critical because it frequently involves blaming other people. It affects relationships within the team and puts the change process under pressure. The doing stage is also critical because of the tendency to overcrowd and attempt too much. Similarly, the doing stage on level 3 can cause the organisation to lose its balance or, conversely, it can choke on too much change. Sustaining on levels 3 and 4 is critical so that the change may survive and produce its desired effect.

In our experience, there is a danger of regression, particularly at phases II and III. As the individual experiences the team's denial and as the team experiences the group's denial, it is often noticed that the individual or the team can lose its confidence and slip back into a denial mode. The presence of a consultant can be significant in confronting this tendency and in helping the manager and the team to process what is going on and remain firm in their convictions. If the consultant can facilitate the emergence of valid information, help generate free and informed choice and internal commitment, this danger can be alerted and averted (Argyris, 1970).

The theory and practice of organisation development (OD) emphasise the central role of the external consultant in facilitating organisational change. A consultant can facilitate the individual manager, the team, the group and the organisation to attend to the processes within the change effort and identify and work through the stages and phases of the change. A process consultation approach allows the members of the organisation to understand what is going on, particularly at the stress points, and develop the key diagnostic and problem-solving skills to manage change themselves (Argyris, 1970; Schein, 1987; Coghlan, 1988). The process consultant collaborates

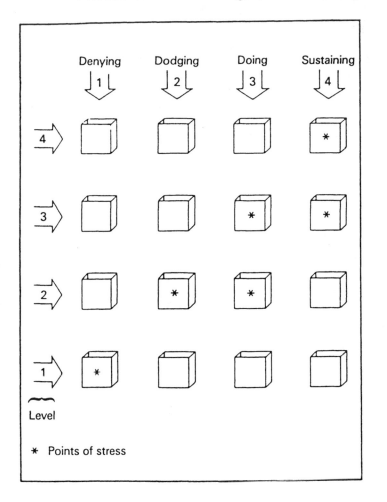

Figure 16.4 *Spaces of interaction between change stages and level of human interaction*

with the members of the organisation in designing the particular activities that help deal with the issues of each stage and move the individual, the team, the group and the organisation through the change phases.

The facilitation of movement from one phase to another of necessity requires awareness and active management of the political processes within an organisation. Denying, dodging and doing activities will contain a core element of political manoeuvring as individuals, teams and coalitions seek to maintain their balance of power. The process consultant must be able to recognise these dynamics and work appropriately with them (Kakabadse and Parker, 1984; Greiner and Schein, 1988).

Conclusions

This framework attempts to provide a map by which the path of organisational change can be charted and thereby better managed. It identifies some critical points on the map that require special attention and management so that the change may not be diverted or lost. It is based on the Kubler-Ross model and develops it by adding the complexity of organisational levels. It is congruent with the Lewinian approaches to change that are developed in organisation development and, thereby, provides a framework whereby OD practitioners can further understand and facilitate the dynamics of organisational change.

References

Allen, T. (1977) *Managing the Flow of Technology*. Cambridge, MA: MIT Press.
Argyris, C. (1970) *Intervention Theory and Method*. Reading, MA: Addison-Wesley.
Beckhard, R. (1975) 'Strategies for large systems change', *Sloan Management Review*, 16(2): 43–55.
Beckhard, R. and Harris, R. (1987) *Organizational Transitions: Managing Complex Change*, 2nd edn. Reading, MA: Addison-Wesley.
Coghlan, D. (1987) 'Consultation on organisational levels: an intervention framework', *Leadership & Organization Development Journal*, 8(3): 11–16.
Coghlan, D. (1988) 'In defence of process consultation', *Leadership & Organization Development Journal*, 9(2): 27–31.
Greiner, L. and Schein, V.E. (1988) *Power and Organization Development*. Reading, MA: Addison-Wesley.
Kakabadse, A. and Parker, C. (eds) (1984) *Power, Politics, and Organisations*. Chichester: Wiley.
Kubler-Ross, E. (1970) *On Death and Dying*. London: Tavistock.
Lippitt, G. (1982) *Organization Renewal*, 2nd edn. Englewood Cliffs, NJ: Prentice-Hall.
Ottaway, R.N. (1983) 'The change agent: a taxonomy in relation to the change process', *Human Relations*, 36(4): 361–92.
Porter, M.E. (1980) *Competitive Advantage*. New York: Free Press.
Rashford, N.S. and Coghlan, D. (1987) 'Enhancing human involvement in organisations – a paradigm for participation', *Leadership & Organization Development Journal*, 8(1): 17-21.
Rashford, N.S. and Coghlan, D. (1988) 'Organisational levels: a framework for management training and development', *Journal of European Industrial Training*, 12(4): 28–32.
Schein, E.H. (1985) *Organizational Culture and Leadership*. San Francisco: Jossey-Bass.
Schein, E.H. (1987) *Process Consultation, Vol. II: Lessons for Managers and Consultants*. Reading, MA: Addison-Wesley.

17

The short list, or principles of selection

C. Northcote Parkinson

A problem constantly before the modern administration, whether in
government or business, is that of personnel selection. The inexor-
able working of Parkinson's Law ensures that appointments have
constantly to be made and the question is always how to choose the
right candidate from all who present themselves. In ascertaining the
principles upon which the choice should be made, we may properly
consider, under separate heads, the methods used in the past and the
methods used at the present day.

Past methods, not entirely disused, fall into two main categories,
the British and the Chinese. Both deserve careful consideration, if
only for the reason that they were obviously more successful than
any method now considered fashionable. The British method (old
pattern) depended upon an interview in which the candidate had to
establish his identity. He would be confronted by elderly gentlemen
seated round a mahogany table who would presently ask him his
name. Let us suppose that the candidate replied, 'John Seymour.'
One of the gentlemen would then say, 'Any relation of the Duke of
Somerset?' To this the candidate would say, quite possibly, 'No, sir.'
Then another gentleman would say, 'Perhaps you are related, in that
case, to the Bishop of Watminster?' If he said 'No, sir' again, a third
would ask in despair, 'To whom then *are* you related?' In the event
of the candidate's saying, 'Well, my father is a fishmonger in
Cheapside,' the interview was virtually over. The members of the
Board would exchange significant glances, one would press a bell and
another tell the footman, 'Throw this person out.' One name could
be crossed off the list without further discussion. Supposing the next
candidate was Henry Molyneux and a nephew of the Earl of Sefton,
his chances remained fair up to the moment when George Howard
arrived and proved to be a grandson of the Duke of Norfolk. The
Board encountered no serious difficulty until they had to compare the
claims of the third son of a baronet with the second but illegitimate
son of a viscount. Even then they could refer to a Book of
Precedence. So their choice was made and often with the best results.

From C.N. Parkinson, *Parkinson's Law*, Harmondsworth: Penguin, 1986, pp.
26–39.

The Admiralty version of this British method (old pattern) was different only in its more restricted scope. The Board of Admirals were unimpressed by titled relatives as such. What they sought to establish was a service connection. The ideal candidate would reply to the second question, 'Yes, Admiral Parker is my uncle. My father is Captain Foley, my grandfather Commodore Foley. My mother's father was Admiral Hardy. Commander Hardy is my uncle. My eldest brother is a Lieutenant in the Royal Marines, my next brother is a cadet at Dartmouth and my younger brother wears a sailor suit.' 'Ah!' the senior Admiral would say. 'And what made you think of joining the Navy?' The answer to this question, however, would scarcely matter, the clerk present having already noted the candidate as acceptable. Given a choice between two candidates, both equally acceptable by birth, a member of the Board would ask suddenly, 'What was the number of the taxi you came in?' The candidate who said 'I came by bus' was then thrown out. The candidate who said, truthfully, 'I don't know,' was rejected, and the candidate who said 'Number 2351' (lying) was promptly admitted to the service as a boy with initiative. This method often produced excellent results.

The British method (new pattern) was evolved in the late nineteenth century as something more suitable for a democratic country. The Selection Committee would ask briskly, 'What school were you at?' and would be told Harrow, Haileybury, or Rugby, as the case might be. 'What games do you play?' would be the next and invariable question. A promising candidate would reply, 'I have played tennis for England, cricket for Yorkshire, rugby for the Harlequins, and fives for Winchester.' The next question would then be 'Do you play polo?' – just to prevent the candidate's thinking too highly of himself. Even without playing polo, however, he was evidently worth serious consideration. Little time, by contrast, was wasted on the man who admitted to having been educated at Wiggleworth. 'Where?' the chairman would ask in astonishment, and 'Where's that?' after the name had been repeated. 'Oh, in *Lancashire*!' he would say at last. Just for a matter of form, some member might ask, 'What games do you play?' But the reply 'Table tennis for Wigan, cycling for Blackpool, and snooker for Wiggleworth' would finally delete his name from the list. There might even be some muttered comment upon people who deliberately wasted the committee's time. Here again was a method which produced good results.

The Chinese method (old pattern) was at one time so extensively copied by other nations that few people realize its Chinese origin. This is the method of Competitive Written Examination. In China under the Ming Dynasty the more promising students used to sit for the provincial examination, held every third year. It lasted three sessions of three days each. During the first session the candidate wrote three essays and composed a poem of eight couplets. During the second session he wrote five essays on a classical theme. During the third, he wrote five essays on the art of government. The successful candidates (perhaps two per cent) then sat for their final examination at the imperial capital. It lasted only one session, the candidate writing one essay on a current political problem. Of those who were successful the majority were admitted to the civil service, the man with the highest marks being destined for the highest office. The system worked fairly well.

The Chinese system was studied by Europeans between 1815 and 1830 and adopted by the East India Company in 1832. The effectiveness of this method was investigated by a committee in 1854, with Macaulay as chairman. The result was that the system of competitive examination was introduced into the Civil Service in 1855. An essential feature of the Chinese examinations had been their literary character. The test was in a knowledge of the classics, in an ability to write elegantly (both prose and verse) and in the stamina necessary to complete the course. All these features were faithfully incorporated in the Trevelyan-Northcote Report, and thereafter in the system it did so much to create. It was assumed that classical learning and literary ability would fit any candidate for any administrative post. It was assumed (no doubt rightly) that a scientific education would fit a candidate for nothing – except, possibly, science. It was known, finally, that it is virtually impossible to find an order of merit among people who have been examined in different subjects. Since it is impracticable to decide whether one man is better in geology than another man in physics, it is at least convenient to be able to rule them both out as useless. When all candidates alike have to write Greek or Latin verse, it is relatively easy to decide which verse is the best. Men thus selected on their classical performance were then sent forth to govern India. Those with lower marks were retained to govern England. Those with still lower marks were rejected altogether or sent to the colonies. While it would be totally wrong to describe this system as a failure, no one could claim for it the success that had attended the systems hitherto in use. There was no guarantee, to begin with, that the man with the highest marks might not turn out to be off his head; as was sometimes found to be the case. Then again the writing of Greek verse might prove to be the sole accomplishment that some candidates had or would ever have. On occasion, a successful applicant may even have been impersonated at the examination by someone else, subsequently proving unable to write Greek verse when the occasion arose. Selection by competitive examination was never therefore more than a moderate success.

Whatever the faults, however, of the competitive written examination, it certainly produced better results than any method that has been attempted since. Modern methods centre upon the intelligence test and the psychological interview. The defect in the intelligence test is that high marks are gained by those who subsequently prove to be practically illiterate. So much time has been spent in studying the art of being tested that the candidate has rarely had time for anything else. The psychological interview has developed today into what is known as ordeal by house party. The candidates spend a pleasant weekend under expert observation. As one of them trips over the doormat and says 'Bother!' examiners lurking in the background whip out their notebooks and jot down, 'Poor physical co-ordination' and 'Lacks self-control.' There is no need to describe this method in detail, but its results are all about us and are obviously deplorable. The persons who satisfy this type of examiner are usually of a cautious and suspicious temperament, pedantic and smug, saying little and doing nothing. It is quite common, when appointments are made by this method, for one man to be chosen from five hundred applicants, only to be sacked a few weeks later as useless even beyond the standards of his department. Of the various methods of selection so far tried, the latest is unquestionably the worst.

What method should be used in the future? A clue to a possible line of investigation is to be found in one little-publicized aspect of contemporary selective technique. So rarely does the occasion arise for appointing a Chinese translator to the Foreign Office that the method used is little known. The post is advertised and the applications go, let us suppose, to a committee of five. Three are civil servants and two are Chinese scholars of great eminence. Heaped on the table before this committee are 483 forms of application, with testimonials attached. All the applicants are Chinese and all without exception have a first degree from Peking or Amoy and a Doctorate of Philosophy from Cornell or Johns Hopkins. The majority of the candidates have at one time held ministerial office in Formosa. Some have attached their photographs. Others have (perhaps wisely) refrained from doing so. The chairman turns to the leading Chinese expert and says, 'Perhaps Dr Wu can tell us which of these candidates should be put on the short list.' Dr Wu smiles enigmatically and points to the heap. 'None of them any good,' he says briefly. 'But how – I mean, why not?' asks the chairman, surprised. 'Because no good scholar would ever apply. He would fear to lose face if he were not chosen.' 'So what do we do now?' asks the chairman. 'I think,' says Dr Wu, 'we might persuade Dr Lim to take this post. What do you think, Dr Lee?' 'Yes, I think he might,' says Lee, 'but we couldn't approach him ourselves of course. We could ask Dr Tan whether he thinks Dr Lim would be interested.' 'I don't know Dr. Tan,' says Wu, 'but I know his friend Dr Wong.' By then the chairman is too muddled to know who is to be approached by whom. But the great thing is that *all* the applications are thrown into the waste-paper basket, only one candidate being considered, and he a man who did not apply.

We do not advise the universal adoption of the modern Chinese method but we draw from it the useful conclusion that the failure of other methods is mainly due to there being too many candidates. There are, admittedly, some initial steps by which the total may be reduced. The formula 'Reject everyone over 50 or under 20 plus everyone who is Irish' is now universally used, and its application will somewhat reduce the list. The names remaining will still, however, be too numerous. To choose between three hundred people, all well qualified and highly recommended, is not really possible. We are driven therefore to conclude that the mistake lies in the original advertisement. It has attracted too many applications. The disadvantage of this is so little realized that people devise advertisements in terms which will inevitably attract thousands. A post of responsibility is announced as vacant, the previous occupant being now in the House of Lords. The salary is large, the pension generous, the duties nominal, the privileges immense, the perquisites valuable, free residence provided with official car and unlimited facilities for travel. Candidates should apply, promptly but carefully, enclosing copies (not originals) of not more than three recent testimonials. What is the result? A deluge of applications, many from lunatics and as many again from retired army majors with a gift (as they always claim) for handling men. There is nothing to do except burn the lot and start thinking all over again. It would have saved time and trouble to do some thinking in the first place.

Only a little thought is needed to convince us that the perfect advertisement would attract only one reply and that from the right man. Let us begin with an extreme example:

> *Wanted*: Acrobat capable of crossing a slack wire 200 feet above raging furnace. Twice nightly, three times on Saturday. Salary offered £25 per week. No pension and no compensation in the event of injury. Apply in person at Wildcat Circus between the hours of 9 a.m. and 10 a.m.

The wording of this may not be perfect but the *aim* should be so to balance the inducement in salary against the possible risks involved that only a single applicant will appear. It is needless to ask for details of qualifications and experience. No one unskilled on the slack wire would find the offer attractive. It is needless to insist that candidates should be physically fit, sober, and free from fits of dizziness. They know that. It is just as needless to stipulate that those nervous of heights need not apply. They won't. The skill of the advertiser consists in adjusting the salary to the danger. An offer of £1000 per week might produce a dozen applicants. An offer of £15 might produce none. Somewhere between those two figures lies the exact sum to specify the minimum figure to attract anyone actually capable of doing the job. If there is more than one applicant, the figure has been placed a trifle too high.

Let us now take, for comparison, a less extreme example:

> *Wanted*: An archaeologist with high academic qualifications willing to spend fifteen years in excavating the Inca tombs at Helsdump on the Alligator River. Knighthood or equivalent honour guaranteed. Pension payable but never yet claimed. Salary of £2000 per year. Apply in triplicate to the Director of the Grubbenburrow Institute, Sickdale, Ill., USA.

Here the advantages and drawbacks are neatly balanced. There is no need to insist that candidates must be patient, tough, intrepid, and single. The terms of the advertisement have eliminated all who are not. It is unnecessary to require that candidates must be mad on excavating tombs. Mad is just what they will certainly be. Having thus reduced the possible applicants to a maximum of about three, the terms of the advertisement place the salary just too low to attract two of them and the promised honour *just* high enough to interest the third. We may suppose that, in this case, the offer of a KCMG would have produced two applications, the offer of an OBE, none. The result is a single candidate. He is off his head but that does not matter. He is the man we want.

It may be thought that the world offers comparatively few opportunities to appoint slack-wire acrobats and tomb excavators, and that the problem is more often to find candidates for less exotic appointments. This is true, but the same principles can be applied. Their application demands, however – as is evident – a greater degree of skill. Let us suppose that the post to be filled is that of Prime Minister. The modern tendency is to trust in various methods of election, with results that are almost invariably disastrous. Were we to turn, instead, to the fairy stories we learned in childhood, we should realize that at the period to which these stories relate far more satisfactory methods were in use. When the king had to choose a man to marry his eldest or only daughter and so inherit the kingdom, he normally planned some obstacle course from which only the right candidate would emerge with credit; and from which indeed (in many instances) only the right candidate would emerge at all. For imposing such a test the kings of that rather vaguely defined period were well provided with both personnel and equipment. Their establishment included magicians, demons, fairies, vampires, werewolves, giants, and dwarfs. Their territories were supplied with magic mountains, rivers of fire, hidden treasures, and enchanted forests. It might be urged that modern governments are in this respect less fortunate. This, however, is by no means certain. An administrator able to command the services of psychologists, psychiatrists, alienists, statisticians, and efficiency experts is not perhaps in a worse (or better) position than one relying upon hideous crones and fairy godmothers. An administration equipped with movie cameras, television apparatus, radio networks, and X-ray machines would not appear to be in a worse (or better) position than one employing magic wands, crystal balls, wishing wells, and cloaks of invisibility. Their means of assessment would seem, at any rate, to be strictly comparable. All that is required is to translate the technique of the fairy story into a form applicable to the modern world. In this, as we shall see, there is no essential difficulty.

The first step in the process is to decide on the qualities a Prime Minister ought to have. These need not be the same in all circumstances, but they need to be listed and agreed upon. Let us suppose that the qualities deemed essential are (1) Energy, (2) Courage, (3) Patriotism, (4) Experience, (5) Popularity, and (6) Eloquence. Now, it will be observed that all these are general qualities which all possible applicants would believe themselves to possess. The field could readily, of course, be narrowed by stipulating (4) Experience *of lion-taming*, or (6) Eloquence *in Mandarin*. But that is not the way in which we want to narrow the field. We do not want to stipulate a quality in a special form; rather, each quality in an exceptional degree. In other words, the successful candidate must be the most energetic, courageous, patriotic, experienced, popular, and eloquent man in the country. Only one man can answer to that description and his is the only application we want. The terms of the appointment must thus be phrased so as to exclude everyone else. We should therefore word the advertisement in some such way as follows:

Wanted: Prime Minister of Ruritania. Hours of work: 4 a.m. to 11.59 p.m. Candidates must be prepared to fight three rounds with the current heavyweight champion (regulation gloves to be worn). Candidates will die for their country, by painless means, on reaching the age of retirement (65). They will have to pass an examination in parliamentary procedure and will be liquidated should they fail to obtain 95% marks. They will also be liquidated if they fail to gain 75% votes in a popularity poll held under the Gallup Rules. They will finally be invited to try their eloquence on a Baptist Congress, the object being to induce those present to rock and roll. Those who fail will be liquidated. All candidates should present themselves at the Sporting Club (side entrance) at 11.15 a.m. on the morning of September 19. Gloves will be provided, but they should bring their own rubber-soled shoes, singlet, and shorts.

Observe that this advertisement saves all trouble about application forms, testimonials, photographs, references, and short lists. If the advertisement has been correctly worded, there will be only one applicant, and he can take office immediately – well, almost immediately. But what if there is no applicant? That is proof that the advertisement needs rewording. We have evidently asked for something more than exists. So the same advertisement (which is, after all, quite economical in space) can be inserted again with some slight adjustment. The pass mark in the examination can be reduced to 85 per cent with 65 per cent of the votes required in the popularity poll, and only two rounds against the heavyweight. Conditions can be successively relaxed, indeed, until an applicant appears.

Suppose, however, that two or even three candidates present themselves. We shall know that we have been insufficiently scientific. It may be that the pass mark in the examination has been too abruptly lowered – it should have been 87 per cent, perhaps, with 66 per cent in the popularity poll. Whatever the cause, the damage has been done. Two, or possibly three, candidates are in the waiting room. We have a choice to make and cannot waste all the morning on it. One policy would be to start the ordeal and eliminate the candidates who emerge with least credit. There is, nevertheless, a quicker way. Let us assume that all three candidates have all the qualities already defined as essential. The only thing we need do is add one further quality and apply the simplest test of all. To do this, we ask the nearest young lady (receptionist or typist, as the case may be), 'Which would you prefer?' She will promptly point out one of the candidates and so finish the matter. It has been objected that this procedure is the same thing as tossing a coin or otherwise letting chance decide. There is, in fact, no element of chance. It is merely the last-minute insistence on one other quality, one not so far taken into account: the quality of sex appeal.

18

Hiring for the organization, not the job

David E. Bowen, Gerald E. Ledford Jr
and Barry R. Nathan

This article examines a new approach to selection in which employees are hired to fit the characteristics of an organization, not just
the requirements of a particular job. Diverse firms – high- and
low-tech, US and Japanese-owned – are using the approach to
build cultures that rely heavily on self-motivated, committed people
for corporate success. New, often expensive, hiring practices are
changing the traditional selection model. An organizational analysis
supplements a job analysis, and personality attributes are screened
in addition to skills, knowledge, and abilities. We outline the basic
steps of the new selection model and present a case description of
a manufacturing company that used the model in hiring employees.
[. . .]

Selection practices

Conventional selection practices are geared toward hiring employees
whose knowledge, skills, and abilities (KSAs) provide the greatest fit
with clearly defined requirements of specific jobs. Traditional
selection techniques rarely consider characteristics of the organization in which the jobs reside. Traditional techniques also ignore
characteristics of the person that are irrelevant to immediate job
requirements. In common management parlance, the organization
hires new 'hands' or new 'heads' – that is, parts of people.

A new model of selection is emerging, however, that is geared
toward hiring a 'whole' person who will fit well into the specific
organization's culture. It reflects a fundamental reorientation of
the selection process toward hiring 'people', not just KSAs, for
'organizations', not just jobs. This leads to hiring practices that seem
peculiar, and needlessly extravagant, from a traditional human

Abridged from D.E. Bowen, G.E. Ledford Jr and B.R. Nathan, 'Hiring for
the organization, not the job', *Academy of Management Executive*, 5, 4 (1991),
pp. 35–50.

resource standpoint. Consider the hiring practices of three different organizations.

- AFG Industries builds two new float glass plants. The plants use practices such as work teams, extensive training, and skill-based pay that create a high level of employee involvement. The hiring process for factory workers includes screening formal résumés (not job applications), personality testing, pre-employment training that simulates some plant jobs, interviews with panels of managers and/or employees, and a medical exam.
- Sun Microsystems is the fastest-growing US company in the past five years, with annual growth averaging more than 100 percent.[1] Filling open jobs is critical to Sun's effectiveness, phenomenal growth, and profitability. Yet, the hiring process is extremely time-consuming and labor-intensive. Potential hires at all levels are brought into the organization from four to seven times for interviews with up to twenty interviewers. The process is full of ambiguity, lacks formal rules, and demands that all employees engage in problem solving to get themselves hired.
- Toyota (USA) screens 50,000 applications for 3,000 factory jobs in the initial staffing of its plant in Georgetown, Kentucky.[2] Each employee hired invests at least eighteen hours in a selection process that includes a general knowledge exam, a test of attitudes toward work, an interpersonal skills assessment center, a manufacturing exercise designed to provide a realistic job preview of assembly work, an extensive personal interview, and a physical exam.

As we shall see, these organizations adopt unusual hiring practices to find employees who fit the organization and to encourage those who do not fit to seek employment elsewhere. Although potential hires with skills that meet the demands of specific jobs are not ignored, these companies maintain that the person–job fit needs to be supported and enriched by person–organization fit. These companies are willing to invest substantial resources in rigorously assessing this fit. Why and how organizations approach hiring in this way are explored in this article. [. . .]

Each of these organizations is attempting to build a distinctive culture that is intentionally 'fragile', meaning that management relies heavily on self-motivated, committed people for system effectiveness.[3] While all three organizations have a management hierarchy, organizational policies, and other tools of external control, all rely to an unusual degree on employees to make the system work effectively. And they use sophisticated selection systems to hire the whole person whose skills and personality fit the type of organization, not just a job.

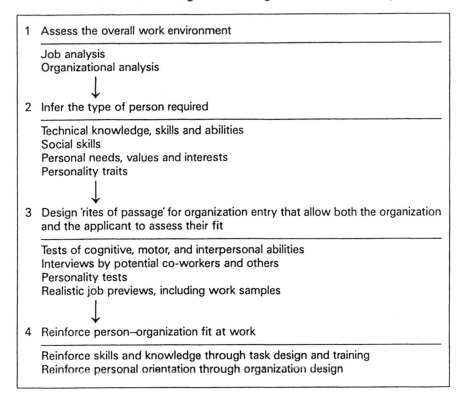

1 Assess the overall work environment

Job analysis
Organizational analysis

↓

2 Infer the type of person required

Technical knowledge, skills and abilities
Social skills
Personal needs, values and interests
Personality traits

↓

3 Design 'rites of passage' for organization entry that allow both the organization
and the applicant to assess their fit

Tests of cognitive, motor, and interpersonal abilities
Interviews by potential co-workers and others
Personality tests
Realistic job previews, including work samples

↓

4 Reinforce person–organization fit at work

Reinforce skills and knowledge through task design and training
Reinforce personal orientation through organization design

Figure 18.1   *A hiring process for person–organization fit*

The new selection model: hiring for person–organization fit

Figure 18.1 presents the new selection model for hiring for person–organization fit. [. . .]

Step one: assess the work environment

The job analysis of the traditional model of selection is also conducted in the new model. It remains instrumental in achieving the fit between individual KSAs and task demands. Alternative job analysis techniques include the position analysis questionnaire, task inventories, and critical incident techniques.[4]

The purpose of an organizational analysis is to define and assess the work environment in terms of the characteristics of the organization, rather than just in terms of the characteristics of a specific job. It identifies the behaviors and responsibilities that lead to organizational effectiveness, and implies the personal characteristics most likely to be associated with such behaviors and responsibilities. Organizational analysis also is important because job analysis data may quickly become outdated as rapidly changing products and technologies reshape employees' jobs. The organization's overall philosophy and values are likely to be more stable and, consequently, the more important long-term focus for fit.

Techniques for organizational analysis are not well-established, largely because there is little research that systematically associates the characteristics of organizations and individual behavior patterns. Managers need to identify the important dimensions of the organization and their implications for the kinds of employees who would best fit those situations. Although organizational analysis techniques are not nearly as well-developed as job analysis techniques, a variety of methods are available. For example, the training field offers guidelines for conducting an organizational analysis as one component of a training needs analysis. Organization characteristics assessed include short- and long-term goals, staffing needs, properties of the environment (for example, stability), and employee perceptions of organization climate. Organizational culture audits have emerged in the last decade that offer both qualitative and quantitative methods for describing an organization's norms and values.[5] Quite promising is a sophisticated Q-sort methodology that assesses the content, integrity, and crystallization of organizational values and matches them with an assessment of individual values.[6] Finally, there is a long-standing approach to diagnosing the characteristics of an organization's four subsystems (individuals, tasks, organizational arrangements, informal organization) that can yield organizational analysis data.[7]

Organization analysis does not replace job analysis. Rather it ensures that important components of the work *context* as well as its content are identified and evaluated for their importance to job success. While many job analyses include evaluations of the work context, the person–organization fit model explicitly recognizes that successful employees have knowledge, skills, abilities, and other personal characteristics that match both the *content* and the *context* of the job.

Step two: infer the type of person required

In step two, managers deal with applicants in terms of who they are, not just what they can do. It is still necessary to infer from the job analysis the KSAs that employees need to be technically competent. However, step two also requires inferring, from the organizational analysis, the needs, values and interests – that is, the personality – an employee must possess to be an effective member of the organization. For example, if the organizational analysis reveals that teamwork is a key norm or value in the setting, then selection tools must be used to find people who are team players. Furthermore, social and interpersonal skills will be necessary, in addition to the cognitive and motor abilities that are the dominant skills-focus of the traditional selection model. [. . .]

Organizations also must pay attention to technical skills needed by the organization. Often applicants with the most appropriate personalities and social skills are not those with the right technical skills. If the organization faces the need to upgrade technical skills quickly, it may be forced to make tradeoffs. Organizations in this situation often place greater weight on personality and social skills, on the grounds that it is easier to train technical skills than change personalities or develop social skills. This can lead to increased short-term training costs and temporary overstaffing. However, if the work technology is complex and training times are long, management may be forced to hire some employees who better fit the organization's technical requirements than its cultural requirements. Douglas Bray, noted pioneer of the AT&T Management Progress Study, considers this tradeoff and suggests that selection decisions about needs, values, and interests may be more critical than those for skills.[8] For example, a desire to learn new jobs is an attribute that cannot be taught easily to employees, as job skills can. You either hire people who have this attribute, or do without.

Step three: design 'rites of passage' that allow the organization and the individual to assess fit

The battery of screens used in the new approach to hiring may seem designed to discourage individuals from taking the job.[9] Yet, these screens have several purposes. First, the use of multiple screening methods, raters, and criteria has long been recommended by researchers as the best approach to hiring.[10] Yet most organizations still hire employees using a single interview with a single interviewer. More sophisticated techniques, if used, typically are reserved for executives and sometimes sales people. Second, multiple screenings not only allow the organization to select employees, but also provide applicants with sufficient realistic information about the work environment so that they can make an informed choice about whether they even want the job. Third, the people who join the organization feel special. They have survived the elaborate rites of passage necessary to join the organization. They experience the sense of accomplishment associated with completing boot camp when entering military service.

A recent *Fortune* article described these fresh approaches as 'The new art of hiring smart'.[11] One ingredient has been increased use of job simulation exercises for assembly workers. These simulations, or work sample tests, help both the person and the organization assess fit. The applicant receives a realistic job preview of the work. The organization has an opportunity to assess applicants' technical skills and, when group interaction is required in an exercise, their interpersonal skills as well. Intelligence tests also seem to be on the rebound.

Sun Microsystems offers a good example of the use of rites of passage to allow mutual assessment of fit. This fast-growing Silicon Valley firm, like many high-technology companies, is constantly changing in response to rapidly developing markets, evolving technologies, and the pace of internal growth. Employees who prefer clear job descriptions, stability, a leisurely pace, and predictability would be unhappy at Sun. The hiring process is such a challenge, and so full of ambiguity, that unsuitable applicants tend to give up before the process is completed. Those hired have survived multiple interviews with many different possible co-workers. A joke at Sun is, 'after seven sets of interviews, we put applicants on the payroll whether they've been hired or not.' The hiring process thus introduces prospective employees to the culture of the organization. [. . .]

Whereas personality tests provide organizations with information about applicants, realistic job previews (RJPs) provide applicants with information about organizations. Examples of RJPs are the Toyota USA job simulations/work sample tests that show applicants the repetitive nature of manufacturing work and the requirements for teamwork. Applicants can then make informed choices about whether they would be satisfied there. 'Turned-off' applicants may drop out of the hiring process. Those hired are more likely to join the organization with a sense of commitment and realistic expectations. Fundamentally, an RJP helps individuals decide if they want to join an organization, based on their own assessment of their personality and how it might fit with a particular type of organization.[12]

Step four: reinforce person–organization fit at work

Selection is clearly the first and, arguably, the most important step in implementing a fragile system philosophy. However, the hiring process must be integrated with, and supported by, the firm's other human resource management practices. [. . .]

Japanese automobile manufacturers operating in the United States provide examples of how to accomplish this. The Japanese 'Auto Alley' in the US provided more than 6,000 assembly jobs in 1989. Key operations include Nissan in Smyrna, Tennessee; Toyota in Georgetown, Kentucky; Honda in Marysville, Ohio; Mazda in Flat Rock, Michigan; and Diamond-Star Motors Corporation in Normal, Illinois.[13] The Japanese have attempted to create a certain type of organization, characterized by now-familiar values of teamwork, consensual decision-making, peer control, egalitarianism, and non-specialized career paths. Broad job classifications encourage employee flexibility, rather than identification with specific jobs. Extensive on-the-job training and job rotation further increase flexibility. Group activities encourage employees to contribute ideas for organizational improvement and promote teamwork. Employment stability helps the organization realize a return on its training and other investments in human resources, and increases employee loyalty to the organization. Thus, a selection system in such organizations typically screens for interest in work variety, social needs and skills, and organization commitment. [. . .]

Benefits and problems from hiring for person–organization fit

Clearly, the new approach to hiring for person–organization fit requires more resources than the traditional selection model. Is it worth the cost? Consider the potential benefits (see Figure 18.2).

Potential benefits

Employee attitudes   Researchers have long proposed that a fit between individual needs and organizational climates and cultures would result in greater job satisfaction and organization commitment.[14] There is ample data documenting that the realistic job previews typically used in the new selection model are associated with higher on-the-job satisfaction.[15] Greater team spirit also is likely when new employees have shared the experience of moving successfully through the demanding rites of passage that lead to organizational entry. [. . .]

Employee behaviors   [. . .] We also have presented a strong case that person–organizational fit will result in employees displaying more of what have been labelled 'organizational citizenship behaviors'. These are behaviors that employees perform above and beyond explicit job requirements. The thinking here is that fitted employees see themselves as really belonging to the organization and willing to invest their own resources in its ongoing maintenance.[16]

Reinforcement of organization design   The effectiveness of Japanese transplants that hire according to this model is common knowledge. [. . .] For example, a study [. . .] found that [such organizations] outperformed their industry on return on sales by an average of 532 percent and outperformed their industry on return on investment by

---

Potential benefits
1   More favorable employee attitudes (such as greater job satisfaction, organization commitment, and team spirit)
2   More desirable individual behaviors (such as better job performance and lower absenteeism and turnover)
3   Reinforcement of organizational design (such as support for work design and desired organizational culture)

Potential problems
1   Greater investment of resources in the hiring process
2   Relatively undeveloped and unproven supporting selection technology
3   Individual stress
4   May be difficult to use the full model where payoffs are greatest
5   Lack of organizational adaptation

Figure 18.2   *Potential benefits and problems with hiring for person–organization fit*

an average of 388 percent.[17] Researchers often argue that the power of such an organization derives from the mutual reinforcement of its parts, including the selection process. The hiring process [. . .] helps select employees who are interested in challenging, responsible, varied jobs and pay systems that reward needed behaviors and performance.

Potential problems

Hiring for person–organization fit may also have its disadvantages (see Figure 18.2).

Greater investment in hiring   This model requires a much greater investment of resources in the hiring process. For example, Mazda in Flat Rock, Michigan spends about $13,000 per employee to staff its plant.[18] It appears that organizations hiring within this model are spending the same time and money on hiring an assembly worker as they do in conducting an executive search.

The costs of making revisions in the hiring process also are different in the new model. A traditional hiring process needs to be revised whenever the requirements of the job change significantly. A hiring process for person–organization fit needs to be changed whenever the business, technological, or cultural requirements of the organization change significantly. This means that changes in hiring practices for person–organization fit are likely to be less frequent but much greater in scope than changes in traditional hiring processes. A change in hiring practices for person–organization fit may well involve a change in how every new employee is hired.

Undeveloped selection technology   The supporting selection technology is still relatively undeveloped and unproven. One problem is the still-thin track record of successfully validating personality tests against job performance. [. . .]

In the context of person–organization fit, techniques for assessing people are more developed than those for assessing work environments. Even on the people side, though, the field is not nearly as sophisticated in measuring work-related personality facets as it is in assessing KSAs. Moreover, there is a great need for techniques of organizational analysis that are as sophisticated as those for job analysis [. . .]. Overall, the challenge in organizational analysis is to: (a) identify relevant underlying dimensions of settings and how they can be measured, (b) determine the major impact on individual attitudes and behaviors, and organizational effectiveness, and (c) determine how such impacts differ depending upon individuals' personality.[19]

Managers may be concerned about the legality of these developing tools. More broadly, managers may be concerned about whether selecting for organization fit is legal. This concern is groundless, in our view. The legal standards for person–organization fit are no different than those for person–job fit. In general, selection procedures that do not result in adverse impact on protected minorities and women are not illegal. If the selection system does result in adverse impact, then evidence of job-relatedness must be presented. Job-relatedness is based on the content, construct, and criterion-related validity of the selection procedures. The procedures we have described establish job-relatedness.

In fact, there may be less adverse impact as a result of hiring for organization fit than in traditional hiring systems. Traditional systems rely mostly on tests of abilities to predict job performance. Intellectual ability tests typically result in adverse impact against minorities, and physical ability tests often result in adverse impact against women. Organization fit, in contrast, is based largely on values, needs, and motives that may be more evenly distributed in the population.

Employee stress   Individuals fitted to 'fragile systems' may find their organizational lives to be more stressful. The firms in the Japanese Auto Alley, [. . .] firms in the Silicon Valley, and so on, which rely on carefully selected people for system effectiveness, are also laying substantial claims to those people's lives. This higher level of involvement at work may be associated with experiencing more stress on the job. These workers have reported that they now take work problems home with them and feel the strains more typically associated with managerial roles.[20]

Difficult to use the full model where the benefits are greatest   A new hiring model may offer the greatest potential benefits to new organizations, such as new plants and startup companies. This is because hiring the right kinds of employees can help establish the desired culture of the organization from the very beginning. In existing organizations that are attempting to change their culture, there may be a long period in which the proportion of employees with unwanted attributes drops through attrition, while the proportion of employees with desired attributes gradually increases due to an improved hiring process. [. . .]

Lack of organizational adaptation   A problem could arise in hiring for the organization if it led to a workforce in which everyone had the same personality profile. The organization might become stagnant because everyone would share the same values, strengths, weaknesses, and blindspots. (Obviously, the issue is the same whether employees all tend to have the same point of view because of the selection system or because of training and socialization.) There has been considerable debate about whether a powerful organizational culture, whatever its source, leads to success or leads to dry rot and lack of innovativeness. There is some evidence, for example, indicating that organizations with little internal variability in employee perspectives perform better in the short run but worse in the long run, presumably as a result of inferior adaptation.[21]

However, we expect that significant internal variability will co-exist with person–organization fit. Even the best selection system is still imperfect; we do not succeed in hiring only the 'right types'. More fundamentally, the hiring process still results in variability on the desired characteristics. Even though all those hired may meet minimum standards, some will be higher than others on the desired characteristics. Finally, employees are not clones of one another just because they are similar on some personality dimensions. We would expect considerable variation on demographic, cultural, and personality dimensions that were not the basis for selection.

The future of hiring for person–organization fit

What does the future hold for this more sophisticated and elaborate approach to employee selection? Will it be adopted by an increasingly large share of corporations?

We believe that hiring for the organization, not the job, will become the only effective selection model for the typical business environment. The defining attributes of this business environment – such as shortened product life cycles, increasingly sophisticated technologies, growing globalization of markets, shifting customer demands – make for very transitory requirements in specific employee jobs. Organizational success in this environment requires hiring employees who fit the overall organization, not those who fit a fixed set of task demands. Employee personalities must fit the management philosophy and values that help define the organization's uniqueness and its fitness for the future.

We also believe that senior managers must become more 'person-oriented' in their own implicit resolution of the person–situation controversy if hiring for person–organization fit is to become a more common approach to selection. Again generally speaking, managers tend to believe that tightly controlled situations are more effective in shaping employee performance than less-structured situations that allow the expression of individual differences. Managers who believe this are more inclined to spend resources on creating strong situations via job descriptions, close supervision, and so on than on sophisticated selection procedures.

Finally, we offer an important caveat to 'person-oriented' managers who are committed to hiring for person–organization fit. They must manage a paradox. They must build strong organizational cultures yet, at the same time, design work situations that are weak enough to allow the unique qualities of individual employees to impact work performance. The key ingredient in balancing this paradox is to create a strong organizational culture with values that empower employees to apply their individual potentials to the conduct of their work. In this way, fragile systems release the employee energy necessary to compete in today's business environment.

Notes

1 See William, E. Sheeline. 'Avoiding growth's perils', *Fortune*, 13 August (1990), p. 55.

2 'Japan's gung-ho US car plants', *Fortune*, 30 January (1989), pp. 78–85.

3 John P. MacDuffie. 'The Japanese auto transplants: challenges to conventional wisdom', *ILR Report*, 26, 1 (1988), pp. 12–18; Huaro Shimada and John Paul MacDuffie, 'Industrial relations and "Humanware", Japanese investments in auto manufacturing in the United States'. Working Paper, Sloan School of Management, MIT (1987).

4 For more detail on job analysis techniques see Benjamin Schneider and Neal Schmitt, *Staffing Organizations*, 2nd edn. (Scott, Foresman, Glenview, IL, 1986).

5 Caren Siehl and Joanne Martin. 'Measuring organizational culture: mixing qualitative and quantitative methods', In M.O. Jones et al. (eds), *Inside Organizations* (Sage, Beverly Hills, 1988).

6 Jennifer Chatman, 'Improving interactional organizational research', *Academy of Management Review*, 14 (1989).

7 Michael Tushman and David Nadler. 'A diagnostic model of organizational behavior'.

8 'Doug Bray: you've got to pick your winners', *Training*, February (1988), pp. 79–81.

9 Richard Pascale, 'Fitting new employees into the company culture', *Fortune*, 28 May (1984), pp. 28–42.

10 For an overview of this issue, see Schneider and Schmitt, *Staffing Organizations*.

11 Brian Dumaine, 'The new art of hiring smart', *Fortune*, 17 August (1987), pp. 78–81.

12 John P. Wanous, *Organizational Entry: Recruitment Selection and Socialization of Newcomers* (Addison-Wesley, Reading, MA, 1980).

13 'Japan's gung-ho US car plants'.

14 See Wanous, *Organizational Entry*, for a discussion of this proposition.

15 For a review of the research findings, see S.C. Premack and J.P. Wanous, 'A meta-analysis of realistic job preview experiments', *Journal of Applied Psychology*, 70 (1985), pp. 706–19.

16 See Chatman, 'Improving'.

17 G.E. Ledford, Jr, T.G. Cummings and R.W. Wright, 'The structure and effectiveness of high involvement organizations'. Working Paper, Center for Effective Organizations, University of Southern California, (1991).

18 William J. Hampton, 'How does Japan Inc. pick its American workers?' *Business Week*, 3 October (1988), pp. 84–8.

19 For a discussion of these issues, see J.L. Holland, 'Some speculation about the investigation of person–environment transactions', *Journal of Vocational Behavior*, 31 (1988), pp. 337–40; R.H. Moos, 'Person–environment congruence in work, school and health-care settings', *Journal of Vocational Behavior*, 31 (1987) pp. 231–47; and J.B. Rounds, R.V. Dawis and L.H. Lofquist, 'Measurement of person–environment fit and prediction of satisfaction in the theory of work adjustment', *Journal of Vocational Behavior*, 31 (1987), pp. 297–318.

20 E.E. Lawler III, 'Achieving competitiveness by creating new organizational cultures and structures', in D.B. Fishman and C. Cherniss (eds), *The Human Side of Corporate Competitiveness* (Sage, Newbury Park, 1990), pp. 69-101.

21 D.R. Denison, *Corporate Culture and Organizational Effectiveness* (Wiley, New York, 1990).

19

When does the recruitment and selection process end? The organisational entry cycle and a horticultural metaphor

Jon Billsberry

How would you respond to the following question: what is recruitment and selection? Most people answer this question by talking about the need to place advertisements, to choose between applicants, or about how to be an effective interviewer. Less commonly, people talk about the need to establish a psychological contract, the analysis of jobs, or selling the organisation. These types of comment tend to emphasise the selection phase of the recruitment and selection process. This is only natural given that this is the stage of the process when you get to meet people and to make judgements about them.

The emphasis on selection also dominates the literature and the activities of researchers. Go to any library and you will find thousands of articles on selection. But try finding something on recruitment or induction and you'll spend a long time searching the shelves. Such is the shortage of work in these areas that the few people who are interested in it are conspicuous (e.g. Sara Rynes, James Breaugh and John Wanous).

The emphasis on selection is unfortunate because it masks the key organisational function of recruitment and selection: to find someone to do a job and to help them become effective as quickly as possible. If you adopt this perspective on recruitment and selection, it encourages you to think about the whole process from the creation of a vacancy until it is filled by someone performing effectively. To demonstrate that this perspective is being adopted, we call the process of finding someone the 'organisational entry process'. This has the distinct advantage that the role of selection is downplayed and the manager is encouraged to think through the whole process required to find an effective employee.

What are the processes of organisational entry? Figure 19.1 shows that there are nine stages to organisational entry that managers need to manage. By a quirk of fate (and a little manipulation) each of

```
┌─────────────────────────────────────────────────────────┐
│              The 9A organisational entry cycle            │
│  1  Approach (design an entry strategy)                    │
│  2  Analysis (job and organisational analysis)            │
│  3  Attraction (interest a pool of candidates)            │
│  4  Assessment (choose the 'best' candidate)              │
│  5  Agreement (negotiate terms and conditions)            │
│  6  Adjustment (manage the anxiety of joining)            │
│  7  Adaptation (help the newcomer adapt)                  │
│  8  Attrition (keep good people)                          │
│  9  Audit (check that the cycle is working effectively)   │
└─────────────────────────────────────────────────────────┘
```

Figure 19.1   *The 9A organisational entry cycle*

these processes begins with the letter A. As a result, I have termed the cycle the '9A organisational entry cycle'. How does it work?

The 9A organisational entry cycle

Approach

Before you begin to do anything, you need to think through your strategy. What are you trying to achieve? How do your intended actions fit in with the human resource strategy and the business strategy of the organisation? What competencies is the organisation keen to acquire? What training can be offered to newcomers? In short, you need to determine the overall shape of your organisational entry process and how it fits in with the organisation's strategy.

Analysis

The core ingredient of any organisational entry process is analysis. As the process tends to be sequential, any mistakes made at this stage will cascade down, perhaps snowballing, through the whole process. At this stage of the process, you need to determine what knowledge, skills, abilities and other attributes are required for people to become effective employees in the job. In addition, you need to understand the environment into which newcomers will be introduced as this will influence how they will behave and perform. This analysis plays a key part in the development of selection criteria which you use to assess applicants. It also helps you understand which recruitment and selection techniques might be useful in attracting or selecting between applicants, e.g. 'The job analysis has shown us that we need someone with high levels of intelligence, so we'll incorporate an intelligence test into the assessment process.'

Attraction

This is the part of the process commonly referred to as recruitment. At this stage in the organisational entry process, you need to decide how you will attract people to apply for the job and how you will handle the associated paperwork. The goal of the recruiter is to attract a small number of highly suitable applicants (Parkinson, 1965; see Chapter 17 in this book).

Assessment

This is the part of the process commonly referred to as selection. During this stage, all of the applicants are compared with the selection criteria using appropriate techniques to assess which of the applicants has the best 'fit'.

Agreement

It is important that due credit is given to the negotiation between the organisation and the prospective employee. At this stage both formal contracts of employment and psychological contracts are formed between the parties which have a considerable impact on the motivation, performance and satisfaction of the new employee. You need to build a specific period into your organisational entry process when you address these important issues. Typically, this stage is subsumed in the assessment phase of the organisational entry process and little attention is given to it.

Adjustment

When people join organisations, they have to adjust to the new job and the new environment. It is a time of great anxiety and transition. It is also a time when newcomers are forming many of their views about their job and the organisation. These have a tremendous effect on motivation but, unfortunately, all too frequently organisations only pay 'lip service' to helping newcomers make this adjustment. You may have heard this part of the process called induction or orientation.

Adaptation

Once newcomers have got over the initial shock of joining the organisation, they then begin the slow process of adapting to the organisation's way of doing things. This adaptation to the organisation's culture is found in most organisations. Where the organisation actively sets out to make people become more in tune with its culture, the process is known as socialisation. This is commonly found in organisations that attempt to make their workplace a 'high commitment (or high involvement) workplace'.

Attrition

There are theoretical arguments and some empirical research (e.g. Schneider, 1987; Bretz et al., 1989; Jordan et al., 1991) showing that when people are unable to adapt to the organisation they are more likely to leave the organisation than those who can adapt to it. In part, this signals that there might have been a failure in the organisational entry process and that people have been recruited that were unsuited to the organisation. However, by no means are all vacancies created from negative attrition. People are promoted, they move on to fresh challenges, or their personal circumstances might mean that they have to change employers. When a vacancy exists, the organisation has to decide whether to fill the vacancy and, if so, how they will do this. As a result, attrition leads to the ignition of the whole organisational entry process.

Audit

As stated earlier, the purpose of organisational entry is to find someone to do a job and to help them become effective as quickly as possible. When someone leaves an organisation it might be a signal that something has gone wrong during the original recruitment of the person. If so, it is important that the organisational entry process is reviewed to see where mistakes occurred so that they are not repeated.

It should be noted that I have interchanged the terms 'process' and 'cycle'. Strictly speaking, the sequence of events is a cycle that begins when a new job is created and ends when the job no longer exists or changes out of all recognition. I have spoken about the organisational entry process to highlight that there are a series of separate operations that you need to work through to be successful.

When does organisational entry finish? A horticultural metaphor

Commonly, selectors think recruitment and selection are finished when they send out an offer letter which is accepted. As the previous discussion illustrates, this view ignores some key stages in organisational entry. And it is a symptom of the traditional view of recruitment and selection which places the selection phase on a pedestal. This is perhaps best illustrated with a metaphor: a horticultural metaphor seems appropriate.[1]

A gardener wakes up one morning to find that overnight thieves have stolen the ornamental pot containing a number of plants that formed the centrepiece in a prize winning border (headhunters have a habit of doing this). As the BBC programme 'Gardener's World' is to visit in a few months to film the garden in full bloom, he has to do something about it. He needs to find a replacement.

As he stands, rather dismayed, looking at the border, he realises that he has several options. His initial reaction is to rush to the garden centre to purchase another ornamental pot and replant it in a similar fashion and thereby re-create what had existed. But he pauses; he has a 'development opportunity'. Could he make things even better? Had the thieves done him a favour? That pot had always been a bit of a problem, it had come with the garden and had always seemed such a formidable, if impressive, thing. Perhaps a different type of centrepiece, maybe a flowering tree? But now that it's gone, the other plants in the border seem much more prominent and much more attractive. Perhaps, rather than finding another centrepiece, he could replace the pot with something that helps the others stand out even more. Eventually, he chooses this option and decides to buy some smaller shrubs that will enhance the other plants in the border. His choice is limited by the nature of the soil and the sunlight and so he needs to carry out quite a lot of analysis to identify suitable plants.

Where to buy the plants? He has several options, but as time is tight, he decides to get in the car and go straight to his local garden centre which he knows has the sort of plants he's looking for. At the garden centre, the experienced gardener chooses his new shrubs quite easily as he knows what he's looking for. He spends more time choosing the right fertiliser and compost so that the new plants will bed in quickly.

Before planting the new shrubs he spends a lot of time preparing the border and getting the conditions just right for the new plants. During the first week of planting he attends daily to the new plants, making sure they are correctly watered and haven't been attacked by predatory birds. Over the next two months he works with the plants every week to ensure that they develop in the way that he wants to complement the other flowers in the border.

A few months later when the 'Gardener's World' film crew appear, the gardener and the producer discuss the border. It has changed much since the producer first saw the garden and decided to highlight it. They both agree that the border is just as good as before; perhaps even better.

Notes

1 An earlier version of this horticultural metaphor was written by the author for the Open University Business School course B800 Foundations of Senior Management.

References

Bretz, R.D., Ash, R.A. and Dreher, G.F. (1989) 'Do people make the place? An examination of the attraction-selection-attrition hypothesis', *Personnel Psychology*, 42: 561–81.

Jordan, M., Herriot, P. and Chalmers, C. (1991) 'Testing Schneider's ASA theory', *Applied Psychology: An International Review*, 40: 47–53.

Parkinson, C.N. (1965) *Parkinson's Law*. London: Penguin.

Schneider, B. (1987) 'The people make the place', *Personnel Psychology*, 40: 437–53.

PART 4
DECISION MAKING AND TEAMS

20

Satisficing

Irving L. Janis and Leon Mann

The most influential hypothesis concerning the way administrative man arrives at a new policy has been formulated by Herbert Simon (1976). The decision maker, according to Simon, *satisfices*, rather than maximizes; that is, he looks for a course of action that is 'good enough', that meets a minimal set of requirements. Businessmen, for example, often decide to invest in a new enterprise if they expect it to return a 'satisfactory profit', without bothering to compare it with all the alternative investments open to them. Sometimes more than one criterion is used, but always it is a question of whether the given choice will yield a 'good enough' outcome. An executive looking for a new job, for example, is likely to settle for the first one to come along that meets his minimal requirements – satisfactory pay, good chance for advancement, adequate working conditions, and location within commuting distance of his home. The satisficing strategy involves a more superficial search for information and less cognitive work than maximizing. All that the person has to do is consider alternative courses of action sequentially until one that 'will do' is found.

Simon argues convincingly that the satisficing approach fits the limited information-processing capabilities of human beings. The world is peopled by creatures of 'bounded or limited rationality', he says, and these creatures constantly resort to gross simplifications when dealing with complex decision problems. Man's limited ability to foresee future consequences and to obtain information about the variety of available alternatives inclines him to settle for a barely 'acceptable' course of action that is 'better than the way things are

Abridged from I.L. Janis and L. Mann, *Decision Making: A Psychological Analysis of Conflict, Choice and Commitment*. New York: Free Press, pp. 25–7.

now'. He is not inclined to collect information about all the complicated factors that might affect the outcome of his choice, to estimate probabilities, or to work out preference orderings for many different alternatives. He is content to rely on 'a drastically simplified model of the buzzing, blooming confusion that constitutes the real world' (Simon, 1976: xxix).

According to Johnson (1974), executives often feel so uncertain about the outcome of what seems to be the best choice that they forgo it in order to play safe: they gravitate toward a more conventional, 'second-best' choice that will cause little immediate disturbance or disapproval because it will be seen as 'acceptable' by superiors and peers who will review the decision and by subordinates who will implement it. Cyert and March (1963) suggest that the more uncertainty there is about a long-term outcome, the greater the tendency to make a policy decision on the basis of its short-term acceptability within the organization.

Organizational theorists assume that individuals use a satisficing strategy in personal decisions as well as organizational decisions (Etzioni, 1968; Miller and Starr, 1967; Simon, 1976; Young, 1966). As Etzioni puts it, 'Simon's important distinction between optimizing and "satisficing" . . . is . . . independent of any socio-political system. It applies as much to a consumer in a supermarket as to the President of the United States' (1968: 253). Whenever the consumer, the president, or anyone else is looking only for a choice that offers some degree of *improvement* over the present state of affairs, his survey, analysis, and evaluation are usually limited to just two alternatives – a new course of action that has been brought to his attention and the old one he has been pursuing. If neither meets his minimal requirements, he continues to look for other alternatives until he finds one that does. Consequently, the use of a satisficing strategy does not preclude contemplating a fairly large number of alternatives, but they are examined *sequentially*, with no attempt to work out a comparative balance sheet of pros and cons.

The simplest variant of the satisficing strategy takes the form of relying upon a single formula as the sole decision rule, which comes down to using only one criterion for a tolerable choice. Paradoxically, this crude approach often characterizes the decision-making behavior of people who are facing major personal decisions that will affect their future health or welfare. Men and women in serious trouble are likely to consult whichever physician or lawyer is recommended by a trusted friend and then to accept whatever course of action the adviser recommends, without spending the money and effort required to get a second opinion. The sole decision rule in such cases is often simply 'Tell a qualified expert about your problem and do whatever he says – that will be good enough.' Simple decision rules are also prevalent in consumer behavior. Studies of consumer purchases indicate that people in shops and supermarkets sometimes buy on impulse, without any advance planning or deliberation (Engel et al., 1968; Hansen, 1972). The person notices something attractive that he would like to have, and, if the price is within the range he regards as 'reasonable', he immediately decides to buy it. A similar decision rule may come into play when a customer impulsively decides to appropriate an attractive piece of merchandise if he sees that no one in the store is looking.

References

Cyert, R.M. and March, J.G. (1963) *A Behavioral Theory of the Firm*. Englewood Cliffs, NJ: Prentice-Hall.

Engel, J.F., Kollat, D.J. and Blackwell, R.D. (1968) *Consumer Behavior*. New York: Holt, Rinehart and Winston.

Etzioni, A. (1968) *The Active Society*. New York: Free Press.

Hansen, F. (1972) *Consumer Choice Behavior*. New York: Free Press.

Johnson, R.J. (1974) 'Conflict avoidance though acceptable decisions', *Human Relations*, 27: 71–82.

Miller, D.W. and Starr, M.K. (1967) *The Structure of Human Decisions*. Englewood Cliffs, NJ: Prentice-Hall.

Simon, H.A. (1976) *Administrative Behavior: a Study of Decision-Making Processes in Administrative Organization*, 3rd edn. New York: Free Press.

Young, S. (1966) *Management: a Systems Analysis*. Glenview, IL: Scott, Foresman.

21

Limited rationality

James March

Studies of decision making in the real world suggest that not all alternatives are known, that not all consequences are considered, and that not all preferences are evoked at the same time. Instead of considering all alternatives, decision makers typically appear to consider only a few and to look at them sequentially rather than simultaneously. Decision makers do not consider all consequences of their alternatives. They focus on some and ignore others. Relevant information about consequences is not sought, and available information is often not used. Instead of having a complete, consistent set of preferences, decision makers seem to have incomplete and inconsistent goals, not all of which are considered at the same time. The decision rules used by real decision makers seem to differ from the ones imagined by decision theory. Instead of considering 'expected values' or 'risk' as those terms are used in decision theory, they invent other criteria. Instead of calculating the 'best possible' action, they search for an action that is 'good enough'.

As a result of such observations, doubts about the empirical validity and usefulness of the pure theory of rational choice have been characteristic of students of actual decision processes for many years. Rational choice theories have adapted to such observations gradually by introducing the idea that rationality is limited. The core notion of limited rationality is that individuals are intendedly rational. Although decision makers try to be rational, they are constrained by limited cognitive capabilities and incomplete information, and thus their actions may be less than completely rational in spite of their best intentions and efforts.

In recent years, ideas of limited (or bounded) rationality have become sufficiently integrated into conventional theories of rational choice to make limited rationality viewpoints generally accepted. They have come to dominate most theories of individual decision making. They have been used to develop behavioral and evolutionary theories of the firm. They have been used as part of the basis for theories of transaction cost economics and game theoretic,

Abridged from J. March, *A Primer on Decision Making*, New York: Free Press, 1994, pp. 8–15.

information, and organizational economics. They have been applied to decision making in political, educational, and military contexts.

Information constraints

Decision makers face serious limitations in attention, memory, comprehension, and communication. Most students of individual decision making seem to allude to some more or less obvious biological constraints on human information processing, although the limits are rarely argued from a strict biological basis. In a similar way, students of organizational decision making assume some more or less obvious information constraints imposed by methods of organizing diverse individuals:

1 *Problems of attention* Time and capabilities for attention are limited. Not everything can be attended to at once. Too many signals are received. Too many things are relevant to a decision. Because of those limitations, theories of decision making are often better described as theories of attention or search than as theories of choice. They are concerned with the way in which scarce attention is allocated.

2 *Problems of memory* The capabilities of individuals and organizations to store information are limited. Memories are faulty. Records are not kept. Histories are not recorded. Even more limited are individual and organizational abilities to retrieve information that has been stored. Previously learned lessons are not reliably retrieved at appropriate times. Knowledge stored in one part of an organization cannot be used easily by another part.

3 *Problems of comprehension* Decision makers have limited capacities for comprehension. They have difficulty organizing, summarizing, and using information to form inferences about the causal connections of events and about relevant features of the world. They often have relevant information but fail to see its relevance. They make unwarranted inferences from information, or fail to connect different parts of the information available to them to form a coherent interpretation.

4 *Problems of communication* There are limited capacities for communicating information, for sharing complex and specialized information. Division of labor facilitates mobilization and utilization of specialized talents, but it also encourages differentiation of knowledge, competence, and language. It is difficult to communicate across cultures, across generations, or across professional specialties. Different groups of people use different frameworks for simplifying the world.

As decision makers struggle with these limitations, they develop procedures that maintain the basic framework of rational choice but modify it to accommodate the difficulties. Those procedures form the core of theories of limited rationality.

Coping with information constraints

Decision makers use various information and decision strategies to cope with limitations in information and information-handling capabilities. Much of contemporary research on choice by individuals and organizations focuses on those coping strategies, the ways choices are made on the basis of expectations about the future but without the kind of complete information that is presumed in classical theories of rational choice.

The psychology of limited rationality

Psychological studies of individual decision making have identified numerous ways in which decision makers react to cognitive constraints. They use stereotypes in order to infer unobservables from observables. They form typologies of attitudes (liberal, conservative) and traits (dependent, extroverted, friendly) and categorize people in terms of the typologies. They attribute intent from observing behavior or the consequences of behavior. They abstract 'central' parts of a problem and ignore other parts. They adopt understandings of the world in the form of socially developed theories, scripts, and schemas that fill in missing information and suppress discrepancies in their understandings.

The understandings adopted tend to stabilize interpretations of the world. For the most part, the world is interpreted and understood today in the way it was interpreted and understood yesterday. Decision makers look for information, but they see what they expect to see and overlook unexpected things. Their memories are less recollections of history than constructions based on what they thought might happen and reconstructions based on what they now think must have happened, given their present beliefs.

A comprehensive review of psychological studies of individual information processing and problem solving would require more space and more talent than are available here. The present intention is only to characterize briefly a few of the principal speculations developed as a result of that research, in particular speculations about four fundamental simplification processes: editing, decomposition, heuristics, and framing.

Editing   Decision makers tend to edit and simplify problems before entering into a choice process, using a relatively small number of cues and combining them in a simple manner. Complex problems or situations are simplified. Search may be simplified by discarding some available information or by reducing the amount of processing done on the information. For example, decision makers may attend to choice dimensions sequentially, eliminating all alternatives that are not up to standards on the first dimension before considering information from other dimensions. In other situations, they may consider all information for all alternatives, but weight the dimensions equally rather than weight them according to their importance.

Decomposition Decision makers attempt to decompose problems, to reduce large problems into their component parts. The presumption is that problem elements can be defined in such a way that solving the various components of a problem individually will result in an acceptable solution to the global problem. For example, a decision maker might approach the problem of allocating resources to advertising projects by first decomposing the global advertising problem of a firm into subproblems associated with each of the products, then decomposing the product subproblems into problems associated with particular geographic regions.

One form of decomposition is working backward. Some problems are easier to solve backward than forward because, like mazes, they have only a few last steps but many first steps. Working backward is particularly attractive to decision makers who accept a 'can do' decision making ideology, because it matches an activist role. Working backward encourages a perspective in which decision makers decide what they want to have happen and try to make it happen.

Decomposition is closely connected to such key components of organizing as division of labor, specialization, decentralization, and hierarchy. An important reason for the effectiveness of modern organization is the possibility of decomposing large complex tasks into small independently manageable ones. In order for decomposition to work as a problem solving strategy, the problem world must not be tightly interconnected. For example, if actions taken on one advertising project heavily affect the results of action on others, deciding on the projects independently will produce complications. The generality of decomposition strategies suggests that the world is, in fact, often only loosely interconnected, so subproblems can be solved independently. But that very generality makes it likely that decomposition will also be attempted in situations in which it does not work.

Heuristics Decision makers recognize patterns in the situations they face and apply rules of appropriate behavior to those situations. Studies of expertise, for example, generally reveal that experts substitute recognition of familiar situations and rule following for

calculation. Good chess players generally do more subtle calculations than novices, but their great advantage lies less in the depth of
their analysis than in their ability to recognize a variety of situations
and in their store of appropriate rules associated with situations.
Although the problem solving of expert salespersons has been
subjected to less research, it appears to be similar.

As another example, people seem not to be proficient at calculating the probability of future events by listing an elaborate decision
tree of possible outcomes. However, they are reasonably good at
using the output of memory to tell them how frequently similar
events have occurred in the past. They use the results of memory as
a proxy for the projection of future probability.

Such procedures are known to the literature of problem solving
and decision making as 'heuristics'. Heuristics are rules-of-thumb for
calculating certain kinds of numbers or solving certain kinds of
problems. Although psychological heuristics for problem solving are
normally folded into a discussion of limited rationality because they
can be interpreted as responses to cognitive limitations, they might
as easily be interpreted as a version of rule-following behavior that
follows a logic quite different from a logic of consequence.

Framing   Decisions are framed by beliefs that define the problem to
be addressed, the information that must be collected, and the
dimensions that must be evaluated. Decision makers adopt paradigms to tell themselves what perspective to take on a problem, what
questions should be asked, and what technologies should be used to
ask the questions. Such frames focus attention and simplify analysis.
They direct attention to different options and different preferences.
A decision will be made in one way if it is framed as a problem of
maintaining profits and in a different way if it is framed as a
problem of maintaining market share. A situation will lead to
different decisions if it is seen as being about 'the value of
innovation' rather than 'the importance of not losing face'.

Decision makers typically frame problems narrowly rather than
broadly. They decide about local options and local preferences,
without considering all tradeoffs or all alternatives. They are
normally content to find a set of sufficient conditions for solving a
problem, not the most efficient set of conditions. Assigning proper
weights to things in the spatial, temporal, and causal neighborhood
of current activity as opposed to things that are more distant
spatially, temporally, or causally is a major problem in assuring
decision intelligence. It is reflected in the tension between the frames
of decision makers, who often seem to have relatively short horizons,
and the frames of historians, who (at least retrospectively) often have
somewhat longer horizons.

The frames used by decision makers are part of their conscious and unconscious repertoires. In part they are encased in early individual experiences that shape individual approaches to problems. In part they are responsive to the particular sequences of decision situations that arise. There is a tendency for frames to persist over a sequence of situations. Recently used frames hold a privileged position, in part because they are more or less automatically evoked in a subsequent situation. In addition, past attention strengthens both a decision maker's skills in using a frame and the ease of justifying action to others within the frame.

These internal processes of developing frames and using them are supplemented by an active market in frames. Decision makers adopt frames that are proposed by consultants, writers, or friends. They copy frames used by others, particularly others in the same profession, association, or organization. Consequential decision making itself is, of course, one such frame. Prescriptive theories of decision making seek to legitimize a consequential frame for considering decisions, one that asks what the alternatives are, what their expected consequences are, and what the decision maker's preferences are.

22

Groupthink

Irving L. Janis

'How could we have been so stupid?' President John F. Kennedy asked after he and a close group of advisers had blundered into the Bay of Pigs invasion. For the last two years I have been studying that question, as it applies not only to the Bay of Pigs decision makers but also to those who led the United States into such other major fiascos as the failure to be prepared for the attack on Pearl Harbor, the Korean War stalemate, and the escalation of the Vietnam War.

Stupidity certainly is not the explanation. The men who participated in making the Bay of Pigs decision, for instance, comprised one of the greatest arrays of intellectual talent in the history of American Government – Dean Rusk, Robert McNamara, Douglas Dillon, Robert Kennedy, McGeorge Bundy, Arthur Schlesinger Jr, Allen Dulles, and others.

It also seemed to me that explanations were incomplete if they concentrated only on disturbances in the behavior of each individual within a decision-making body: temporary emotional states of elation, fear, or anger that reduce a man's mental efficiency, for example, or chronic blind spots arising from a man's social prejudices or idiosyncratic biases.

I preferred to broaden the picture by looking at the fiascos from the standpoint of group dynamics as it has been explored over the past three decades, first by the great social psychologist Kurt Lewin and later in many experimental situations by myself and other behavioral scientists. My conclusion after poring over hundreds of relevant documents – historical reports about formal group meetings and informal conversations among the members – is that the groups that committed the fiascos were victims of what I call 'groupthink'.

'Groupy'

In each case study, I was surprised to discover the extent to which each group displayed the typical phenomena of social conformity

From I.L. Janis, 'Groupthink', in B. Straw (ed.), *Psychological Dimensions of Organizational Behavior*, New York: Macmillan, pp. 514–22; originally from *Psychology Today Magazine*, 1971.

that are regularly encountered in studies of group dynamics among ordinary citizens. For example, some of the phenomena appear to be completely in line with findings from social-psychological experiments showing that powerful social pressures are brought to bear by the members of a cohesive group whenever a dissident begins to voice his objections to a group consensus. Other phenomena are reminiscent of the shared illusions observed in encounter groups and friendship cliques when the members simultaneously reach a peak of 'groupy' feelings.

Above all, there are numerous indications pointing to the development of group norms that bolster morale at the expense of critical thinking. One of the most common norms appears to be that of remaining loyal to the group by sticking with the policies to which the group has already committed itself, even when those policies are obviously working out badly and have unintended consequences that disturb the conscience of each member. This is one of the key characteristics of groupthink.

1984

I use the term *groupthink* as a quick and easy way to refer to the mode of thinking that persons engage in when *concurrence seeking* becomes so dominant in a cohesive ingroup that it tends to override realistic appraisal of alternative courses of action. Groupthink is a term of the same order as the words in the newspeak vocabulary George Orwell used in his dismaying world of *Nineteen Eighty-Four*. In that context, groupthink takes on an invidious connotation. Exactly such a connotation is intended, since the term refers to a deterioration in mental efficiency, reality testing, and moral judgments as a result of group pressures.

The symptoms of groupthink arise when the members of decision-making groups become motivated to avoid being too harsh in their judgments of their leaders' or their colleagues' ideas. They adopt a soft line of criticism, even in their own thinking. At their meetings, all the members are amiable and seek complete concurrence on every important issue, with no bickering or conflict to spoil the cozy, 'we-feeling' atmosphere.

Kill

Paradoxically, soft-headed groups are often hard-hearted when it comes to dealing with outgroups or enemies. They find it relatively easy to resort to dehumanizing solutions – they will readily authorize bombing attacks that kill large numbers of civilians in the name of the noble cause of persuading an unfriendly government to negotiate at the peace table. They are unlikely to pursue the more difficult and controversial issues that arise when alternatives to a harsh military solution come up for discussion. Nor are they inclined to raise ethical issues that carry the implication that *this fine group of ours, with its humanitarianism and its high-minded principles, might be capable of adopting a course of action that is inhumane and immoral.*

Norms

There is evidence from a number of social-psychological studies that as the members of a group feel more accepted by the others, which is a central feature of increased group cohesiveness, they display less overt conformity to group norms. Thus we would expect that the more cohesive a group becomes, the less the members will feel constrained to censor what they say out of fear of being socially punished for antagonizing the leader or any of their fellow members.

In contrast, the groupthink type of conformity tends to increase as group cohesiveness increases. Groupthink involves nondeliberate suppression of critical thoughts as a result of internalization of the group's norms, which is quite different from deliberate suppression on the basis of external threats of social punishment. The more cohesive the group, the greater the inner compulsion on the part of each member to avoid creating disunity, which inclines him to believe in the soundness of whatever proposals are promoted by the leader or by a majority of the group's members.

In a cohesive group, the danger is not so much that each individual will fail to reveal his objections to what the others propose but that he will think the proposal is a good one, without attempting to carry out a careful, critical scrutiny of the pros and cons of the alternatives. When groupthink becomes dominant, there also is considerable suppression of deviant thoughts, but it takes the form of each person's deciding that his misgivings are not relevant and should be set aside, that the benefit of the doubt regarding any lingering uncertainties should be given to the group consensus.

Stress

I do not mean to imply that all cohesive groups necessarily suffer from groupthink. All ingroups may have a mild tendency toward groupthink, displaying one or another of the symptoms from time to time, but it need not be so dominant as to influence the quality of the group's final decision. Neither do I mean to imply that there is anything necessarily inefficient or harmful about group decisions in general. On the contrary, a group whose members have properly defined roles, with traditions concerning the procedures to follow in pursuing a critical inquiry, probably is capable of making better decisions than any individual group member working alone.

The problem is that the advantages of having decisions made by groups are often lost because of powerful psychological pressures that arise when the members work closely together, share the same set of values, and, above all, face a crisis situation that puts everyone under intense stress.

The main principle of groupthink, which I offer in the spirit of Parkinson's Law, is this: *The more amiability and esprit de corps there is among the members of a policy-making ingroup, the greater the danger that independent critical thinking will be replaced by groupthink, which is likely to result in irrational and dehumanizing actions directed against outgroups.*

Symptoms

In my studies of high-level governmental decision makers, both civilian and military, I have found eight main symptoms of groupthink.

Invulnerability

Most or all of the members of the ingroup share an *illusion* of invulnerability that provides for them some degree of reassurance about obvious dangers and leads them to become overoptimistic and willing to take extraordinary risks. It also causes them to fail to respond to clear warnings of danger.

The Kennedy ingroup, which uncritically accepted the Central Intelligence Agency's disastrous Bay of Pigs plan, operated on the false assumption that they could keep secret the fact that the United States was responsible for the invasion of Cuba. Even after news of the plan began to leak out, their belief remained unshaken. They failed even to consider the danger that awaited them: a worldwide revulsion against the US.

A similar attitude appeared among the members of President Lyndon B. Johnson's ingroup, the 'Tuesday Cabinet' which kept escalating the Vietnam War despite repeated setbacks and failures. 'There was a belief', Bill Moyers commented after he resigned, 'that if we indicated a willingness to use our power, they [the North Vietnamese] would get the message and back away from an all-out confrontation . . . There was a confidence – it was never bragged about, it was just there – that when the chips were really down, the other people would fold.'

A most poignant example of an illusion of invulnerability involves the ingroup around Admiral H. E. Kimmel, which failed to prepare for the possibility of a Japanese attack on Pearl Harbor despite repeated warnings. Informed by his intelligence chief that radio contact with Japanese aircraft carriers had been lost, Kimmel joked about it: 'What, you don't know where the carriers are? Do you mean to say that they could be rounding Diamond Head [at Honolulu] and you wouldn't know it?' The carriers were in fact moving full-steam toward Kimmel's command post at the time. Laughing together about a danger signal, which labels it as a purely laughing matter, is a characteristic manifestation of groupthink.

Rationale

As we see, victims of groupthink ignore warnings; they also collectively construct rationalizations in order to discount warnings and other forms of negative feedback that, taken seriously, might lead the group members to reconsider their assumptions each time they recommit themselves to past decisions. Why did the Johnson ingroup avoid reconsidering its escalation policy when time and again the expectations on which they based their decisions turned out to be wrong? James C. Thompson Jr, a Harvard historian who spent five years as an observing participant in both the State Department and the White House, tells us that the policymakers avoided critical discussion of their prior decisions and continually invented new rationalizations so that they could sincerely recommit themselves to defeating the North Vietnamese.

In the fall of 1964, before the bombing of North Vietnam began, some of the policymakers predicted that six weeks of air strikes would induce the North Vietnamese to seek peace talks. When someone asked, 'What if they don't?', the answer was that another four weeks certainly would do the trick.

Later, after each setback, the ingroup agreed that by investing just a bit more effort (by stepping up the bomb tonnage a bit, for instance), their course of action would prove to be right. *The Pentagon Papers* bear out these observations.

In *The Limits of Intervention*, Townsend Hoopes, who was Acting Secretary of the Air Force under Johnson, says that Walt W. Rostow in particular showed a remarkable capacity for what has been called 'instant rationalization'. According to Hoopes, Rostow buttressed the group's optimism about being on the road to victory by culling selected scraps of evidence from news reports or, if necessary, by inventing 'plausible' forecasts that had no basis in evidence at all.

Admiral Kimmel's group rationalized away their warnings, too. Right up to December 7, 1941, they convinced themselves that the Japanese would never dare attempt a full-scale surprise assault against Hawaii because Japan's leaders would realize that it would precipitate an all-out war which the United States would surely win. They made no attempt to look at the situation through the eyes of the Japanese leaders – another manifestation of groupthink.

Morality

Victims of groupthink believe unquestioningly in the inherent morality of their ingroup; this belief inclines the members to ignore the ethical or moral consequences of their decisions.

Evidence that this symptom is at work usually is of a negative kind – the things that are left unsaid in group meetings. At least two influential persons had doubts about the morality of the Bay of Pigs adventure. One of them, Arthur Schlesinger, Jr, presented his strong objections in a memorandum to President Kennedy and Secretary of State Rusk but suppressed them when he attended meetings of the Kennedy team. The other, Senator J. William Fulbright, was not a member of the group, but the President invited him to express his misgivings in a speech to the policymakers. However, when Fulbright finished speaking the President moved on to other agenda items without asking for reactions of the group.

David Kraslow and Stuart H. Loory, in *The Secret Search for Peace in Vietnam*, report that during 1966 President Johnson's ingroup was concerned primarily with selecting bomb targets in North Vietnam. They based their selections on four factors – the military advantage, the risk to American aircraft and pilots, the danger of forcing other countries into the fighting, and the danger of heavy civilian casualties. At their regular Tuesday luncheons, they weighed these factors the way school teachers grade examination papers, averaging them out. Though evidence on this point is scant, I suspect that the group's ritualistic adherence to a standardized procedure induced the members to feel morally justified in their destructive way of dealing with the Vietnamese people – after all, the danger of heavy civilian casualties from US air strikes was taken into account on their checklists.

Stereotypes

Victims of groupthink hold stereotyped views of the leaders of enemy groups; they are so evil that genuine attempts at negotiating differences with them are unwarranted, or they are too weak or too stupid to deal effectively with whatever attempts the ingroup makes to defeat their purposes, no matter how risky the attempts are.

Kennedy's groupthinkers believed that Premier Fidel Castro's air force was so ineffectual that obsolete B-26s could knock it out completely in a surprise attack before the invasion began. They also believed that Castro's army was so weak that a small Cuban-exile brigade could establish a well-protected beachhead at the Bay of Pigs. In addition, they believed that Castro was not smart enough to put down any possible internal uprisings in support of the exiles. They were wrong on all three assumptions. Though much of the blame was attributable to faulty intelligence, the point is that none of Kennedy's advisers even questioned the CIA planners about these assumptions.

The Johnson advisers' sloganistic thinking about 'the Communist apparatus' that was 'working all around the world' (as Dean Rusk put it) led them to overlook the powerful nationalistic strivings of the North Vietnamese government and its efforts to ward off Chinese domination. The crudest of all stereotypes used by Johnson's inner circle to justify their policies was the domino theory ('If we don't stop the Reds in South Vietnam, tomorrow they will be in Hawaii and next week they will be in San Francisco', Johnson once said). The group so firmly accepted this stereotype that it became almost impossible for any adviser to introduce a more sophisticated viewpoint.

In the documents on Pearl Harbor, it is clear to see that the Navy commanders stationed in Hawaii had a naive image of Japan as a midget that would not dare to strike a blow against a powerful giant.

Pressure

Victims of groupthink apply direct pressure to any individual who momentarily expresses doubts about any of the group's shared illusions or who questions the validity of the arguments supporting a policy alternative favored by the majority. This gambit reinforces the concurrence-seeking norm that loyal members are expected to maintain.

President Kennedy probably was more active than anyone else in raising skeptical questions during the Bay of Pigs meetings, and yet he seems to have encouraged the group's docile, uncritical accept-ance of defective arguments in favor of the CIA's plan. At every meeting, he allowed the CIA representatives to dominate the discussion. He permitted them to give their immediate refutations in response to each tentative doubt that one of the others expressed, instead of asking whether anyone shared the doubt or wanted to pursue the implications of the new worrisome issue that had just been raised. And at the most crucial meeting, when he was calling on each member to give his vote for or against the plan, he did not call on Arthur Schlesinger, the one man there who was known by the President to have serious misgivings.

Historian Thompson informs us that whenever a member of Johnson's ingroup began to express doubts, the group used subtle social pressures to 'domesticate' him. To start with, the dissenter was made to feel at home, provided that he lived up to two restrictions: (1) that he did not voice his doubts to outsiders, which would play into the hands of the opposition; and (2) that he kept his criticisms within the bounds of acceptable deviation, which meant not challenging any of the fundamental assumptions that went into the group's prior commitments. One such 'domesticated dissenter' was Bill Moyers. When Moyers arrived at a meeting, Thompson tells us, the President greeted him with 'Well, here comes Mr Stop-the Bombing.'

Self-censorship

Victims of groupthink avoid deviating from what appears to be group consensus; they keep silent about their misgivings and even minimize to themselves the importance of their doubts.

As we have seen, Schlesinger was not at all hesitant about presenting his strong objections to the Bay of Pigs plan in a memorandum to the President and the Secretary of State. But he became keenly aware of his tendency to suppress objections at the White House meetings. 'In the months after the Bay of Pigs I bitterly reproached myself for having kept so silent during those crucial discussions in the cabinet room', Schlesinger writes in *A Thousand Days*. 'I can only explain my failure to do more than raise a few timid questions by reporting that one's impulse to blow the whistle on this nonsense was simply undone by the circumstances of the discussion.'

Unanimity

Victims of groupthink share an *illusion* of unanimity within the group concerning almost all judgments expressed by members who speak in favor of the majority view. This symptom results partly from the preceding one, whose effects are augmented by the false assumption that any individual who remains silent during any part of the discussion is in full accord with what the others are saying.

When a group of persons who respect each other's opinions arrives at a unanimous view, each member is likely to feel that the belief must be true. This reliance on consensual validation within the group tends to replace individual critical thinking and reality testing, unless there are clear-cut disagreements among the members. In contemplating a course of action such as the invasion of Cuba, it is painful for the members to confront disagreements within their group, particularly if it becomes apparent that there are widely divergent views about whether the preferred course of action is too risky to undertake at all. Such disagreements are likely to arouse anxieties about making a serious error. Once the sense of unanimity is shattered, the members no longer can feel complacently confident about the decision they are inclined to make. Each man must then face the annoying realization that there are troublesome uncertainties and he must diligently seek out the best information he can get in order to decide for himself exactly how serious the risks might be. This is one of the unpleasant consequences of being in a group of hardheaded, critical thinkers.

To avoid such an unpleasant state, the members often become inclined, without quite realizing it, to prevent latent disagreements from surfacing when they are about to initiate a risky course of action. The group leader and the members support each other in playing up the areas of convergence in their thinking, at the expense of fully exploring divergencies that might reveal unsettled issues.

'Our meetings took place in a curious atmosphere of assumed consensus', Schlesinger writes. His additional comments clearly show that, curiously, the consensus was an illusion – an illusion that could be maintained only because the major participants did not reveal their own reasoning or discuss their idiosyncratic assumptions and vague reservations. Evidence from several sources makes it clear that even the three principals – President Kennedy, Rusk and McNamara – had widely differing assumptions about the invasion plan.

Mindguards

Victims of groupthink sometimes appoint themselves as mindguards to protect the leader and fellow members from adverse information that might break the complacency they shared about the effectiveness and morality of past decisions. At a large birthday party for his wife, Attorney General Robert F. Kennedy, who had been constantly informed about the Cuban invasion plan, took Schlesinger aside and asked him why he was opposed. Kennedy listened coldly and said, 'You may be right or you may be wrong, but the President has made his mind up. Don't push it any further. Now is the time for everyone to help him all they can.'

Rusk also functioned as a highly effective mindguard by failing to transmit to the group the strong objections of three 'outsiders' who had learned of the invasion plan – Undersecretary of State Chester Bowles, USIA Director Edward R. Murrow, and Rusk's intelligence chief, Roger Hilsman. Had Rusk done so, their warnings might have reinforced Schlesinger's memorandum and jolted some of Kennedy's ingroup, if not the President himself, into reconsidering the decision.

Products

When a group of executives frequently displays most or all of these interrelated symptoms, a detailed study of their deliberations is likely to reveal a number of immediate consequences. These consequences are, in effect, products of poor decision-making practices because they lead to inadequate solutions to the problems under discussion.

First, the group limits its discussions to a few alternative courses of action (often only two) without an initial survey of all the alternatives that might be worthy of consideration.

Second, the group fails to reexamine the course of action initially preferred by the majority after they learn of risks and drawbacks they had not considered originally.

Third, the members spend little or no time discussing whether there are nonobvious gains they may have overlooked or ways of reducing the seemingly prohibitive costs that made rejected alternatives appear undesirable to them.

Fourth, members make little or no attempt to obtain information from experts within their own organizations who might be able to supply more precise estimates of potential losses and gains.

Fifth, members show positive interest in facts and opinions that support their preferred policy; they tend to ignore facts and opinions that do not.

Sixth, members spend little time deliberating about how the chosen policy might be hindered by bureaucratic inertia, sabotaged by political opponents, or temporarily derailed by common accidents. Consequently, they fail to work out contingency plans to cope with foreseeable setbacks that could endanger the overall success of their chosen course.

Support

The search for an explanation of why groupthink occurs had led me through a quagmire of complicated theoretical issues in the murky area of human motivation. My belief, based on recent social-psychological research, is that we can best understand the various symptoms of groupthink as a mutual effort among the group members to maintain self-esteem and emotional equanimity by providing social support to each other, especially at times when they share responsibility for making vital decisions.

Even when no important decision is pending, the typical administrator will begin to doubt the wisdom and morality of his past decisions each time he receives information about setbacks, particularly if the information is accompanied by negative feedback from prominent men who originally had been his supporters. It should not be surprising, therefore, to find that individual members strive to develop unanimity and *esprit de corps* that will help bolster each other's morale, to create an optimistic outlook about the success of pending decisions, and to reaffirm the positive value of past policies to which all of them are committed.

Pride

Shared illusions of invulnerability, for example, can reduce anxiety about taking risks. Rationalizations help members believe that the risks are really not so bad after all. The assumption of inherent morality helps the members to avoid feelings of shame or guilt. Negative stereotypes function as stress-reducing devices to enhance a sense of moral righteousness as well as pride in a lofty mission.

The mutual enhancement of self-esteem and morale may have functional value in enabling the members to maintain their capacity to take action, but it has maladaptive consequences in so far as concurrence-seeking tendencies interfere with critical, rational capacities and lead to serious errors of judgment.

While I have limited my study to decision-making bodies in government, groupthink symptoms appear in business, industry and any other field where small, cohesive groups make the decisions. It is vital, then, for all sorts of people – and especially group leaders – to know what steps they can take to prevent groupthink.

Remedies

To counterpoint my case studies of the major fiascos, I have also investigated two highly successful group enterprises, the formulation of the Marshall Plan in the Truman Administration and the handling of the Cuban missile crisis by President Kennedy and his advisers. I have found it instructive to examine the steps Kennedy took to change his group's decision-making processes. These changes ensured that the mistakes made by his Bay of Pigs ingroup were not repeated by the missile-crisis ingroup, even though the membership of both groups was essentially the same.

The following recommendations for preventing groupthink incorporate many of the good practices I discovered to be characteristic of the Marshall Plan and missile-crisis groups:

1   The leader of a policy-forming group should assign the role of critical evaluation to each member, encouraging the group to give high priority to open airing of objections and doubts. This practice needs to be reinformed by the leader's acceptance of criticism of his own judgments in order to discourage members from soft-pedaling their disagreements and from allowing their striving for concurrence to inhibit critical thinking.
2   When the key members of a hierarchy assign a policy-planning mission to any group within their organization, they should adopt an impartial stance instead of stating preferences and expectations at the beginning. This will encourage open inquiry and impartial probing of a wide range of policy alternatives.

3   The organization routinely should set up several outside policy-planning and evaluation groups to work on the same policy question, each deliberating under a different leader. This can prevent the insulation of an ingroup.

4   At intervals before the group reaches a final consensus, the leader should require each member to discuss the group's deliberations with associates in his own unit of the organization – assuming that those associates can be trusted to adhere to the same security regulations that govern the policy-makers – and then to report back their reactions to the group.

5   The group should invite one or more outside experts to each meeting on a staggered basis and encourage the experts to challenge the views of the core members.

6   At every general meeting of the group, whenever the agenda calls for an evaluation of policy alternatives, at least one member should play devil's advocate, functioning as a good lawyer in challenging the testimony of those who advocate the majority position.

7   Whenever the policy issue involves relations with a rival nation or organization, the group should devote a sizable block of time, perhaps an entire session, to a survey of all warning signals from the rivals and should write alternative scenarios on the rivals' intentions.

8   When the group is surveying policy alternatives for feasibility and effectiveness, it should from time to time divide into two or more subgroups to meet separately, under different chairmen, and then come back together to hammer out differences.

9   After reaching a preliminary consensus about what seems to be the best policy, the group should hold a 'second-chance' meeting at which every member expresses as vividly as he can all his residual doubts, and rethinks the entire issue before making a definitive choice.

How

These recommendations have their disadvantages. To encourage the open airing of objections, for instance, might lead to prolonged and costly debates when a rapidly growing crisis requires immediate solution. It also could cause rejection, depression and anger. A leader's failure to set a norm might create cleavage between leader and members that could develop into a disruptive power struggle if the leader looks on the emerging consensus as anathema. Setting up outside evaluation groups might increase the risk of security leakage. Still, inventive executives who know their way around the organizational maze probably can figure out how to apply one or another of the prescriptions successfully, without harmful side effects.

They also could benefit from the advice of outside experts in the administrative and behavioral sciences. Though these experts have much to offer, they have had few chances to work on policy-making machinery within large organizations. As matters now stand, executives innovate only when they need new procedures to avoid repeating serious errors that have deflated their self-images.

In this era of atomic warheads, urban disorganization and eco-catastrophes, it seems to me that policymakers should collaborate with behavioral scientists and give top priority to preventing groupthink and its attendant fiascos.

23

Reaping the benefits of teamwork

Adrian Furnham

Nearly all of us work with other people. Most of us are inter-dependent in the sense that we have to help, support and reward each other at work. No one can whistle a symphony; it takes the team effort of an orchestra to play it. Whether we call them groups, sections, squads or teams, most of us realise how much our productivity and satisfaction is due to them. This pretty obvious point is now the latest management obsession.

Management science, if there can be such a thing, is notoriously faddish. Not long ago it was strategic planning that was the key to organisational success. Then it had to do with organisation structure. After that the gurus said that once the corporate culture (another oxymoron) was right, Eldorado was just around the corner!

All these solve-all solutions have now reached their sell-by date. But there is, fortunately, a new solution to all the hard-pressed manager's needs. Teamwork, it seems, will solve all your problems and lead to happy, healthy, productive workers.

So business sections of bookshops bulge with books, nearly always written by people called Chuck, Randy or Ed, on teams and team-work. They rejoice under crypto-sporting titles such as *Team-Power*, or *How To Be a Team Player: Winning Big*. Their message is simple: the power of the waterfall is nothing but a lot of drips working together. No matter how great a warrior he might be, a chief cannot do battle without his indians.

What supporters of the team concept argue is this: bearing in mind that management is the art of getting things done through people, you need to let your people know what your goals are – what you want to accomplish, why you want to accomplish it, how they will benefit from it and the role they will play in accomplishing it. This is another way of saying that the members of the management team must be able to identify themselves individually with the company's overall goals. No chief executive, no top management group ever reached these goals by themselves. Unless the entire management team is aboard, the company will never get there.

From A. Furnham, 'Reaping the benefits of teamwork', *Financial Times*, 19 May 1993.

What has caused this explosion in restating the obvious? The answer is partly in the American obsession with the Japanese, who are still perceived by the Pearl Harbor generation as mindless, but highly disciplined, killers. The post-war Japanese miracle has puzzled – indeed terrified – the Americans. What is the Japanese secret of success? Answer – teamwork.

The Japanese come from a collectivistic culture and hence naturally do things in groups or teams. We in the Anglo-Saxon world come from an individualistic culture, which selects on, rewards and values individual effort. No matter how much teamwork achieves in our culture, the results tend to get identified with a single name. We therefore have to endure various mildly humiliating training courses (many in the great outdoors) to encourage team-work because it is not natural to us. While it is true that no member of a boat crew is praised for the individuality of their rowing, this is an exception to the rule. The Japanese, I presume, don't feel obligated to attend individualism courses to learn how to 'become their own person', or 'do things their own way'. They are natural collectivistic team players.

This individualism in our culture runs deep. We are, however, loyal to some groups: usually those we have been forced to join, or with whom we have endured hardship and difficulty. Family, school classmates and fellow military conscripts often do command our loyalty. But, because we don't have jobs for life and find it easier to get promotion by moving between organisations, we rarely stay long enough in a team to be really part of it.

The life of a team goes through various stages: forming (the getting together); storming (arguing over who does what, who is leader, etc.); norming (the acceptable explicit and implicit rules); performing (actually working well after the early stages have occurred); finally, teams go through mourning (when they break up). But all this takes time and many of us never really stay long enough in a particular team to appreciate its worth.

But how seriously do companies which have swallowed the team solution really take the idea? Yes, they do talk it up; go on endless (and expensive) courses; they even partly restructure sections into 'new teams'. Yet very, very few reward the team, rather than the individual. Most performance management systems (the euphemism for how pay is determined) are explicitly geared to the individual. Yes, teamwork in the sense of contribution to the team may be a criterion which is rated, but it is usually only one of many. Also, we rarely hire people with a team in mind or indeed hire whole teams.

Michael Winner got it right when he said: 'Team effort is a lot of people doing what I say.' The teamwork philosophy of co-operation, interdependence and group loyalty is counter-cultural.

Our business heroes are for the most part egocentric, rugged individuals, not team players. Teamwork may be a really good idea, but don't fool yourself either that it is a total solution or that a couple of fuzzy warm courses will do the trick.

24

Team roles and a self-perception inventory

R. Meredith Belbin

Not so long ago nearly every firm was run by a boss, or a 'governor' as he was sometimes quite accurately called. In every sense he was the manager. Nowadays most middle-sized and large firms, and almost all institutions, are run by small management teams. Each team member may carry the designation 'manager' but the word has largely lost its original meaning: it no longer implies an authority figure and may refer merely to someone holding a position of responsibility.

The shift in power and authority away from the individual and towards a team owes something to the climate of our times. The concentration of power tends to corrupt, so that it is better to share power. The more educated the population entering into employment, the greater the desire for some say in management. On both moral and intellectual grounds it is unacceptable to many that one person should make all the important decisions. And then there is the sheer difficulty of doing so. The decision-making business has to embrace changing technology, competition that is international as well as domestic, and the administrative problems of running a company in a world that is becoming increasingly complicated. The lone helmsman, whatever his ability, is prone to mistakes and oversights which reflect the limitations of his knowledge and experience. The management team has become the stable alternative, a means of running a company effectively so long as the right combination of people can be found.

For many years the qualities of the individual manager have been a focal point of interest: those of a successful management team are less well understood. A team is more difficult to study than a person. [. . .]

The material which forms the body of this book is the product of over nine years of original research, most of which was conducted at the Administrative Staff College, Henley, by the Industrial Training

Abridged from R.M. Belbin, *Management Teams*, Oxford: Butterworth Heinemann, 1981, pp. ix–x, 76–8, 153–7.

Research Unit from Cambridge. The work centred mainly round the composition of teams, according to various hypotheses and designs. One hundred and twenty management teams were formed in an experimental way, mostly with six members in each team. Team effectiveness was measured in terms of financial results in a management game. [. . .]

Central to the approach developed as an outcome of these experiments has been the concept of team-role. This defines the ways in which members with characteristic personalities and abilities contribute to a team. Useful team-roles are limited in number and the success of a team depends on their interlocking pattern and how well they are discharged. Given certain information on the team-roles to which members of a team are predisposed by nature and ability, we can give a fair estimate of whether that team is likely to succeed or fail in meeting its objectives. Lastly, and perhaps most importantly, our team-building theories and ideas have been made operational in a number of organizations and companies in the UK and Australia. [. . .]

A self-perception inventory

This inventory was developed from a number of earlier versions which had been designed to give Henley members a simple means of assessing their best team-roles.

Directions

For each section distribute a total of ten points among the sentences which you think best describe your behaviour. These points may be distributed among several sentences: in extreme cases they might be spread among all the sentences, or ten points may be given to a single sentence. Enter the points in Table 24.1.

Table 24.1   *Points table for self-perception inventory*

Section	Item a	b	c	d	e	f	g	h
I								
II								
III								
IV								
V								
VI								
VII								

I What I believe I can contribute to a team:
   (a) I think I can quickly see and take advantage of new opportunities.
   (b) I can work well with a very wide range of people.
   (c) Producing ideas is one of my natural assets.
   (d) My ability rests in being able to draw people out whenever I detect they have something of value to contribute to group objectives.
   (e) My capacity to follow through has much to do with my personal effectiveness.
   (f) I am ready to face temporary unpopularity if it leads to worthwhile results in the end.
   (g) I am quick to sense what is likely to work in a situation with which I am familiar.
   (h) I can offer a reasoned case for alternative courses of action without introducing bias or prejudice.

II If I have a possible shortcoming in teamwork, it could be that:
   (a) I am not at ease unless meetings are well structured and controlled and generally well conducted.
   (b) I am inclined to be too generous towards others who have a valid viewpoint that has not been given a proper airing.
   (c) I have a tendency to talk a lot once the group gets on to new ideas.
   (d) My objective outlook makes it difficult for me to join in readily and enthusiastically with colleagues.
   (e) I am sometimes seen as forceful and authoritarian if there is a need to get something done.
   (f) I find it difficult to lead from the front, perhaps because I am overresponsive to group atmosphere.
   (g) I am apt to get too caught up in ideas that occur to me and so lose track of what is happening.
   (h) My colleagues tend to see me as worrying unnecessarily over detail and the possibility that things may go wrong.

III When involved in a project with other people:
   (a) I have an aptitude for influencing people without pressurizing them.
   (b) My general vigilance prevents careless mistakes and omissions being made.
   (c) I am ready to press for action to make sure that the meeting does not waste time or lose sight of the main objective.
   (d) I can be counted on to contribute something original.
   (e) I am always ready to back a good suggestion in the common interest.

(f) I am keen to look for the latest in new ideas and developments.

(g) I believe my capacity for cool judgement is appreciated by others.

(h) I can be relied upon to see that all essential work is organized.

IV My characteristic approach to group work is that:
   (a) I have a quiet interest in getting to know colleagues better.
   (b) I am not reluctant to challenge the views of others or to hold a minority view myself.
   (c) I can usually find a line of argument to refute unsound propositions.
   (d) I think I have a talent for making things work once a plan has to be put into operation.
   (e) I have a tendency to avoid the obvious and to come out with the unexpected.
   (f) I bring a touch of perfectionism to any team job I undertake.
   (g) I am ready to make use of contacts outside the group itself.
   (h) While I am interested in all views I have no hesitation in making up my mind once a decision has to be made.

V I gain satisfaction in a job because:
   (a) I enjoy analysing situations and weighing up all the possible choices.
   (b) I am interested in finding practical solutions to problems.
   (c) I like to feel I am fostering good working relationships.
   (d) I can have a strong influence on decisions.
   (e) I can meet people who may have something new to offer.
   (f) I can get people to agree on a necessary course of action.
   (g) I feel in my element where I can give a task my full attention.
   (h) I like to find a field that stretches my imagination.

VI If I am suddenly given a difficult task with limited time and unfamiliar people:
   (a) I would feel like retiring to a corner to devise a way out of the impasse before developing a line.
   (b) I would be ready to work with the person who showed the most positive approach, however difficult he might be.
   (c) I would find some way of reducing the size of the task by establishing what different individuals might best contribute.
   (d) My natural sense of urgency would help to ensure that we did not fall behind schedule.
   (e) I believe I would keep cool and maintain my capacity to think straight.
   (f) I would retain a steadiness of purpose in spite of the pressures.

(g) I would be prepared to take a positive lead if I felt the group was making no progress.

(h) I would open up discussions with a view to stimulating new thoughts and getting something moving.

VII With reference to the problems to which I am subject in working in groups:

(a) I am apt to show my impatience with those who are obstructing progress.

(b) Others may criticize me for being too analytical and insufficiently intuitive.

(c) My desire to ensure that work is properly done can hold up proceedings.

(d) I tend to get bored rather easily and rely on one or two stimulating members to spark me off.

(e) I find it difficult to get started unless the goals are clear.

(f) I am sometimes poor at explaining and clarifying complex points that occur to me.

(g) I am conscious of demanding from others the things I cannot do myself.

(h) I hesitate to get my points across when I run up against real opposition.

To interpret the self-perception inventory you should now look at the analysis sheet in Table 24.2.

Table 24.2   *Self-perception inventory analysis sheet*

Transpose the scores taken from Table 24.1, entering them section by section. Then add up the points in each column to give a total team-role distribution score. [See Table 24.4 for symbols.]

Section	IM	CO	SH	PL	RI	ME	TW	CF
I	g	d	f	c	a	h	b	e
II	a	b	e	g	c	d	f	h
III	h	a	c	d	f	g	e	b
IV	d	h	b	e	g	c	a	f
V	b	f	d	h	e	a	c	g
VI	f	c	g	a	h	e	b	d
VII	e	g	a	f	d	b	h	c
Total								

Table 24.3   *Table of norms for SPI (sample size = 78)*

	Low 0–33%	Average 33–66%	High 66–85%	Very high 85–100%	Average score
IM	0–6	7–11	12–16	17–23	10.0
CO	0–6	7–10	11–13	14–18	8.8
SH	0–8	9–13	14–17	18–36	11.6
PL	0–4	5–8	9–12	13–29	7.3
RI	0–6	7–9	10–11	12–21	7.8
ME	0–5	6–9	10–12	13–19	8.2
TW	0–8	9–12	13–16	17–25	10.9
CF	0–3	4–6	7–9	10–17	5.5

[Use this table to spot your two highest team-roles]

Interpretation of total scores and further notes

The highest score on team-role will indicate how best the respondent can make his or her mark in a management or project team. The next highest scores can denote back-up team roles towards which the individual should shift if for some reason there is less group need for a primary team-role.

The two lowest scores in team-role imply possible areas of weakness. But rather than attempting to reform in this area the manager may be better advised to seek a colleague with complementary strengths. [. . .]

The table of norms in Table 24.3 is based on scores of a cross-section of managers from various functions and industries. [. . .]

Experience with the self-perception inventory [SPI] indicates that the most preferred team-role for executives is shaper and the least preferred is completer. We can therefore conjure up the image of the typical manager as good at initiating things, being pushy, outgoing and reactive, but weak in follow-through. But such a conclusion should be treated with some reservation because in every questionnaire there is a tendency for some responses to be more popular than others. It is useful therefore to see how individual respondents compare with executives in general.

Conclusion

The eight types of people identified as useful to have in teams form our comprehensive list. After half a decade of industrial experience in composing teams we could not find any other useful team-role to add. This does not mean that people may not be welcome in teams for their personal qualities, like a sense of humour, or for their technical knowledge, as befits a specialist. It is that such people

Table 24.4   *Useful people to have in teams*

Team-role	Symbol	Typical features	Positive qualities	Allowable weaknesses
Implementer	IM	Conservative, dutiful, predictable	Organizing ability, practical common sense, hard-working, self-discipline	Lack of flexibility, unresponsiveness to unproven ideas
Co-ordinator	CO	Calm, self-confident, controlled	A capacity for treating and welcoming all potential contributors on their merits and without prejudice. A strong sense of objectives	No more than ordinary in terms of intellect or creative ability
Shaper	SH	Highly strung, outgoing, dynamic	Drive and a readiness to challenge inertia, ineffectiveness, complacency or self-deception	Proneness to provocation, irritation and impatience
Plant	PL	Individualistic, serious-minded, unorthodox	Genius, imagination, intellect, knowledge	Up in the clouds, inclined to disregard practical details or protocol
Resource investigator	RI	Extroverted, enthusiastic, curious, communicative	A capacity for contacting people and exploring anything new. An ability to respond to challenge	Liable to lose interest once the initial fascination has passed
Monitor-evaluator	ME	Sober, unemotional, prudent	Judgement, discretion, hard-headedness	Lacks inspiration or the ability to motivate others
Team worker	TW	Socially orientated, rather mild, sensitive	An ability to respond to people and to situations, and to promote team spirit	Indecisiveness at moments of crisis
Completer-finisher	CF	Painstaking, orderly, conscientious, anxious	A capacity for follow-through. Perfectionism	A tendency to worry about small things. A reluctance to 'let go'

cannot take up any generalizable team-role in which they would have definite responsibilities. Good examples of our eight types would prove adequate for any challenge, although not all eight team-roles are necessarily needed.

The procedure for assessing each person in terms of the team which he might best enter was to establish from our psychometric test predictors the two roles for which that person might best be suited – the first role being his most dominant one and the second his best back-up. Hence ME/CF would apply to a person whose main characteristic was that he was clever and had a capacity for impartial judgement but who was also the sort of person who would not be happy with any loose ends that might be left around. RI/TW would indicate an extroverted person who loved exploring new ideas and who communicated and related easily and well with others.

The value of particular team-roles could be demonstrated by constructing teams that were deficient in some given team-role. Although those teams might succeed in capitalizing on their collective strength, any shortcoming in performance usually reflected the fault inherent in their team composition. [. . .]

The useful people to have in teams are those who possess strengths or characteristics which serve a need without duplicating those already there. Teams are a question of balance. What is needed is not well-balanced individuals but individuals who balance well with one another. In that way, human frailties can be underpinned and strengths used to full advantage.

Note

If you wish to read more about Belbin's team-roles, you should consult his later book *Team-Roles at Work* (Butterworth Heinemann, Oxford, 1993).

25

Teams: old myths and a new model

Peter Herriot and Carole Pemberton

Using knowledge through teams

Knowledge is to be found everywhere in the organisation. Everyone from the cleaner to the chief executive has know-how; everyone knows that various things are currently happening, inside and outside the organisation; and everyone knows beyond the present, at least in personal, if not yet in organisational terms. Know-how we define as expertise in how to solve particular sorts of problem on the basis of past experience. 'Knowing that' is possessing information about what's going on at the moment. 'Knowing beyond' means imagining from the viewpoint of the present what we might do in the future.

We already have the *knowledge people*, and their different frameworks of knowing provide the varied perspectives we need for input to the knowledge process. The *knowledge process* is a continuous cycle of actions and learning from their outcomes. Such learning increases knowledge, from which basis new actions are generated. The knowledge process represents the knowledge-based organisation of the future. Its core feature is knowing beyond. It is this combination of facing towards the future while continuously learning from the present that distinguishes the organisational survivors of the next century.

We have the knowledge people. We understand the knowledge process. Yet how can the people's talents be integrated into the organisational process? What, in brief, is *knowledge practice* to be? The integrative approach being adopted by an ever-increasing number of companies is to organise themselves in teams. Table 25.1 demonstrates the increase in teamworking in UK organisations. In response to the enquiry as to what they were doing to respond to new challenges and opportunities within their business environment, 79 per cent cited increased teamworking.[1]

Adapted by P. Herriot from P. Herriot and C. Pemberton, *Competitive Advantage through Diversity*, London: Sage, 1995, pp. 81–99.

Table 25.1 *Responses to business challenges and opportunities*

	Per cent
Creating slimmer and flatter organisations	88
More teamworking	79
More responsive networks	78
More interdependence of functions	71
Procedures resulting in greater flexibility	67
More interdependent organisations	55

Organisations have been busily introducing project teams, focus groups, autonomous work groups, quality circles, multi-function work teams, and top teams in the board room for the last decade. Back in 1982, Peters and Waterman's excellent companies,[2] alas not all so excellent today, were distinguished by their use of small groups. So much so, that the authors called teams 'the basic organisational building blocks'.

How is it, then, that teamworking has seldom transformed organisations into examples of the knowledge process? After all, teamworking is specifically designed to make the most of everyone's knowledge and skills. 'A team opportunity', we are told, 'exists anywhere where hierarchy or organisational boundaries inhibit the skills and perspectives needed for optimal results.'[3] Looking at our own organisations, we might all be tempted to reduce this sentence to, 'A team opportunity exists anywhere.'

So if practice and opportunity are widespread, why the apparent lack of impact? Definitions of teams and their critical success factors suggest some answers. It's not the mechanics but the practice that matters; not the structure itself, but whether it changes the way we work. A true team, according to the textbook, 'is a small number of people with complementary skills who are committed to a common purpose, set of performance goals, and approach for which they hold themselves mutually accountable'.[4] Real teams, as opposed to other sorts of organisational group, have:

- shared leadership roles
- individual and mutual accountability
- specific team purpose that the team itself delivers
- collective work-products
- open-ended discussions and active problem-solving meetings
- measures of collective work-products as performance indicators
- discussions, decisions, and real work.[5]

These aren't just academic definitions – textbook recommendations on how to do things which the author hasn't tested or observed in practice. These are the features of real teams in organisations as diverse as Hewlett-Packard and the Girl Scouts. Just to emphasise the generality, here are the eight critical success factors for an even more diverse set of teams – ranging from the team that investigated the Challenger space shuttle accident, through a football team and a cardiac surgery team, to the people who developed the IBM personal computer:

- a clear elevating goal
- a results-driven structure
- competent team members
- unified commitment
- a collaborative climate
- standards of excellence
- external support and recognition
- principled leadership.[6]

These findings demonstrate that merely bringing a diverse set of people together is certainly no guarantee of success. A lot more has to happen as well. But what if we combined the two lists of features and brought teams together according to those criteria? Surely we'd be on the way to the knowledge process, wouldn't we?

Two pervasive myths

We believe not. We believe that the features that are listed above do indeed distinguish successful from unsuccessful teams. But the successful teams were not necessarily successful *because* of these features alone. Researchers chose to compare teams on the basis of those particular features because they had certain beliefs about what it was important to look at. These views were probably influenced by two long-held myths about how teams work and why they are successful.

The first myth is that you have to get the interpersonal relationships among the group right before you can get down to your real task: the *All Friends Together* myth. The second is related. It is that you have to go through a sequence of stages of group development in a particular order to be successful: the *Seven Stages of Team* myth. Both of these myths focus upon internal interpersonal processes to the exclusion of the relationship of the team to its environment. Perhaps influenced by the mythology, the researchers we have quoted above included only one external team feature in a combined list of 15:

- external support and recognition.

The All Friends Together myth is derived from a long-past period in the history of organisational theory and practice: the so-called human relations era, with its spin-off, the T group. Once we more fully understand and accept ourselves and others, it was optimistically argued, we could work together more effectively. The assumption was that we could be trained to relate better in general, and that this learning would transfer to the workplace. Further, it was implied that we would work better together because we related to each other better.

The glad new dawn of the post-war era generated this hopelessly naive optimism. The evidence, alas, fails to support the myth. There is no evidence that interventions aimed at improving relations between members of the team improve the team's effectiveness at its task.[7] Those interventions into group process which *do* sometimes boost outcomes are about helping people with how best to work together on their task: defining objectives for example, or allocating tasks to the right people.[8]

The Seven Stages of Team myth derives from the same historical period and the same assumptions. Why does a sequence of developmental stages have to be passed through before the team can tackle its task? Because learning about how to operate together has to happen before real work can start. Or rather, more preciously, because we have to 'work hard at our relationships' before we can start the task. This myth was supported by a widely quoted rhyming mnemonic – forming, storming, norming, and performing [9] – still the staple fare provided by many trainers and consultants.

Yet here again, the evidence fails to support the myth. In organisational settings, teams don't spend a lot of time on process. On the contrary, they usually leap rapidly (perhaps too rapidly) into the task they think they have been given. Then they have alternate periods of getting on with their work and changing the way they do it.[10] It's hardly surprising that there is no fixed sequence or pattern. After all, there is a tremendous variety in the nature of the tasks they undertake – resolving problems, devising strategy, achieving a tactical objective, reporting on feasibility, planning and restructuring, running a campaign. Tasks differ in ambiguity and familiarity: imagining a new service or product that people might be persuaded to buy is a much more ambiguous task than designing an improved model of an automobile. Different tasks require different ways of working.[11]

A new model

What we need is a much broader model of teams and teamwork. We are not saying that the process of how team members work together is irrelevant. On the contrary, it is the core of the team concept; our next four chapters are all about processes. What we do argue is that to concentrate on team processes in isolation from the tasks and their context is meaningless. The traditional model has been:

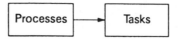

Get the processes right and success at the tasks will follow. We want first of all to reverse the sequence to:

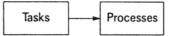

In other words, the nature of the task will determine the ways we tackle it. Then we need to add in the context:

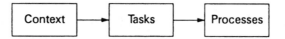

It is the organisational context which sets the tasks that the team has to tackle. However, we also need to add another relationship, as follows:

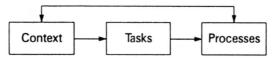

The organisational context has an impact on what sort of work processes are used (for example, it may determine the number and the identity of team members). Also, the processes have an impact on the context, in the sense that the team will seek to influence and persuade its organisational and external clients. Next, we need to add a fourth component, roles:

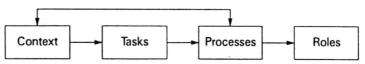

Roles are the different parts people play in helping along each of the processes (which are, in their turn, what gets the tasks done). Finally, we have to remember what it's all for: this is shown in Figure 25.1.

Team members can enjoy their activity no end. Indeed, they can gain great satisfaction in their work and believe, incorrectly, that they are being successful.[12] Ultimately they are evaluated not only by themselves but more importantly by their clients and customers; outcomes matter.

We need now to explore this model in greater depth. We need to

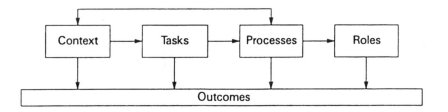

Figure 25.1 *The teamworking model*

understand more fully its components and their relationships. Only then can we decide how to teamwork more effectively.

Context and tasks

First, then, the context in which the team works, and how it determines the tasks:

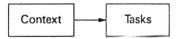

The organisation is the most immediate context, and other organisational members have usually tasked the team to achieve some sort of outcome. Of course, this does not mean that the team may not redefine the task or consider issues that were not in its original remit. What it does mean is that the team has to produce something, normally to a deadline.[13]

The range of tasks a team can be tasked with is infinitely varied. Think of three teams currently operating in your organisation:

- What is their name?
- What are their tasks?
- Along which dimensions do the tasks differ?

The last question is the tough one. It's very hard to think of ways tasks differ apart from difficult, very difficult, and next to impossible. One way is to think of tasks in terms of the knowledge process. Some tasks have a high knowing-beyond component, others imply a large dose of know-how, others again require a great deal of information. See, for example, Table 25.2.

Clearly, organisations exist within a business environment, the condition of which will affect the nature of the task. During recession the dominant tasks are likely to be those requiring less knowing beyond, since most organisations are concerned with short-term survival.

Table 25.2   *Some tasks and their knowledge requirements*

Task	Know beyond	Know-how	Know that
Feasibility study	Low	Medium	High
Problem solution	Medium	High	Medium
Devising strategy	High	Medium	High
Tactical objective	Medium	Medium	High
Restructuring	Medium	Medium	Low
Running a campaign	Medium	High	Medium

Not only does the state of the business environment affect what tasks organisations give to their teams. It also means that organisations themselves are changing. The consequence is that the organisational context in which teams operate is often in a state of flux. The task that the team started off with may well be changed as a consequence, part way through. Think back to the three teams you enumerated from your own organisation:

- Which of them now has a different task from the one it was tasked with at the beginning?
- When and why did this change occur?
- Were there new organisational circumstances which triggered this change?

The variety of primary tasks, then, is immense. But in the knowledge-based organisation, every team has an identical secondary task. It is to increase that knowledge base – to learn. As we work through the team model, then, we have to ask continuously how *both* tasks are being achieved.

In terms of the components we are currently considering, we have to ask:

- Have others in the organisation explicitly tasked the team with learning?
- Do they require from the team an output which demonstrably adds to the knowledge base?
- Have they established systems which capture the team's outputs and make them available for others?

Tasks and processes

The second relationship in our team model is between tasks and processes:

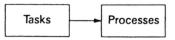

Table 25.3   *Some tasks and their process requirements*

	Motivation and momentum	Issues and ideas	Managing boundaries	Evaluating progress and outcomes
Feasibility study	High	Low	Medium	Medium
Problem solution	Medium	High	High	Medium
Devising strategy	Low	High	Low	Medium
Tactical objective	High	Low	Medium	High
Restructuring	Low	Medium	High	High
Running a campaign	High	Medium	Medium	High

We believe there are four processes necessary if teams are to achieve their tasks -- both their primary task, and their task of learning. They are:

- achieving motivation and momentum
- defining issues and getting ideas
- managing the boundaries
- evaluating progress and outcomes.

All of these processes are necessary if tasks are to be completed. However, they may well differ in their importance for different kinds of task. Table 25.3 gives some examples.

Take the example of reaching a tactical objective: the need to maintain motivation is high since the task is not inherently of great interest. However, there is little need for ideas, since the objective may be a routine one. Boundaries need to be managed but, more important, progress has to be evaluated. This evaluation is vital since tactical objectives are usually specific and progress can be estimated.

Some processes may be very important at particular points in the time span of tasks. For example:

- Issues and ideas are going to be crucial near the beginning of the strategy-making task.
- Managing boundaries will be important at the end of a problem-solving task when the solution has to be sold to the problem's owners.
- Keeping motivation and momentum going will prevent a campaign from sagging in the middle.
- Constant evaluation of progress will ensure that the tactical objective is adhered to.
- Evaluation of progress and outcome is essential for the universal task of learning, which cannot occur unless activity is reflected upon.

So, as we have shown, the nature of the task affects which processes are important and when.

Context and processes

The third relationship in our model is that between context and processes:

Components include:

- the cooperation others in the organisation give or fail to give the team
- the time pressure they put the team under – they usually set the deadlines
- the resources they allocate for the team's use
- the degree of autonomy they allow the team.

All of these are contextual features which affect how well the four basic processes work.

As we all know from bitter experience:

- It's hard to keep up momentum if you haven't been given the resources; and motivation is difficult to summon up if you believe that lack of resources indicates no-one's really interested in what you're doing.
- You don't have time for issues and ideas or for evaluating progress if they're on your back all the time for an answer. In other words, you don't have time for innovation or learning.
- There's no room to define issues and there's little motivation to succeed if they take away your autonomy by telling you precisely what the problem is and precisely how to tackle it.

Now think of a team of which you are currently a member:

- In what ways do others in the organisation support and help you?
- In what ways do others hinder you from achieving your task?
- What efforts do you make to maximise support and minimise hindrances?
- How successful are these efforts?

These last two questions direct our attention to the two-way nature of the relationship in our model between context and processes. Teams actively seek to manage their context. They:

- protect their boundaries
- buffer themselves against pressure and threats
- promote their cause to important people
- keep their ears to the political ground
- and make alliances with other teams.[14]

They coordinate what they're doing with suppliers and colleagues, and negotiate specifications and deadlines with customers. They scan their business sector and competitors for ideas, both marketing and technical. And they keep or gradually release as appropriate the team's secrets. So teams aren't necessarily at the mercy of their environment – they influence it too.

Processes and roles

The next relationship in our model is that between processes and roles:

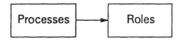

We believe not only that different processes require different roles, but also that the role-playing skills available affect how well each of our four basic processes actually operates in practice: the relationship is two-way.

There is already a large number of different theoretical frameworks relating to team roles. We have earlier outlined the best-known set of team role definitions, that of Belbin.[15] However, it's important to note that despite its widespread use, there is little published evidence to demonstrate that these roles are used and work in the organisational setting when real tasks are to be tackled by real teams. On the contrary, Belbin's team roles were derived from observations of senior managers engaged in simulation exercises. Where the task isn't real, attention focuses inevitably on roles which become objects of attention in their own right, divorced from the task. Furthermore, recent research indicates that Belbin's measure of the roles lacks reliability and validity.[16] In other words, people's scores vary considerably from one completion of the questionnaire to the next; and the scores obtained don't justify the division of roles into the eight which Belbin proposed.

We propose instead to differentiate four basic ways of approaching and understanding task situations. We will call these 'roles', even though they are more general and broad-ranging than the term usually implies. Each individual prefers one of these four roles, and each of the four team processes is dependent on particular roles being played. We can attach role labels to them:[17]

- traditionalists
- visionaries
- catalysts
- loyalists.

These roles have the following characteristics:

- *Traditionalists* prefer to gather all the pertinent facts and consider them dispassionately. They are pretty good at coming to logical, reasonable decisions and at making existing systems run efficiently. They are weak at responding to change (the existing systems won't work), and they tend to avoid situations where subjective and personal factors predominate.
- *Visionaries*, too, like to be analytic and logical, but they prefer situations where there isn't much clear information available. They can see the big picture and devise new systems and projects. However, they are weak at following through on detail, and they tend to avoid situations where the facts are established and where feelings and emotions are involved.
- *Catalysts* like developing their own and other people's skills and talents. They are good at getting people to work together and at handling people problems. However, they are impatient with routine, and they don't like getting involved in decisions which may cause conflict.
- *Loyalists* are pragmatists, who will do whatever is needed to help colleagues or clients. They have a compassionate concern for the common good, and are concerned to make things work efficiently and harmoniously. They may fail to notice change, however, particularly in areas where they have laboured themselves; and they don't like taking decisions which can cause conflict.

Our four roles are to be found all over organisations. However, some roles are more likely to be preferred by particular categories of employee, since they self-select into and are selected for these categories on the basis of what they prefer and are good at. Try speculating, for example, on the role most likely to be preferred by top managers, by secretaries, by middle managers.

What is important here is to tease out how our four processes relate to these four roles. For if a team needs all four processes to occur, and if different roles are needed for different processes, then it follows that the team needs different roles to be played (Figure 25.2).

We are suggesting, then, that:

- *Catalysts* are needed to enhance the team's *motivation* and cohesion, and *loyalists* to keep the *momentum* going so as to achieve the task.
- *Visionaries* are required for identifying the *issues* within the broad picture, *catalysts* for ensuring that *ideas* see the light of day.
- *Catalysts*, with their preference for handling people issues, are useful in *managing boundaries*. So are *loyalists*, who will dutifully

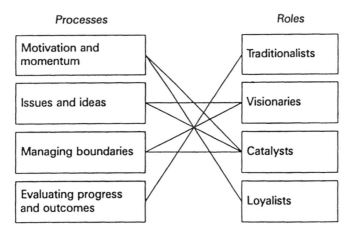

Figure 25.2 *Team processes and their role requirements*

protect their colleagues from outside threat, and *visionaries* who know about the rest of the organisation.
- *Traditionalists* will come into their own when *evaluating* progress and outcomes, as they direct their unsentimental gaze at the hard realities.

So different processes need different roles; and the under- or over-representation of people willing and able to play these roles will profoundly affect task achievement.

Components and outcomes

The final relationship we have to consider in the model is that between all its other components and the outcomes:

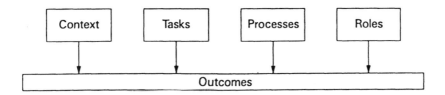

Note the plurality of 'outcomes'. The evidence we have is based almost entirely on primary outcomes – whether or not the task which was set the team was successfully achieved. Yet there is always a secondary outcome in the knowledge-based organisation: did any learning occur? We cannot go along with the hard-nosed bottom-line argument of Shea and Guzzo: 'We believe that real-world, real-time group effectiveness is what matters, and that it boils down to the production of designated products or the delivery of contracted services, per specification'.[18] This is true, but it is only half the truth. It is quite possible that the successful achievement of the primary task makes it less likely that learning will occur. On the assumption that learning happens especially when failure occurs, this is a reasonable hypothesis. It's likely, though, that we learn from failure because failure isn't usually what we plan for or expect. It's the failure to fulfil our expectations that forces us to reflect on what happened and learn from it. Things may go quite contrary to our plans and expectations, but we may successfully adapt and achieve our task in the end. We've learned from success, but success gained the hard way. So learning as well as task achievement or failure is an outcome; and learning can result from both failure and unexpected achievement.

The second reason for using the plural 'outcomes' in the model is that there are always additional outcomes to the achievement of the task. There are all sorts of unforeseen systemic consequences of action, some favourable, others not. This is why evaluating outcomes is such an important process. It's not a mechanical checking off of outputs against objectives. Rather, it's an intelligent and thorough look at the multiple ripples caused by the team throwing its stone into the organisational pool.

But back to the team's primary task. What determines a successful outcome? We started the chapter with two lists of features of successful teams. Now that we have a model, we can be more sophisticated. We would expect:

- context to be crucial, since others in the organisation usually set the task, expect the outcomes, and provide the resources
- task to be vital, since task type and task difficulty clearly make task achievement more or less probable
- processes to be important, since all four processes are necessary for the team to approach the task, continue addressing it, and keep their client on-side
- roles to play a part, since tasks can't be undertaken and processes can't be carried through unless people with the right skills and knowledge are prepared to contribute them.

Which of these four components of the model contributes most to task achievement? Perhaps this is a meaningless question, since they are all so closely related. It is probably just as much the quality of these relationships as the components themselves which explains success. However, one thing we can say. The team's organisational context and how the team manages it are more important than we've so far realised.[19] After all, others in the organisation:

- oriented the team towards its task
- provided it with its resources

- set its final deadline
- monitor its progress.

This degree of dependency can make it very difficult for the team to keep the necessary autonomy (particularly important when it's defining issues and having ideas about how to tackle them). How the team manages its boundary relationships is crucial. Recent research on 45 teams developing new high tech products[20] showed that senior management rated the team's performance and innovation more highly in various areas when the team took care of several boundary relationships, as follows:

- If people in the team adopted an ambassadorial role towards others in the organisation, that is
  — persuading them of the team's importance
  — lobbying for support for the team's decisions
  — reporting progress toward task achievement
  — watching out for threats, changes in strategy or politics
  — deflecting interference and excessive demands,
  then the team was more likely to meet its budgets and schedules and to be considered innovative.
- If people in the team coordinated the technical task issues and cooperated with other teams, then the team was likely to be rated more innovative.
- But if the team spent a lot of time scanning its environment for marketing and technical ideas, then performance was rated lower. Perhaps a case of paralysis by analysis, or perhaps a lack of confidence. After all, a history of prior success can boost a team's performance no end.[21]
- Finally, if the team imports other people from its own or other organisations into the team, then it performs better (but it's less satisfied and cohesive).[22]

So there are a wide variety of team success factors; but perhaps the most crucial are about how the team manages its context.

Summary

- Teamworking is a way of integrating individuals' knowledge into the organisational knowledge process.
- Our concepts of teamworking have been held back by two pervasive myths: the All Friends Together myth and the Seven Stages of Team myth.
- A new model of teamworking includes the elements of context, tasks, processes, roles, and outcomes.

- Tasks are taken to include both the specific set task and the task of learning.
- Different tasks require predominantly different processes.
- Processes are four in number: achieving motivation and momentum; defining issues and getting ideas; managing the team boundaries; evaluating progress and outcomes.
- Different processes require predominantly different roles.
- Roles are four in number: traditionalists, visionaries, catalysts, and loyalists.
- The most under-rated predictor of team success is the process of how it manages its boundaries.

Notes

1 C. Coulson-Thomas and T. Coe, *The Flat Organisation: Philosophy and Practice* (British Institute of Management, Corby, 1991).

2 T.J. Peters and R.H. Waterman, *In Search of Excellence: Lessons from American's Best-run Companies* (Harper and Row, New York, 1982).

3 J.R. Katzenbach and D.K. Smith, 'The discipline of teams', *Harvard Business Review*, 71, 2 (1993), pp. 111–20.

4 Ibid., p. 112.

5 Ibid., p. 113.

6 C.E. Larson and F.M.J. Lafasto, *Teamwork: What Must Go Right/What Can Go Wrong* (Sage, Newbury Park, CA, 1989).

7 E. Sundstrom, K.P. De Meuse and D. Futnell, 'Work teams: applications and effectiveness', *American Psychologist*, 45 (1990), pp. 120–33.

8 R.A. Guzzo and G.P. Shea, 'Group performance and intergroup relations in organisations', in M.D. Dunnette and L.M. Hough (eds), *Handbook of Industrial and Organisational Psychology*, 2nd edn, vol. 3 (Consulting Psychologists Press, Palo Alto, CA, 1991).

9 B.W. Tuckman, 'Developmental sequence in small groups', *Psychological Bulletin*, 63 (1965), pp. 384–99.

10 C.J.G. Gersick, 'Time and transition in work teams: toward a new model of group development', *Academy of Management Journal*, 31, 1 (1988), pp. 9–41.

11 Larson and Lafasto, *Teamwork*.

12 D.L. Gladstein, 'Groups in context: a model of task group effectiveness', *Administrative Science Quarterly*, 29 (1984), pp. 499–517.

13 C.J.G. Gersick, 'Time and transition'.

14 D.G. Ancona and D.F. Caldwell, 'Bridging the boundary: external activity and performance in organisational teams', *Administrative Science Quarterly*, 37 (1992), pp. 634–65.

15 R.M. Belbin, *Management Teams: Why they Succeed or Fail* (Heinemann, London, 1981).

16 A. Furnham, H. Steele and D. Pendleton, 'A psychometric assessment of the Belbin Team-Role Self Perception Inventory', *Journal of Occupational and Organisational Psychology*, 66, 3 (1993), pp. 245–57.

17 I.B. Myers, *Myers-Briggs. Type Indicator* (Consulting Psychologists Press, Palo Alto, CA, 1988).

18 G.P. Shea and R.A. Guzzo, 'Group effectiveness: what really matters?' *Sloan Management Review*, 28 (1987), pp. 25–31.

19 Ibid.
20 Ancona and Caldwell, 'Bridging the boundary'.
21 Shea and Guzzo, 'Group effectiveness'.
22 D.G. Ancona, 'Outward bound: strategies for team survival in the organisation', *Academy of Management Journal*, 33 (1990), pp. 334–65.

26

The trouble with teams

The Economist

Togetherness has its perils

Peter Cook, a British satirist who died on January 9th [1995], loved to poke fun at British private schools and their cult of team spirit. But if you listened to management theorists, you would think that these schools had unwittingly stumbled upon the magic secret of business success. With teams all the rage, management theorists are earning fat fees by proffering advice on how to build them and how to inculcate team spirit.

At first sight, the virtues of teamwork look obvious. Teams make workers happier, by giving them the feeling that they are shaping their own jobs. They increase efficiency by eliminating layers of managers whose job was once to pass orders downwards. And, in principle, they enable a company to draw on the skills and imagination of a whole workforce, instead of relying on specialists to watch out for mistakes and suggest improvements.

Having started with corporate giants such as Toyota, Motorola, and General Electric, the fashion for teams has spread rapidly. A recent survey suggested that 'cell manufacturing' – in which small groups of workers make entire products – is being experimented with at more than half of America's manufacturing plants. And teams are growing more powerful as well as more numerous. Their task was at first to execute decisions under the supervision of managers, not to make decisions. The current fashion, however, is for self-management.

Companies as different as Xerox (office equipment), Monsanto (chemicals) and Johnsville Sausage (you guessed) are allowing teams to decide on everything from hiring and firing to organising the flow of work. At New United Motor Manufacturing, a joint venture run in Fremont, California, by General Motors and Toyota, teams of workers elect their own leaders and invent ways of improving quality and efficiency.

Hewlett-Packard, a computer maker, has gone even further in mixing the specialisms represented in single teams. Its teams bring together engineers, technical writers, marketing managers, lawyers, purchasing professionals and shop-floor workers. At Corning's ceramics plant in Erwin, New York, teams are fed business information so that they can understand how their plant is faring in the market. Informed workers, it is assumed, are less likely to make unreasonable wage demands.

Still, it would not surprise every inmate of a British private school to learn that teams are not always flawless ways to motivate and inspire people. Like many management fads, the one for teams is beginning to produce its trickle of disappointments. A.T. Kearney, a consultancy that continues to favour teams, found in a survey that nearly seven out of ten teams fail to produce the desired results.

A common error, says A.T. Kearney, is to create teams instead of taking more radical decisions. In many businesses it is still more effective to automate work than to reorganise the workforce. A few years ago Sweden's Volvo was praised for introducing self-governing teams in its car factories in Kalmar and Uddevalla, in order to make the work more interesting. More interesting it duly became, but also so expensive that the company was forced to close the experimental plants and concentrate production at Gothenburg, on a traditional assembly line.

Even when creating teams really is the appropriate solution to a firm's problem, managers often make a hash of running them. A typical mistake is the failure to set clear objectives. Another is to introduce teams without changing the firm's pattern of appraisal and reward from an individual to a collective system. That can send the workforce fatally mixed signals: employees are expected on the one hand to pull together, on the other to compete for individual rewards.

Teamwork, moreover, costs money, the biggest additional expense being training. Not unreasonably, members of supposedly 'self-managing' teams start wondering how to manage. This gives birth to an epidemic of woolly courses on 'conflict management' and 'stress resolution'. Meetings swallow time as 'empowered' workers break off from the tedium of making things and chat endlessly instead about 'process improvement' or 'product imperfections'.

Although many such courses are superfluous, advocates of team-based production concede that the best teams are made up of people with broad enough skills to step easily into each other's shoes. Providing such 'cross-training', as the theorists call it, is arduous. In some of the more complicated team structures, such as those in chemical plants, it can take team members six to ten years to learn all the jobs they might be called upon to do.

The iron law of oligarchy

However, the chief problem with teams is political. Almost invariably, their creation undermines some existing distribution of power in a firm. Middle managers often see shop-floor teams as a threat to their authority, and perhaps to their livelihoods; many workers see teams as a source of division and a goad to overwork. On at least two occasions American unions have used the National Labor Relations Act of 1935 (which makes it unlawful for an employer to dominate or interfere with the formation or administration of a labour organisation) to foil attempts to introduce teamwork.

Besides, although the cheery vocabulary of teamwork makes excitable use of words such as 'empowerment', teams usually replace top-down managerial control with peer pressure, a force that is sometimes no less coercive. 'People try to meet the team's expectations,' says one worker at New United Motor in Fremont, 'and under peer pressure they end up pushing themselves too hard.'

Some workers may prefer being told what to do to shouldering the burden of decisions themselves. Those who welcome responsibility sometimes find it hard to discipline their wayward colleagues. And there is always a danger that teams will impose a deadly uniformity and stifle the special qualities of individuals. As many a graduate of Britain's private schools will tell you, such places made little use of the brainy wimp who hated rugby and spent a childhood shivering on the sidelines. That, in a way, was Peter Cook's point, and one that management theorists have been slow to notice.

PART 5
DEVELOPING STAFF

27

The Peter Principle

Laurence J. Peter and Raymond Hull

When I was a boy I was taught that the men upstairs knew what they were doing. I was told, 'Peter, the more you know, the further you go.' So I stayed in school until I graduated from college and then went forth into the world clutching firmly these ideas and my new teaching certificate. During the first year of teaching I was upset to find that a number of teachers, school principals, supervisors and superintendents appeared to be unaware of their professional responsibilities and incompetent in executing their duties. For example my principal's main concerns were that all window shades be at the same level, that classrooms should be quiet and that no one step on or near the rose beds. The superintendent's main concerns were that no minority group, no matter how fanatical, should ever be offended and that all official forms be submitted on time. The children's education appeared farthest from the administrator mind.

At first I thought this was a special weakness of the school system in which I taught so I applied for certification in another province. I filled out the special forms, enclosed the required documents and complied willingly with all the red tape. Several weeks later, back came my application and all the documents!

No, there was nothing wrong with my credentials; the forms were correctly filled out; an official departmental stamp showed that they had been received in good order. But an accompanying letter said, 'The new regulations require that such forms cannot be accepted by the Department of Education unless they have been registered at the Post Office to ensure safe delivery. Will you please remail the forms to the Department, making sure to register them this time?'

From L.J. Peter and R. Hull, *The Peter Principle*, London, Souvenir, 1994, pp. 19–27.

I began to suspect that the local school system did not have a monopoly on incompetence.

As I looked further afield, I saw that every organization contained a number of persons who could not do their jobs.

A universal phenomenon

Occupational incompetence is everywhere. Have you noticed it? Probably we all have noticed it.

We see indecisive politicians posing as resolute statesmen and the 'authoritative source' who blames his misinformation on 'situational imponderables'. Limitless are the public servants who are indolent and insolent; military commanders whose behavioral timidity belies their dreadnought rhetoric, and governors whose innate servility prevents their actually governing. In our sophistication, we virtually shrug aside the immoral cleric, corrupt judge, incoherent attorney, author who cannot write and English teacher who cannot spell. At universities we see proclamations authored by administrators whose own office communications are hopelessly muddled; and droning lectures from inaudible or incomprehensible instructors.

Seeing incompetence at all levels of every hierarchy – political, legal, educational and industrial – I hypothesized that the cause was some inherent feature of the rules governing the placement of employees. Thus began my serious study of the ways in which employees move upward through a hierarchy, and of what happens to them after promotion.

For my scientific data hundreds of case histories were collected. Here are three typical examples.

Municipal government file, case no. 17

J.S. Minion[1] was a maintenance foreman in the public works department of Excelsior City. He was a favorite of the senior officials at City Hall. They all praised his unfailing affability.

'I like Minion,' said the superintendent of works. 'He has good judgment and is always pleasant and agreeable.'

This behavior was appropriate for Minion's position: he was not supposed to make policy, so he had no need to disagree with his superiors.

The superintendent of works retired and Minion succeeded him. Minion continued to agree with everyone. He passed to his foreman every suggestion that came from above. The resulting conflicts in policy, and the continual changing of plans, soon demoralized the department. Complaints poured in from the Mayor and other officials, from taxpayers and from the maintenance-workers' union.

Minion still says 'Yes' to everyone, and carries messages briskly back and forth between his superiors and his subordinates. Nominally a superintendent, he actually does the work of a messenger. The maintenance department regularly exceeds its budget, yet fails to fulfill its program of work. In short, Minion, a competent foreman, became an incompetent superintendent.

Service industries file, case no. 3

E. Tinker was exceptionally zealous and intelligent as an apprentice at G. Reece Auto Repair Inc., and soon rose to journeyman mechanic. In this job he showed outstanding ability in diagnosing obscure faults, and endless patience in correcting them. He was promoted to foreman of the repair shop.

But here his love of things mechanical and his perfectionism become liabilities. He will undertake any job that he thinks looks interesting, no matter how busy the shop may be. 'We'll work it in somehow,' he says.

He will not let a job go until he is fully satisfied with it.

He meddles constantly. He is seldom to be found at his desk. He is usually up to his elbows in a dismantled motor and while the man who should be doing the work stands watching, other workmen sit around waiting to be assigned new tasks. As a result the shop is always overcrowded with work, always in a muddle, and delivery times are often missed.

Tinker cannot understand that the average customer cares little about perfection – he wants his car back on time! He cannot understand that most of his men are less interested in motors than in their pay checks. So Tinker cannot get on with his customers or with his subordinates. He was a competent mechanic, but is now an incompetent foreman.

Military file, case no. 8

Consider the case of the late renowned General A. Goodwin. His hearty, informal manner, his racy style of speech, his scorn for petty regulations and his undoubted personal bravery made him the idol of his men. He led them to many well-deserved victories.

When Goodwin was promoted to field marshal he had to deal, not with ordinary soldiers, but with politicians and allied generalissimos.

He would not conform to the necessary protocol. He could not turn his tongue to the conventional courtesies and flatteries. He quarreled with all the dignitaries and took to lying for days at a time, drunk and sulking, in his trailer. The conduct of the war slipped out of his hands into those of his subordinates. He had been promoted to a position that he was incompetent to fill.

An important clue!

In time I saw that all such cases had a common feature. The employee had been promoted from a position of competence to a position of incompetence. I saw that, sooner or later, this could happen to every employee in every hierarchy.

Hypothetical case file, case no. 1

Suppose you own a pill-rolling factory, Perfect Pill Incorporated. Your foreman pill roller dies of a perforated ulcer. You need a replacement. You naturally look among your rank-and-file pill rollers.

Miss Oval, Mrs Cylinder, Mr Ellipse and Mr Cube all show various degrees of incompetence. They will naturally be ineligible for promotion. You will choose – other things being equal – your most competent pill roller, Mr Sphere, and promote him to foreman.

Now suppose Mr Sphere proves competent as foreman. Later, when your general foreman, Legree, moves up to Works Manager, Sphere will be eligible to take his place.

If, on the other hand, Sphere is an incompetent foreman, he will get no more promotion. He has reached what I call his 'level of incompetence'. He will stay there till the end of his career.

Some employees, like Ellipse and Cube, reach a level of incompetence in the lowest grade and are never promoted. Some, like Sphere (assuming he is not a satisfactory foreman), reach it after one promotion.

E. Tinker, the automobile repair-shop foreman, reached his level of incompetence on the third stage of the hierarchy. General Goodwin reached his level of incompetence at the very top of the hierarchy.

So my analysis of hundreds of cases of occupational incompetence led me on to formulate *The Peter Principle*:

> In a hierarchy every employee tends to rise to his level of incompetence.

A new science!

Having formulated the Principle, I discovered that I had inadvertently founded a new science, hierarchiology, the study of hierarchies.

The term 'hierarchy' was originally used to describe the system of church government by priests graded into ranks. The contemporary meaning includes any organization whose members or employees are arranged in order of rank, grade or class.

Hierarchiology, although a relatively recent discipline, appears to have great applicability to the fields of public and private administration.

This means you!

My Principle is the key to an understanding of all hierarchal systems, and therefore to an understanding of the whole structure of civilization. A few eccentrics try to avoid getting involved with hierarchies, but everyone in business, industry, trade-unionism, politics, government, the armed forces, religion and education is so involved. All of them are controlled by the Peter Principle.

Many of them, to be sure, may win a promotion or two, moving from one level of competence to a higher level of competence. But competence in that new position qualifies them for still another promotion. For each individual, for *you*, for *me*, the final promotion is from a level of competence to a level of incompetence.

So, given enough time – and assuming the existence of enough ranks in the hierarchy – each employee rises to, and remains at, his level of incompetence. *Peter's Corollary* states:

In time, every post tends to be occupied by an employee who is incompetent to carry out its duties.

Who turns the wheels?

You will rarely find, of course, a system in which *every* employee has reached his level of incompetence. In most instances, something is being done to further the ostensible purposes for which the hierarchy exists.

Work is accomplished by those employees who have not yet reached their level of incompetence.

Notes

1 Some names have been changed, in order to protect the guilty.

28

How managers can become developers

Alan Mumford

Work-based learning, in which managers recognise and take advantage of learning opportunities in the course of their everyday work, can be a more powerful way of developing people than formal, set-piece management development courses which are seen as being tacked on to the job of managing.

The manager of a hotel is called from his office. An angry customer has complained to the receptionist that he had been interrupted in his bedroom three times in the space of half an hour, by a cleaner, the housekeeper, and someone checking the minibar. The manager takes his new deputy with him – 'an interesting experience for you' – and they both listen while the customer repeats his complaint.

The manager goes through the reasons why three different employees arrived in such a short space of time: 'It is, of course, part of our policy of providing excellent service.' The customer departs, still expressing dissatisfaction.

The hotel manager and deputy return to the manager's room. The manager sits behind his desk, blows out his cheeks and says 'So how would you have handled him?'

A great deal of management development occurs in this way. An unplanned experience, a question from one manager to another, a discussion reviewing facts and opinions, a decision about what to do in a similar situation. Potentially these are all the elements of an effective learning cycle.

There are some other things we know about this kind of experience. First, managers constantly claim that they learn from such experiences. Secondly, they rarely recognise at the time that they are 'learning' – they think they are simply 'managing'. Thirdly, they may not have been introduced to the idea of a complete process in which the elements of learning are balanced. Finally and most significant, helpful interventions by the boss are all too rare.

There are three main developments in the increasing provision of work-based learning for managers. Although they overlap both

Abridged from A. Mumford, 'How managers can become developers', *Personnel Management*, June 1993, pp. 42–5.

chronologically and in terms of content, they have been action learning (Reg Revans), the learning organisation (Peter Senge, Mike Pedler, John Burgoyne, Tom Boydell), and the competency approach (Richard Boyatzis).

The shift towards work-based learning has occurred in part because of the powerful intellectual contribution of such people, but an even more important driving factor, perhaps, has been the demands of consumers for valid and relevant development.

In fact, the three parts of the theoretical drive towards work-based learning coincide with the accidental reality of informal development stressed in the hotel scenario above. Not only are they all centred on learning from real work, they all demand that management development should succeed in putting life into an old management responsibility. If we accept that managers have a major responsibility for developing those who work with them, all these themes demand a major effort from those managers.

In the UK the competency approach adopted through the Management Charter Initiative – with its emphasis on applied prior learning or crediting competence – will require successful intervention by bosses in a form which has not seriously been tackled in most organisations.

The stimulus provided by the theories mentioned above, and the demand from managers for effective help with their development, mean we have to combine three elements to produce an effective management development system:

Self-development A recognition that individuals can learn but are unlikely to be taught, and that the initiative for development often rests with the individual.

Organisation-derived development The development of those systems of formal development beloved of personnel and management development specialists.

Boss-derived development Those actions undertaken by a senior manager with others, most frequently around real problems at work.

Formal management development systems insist that managers appraise, identify development needs, and provide time and money for people to attend courses. These are valuable and necessary processes through which we try to balance the often frantic pressures at work with more effective and planned attention to performance and development. These formal processes could certainly be improved and extended.[1]

The significance of the case I am making can be assessed in at least two ways. If my analysis of the three major current themes of management development is accurate, how far do current formal schemes effectively provide the enhanced role of the boss in developing others?

A slightly different form of test could be applied by looking at the resources currently devoted to helping managers to help others to learn. If we add up the days devoted to designing appraisal schemes and to running courses on effective appraisal, and compare that with the time devoted in most organisations to how managers can assist in the development of others, the disproportion is staggering. Some organisations run courses on how to be an effective coach or mentor. Useful though these can be, they all too often give managers the idea that the process of developing others is something which is added on to management as a special activity, not an integral part of the process itself.

There are a number of things we have to do to enable managers to develop others more effectively – including establishing why it is important, giving them a better understanding of the learning process, and developing the skills involved. The starting point for managers must be the managerial situation which provides the opportunity for development.

- A boss arrives in a subordinate's office at 8.30 a.m. one Tuesday and says: 'I have been thinking about that problem with client Y you raised with me. I think it might mean not just a specific problem of that kind but something that runs across several. Why don't we get together for two hours on Friday, review what the issues are and how we might tackle them?'
- A customer phones with a quality problem arising from a recent major delivery. They want the supplier to send their production manager and quality manager to see the reality of the problem on the customer's side. The production manager decides to take a graduate trainee with him, saying 'Keep your eyes open, take notes and we will talk about it afterwards.'
- A director close to retirement has been given a significant project to do, and recruits a young man thought to have high potential as the finance department's representative. After the first two meetings of the project group the director calls this person in and says: 'I would just like to talk over some of the things that are happening on the group. How do you think things are going?'

These examples, like the hotel case with which we began, contain some recognition on the part of the boss (or, in the last case, the mentor) that the work situation offered an opportunity for learning. Unfortunately such examples are relatively rare, and that is why our first concern in helping managers to help others learn must be on helping them to recognise opportunities, and then to use them more effectively.

The Big O

Managers and, sadly, some management development advisers think too often in terms of what I call the Big O: 'We have this splendid chance for you to move from sales into marketing.' Even more to the point: 'We are moving you to work for Jane Smith instead of John Brown. You will find she is a quite different sort of manager.'

Presenting individuals with this kind of opportunity is usually better than not providing them with an opportunity at all. However, we need to give much more detailed attention to exactly what kind of learning opportunities are likely to exist within the Big O. What new experiences will be on offer? What are the differences in the work? Who are the new and different people the younger manager may encounter?

The best way to help managers to help others is to get them to start by considering the kind of experiences from which they have learned. The following exercise has the advantage of being both simple and immensely productive:

Identify the two most helpful learning experiences you have had, and the two most unhelpful.

Once the general ground of learning from experience has been established, it is possible to go to a more specific exercise:

Think of an experience of being helped by another manager. What was the experience, and what did the other manager do to help you?

It is possible to ask people to do these exercises without any stimulus or suggestion of what they might consider. An alternative or supplementary approach is to give them a list of situations in which a manager can offer assistance to others. The list is lengthy but includes learning from a new project, membership of a task force, confronting difficult colleagues and reviewing completed tasks.[2]

The crucial point when helping managers to recognise such opportunities is to get them to consider first the activity or the situation, and not to ask them to think initially about learning opportunities at all. Managers think in terms of activities, not learning opportunities!

It is often a discovery for managers that things they have considered purely as work activities are learning opportunities as well. Like the Molière character who discovered he had been speaking prose all his life, they can be helped to see what they have always taken to be 'natural work' can be used also as a creative learning opportunity.

Our main concern must be to facilitate learning through our understanding of real work in the manager's world, rather than attempting to impose separate management development processes. Take the following examples:

- A manager does a lot of coaching and counselling informally, finding it effective and less threatening than to be called into the manager's office. They just sit down with someone and say: 'How is it going? Tell me what you are working on.' That gives the people a chance to raise things with the manager without making too big a thing of it.
- A factory manager is involved in making the arrangements to close down his factory over a nine-month period. He arranges a meeting with all his subordinates in a group where they discuss each week what has happened, how their plans are going and what actions need to be taken. Then at the end of it he sets aside 20 minutes to ask what they have all learned from what they have done that week, and whether there is there anything they should do differently.

The major message we have to convey to managers in helping them to help others is that we are not encouraging them to take up totally new activities. Managers do not talk about coaching much, unless they have been on a coaching course. They talk about problem solving; we should start from there, not from 'How to be a good coach'.

However, what we are adding to their normal understanding of their managerial work is an extra dimension, explicitly involving learning. Learning should be drawn out from the managerial experience, not bolted on as a quite different extra. For people fully to get the benefit from that experience they need to understand some concepts and techniques which will help them to learn more effectively. One, the learning cycle, was introduced at the beginning of this article. The factory manager quoted above is engaged in the reviewing stage of the learning cycle.

Two important practical points emerge from thinking about this kind of approach. The first is that if you simply suggest to a boss that they ought to lead a learning review, the response is not likely to be favourable unless they have already had some kind of introduction built on their own experience. Even more significant, the idea of a review is very much a managerial concept, not just a learning one. Managers are used to the idea of looking back to see whether things worked out, and if not why not.

For most managers most of the time, helping others with learning will mean retrospectively reviewing an experience rather than the prospective planning of learning from a future experience. Of course we need to encourage the latter, but retrospective analysis is not only more in tune with the way in which managers behave in other respects of their managerial life, it also provides immediate practical examples through which a manager can be encouraged to work.

Wrong emphasis

Perhaps this is why some formal management development processes have not worked as effectively in the past as we would have liked. We have put too much emphasis on planning ahead, and not enough on enabling managers to use, understand and then build on their past learning experiences. Once managers have been engaged in helping to interpret, re-interpret and better understand their past work experiences, they can be encouraged to help others to go through the same process. Beyond this there lies the rosy future of better identified future learning opportunities.

In a sense there is plenty of anecdotal evidence that the kind of approach suggested here can work. Some managers have always given time and attention to the development of their subordinates. The question is not whether some managers do it naturally, but whether we can encourage more managers to do it, equally naturally but with some previous encouragement and thought.

My experience on this is hopeful. I find managers are intrigued [and] stimulated [by] and enjoy the kind of activities described here. Again comparisons can be drawn with appraisal training. All too often this is approached by the management developer with a firmness of purpose only equalled by the unwillingness of managers to participate. The situations and processes described here recognise and build on things which managers are aware of, rather than imposing something which is all too often outside their experience and their sense of commitment.

Managers develop others for a variety of reasons. Sometimes the formal system instructs them to do so. Sometimes they expect to reduce problems by increasing the ability of their subordinates to handle problems on their own. Nor should we ignore less self-centred reasons. For at least some of them what I call the principle of reciprocity occurs. Managers like helping to develop others not just because of the direct return in the sense of performance, but because they get a glow of satisfaction from having helped someone.

The task of helping managers to develop others does not have to be as difficult as management development systems have seemed to make it, if we base our guidance on using real situations, rather than contriving special management development processes.

Notes

1 Alan Mumford, *Management Development: Strategies for Action*, 2nd edn (IPM, 1993).

2 Peter Honey and Alan Mumford, *Manual of Learning Opportunities* (Honey, 1989).

29

Special needs, different solutions

Alan Mumford

Women managers – a natural disproportion?

At least 40 per cent of the UK workforce are women, according to the 1987 *Labour Force Survey*, yet at 27 per cent the proportion of women managers is much lower (and the figure of 8 per cent for women directors illustrates the point even more dramatically). There can, broadly, be two views about this disparity. One would be that the disproportionately fewer women managers and directors reflect women's actual competence or their own 'natural' career choices. A second view is that this disproportion is inappropriate either ethically or in terms of effective use of resources.

Attention to this subject is a relatively new phenomenon. Tom Roberts's book,[1] in many ways an excellent guide to orthodox management development, does not mention women at all, even in the 1974 edition. I remember the disbelief of many readers when a survey of which I was the lead author[2] suggested that the training needs of women managers might be different from those of their male colleagues. We have moved on a long way since then in terms of recognizing the issue, and to some extent in terms of under- standing; but we have perhaps moved less far towards effective action. One of the problems is recognizing precisely what the issues actually are, and then what objectives might be appropriate for the development of women managers.

I can already sense the objections forming in the minds of two different types of reader. One group may be feeling that there is a simple explanation for the lower proportion of women managers, and that a more detailed analysis of the issue is unnecessary. Others may feel that to give a special section to women managers is to place them in a ghetto. In this group will be the 'cream rises to the top' sub-group, which will include some successful women. Such people tend to argue that although there are special problems for women leaders, it is the successful overcoming of those problems which demonstrates that you are special as a leader and not as a woman.

From A. Mumford, *Management Development*, 2nd edn, London: Institute of Personnel Management, 1993, pp. 178–92.

They therefore deprecate any special measures to redress the balance on the grounds that they lead to tokenism or to reducing the value accorded to achieved success.

The proposition that the lower proportion of women managers is in some sense 'natural' appears in its most respectable form in terms of career choice. It is argued that women as child bearers actually leave employment at a crucial time in terms of their possible development as managers, and that many of them neither want nor expect managerial careers. Organizational attitudes which mirror that expectation are therefore thought to be understandable and proper. This view is deeply engrained in some women and in many male-dominated organizations.

However, the major shift in women's views about their own lives, and the change in their expectations and wants about their careers, have created a considerable 'push' for a change of attitude. This has been matched by 'pull' in some organizations, notably by some of the major banks. To some extent encouraged by national debate, if not action, generated by the Equal Opportunities Commission, and to some extent fuelled by recognition of their own needs, organizations are gradually becoming less accepting of traditional views about women's careers. The word 'expectations' is extremely important here. A small minority of people who are prepared to fight hard and push has gradually been augmented by a larger number whose previous negative expectations have to some extent been changed by the apparent success of the pushers.

Formal management development action taken to change both the actuality and the expectations about career opportunities for women includes:

- developing a clear policy statement directed at increasing the number of women managers and accompanying it with procedures and monitoring processes
- reviewing selection processes and selection criteria in order to control, if not eliminate, bias against women
- developing special arrangements such as extended maternity leave, career breaks with accompanying fast track training processes to enable women to return to work more quickly or more effectively.

The second type of 'it is only natural' response to the lower number of women managers is more difficult to define and counter. It essentially revolves around questions of how women perform as managers and how their performance is perceived by their surrounding male colleagues. This already difficult issue is then complicated by a second question. Should women managers behave like men managers anyway, or should they behave differently? Or should more male managers try to employ the supposedly characteristic female processes evidenced by some successful women managers?

Both men and women tend to agree that women managers behave differently from their male colleagues. While women who accept the 'difference' argument will tend to say 'different but as good as', men will, more characteristically, say 'different and less effective than'. Some women managers, or course, do not accept that there is a difference in how they carry out their work, and an American article[3] based on a matched study of 2,000 managers showed that women do not manage differently from men. This research evidence might seem to support the views of those successful women who tend to argue that there is no basis for claiming that women managers are different (although it says nothing about the proposition that they are actually held back).

We are faced with a number of stereotypes: of men about women, of women about men, of women about themselves. Some men point to the success of a small number of political leaders. There is, indeed, a small group of highly successful women politicians, some of them coming from even more unlikely environments than our own Margaret Thatcher. The success of Golda Meir, Indira Gandhi, Mrs Bandaranaike, Benazir Bhutto and some lesser known Scandinavian politicians may seem to support the stereotype 'it shows what can be done without laws on equal opportunities.' Yet senior women remain a tiny minority in politics, in the judiciary, in the civil service and local government.

No woman in industry or commerce has run a huge organization and received a damehood. Such female role models as there are in industry and commerce, like Anita Roddick of Body Shop or Steve Shirley of F International, tend to be important but atypical. As Marshall[4] points out, much of early discussion of women managers concentrated on the belief that men and women managers operated in essentially the same way in order to facilitate a more positive view of women's potential. She argues that these similarities have been overstated at the expense of legitimate and useful differences.

> Women tend to emphasise people management over task structuring, whilst men have opposite priorities; women are often inhibited in exercising position power because other people reject or undermine their use of authority, stereotype them in devalued female roles.

Like other authors, she comments on the male emphasis on individualism, competition and control (in contrast to interdependence, collaboration and acceptance) as defining the values to which women managers are supposed to adhere if they wish to join the managerial club.

Writers who have highlighted these competing styles and values between men and women have not made the task of management development any easier; but they may have made it more effective. They have also helped to persuade some men to view some of their own values differently. If women have the capacity not only to be different but to be usefully and effectively different by bringing to the party some female styles and values as well as some effective male attributes, might not the reverse also apply? The article by Simmons[5] shows what can be achieved by causing men to question whether breaking gender bounds will lead to more effective management.

There has been a shift among organizations and women themselves about careers and managerial jobs. There has also been an accompanying shift in the expectations of a minority of men about women with whom they share their lives. Women will no longer necessarily surrender their careers either to the demands of child bearing or to their husbands' careers. The issue of dual-career families is the sharpest instance of this. This is particularly significant because the social circumstances of women – when they are married and have children – often make planned career development more difficult. It is understandable, although not appropriate, that the (often male) management development adviser should accept these difficulties rather than try to overcome them. Yet they are difficulties which will increasingly need to be overcome for men as well. Cavalier assumptions that men will go where they are sent, and that wives will go with them, have ceased to be tenable – for men or women.

Up till now women managers have coped with the difficulties involved in a different way from men. According to one UK survey,[6] 39 per cent of women managers were unmarried, divorced or widowed, as against 8 per cent of men (the difference is slightly larger in the United States). The appropriate inference is not that more men ought to be similarly lonely or 'available', but that this should not be an apparently necessary requirement for so many women.

The personnel function and the management development specialism point to another special feature of women managers. There has been a tendency to push them into 'caring functions'. To some extent this process is a reflection of societal stereotypes of desired female behaviour, of the failure to provide effective choice at school and of subsequent early career choice. The fact that we are more likely to find a female personnel director than production director is much more likely to be the product of these earlier factors than later career development in any particular organization. Although in some respects the role model offered by Margaret Thatcher as the toughest man in her cabinet is unfortunate, her success in carrying out her chief executive role is important. What is needed is some more role models of women moving not through the caring departments (as they used to be considered) of Education or Social Services, but through the Department of Trade and Industry, the Foreign Office and the Treasury.

Women managers – different development needs?

Women managers actually face a different situation from men managers. The predominant managerial style is most likely to be male in orientation. The woman manager is therefore faced with the issue of whether, and how, to adopt managerial forms of behaviour which may contradict or conflict with her existing style of behaviour. Some women have obviously long since adopted male forms of behaviour and have no problems of such adaptation. For others the need to adapt may include:

- coping with competition
- adopting at least some of the behaviour of male clubs (post-work socializing, discussion of predominantly male sports)
- the use of personal and role power
- developing individual self-awareness
- acquiring a positive self-image as a woman manager
  — self-confidence and assertiveness skills
  — dealing with stress.

The real issue for most women managers is how to handle the fact of being a woman within what is likely to be a majority group of male managers in an organization which has little sympathy for and understanding of the contribution that women might make, let alone their potentially different contribution. It should also be emphasized that at least some women managers will choose to follow the line indicated by Marshall[7] in which adaptation to male domination is not seen as the only recourse.

Women managers – different development processes?

It is not surprising that male attitudes and behaviour on courses tend to follow the stereotypes about women found in the real world outside. Behaviour which is seen in men by men as normal, managerial assertiveness is seen by men in women as aggressive and strident. Women who do not behave according to the other kinds of stereotype are similarly pushed towards the supposedly 'feminine' behaviour corner. Women are expected to be concerned about the comfort of the group, to pour out the tea, to express emotion rather than to conceal it. They are treated with a form of superficial gallantry which emphasizes that they are being treated as a woman not as a manager. Alternatively their capacities are belittled by reference to their sexuality: 'I bet it's difficult having a serious discussion with a beauty like Jane in the group.'

Because of the difficulties women have in largely male managerial training and education situations, and because of the view that they have special needs anyway, women-only training groups were developed. There are two conflicting arguments over this. One says that since women have to survive in a predominantly male environment, it is unreal to provide them with women-only management training. Whatever else this may achieve, the absence of men will create a future problem of transferring any learning achieved. The alternative view is that the absence of men removes some unnecessary obstacles to learning, opens opportunities for more women to be more experimental with behaviour which may be helpful to them subsequently in the male environment. I am not aware of any research which provides a clear basis for deciding which of these views is true. There is evidence that a number of women feel they have benefited from women-only courses, in the ways indicated above. It is also the case that since some women nowadays are less prepared to accept inappropriate male behaviour towards them on courses, mixed courses can sometimes become a battleground for male/female issues rather than a learning experience related to the original objectives. It is argued on the other hand, by both men and women, that emphasizing differences by setting up women-only experiences is unhelpful.

It may be that the most useful process is to create special learning experiences for women to help them define and deal with the male world. So strategies for working cooperatively together, for understanding their relationships with men, and perhaps creating processes for challenging stereotypes all provide an appropriate focus. It is not so clear that women-only courses dealing with general management skills and requirements are desirable. Perhaps here the argument of enabling women to behave differently is less clearly dominant, as compared with the requirement for them to work even in a training context with male colleagues.

It will be noted that I am writing as a man who cannot possibly have the same recognition of the balance of feeling and requirement that a woman adviser might have. So an additional point might well be that the choice of whether to make an activity women-only should depend not only on the adviser (whether male or female) but on whether the prospective female participants actually want it that way. The case for women-only groups is well set out by Marshall.

The presence of men may be an inhibitor both to achieved learning and the expression of it by women. A related issue concerns whether women's learning processes differ from those of men. The common stereotype of the emotional and intuitive woman can be expressed in learning terms by saying that women are less responsive to hard rational approaches to learning and more responsive to particular situations and feelings. The view of women as intuitive certainly implies that their learning processes will be different from men's. One part of the answer may rest in those characteristics which women are said to share – the preference for a supportive, co-operative environment in which to learn as compared with the more characteristically competitive environment favoured by men.

However, this environmental point does not deal with the basic issue of whether women as a whole differ from men in their learning processes. On the Honey/Mumford Learning Styles Questionnaire (LSQ), the norms for 174 women differed scarcely at all from men on the Reflector and Theorist dimensions, and by only one point on the Activist (higher for women) and Pragmatist (lower for women) scores. These differences are not at a level of significance which suggests that women characteristically learn differently from men. The admittedly small sample of women in my director research similarly did not differ from their male director counterparts. The information on our LSQ is, however, different from that found by David Kolb in his Learning Styles Inventory (LSI).[8] On his dimensions, women have a much higher preference for what he calls 'abstract conceptualization', as compared with 'concrete experience'. The male scores are almost exactly opposite to the female on these dimensions. The difference in results from the LSQ may be related to the fact that the LSI brings in 'feelings' in a more overt way. My conclusion is that learning experiences should not be designed according to a stereotyped view that women will learn differently; they should be designed according to the nature of the particular group or the particular individual.

Nor is there any evidence that women learn better or worse from any particular kind of learning opportunity as compared with men. They are just as likely to learn or not learn from real tasks, projects, bosses, courses, as men are. The only area in which there may be some significant difference is that of the use of boss, colleagues or mentors. Here learning opportunities may be influenced by the stereotypes and actualities of male/female behaviour. In the scarce literature on learning from boss and colleagues there is no reference to women learning differently from men, nor is it my experience that this is so. But there may well be extra inhibitions and difficulties. The only area in which this has been researched has been that of mentors. For some time it was thought that women could only get on in an organization dominated by men by having a mentor; inevitably the mentor was most often a man. More recently, of course, female mentors have become available. Again the evidence slowly coming to hand conflicts with stereotypes. The assumption that a male mentor and a female protégée will inevitably provoke jealousy in others, and particularly the suspicion that the relationship has a sexual base, has been examined by Bowey.[9] This article shows that, comparing male and female mentors of females:

- the sexual issue was not large and was quite manageable
- resentment is created irrespective of whether the mentor was male or female
- there are positive benefits for both male and female mentors and their protégées both at and outside work.

Kram[10] offers rather less comfortable evidence. In her view 'collusion in stereotypical behaviours encourages women to maintain feelings of dependency and incompetence.' Clutterbuck[11] gives a useful review of the particular problems of male/female mentoring.

You may wish to test your own position, and your organization's, on a number of the issues raised here about women managers.

Exercise

1   What are my beliefs about why there are proportionately fewer women managers than there are women at work?
2   What do I believe my organization's beliefs to be?
3   Does my organization have any clear policies about women managers, and procedures to implement those policies?
4   What is my view about the existence of differences between the way in which a woman manager and a male manager will work?
5   Are there different management development needs for women?
6   What is my view and practice on the provision of women-only groups?
7   Do women learn differently from men? If so in what way?

Multinational needs

There are three major aspects which make management development in multinational organizations different from those which have a single national base:

- *differences in national culture*, with consequent differences, required styles and behaviours of managers
- *mixed management teams*, which require the effective integration of different cultures and styles

- *different management development systems*, involving a recognition that a system which works in one country may not work at all or in certain respects in another.

The major work of practical value on cultural issues in management development is still Hofstede.[12] Because his research was conducted in one major organization with a strong managerial culture, the differences in national style that he drew out were identifiably national rather than influenced by organizational structure, techniques or processes. Hofstede described culture as 'a collective programming of the mind'. In his research he found that value patterns differed along four main dimensions:

- large or small power distance
- strong or weak uncertainty avoidance
- individualism versus collectivism
- masculinity versus femininity.

The details of his definitions of these dimensions, and the attribution of them to particular countries, can be found in his book (see Chapter 32). We need only note here that he provides a research-based process for enabling managers to move beyond simply recognizing that people from other countries are different – and because they are different necessarily inferior or less effective! Working abroad, or working in your own country with managers from other countries, creates culture shock because your expectation of the right way of doing things differs from those of other countries. Those difficulties are, of course, exacerbated by language. The old joke about the United States and England being countries separated by a common language has the major merit of reminding us that it is all too easy to believe that another person has understood you. When the other person's language is not English, the difficulties that arise are often clearer, although equally the subject of horror stories and jokes.

The ethics of managers are another aspect of cultural belief. Some years ago I took part in a television programme and was fascinated to see how British-based managers attempted to defend the operation of different ethical practices outside the UK as compared with those they would use at home. An interesting analysis of this kind of issue occurred on some courses run for the Swedish company SAS. Participants were asked to list the values most important to them. An overwhelming majority of Swedish participants chose honesty as the most important; the value of honesty was not mentioned in the top fifteen by North American participants. Instead they listed competition, liberty and freedom. Competition is not an important value for Swedish managers or for Japanese managers. Different views about such issues were also found in Weinshall and Raveh.[13] Even more explicitly, they found that, in a case study about management failure, 2 per cent of French managers said 'fire him'; but 80 per cent of the American managers offered this solution.

The research studies here are important not least because they sometimes contradict stereotypes or perhaps provide clarification of the existence of a stereotype. As throughout this book, however, it is necessary to warn against generalization. Of course the casual informality of many American managers demonstrates the truth of a stereotype: but informality in personal relationships does not necessarily go with informality in communication within the managerial hierarchy. In a study I did of German and English managers, one group complained that the other was far too bound by rules of precedent and hierarchy. The British managers were astonished to find that it was the Germans who were making this complaint about them!

The question of the tightness of structure and responsibility, and the degree of openness in managerial relationships, is especially important in management development. Many UK and American books nowadays advocate much looser managerial relationships and concepts of teamwork which other countries, particularly in Asia and Africa, find quite bewildering and unusable.

It is therefore a major problem to adapt to the culture of a country when you are the expatriate manager. It is additionally difficult to manage cross-cultural relationships when you are participating in a mixed team of managers from several different cultures. I have worked with an American director working in England for an American multinational. Members of his team were predominantly British, but he also had several Germans, two other Americans and one solitary Frenchman. It so happened that he was extremely competent and flexible in his way of dealing with people; but even he had problems in trying to adapt his approach to the differing demands not merely of individuals, but of individuals with quite strong national characteristics. These factors affect the design and implementation of management development systems and influence perceptions about that implementation.

The comments about different cultures and management styles are significant for the design of systems. An appraisal scheme built on free and open exchange, including self-appraisal, may be well accepted in the United States, partially accepted in the United Kingdom and not accepted at all in some other countries. There has further been a major change in the patterns of job movement. The opportunities that used to exist in multinationals to send people abroad for a desirable period of experience in other countries are now much reduced. Understandably many countries prefer, and need, to develop their own managers instead of creating vacancies for managers from the parent organization. Desirable as it is that other countries should look after their own needs, this has substantially reduced certain kinds of management development opportunity for people from the parent company. An unfortunate consequence of this is that parent company senior managers may increasingly have had only visiting experience of the countries for which they may have senior responsibility at corporate headquarters. As Laurent[14] has shown, perceptions about careers and what it takes to develop careers may differ. American managers relate career to 'ambition and drive', while French managers see it as 'being labelled as having high potential'.

From a systematic management development point of view it may well be that the opportunities for posting abroad are diminishing at exactly the time when there is greater understanding of what needs to be done in order to make for a successful management appointment abroad! The advantages of distance and greater autonomy, which in many respects provide a good test of management competence, have to be balanced against the more solitary and isolated nature of the manager's work. There may well be greater risks, both political and commercial, involved in working abroad. And domestic problems can contribute to failure at least as often as they contribute to success. There is also the re-entry difficulty, which is now more problematic than it is for spacecraft. Finding the right slot at the right time for the returning manager, or even promising to do so before his departure abroad, can cause major headaches.

The main problem is the ethnocentric view of the world, held in the corporate headquarters of a multinational in the UK. It is not only that other countries and other cultures may respond negatively to the UK style. They may well have a substantially different view of appropriate management development practices. It is true that some British managers are as tired of hearing about the more effective Japanese practices as their predecessors were of hearing about the United States in the 1960s. [. . .]

There is one further aspect of cultural differences to be discussed. We have yet to see in the UK the evolution of managers from minority ethnic groups. In proportion to the population they are fewer than women, who have already started on the journey which will lead out of the ghetto. The main steps taken by ethnic minorities seem so far to have been into local government rather than industry or commerce. Cheap laughs are available to anyone on the occasional excesses of programmes on anti-racism. But the issue cannot be laughed away, since it involves ethics and/or the allocation of managerial resources.

Graduates

A number of organizations recruit graduates primarily to fill immediate technical or functional needs. After time, experience, and achieved performance they merge into the totality of the unit they have joined and their development as managers follows the normal path for that organization.

Other organizations recruit graduates less for such immediate technical or functional purposes than to create a pool of intelligent people with high potential as a means of providing for management of the future. The difference in objectives and immediate location for these two different kinds of graduate recruitment illustrates the problems that arise. Whereas the first group go into a proper job, although admittedly it may be below their intellectual level or ambition, the latter group often go into no clear functional stream.

The problems experienced by management trainees over the years recur, although they do seem to have diminished since the awful days of the 1950s. The problem of the Cook's tour, where graduates were hurtled around a number of departments for a few weeks or months at a time with no proper job at any staging point, were well known by the early 1960s. Few organizations now fall into that trap. More frequently organizations will put graduates or management trainees into departments for more substantial periods, or will employ them on specific tasks or projects. Not only is this something which intelligent graduates now demand, but it is something which organizations themselves have come to recognize as necessary if they are to make any judgement about the actual capacity of the graduates recruited.

There is no mystery about what to do with graduates. There needs to be a formal development programme for them which will include appropriate courses, they need to have assignments in particular units or departments long enough to establish that they have done a definable piece of work. If sharp distinctions are made between themselves and others of equivalent age but with no degree, the expectations and motivation of non-degree people will be reduced.

Of course one of the prime issues here is the same as for more experienced managers: whether the process of learning from the experiences offered to graduate entrants is actually effective in learning terms. Barrington's book[15] is an excellent guide to some aspects of this whole graduate training process, precisely because it focuses on issues about learning and not simply on issues about moving people between jobs.

[. . .] Some stereotypical thinking about MBA recruits has become firmly entrenched in a number of organizations. They are seen as expensive recruits who want to do the managing director's job before they have shown that they can manage a department. They are characterized as arrogant, as possessing intellectual and analytical skills rather than the practical skills on which so much effective management is believed to be based. Of course, if all organizations believed this then no business school would be able to run a traditional MBA programme. So the traditional picture is partial rather than complete. (Although some criticisms of the content and learning processes of traditional programmes are valid.) Current developments in MBA programmes all emphasize relevance and reality, whether they be the City University programme based around competencies or the IMC programme based on action learning. It does seem likely that the associated development of programmes which focus on particular organizational needs, whether on a consortium basis or an individual organization, will provide both greater demands and greater opportunities for effective management development. There is undoubtedly a group of young managers who want the discipline and structure of a formal MBA, but who also want it conducted in terms of more appropriate general management processes and more specific relevance to their own organization. The future growth of MBA programmes is more likely in this area than in that of providing open programmes offering a career break to middle managers.

Notes

1 T. Roberts, *Developing Effective Managers* (IPM, 1974).

2 Training Survey Unit, *Survey on Management Training and Development* (Department of Employment, 1971).

3 S. Fraker, 'Why women aren't getting to the top', *Fortune Magazine*, April (1984).

4 J. Marshall, 'Women managers', in A. Mumford (ed.), *A Handbook of Management Development* (Gower, 1991).

5 M. Simmons, 'Undoing men's gender conditioning', *Industrial and Commercial Training*, November (1986).

6 B. Alban Metcalfe, *Career Development of British Managers* (British Institute of Management, 1984).

7 Marshall, 'Women managers'.

8 D. Kolb, *Experiential Learning* (Prentice-Hall, 1984).

9 D. Bowey, 'Were men meant to mentor women?', *Training and Development*, February (1985).

10 K. Kram, 'Phases of the mentor relationship', *Academy of Management Journal*, 16, 4 (1983).

11 D. Clutterbuck, *Everyone Needs a Mentor*, 2nd edn (IPM, 1991).

12 G. Hofstede, *Culture's Consequences* (Sage, 1980).

13 T.D. Weinshall and Y.A. Raveh, *Managing Growing Organisations* (Wiley, 1983).

14 A. Laurent, 'The cross cultural puzzle', *Human Resource Management*, 25(1) (Spring 1986).

15 A. Barrington, *Learning about Management*, (McGraw Hill, 1985).

30

Appraisal: an idea whose time has gone?

Clive Fletcher

Has your organisation's basic approach to performance appraisal altered much recently? It certainly should have. Reflect for a moment on the radical restructuring most organisations have undergone in the last few years. They have become more organic and less mechanistic, with fewer levels and more flexible modes of operating.

Increasingly, managers have to build and manage teams that cross organisational, and sometimes national, boundaries and which may last only as long as the immediate task. Because of delayering, they also have to deal with more information and take on more responsibilities.

The kinds of staff they manage are changing too, with an increasing proportion of them possessing professional and technical qualifications. Various philosophies of management practice have had a widespread influence – performance management, the competency movement, TQM and so on.

These and other developments have far-reaching implications for appraisal practice, though the second stage of the IPM's performance management study demonstrated that quite a few organisations were still operating rather traditional appraisal schemes of doubtful relevance to their circumstances and needs.[1]

This article will try to draw out some of the trends in appraisal that arise from the changes of recent years, looking at them in terms of the aims and ownership of appraisal, who appraises and the content of appraisal.

Aims and ownership

The advent of performance management systems (PMSs), with their strategic approach to managing organisational and individual performance, places performance appraisal in a central role in a more integrated and dynamic set of HR policies. Potentially, this offers an

Abridged from C. Fletcher, 'Appraisal: an idea whose time has gone?', *Personnel Management*, September 1993, pp. 34–7.

opportunity for appraisal to achieve more than it alone could do in the past.

For example, it resolves one of the more persistent problems of appraisal – that of having a multiplicity of often conflicting aims. The typical appraisal system tries to act as a vehicle for motivating people and improving performance (through objective setting), as a means of assessing performance and distributing rewards equitably (through the use of performance-related pay and ratings) and as a development tool – all in one session.

The dissatisfaction registered by over 80 per cent of companies with their appraisal schemes is testimony to the problems this approach runs into, the main ones being that all this sets an overly demanding agenda for a single procedure and that the imminence of reward decisions tends to block constructive discussion of development needs.

The advantage of performance management is that it offers the opportunity for objective setting and review, and PRP, to be separated out from the other functions of appraisal, a practice which research has long suggested to be the best way forward. Organisations operating a sophisticated PMS are tending to have a session on objective setting and review tied in to the start of the business year, with a more developmentally oriented appraisal session at a later date. Any performance-related pay element is usually related to the former.

Another feature of PMS is that it is supposed to be line-driven. It follows that, if appraisal is a key element of PMS, that too should move out of its personnel department home and become owned by the line. Getting line managers involved in the development of appraisal systems is not new, of course, though neither has it been very common.[2]

However, going beyond this and getting the line to take on significant aspects of implementing and running appraisal has only really come into the picture with performance management. Greater line management ownership should help focus the process more effectively on the needs of appraisers and appraisees and raise commitment to making it work.

But unless the transfer of this responsibility is handled carefully, with ample back-up support from the personnel specialists, the effectiveness of the appraisal systems put in place has been found to suffer.

Who appraises?

With fewer management layers and more direct reports to each manager, increased use of matrix or project management and greater geographical spread of staff, the old principle of the immediate boss carrying out the appraisal becomes unworkable in many instances. A manager may have too many appraisees to deal with, or see them too infrequently to know how they are doing. An appraisee may work for several different bosses throughout the year. Who, then, should be the appraiser?

There have been a variety of responses to this problem. Increased use of self-appraisal is one; who else sees as much of his or her performance as the appraisee? This helps, but it is not without problems; it will only be useful where the expectations generated by the introduction of self-appraisal have been carefully managed and where the appraisers have been trained to use it. At least one study has shown how self-appraisal can lead to appraisees feeling they have less influence over the appraisal and expressing more disagreement where these conditions are not met.[3]

While a combination of self and superior appraisal is still the most common one, the involvement of peers, other bosses and even of subordinates as appraisers is gaining popularity. An interesting example of this is the much disputed teachers' appraisal scheme, which is based on a degree of self-assessment (encouraged but not compulsory), on at least two classroom observation sessions, and on other sources of information, including people who have knowledge of the person's work. The latter would be mainly peers for most teachers, but for head teachers it could include governors, parents and education authority officers.

The appraiser has the task of approaching these sources and is required by the regulations to consult the appraisee about it first. The DES circular on teacher appraisal says: 'During such consultation, appraisees should be given the opportunity to express their views about the principle of collecting information from the particular people involved and the method of collection.'

The question of allowing the appraisees to have some say in who comments on their performance also arises in upward appraisal. Many organisations have for some years included some very mild gestures in this direction in the form of headings on the appraisees' preparation form that invited them to identify things that 'management' could do to help them improve performance.

Recently some UK organisations have taken this further; one major oil company, for example, has included an item on the preparation form that asks the appraisee to identify occasions in the last year on which the appraiser could have provided them with more support.

A more common approach, though, is to have an external agency send questionnaires to a manager's subordinates, seeking their views on various aspects of their boss's performance; the results are then collated into a report which is discussed in a feedback session between the manager and a consultant or someone designated for the role within the organisation. Among the UK organisations which have used upward appraisal to at least a limited extent are W.H. Smith, BP Exploration, American Express and Rank Xerox. The practice is much more widespread in the USA.

It has been suggested that upward appraisal has the advantages of both facilitating the empowerment of employees and making appraisal decisions more defensible against legal challenge (because they are based on a wider assessment input).[4] But inevitably there are some difficulties, such as the frequently voiced concern either that the managers being so appraised will feel their position to be undermined and react badly or that their subordinates will not be frank enough to make any meaningful comments anyway, or both.

The conditions for upward appraisal to work would seem to include anonymity for the subordinate respondents; a manager having enough subordinates to facilitate that anonymity and also to ensure a reasonable sample on which to base feedback; the focus of upward appraisal being on those aspects of managerial performance that subordinates are most able to comment on (that is, various aspects of staff management); and a sufficient degree of trust being built up to gain the manager's support for the exercise.

Upward appraisal is likely to become more frequently used in the next few years, but it is really an occasional, additional development activity rather than an integral and regular part of the appraisal process.

Finally, as far as who appraises is concerned, the practice of having several bosses contribute to the appraisal process has become common in matrix management organisations. Typically, this involves one line manager – or sometimes a functional head – consulting the appraisee's other bosses over the period in question and trying to feed back a representative view based on their replies.

Putting their cards on the table

Being assessed by peers and subordinates can be a daunting process, according to a senior manager at American Express who has seen upward appraisal slowly gain acceptance at the credit card multinational.

Currently used in isolation from pay and other annual assessment methods, it is a symbol of the approval which upward appraisal has achieved that this kind of evaluation is soon to be built into the mainstream appraisal system at Amex.

Peter Hall, division vice president of American Express' European operating centre in Brighton, said that around 300 managers in the UK have experienced upward appraisal since it was first rolled out from the US three years ago.

Forming one part of a general leadership seminar, managers are shown two questionnaires, one filled in by peers, the other by subordinates. Each survey consists of around 70 questions and is first given to the manager to digest before a personnel specialist takes them through the results. More detailed comments outside the scope of the specific questions are also passed on and discussed.

The personnel professional takes on an interpretative and counselling role, helping the manager to design an action plan. These briefing sessions last around an hour and begin with the good news before tackling weaker areas which need work.

All management scores are added to the American Express statistical norms, which are updated so that every manager can compare themselves to their equivalents throughout the organisation. This is the only company-wide use of the data: there is no divisional or departmental analysis of upward appraisals.

Hall says that the questionnaires pick out management skills such as listening and being able to deal with bad news: 'If a member of staff gets shot every time they have to give a manager bad news, then no one wants to go to their boss with bad news.'

He said that one of the surprising, and potentially intimidating, aspects of the process is the accuracy of subordinate opinions. 'The first time it's quite daunting. You don't know what you are going to hear. The perceptions of people around you are pretty accurate: they know your weaknesses.'

Managers are encouraged to talk through their action plan with their own bosses as well as the team which filled in the questionnaires. All subordinate and peer opinions remain anonymous, so managers take the opportunity to thank their team for co-operating and confirm which of their weaker areas they will be attempting to improve.

As the technique has been used for three years, there are managers who have had a chance to see a second group of questionnaires and measure their progress. 'You can actually see the needle move,' says Hall. 'If you work hard, things actually go off the bottom of your list of problems and are replaced by new issues.'

As upward appraisal becomes embedded into the company culture, Hall has found that subordinates may not pull their punches when assessing their managers' worth but are keen to help them change: 'There is a great spirit of openness, and the process is starting to become a way of life.'

The content of appraisal

As already indicated, for some companies appraisal as such now seems to be more about the short- and medium-term development of individuals and their performance – because objective-setting is regarded as a different aspect of PMS.

What form does the content of appraisal take in this context? The adoption of a competency framework for describing performance development has become popular, and this is often a part of the appraisal process. The use of ratings to compare individuals (even overall performance ratings), for so long a central element of appraisal forms and process, is now declining; Zeneca is an interesting example of this.[5]

Perhaps the views of W. Edwards Deming, the 'guru' of total quality, have been one of the influences here. He has suggested that performance appraisal is one of the seven deadly diseases of current management practice.[6] Among other things, he argues that appraisal does harm because managers cannot effectively differentiate between individual staff and organisational systems as the cause in performance variation and that the latter rather than the former are the major factor.

Deming's ideas have had some impact on appraisal practice; for example, it is reported that Ford in the USA has been experimenting with reducing the appraisal categories from nine to three; it has taken on Deming's point that most people perform within the limitations of the system and has decided that only 5 to 11 per cent of staff should be rated higher or lower than the middle category.[7]

However, the downsizing and delayering in so many organisations has taken its toll of promotion opportunities, with the result that, where appraisal does focus on development, that development is much more about improving competence and performance through in-the-job activities and lateral moves than simple upward progression.

As with most aspects of the changes in appraisal practice, appraisers usually need training to take on this wider development role successfully. Another facet of this, and one that is important in managing appraisee expectations in a developmentally oriented appraisal system, is that the formal assessment of promotability and potential is less likely to be on the agenda.

The well-documented rise in the use of assessment centres and psychometric tests includes their application in this area.[8] Instead of relying on the inevitably rather limited perspective of the appraiser to identify the key personnel for the future, many companies have opted to use more objective and sophisticated assessment procedures. In these circumstances, appraisal continues to have a role as a first step in the chain, but the actual decisions tend to become more reliant on these other techniques.

The future of appraisal

What do all these changes (and there are many more than there is space to detail in a short article) and their associated trends in appraisal practice add up to? What we are seeing is the demise of the traditional, monolithic appraisal system.

Doubtless the idea of a universally applied, personnel-driven, standard procedure that stays rigidly in place (perhaps kept there by the weight of its own paperwork) within the organisation for years on end will lumber on in some quarters for a while yet, but its days are certainly numbered.

In its place are evolving a number of separate but linked processes, applied in different ways according to the needs of local circumstances and staff levels. The various elements in this may go by a variety of names, and perhaps the term 'appraisal' has in some ways outlived its usefulness.

Notes

1 *Performance Management in the UK: an Analysis of the Issues* (IPM, 1992).

2 Bob Scott 'Evolution of an appraisal programme', *Personnel Management*, August (1983).

3 L. Robertson et al., 'Self appraisal and perceptions of the appraisal discussion: a field experiment', *Journal of Organizational Behavior*, 14 (1993), pp. 129–42.

4 T. Redman and E. Snape, 'Upward and onward: can staff appraise their managers?', *Personnel Review*, 21 (1992), pp. 32–46.

5 Angela Sheard , 'Learning to improve performance', *Personnel Management*, November (1992).

6 W. Edwards Deming, *Out of the Crisis* (MIT Institute for Advanced Engineering Study, Cambridge, MA, 1986).

7 K.P. Carson, R.L. Cardy and G.H. Dobbins, 'Performance appraisal as effective management or as deadly management disease; two initial empirical investigations', *Group and Organization Studies*, 16 (1991), pp. 143–59.

8 W. Mabey, 'The growth of test use', *Selection and Development Review*, 8, 3 (1992), pp. 6–8; V. J. Shackleton and S. Newell, 'Management selection: a comparative survey of methods used in top British and French companies', *Journal of Occupational Psychology*, 64 (1991), pp. 23–6.

31

Managing individual behavior: bringing out the best in people

Stephen L. Fink

Effective managers learn to view organizational life from a number of different perspectives. From a broad perspective, they need to understand the overall system and to think in long-range terms. From a narrower perspective, they should know how groups function and how to build effective teamwork. However, when it comes right down to getting something done, the individual must do it, and the most competent managers understand just how to bring out the best in the people who work for them. [. . .]

What ye sow, so shall ye reap

W. Edwards Deming developed a demonstration of a worker's plight in a situation where performance improvement was demanded but simultaneously made impossible – by the very management who had designed the work. The exercise is called *The Bead Factory*. In the bead factory the worker is required to scoop 50 beads from a box containing a mixture of white and red beads. There are many more white ones than red ones, with the red beads signifying defects. The worker's task is to minimize the number of red beads in each scoopful. Five or six workers take turns, and each gets repeated opportunities to improve performance. A supervisor records the results and keeps up the pressure for quality improvement. Despite the fact that there is no real way to improve performance, that the number of red and white beads in a scoop occurs in random fashion, each worker believes that he or she has control over the work and, given enough practice, can do better. The supervisor also behaves as though that were true. By the end of the exercise, the workers feel the discouragement and helplessness often reported by employees who are expected to demonstrate improved performance over time but who have no control over key factors that affect their

Abridged from S.L. Fink, 'Managing individual behavior: bringing out the best in people', in A.R. Cohen, *The Portable MBA in Management*, New York: Wiley, 1993, pp. 71, 103.

performance. Instead of recognizing that the problem is in the technology itself, which only management can change, the manager will tend to perceive the employee as the problem.

The important message here is that the label *difficult employee* might easily show a displacement of management's failure to establish the appropriate setting, technology, or reward system for the job. In order for employees to be held truly accountable for their performance, they must be empowered to exercise their own control over it. The irony is that many managers refuse to give employees that control yet hold them accountable anyway. Then they wonder why an employee's performance is not up to expectations.

PART 6
DIVERSITY IN ORGANISATIONS

32

The cultural relativity of organizational practices and theories

Geert Hofstede

Management and national cultures

A key issue for organization science is the influence of national cultures on management. Twenty or even ten years ago, the existence of a relationship between management and national cultures was far from obvious to many, and it may not be obvious to everyone even now. In the 1950s and 1960s, the dominant belief, at least in Europe and the USA, was that management was something universal. There were principles of sound management, which existed regardless of national environments. If national or local practice deviated from these principles, it was time to change local practice. In the future, the universality of sound management practices would lead to societies becoming more and more alike. This applied even to the poor countries of the Third World, which would become rich as well and would be managed just like the rich countries. Also the differences between management in the First and Second World (capitalist and socialist) would disappear; in fact, under the surface they were thought to be a lot smaller than was officially recognized. This way of thinking, which dominated the 1950s and 1960s, is known as the 'convergence hypothesis'.

During the 1970s the belief in the unavoidable convergence of management practices waned. It was too obviously in conflict with the reality we saw around us. At the same time supranational organizations like the European Common Market, which were

From G. Hofstede, 'The cultural relativity of organizational practices and theories', in J. Drew, *Readings in International Enterprise*, London: Routledge and Open University, pp. 140–58.

founded very much on the convergence belief, had to recognize the stubbornness of national differences. Even within existing nations, regional differences became more rather than less accentuated. The Welsh, the Flemish, the Basques, the Bangladeshi, the Quebecois defended their own identity, and this was difficult to reconcile with a management philosophy of convergence. It slowly became clear that national and even regional cultures do matter for management. The national and regional differences are not disappearing; they are here to stay. In fact, these differences may become one of the most crucial problems for management – in particular for the management of multinational, multicultural organizations, whether public or private.

The importance of nationality

Nationality is important to management for at least three reasons. The first, very obviously, is political. Nations are political units, rooted in history, with their own institutions, forms of government, legal systems, educational systems, labor and employers' association systems. Not only do the formal institutions differ, but even if we could equalize them, the informal ways of using them differ. For example, formal law in France protects the rights of the individual against the state much better than formal law in Great Britain or Holland. However, few French citizens have ever won court cases against the state, whereas this happens quite regularly in Holland or Britain. Such informal political realities are quite resistant to change.

The second reason why nationality is important is sociological. Nationality or regionality has a symbolic value to citizens. We all derive part of our identity from it; it is part of the 'who am I?'. The symbolic value of the fact of belonging to a nation or region has been and still is sufficient reason for people to go to war, when they feel their common identity to be threatened. National and regional differences are felt by people to be a reality – and therefore they are a reality.

The third reason why nationality is important is psychological. Our thinking is an effect of early life experiences in the family and later educational experiences in schools and organizations, which are not the same across national borders. In a classroom, I can easily demonstrate the process of conditioning by experience. For this purpose I use an ambiguous picture: one that can be interpreted in two different ways. One such picture represents either an attractive young girl or an ugly old woman, depending on the way you look at it. In order to demonstrate the process of conditioning, I ask one half of the class to close their eyes. To the other half, I show for five seconds a slightly changed version of the picture, in which only the young girl can be seen. Then I ask the other half to close their eyes, and to the first half I show, also for five seconds, a version in which only the old woman can be seen. After this preparation, I show the ambiguous picture to everyone at the same time. The results are amazing: the vast majority of those 'conditioned' by seeing the young girl first, now see only the young girl in the ambiguous picture; and most of those 'conditioned' by seeing the old woman first can see only the old woman afterwards.

Mental programming

This very simple experiment shows that as a teacher I can in five seconds condition a randomly taken half of a class to see something else in a picture than would the other half. If this is so, how much stronger should the differences in perception of the same reality be between people who have been 'conditioned' by different educational and life experiences not for a mere five seconds, but for twenty, thirty, or forty years? Through our experiences we become 'mentally programmed' to interpret new experiences in a certain way. My favorite definition of 'culture' is precisely that its essence is collective mental programming: it is that part of our conditioning that we share with other members of our nation, region, or group but not with members of other nations, regions, or groups.

Examples of differences in mental programming between members of different nations can be observed all around us. One source of difference is, of course, language and all that comes with it, but there is much more. In Europe, British people will form a neat queue whenever they have to wait; not so, the French. Dutch people will as a rule greet strangers when they enter a small, closed space like a railway compartment, doctor's waiting-room, or lift; not so, the Belgians. Austrians will wait at a red pedestrian traffic light even when there is no traffic; not so the Dutch. Swiss tend to become very angry when somebody – say, a foreigner – makes a mistake in traffic; not so the Swedes. All these are part of an invisible set of mental programs which belongs to these countries' national cultures.

Such cultural programs are difficult to change, unless one detaches the individual from his or her culture. Within a nation or a part of it, culture changes only slowly. This is the more so because what is in the minds of the people has also become crystallized in the institutions mentioned earlier: government, legal systems, educational systems, industrial relations systems, family structures, religious organizations, sports clubs, settlement patterns, literature, architecture, and even scientific theories. All these reflect traditions and common ways of thinking, which are rooted in the common culture but may be different for other cultures. The institutions constrain and reinforce the ways of thinking on which they are based. One well known mechanism by which culturally determined ways of thinking perpetuate themselves is the self-fulfilling prophecy. If, for example, the belief is held that people from a certain minority are irresponsible, the institutions in such an environment will not admit these people into positions of responsibility: never being given responsibility, minority people will be unable to learn it, and very likely they will actually behave irresponsibly. So, everyone remains caught in the belief – including, probably, the minority people themselves. Another example of the self-fulfilling prophecy: if the dominant way of thinking in a society is that all people are ultimately motivated by self-interest, those who do not pursue self-interest are considered as deviant. As it is unpleasant to be deviant, most people in such an environment will justify whatever they want to do with some reference to self-interest, thereby reinforcing the dominant way of thinking. People in such a society cannot even imagine motives that cannot be reduced to self-interest.

National character

This article shall be limited to national cultures, excluding cultural differences between groups within nations; such as, those based on regions, social classes, occupations, religion, age, sex, or even families. These differences in culture within nations, of course, do exist, but for most nations we can still distinguish some ways of thinking that most inhabitants share and that we can consider part of their national culture or national character. National characters are more clearly distinguishable to foreigners than to the nationals themselves. When we live within a country, we do not discover what we have in common with our compatriots, only what makes us different from them.

Statements about national culture or national character smell of superficiality and false generalization. There are two reasons for this. First, there is no commonly accepted language to describe such a complex thing as a 'culture'. We meet the same problem if we want to describe someone's 'personality': we risk being subjective and superficial. In the case of 'personality', however, psychology has at least developed terms like intelligence, energy level, introversion-extroversion and emotional stability, to mention a few, which are more or less commonly understood. In the case of 'culture', such a scientific language does not exist. In the second place, statements about national character have often been based on impressions only, not on systematic study. Such statements can indeed be considered false generalizations.

A research project across fifty countries

My own research into national cultures was carried out between 1967 and 1978. It has attempted to meet the two objectives I just mentioned: to develop a commonly acceptable, well-defined, and empirically based terminology to describe cultures; and to use systematically collected data about a large number of cultures, rather than just impressions. I obtained these data more or less by accident. From 1967 to 1971 I worked as a psychologist on the international staff of a large multinational corporation. As part of my job I collected data on the employees' attitudes and values, by means of standardized paper-and-pencil questionnaires. Virtually all employees of the corporation were surveyed, from unskilled workers to research scientists in many countries around the globe. Then from 1971 to 1973 the surveys were repeated once more with the same group of employees. All in all the corporation collected over 116,000 questionnaires which were stored in a computerized data bank. For 40 countries, there were sufficient data for systematic analysis.

It soon appeared that those items in the questionnaires that dealt with employee values rather than attitudes showed remarkable and very stable differences between countries. By an attitude I mean the response to a question like 'how do you like your job?' or 'how do you like your boss?' By a value I mean answers to questions of whether people prefer one type of boss over another, or their choice of factors to describe an ideal job. Values indicate their desires, not their perceptions of what actually went on. These values, not the attitudes, reflect differences in mental programming and national character.

These differences, however, were always statistical in nature. Suppose people were asked whether they strongly agreed, agreed, were undecided, disagreed, or strongly disagreed with a certain value statement. In such a case we would not find that all employees in country A agreed and all in country B disagreed; instead we might find that 60 per cent of the employees in country A agreed, while only 40 per cent in country B agreed. Characterizing a national culture does not mean that every individual within that culture is mentally programmed in the same way. The national culture found is a kind of average pattern of beliefs and values, around which individuals in the country vary. For example, I found that, on average, Japanese have a greater desire for a strong authority than English; but some English have a greater desire for a strong authority than quite a few Japanese. In describing national cultures we refer to common elements within each nation, but we should not generalize to every individual within that nation.

In 1971 I went as a teacher to an international business school, where I asked the course participants, who were managers from many different countries, to answer the same values questions we used in the multinational corporation. The answers revealed the same type of pattern of differences between countries, showing that we were not dealing with a phenomenon particular to this one company. Then in my later research, from 1973 to 1979, at the European Institute for Advanced Studies in Brussels, I looked for other studies comparing aspects of national character across countries. I found about forty such studies comparing five or more countries which showed differences confirming the ones found in the multinational corporation. All this material together forms the basis for my book *Culture's Consequences* (Hofstede, 1980). Later, supplementary data became available for another ten countries and three multi-country regions, thereby raising the total number of countries to fifty (Hofstede, 1983).

Four dimensions of national culture

My terminology for describing national cultures consists of four different criteria which I call 'dimensions' because they occur in nearly all possible combinations. They are largely independent of each other:

1   Individualism versus Collectivism;
2   large or small Power Distance;
3   strong or weak Uncertainty Avoidance;
4   Masculinity versus Femininity.

The research data have allowed me to attribute to each of the forty countries represented in the data bank of the multinational corporation an index value (between 0 and about 100) on each of these four dimensions.

The four dimensions were found through a combination of multivariate statistics (factor analysis) and theoretical reasoning. The cases analysed in the factor analysis were the forty countries; the variables were the mean scores or answer percentages for the different value questions, as produced by the multinational corporation's employees within these countries. This factor analysis showed that 50 per cent of the variance in answer patterns between countries on the value questions could be explained by three factors, corresponding to the dimensions 1 + 2, 3, and 4. Theoretical reasoning led to the further splitting of the first factor into two dimensions. The theoretical reasoning meant that each dimension should be conceptually linkable to some very fundamental problem in human societies, but a problem to which different societies have found different answers. These are the issues studied in primitive, non-literate societies by cultural anthropologists, such as the distribution of power, or the distribution of roles between the sexes. There is no reason why such issues should be relevant only for primitive societies.

Individualism versus collectivism

The first dimension is labeled 'Individualism versus Collectivism'. The fundamental issue involved is the relation between an individual and his or her fellow individuals. At one end of the scale we find societies in which the ties between individuals are very loose. Everybody is supposed to look after his or her own self-interest and maybe the interest of his or her immediate family. This is made possible by a large amount of freedom that such a society leaves individuals. At the other end of the scale we find societies in which the ties between individuals are very tight. People are born into collectivities or ingroups which may be their extended family (including grandparents, uncles, aunts, and so on), their tribe, or their village. Everybody is supposed to look after the interest of his or her ingroup and to have no other opinions and beliefs than the opinions and beliefs in their ingroup. In exchange, the ingroup will protect them when they are in trouble. We see that both the Individualist and the Collectivist society are integrated wholes, but the Individualist society is loosely integrated, and the Collectivist society tightly integrated.

All fifty countries can be placed somewhere along the Individualist–Collectivist scale. On the basis of the answers obtained on the questionnaire in the multinational corporation, each country was given an Individualism index score. The score is such that 100 represents a strongly Individualist society, and 0 a strongly Collectivist society: all 50 countries are somewhere between these extremes.

It appears that the degree of Individualism in a country is statistically related to that country's wealth. Table 32.1 shows the list of countries used, and Figure 32.1 shows vertically the Individualism index scores of the 50 countries, and horizontally their wealth, expressed in their gross national product per capita at the time the surveys were taken (around 1970). We see evidence that wealthy countries are more Individualist and poor countries more Collectivist. Very Individualist countries are the US, Great Britain, the Netherlands; very Collectivist are Colombia, Pakistan, and Taiwan. In the middle we find Japan, India, Austria, and Spain.

Power distance

The second dimension is labeled 'Power Distance'. The fundamental issue involved is how society deals with the fact that people are

Table 32.1   *The countries and regions*

ARA	Arab countries (Egypt, Lebanon, Libya, Kuwait, Iraq, Saudi Arabia, UAE)	JAM	Jamaica
		JPN	Japan
		KOR	South Korea
ARG	Argentina	MAL	Malaysia
AUL	Australia	MEX	Mexico
AUT	Austria	NET	Netherlands
BEL	Belgium	NOR	Norway
BRA	Brazil	NZL	New Zealand
CAN	Canada	PAK	Pakistan
CHL	Chile	PAN	Panama
COL	Colombia	PER	Peru
COS	Costa Rica	PHI	Philippines
DEN	Denmark	POR	Portugal
EAF	East Africa (Kenya, Ethiopia, Zambia)	SAF	South Africa
		SAL	Salvador
EQA	Ecuador	SIN	Singapore
FIN	Finland	SPA	Spain
FRA	France	SWE	Sweden
GBR	Great Britain	SWI	Switzerland
GER	Germany	TAI	Taiwan
GRE	Greece	THA	Thailand
GUA	Guatemala	TUR	Turkey
HOK	Hong Kong	URU	Uruguay
IDO	Indonesia	USA	United States of America
IND	India	VEN	Venezuela
IRA	Iran	WAF	West Africa (Nigeria, Ghana, Sierra Leone)
IRE	Ireland		
ISR	Israel	YUG	Yugoslavia
ITA	Italy		

unequal. People are unequal in physical and intellectual capacities. Some societies let these inequalities grow over time into inequalities of power and wealth; the latter may become hereditary and no longer related to physical and intellectual capacities at all. Other societies try to play down inequalities in power and wealth as much as possible. Surely, no society has ever reached complete equality, because there are strong forces in society that perpetuate existing inequalities. All societies are unequal, but some are more unequal than others. This degree of inequality is measured by the Power Distance scale, which also runs from 0 (small Power Distance) to 100 (large Power Distance).

In organizations, the level of Power Distance is related to the degree of centralization of authority and the degree of autocratic leadership. This relationship shows that centralization and autocratic leadership are rooted in the 'mental programming' of the members of a society, not only of those in power but also of those at the bottom of the power hierarchy. Societies in which power tends to be distributed unequally can remain so because this situation satisfies

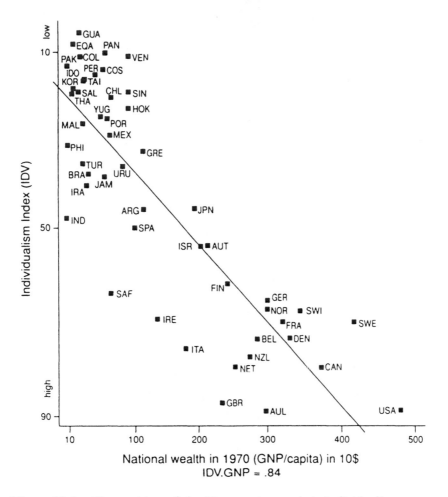

Figure 32.1   *The position of the 50 countries on their Individualism index (IDV) versus their 1970 national wealth (per capita GNP)*

the psychological need for dependence of the people without power. We could also say that societies and organizations will be led as autocratically as their members will permit. The autocracy exists just as much in the members as in the leaders: the value systems of the two groups are usually complementary.

In Figure 32.2 Power Distance is plotted horizontally and Individualism–Collectivism vertically. The Philippines, Venezuela, India, and others show large Power Distance index scores, but also France and Belgium score fairly high. Denmark, Israel, and Austria score low. We see that there is a global relationship between Power Distance and Collectivism: Collectivist countries always show large Power Distances, but Individualist countries do not always show small Power Distances. The Latin European countries – France,

Power Distance Index (PDI)

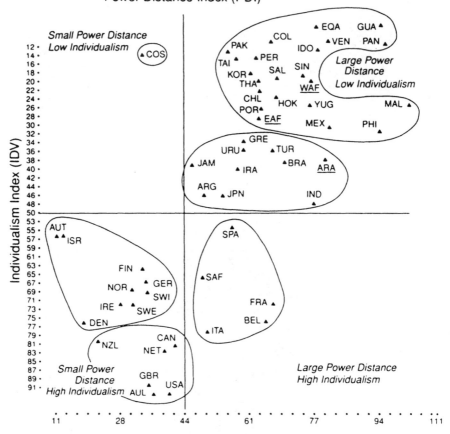

Figure 32.2   *The position of the 50 countries on the Power Distance and Individualism scales*

Belgium, Italy, and Spain, plus marginally South Africa – show a combination of large Power Distances plus Individualism. The other wealthy Western countries all combine smaller Power Distance with Individualism. All poor countries are Collectivist with larger Power Distances.

Uncertainty Avoidance

The third dimension is labeled 'Uncertainty Avoidance'. The fundamental issue involved here is how society deals with the fact that time runs only one way; that is, we are all caught in the reality of past, present and future, and we have to live with uncertainty because the future is unknown and always will be. Some societies socialize their members into accepting this uncertainty and not becoming upset by it. People in such societies will tend to accept each day as it comes. They will take risks rather easily. They will not work as hard. They will be relatively tolerant of behavior and opinions different from their own because they do not feel threatened by them. Such societies can be called 'weak Uncertainty Avoidance' societies; they are societies in which people have a natural tendency to feel relatively secure.

Other societies socialize their people into trying to beat the future. Because the future remains essentially unpredictable, in those societies there will be a higher level of anxiety in people, which becomes manifest in greater nervousness, emotionality, and aggressiveness. Such societies, called 'strong Uncertainty Avoidance' societies, also have institutions that try to create security and avoid risk. We can create security in three ways. One is technology, in the broadest sense of the word. Through technology we protect ourselves from the risks of nature and war. We build houses, dikes, power stations, and ICBMs which are meant to give us a feeling of security. The second way of creating security is law, again in the broadest sense of the word. Through laws and all kinds of formal rules and institutions, we protect ourselves from the unpredictability of human behavior. The proliferation of laws and rules implies an intolerance of deviant behaviors and opinions. Where laws cannot be made because the subject is too fuzzy, we can create a feeling of security by the nomination of experts. Experts are people whose word we accept as a kind of law because we assume them to be beyond uncertainty. The third way of creating a feeling of security is religion, once more in the broadest sense of the word. This sense includes secular religions and ideologies, such as Marxism, dogmatic capitalism, or movements that preach an escape into meditation. Even science is included. All human societies have their religions in some way or another. All religions, in some way, make uncertainty tolerable, because they all contain a message that is beyond uncertainty, that helps us to accept the uncertainty of today because we interpret experiences in terms of something bigger and more powerful that transcends personal reality. In strongly Uncertainty Avoiding societies we find religions which claim absolute truth and which do not tolerate other religions. We also find in such societies a scientific tradition looking for ultimate, absolute truths, as opposed to a more relativist, empiricist tradition in the weak Uncertainty Avoidance societies.

The Uncertainty Avoidance dimension, thus, implies a number of things, from aggressiveness to a need for absolute truth, that we do not usually consider as belonging together. They appear to belong together in the logic of culture patterns, but this logic differs from our own daily logic. Without research we would not have found that, on the level of societies, these things go together.

Figure 32.3 plots the Uncertainty Avoidance index for fifty

Power Distance Index

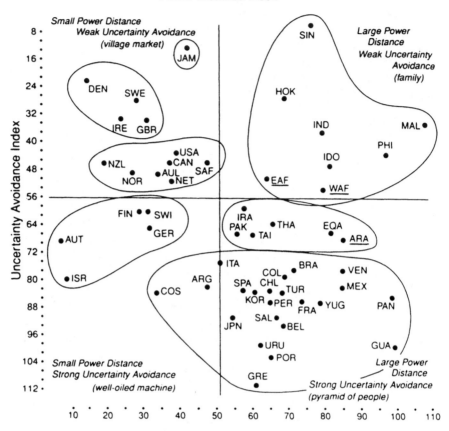

Figure 32.3 *The position of the 50 countries on the Power Distance and Uncertainty Avoidance scales*

countries along the vertical axis, against the Power Distance index on the horizontal axis. We find several clusters of countries. There is a large cluster of countries with strong Uncertainty Avoidance and large Power Distance. They are: all the Latin countries, both Latin European and Latin American; Mediterranean countries, such as Yugoslavia, Greece, and Turkey; and Japan plus Korea.

The Asian countries are found in two clusters with large Power Distance and medium to weak Uncertainty Avoidance. Then we find a cluster of German-speaking countries, including Israel and marginally Finland, combining small Power Distance with medium to strong Uncertainty Avoidance.

Both small Power Distance and weak Uncertainty Avoidance are found in Denmark, Sweden, Great Britain, and Ireland, while the Netherlands, USA, Norway, and the other Anglo countries are in the middle.

Masculinity versus femininity

The fourth dimension is labeled 'Masculinity versus Femininity'. The fundamental issue involved is the division of roles between the sexes in society. All societies have to deal with the basic fact that one half of mankind is female and the other male. The only activities that are strictly determined by the sex of a person are those related to procreation. Men cannot have babies. Human societies, however, through the ages and around the globe, have also associated other roles to men only, or to women only. This is called social, rather than biological, sex role division.

All social role divisions are more or less arbitrary, and what is seen as a typical task for men or for women can vary from one society to the other. We can classify societies on whether they try to minimize or to maximize the social sex role division. Some societies allow both men and women to take many different roles. Others make a sharp division between what men should do and what women should do. In this latter case, the distribution is always such that men take the more assertive and dominant roles and women the more service-oriented and caring roles. I have called those societies with a maximized social sex role division 'Masculine' and those with a relatively small social sex role division 'Feminine'. In Masculine societies, the traditional masculine social values permeate the whole society – even the way of thinking of the women. These values include the importance of showing off, of performing, of achieving something visible, of making money, of 'big is beautiful'. In more Feminine societies, the dominant values – for both men and women – are those more traditionally associated with the feminine role: not showing off, putting relationships with people before money, minding the quality of life and the preservation of the environment, helping others, in particular the weak, and 'small is beautiful'. In a Masculine society, the public hero is the successful achiever, the superman. In a more Feminine society, the public sympathy goes to the anti-hero, the underdog. Individual brilliance in a Feminine society is suspect.

Following the procedure used for the other dimensions, each of the fifty countries was given an index score on the Masculinity–Femininity scale: a high score means a more Masculine, a low score a more Feminine country. Figure 32.4 plots the Masculinity index score horizontally and the Uncertainty Avoidance index again vertically. The most Masculine country is Japan; also quite Masculine are the German-speaking countries: Germany, Austria, and Switzerland. Moderately Masculine are a number of Latin countries, such as Venezuela, Mexico, and Italy; also the entire cluster of Anglo countries including some of their former colonies: India and the Philippines.

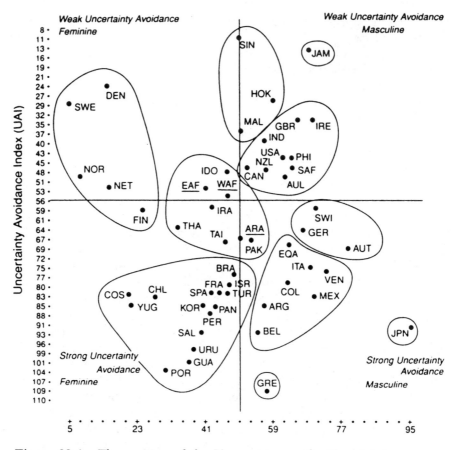

Figure 32.4   *The position of the 50 countries on the Uncertainty Avoidance and Masculinity scales*

On the far end towards the Feminine side we find the four Nordic countries and the Netherlands. Some Latin and Mediterranean countries like Yugoslavia, Chile, Portugal, Spain, and France are moderately Feminine.

Some consequences for management theory and practice

The naive assumption that management is the same or is becoming the same around the world is not tenable in view of these demonstrated differences in national cultures. Consider a few of the ideas about management which have been popularized in the Western literature in the past fifteen years: in particular, about leadership, about models of organization, and about motivation. These theories were almost without exception made in the USA; in fact, the post-Second-World-War management literature is entirely US dominated. This reflects the economic importance of the USA during this period, but culturally the USA is just one country among all others, with its particular configuration of cultural values which differs from that of most other countries.

Leadership

The most relevant dimensions for leadership are Individualism and Power Distance. Let us look at Figure 32.2 again. We find the USA in an extreme position on the Individualism scale (50 out of [the] 50 [countries]) and just below average on the Power Distance scale (16 out of 50). What does the high Individualism score mean? US leadership theories are about leading individuals based on the presumed needs of individuals who seek their ultimate self-interest. For example, the word 'duty', which implies obligations towards others or towards society, does not appear at all in the US leadership theories.

Leadership in a Collectivist society – basically any Third World country – is a group phenomenon. A working group which is not the same as the natural ingroup will have to be made into another ingroup in order to be effective. People in these countries are able to bring considerable loyalty to their job, providing they feel that the employer returns the loyalty in the form of protection, just like their natural ingroup does.

Let us now look at the Power Distance dimension in terms of participative leadership. What does participative leadership US style mean? Individual subordinates are allowed to participate in the leader's decisions; it is the leader who keeps the initiative. Management prerogatives are very important in the USA. Let us remember that on Power Distance, the USA is more or less in the middle zone. In countries with higher Power Distances – such as many Third World countries, but also France and Belgium – individual subordinates as a rule do not want to participate. It is part of their expectations that leaders lead automatically, and such subordinates will, in fact, by their own behavior make it difficult for leaders to lead in any other way. There is very little participative leadership in France and Belgium. If the society is at the same time Collectivist, however, there will be ways by which subordinates in a group can still influence the leader. This applies to all Asian countries. Let us take some countries on the other side, however: Denmark, Sweden, or Israel. In this case, subordinates will not necessarily wait until their boss takes the initiative to let them participate. They will, for example, support forms of employee codetermination in which either individuals or groups can take initiatives towards management. In these cultures there are no management prerogatives that are automatically accepted; anything a boss does may be challenged by the subordinates. Management privileges in particular are much more easily accepted in the USA than in some of the very low Power Distance countries. A similar difference is found in the ratios between management compensation and subordinate compensation.

Organization

In organizations the decisive dimensions of culture are Power Distance and Uncertainty Avoidance. Organizations are devices to distribute power, and they also serve to avoid uncertainty, to make things predictable. So let us look at Figure 32.3 again. My former colleague, Professor James Stevens from INSEAD, once gave the same description of an organizational problem to separate groups of French, West German, and British management students. The problem described a conflict between two departments. The students were asked to determine what was wrong and what should be done to resolve the problem. The French in majority referred the problem to the next higher authority level. The Germans suggested the setting of rules to resolve such problems in the future. The British wanted to improve communications between the two department heads, perhaps by some kind of human relations training. My colleague concluded that the dominant underlying model of an organization for the French was a pyramid, a hierarchical structure held together by the unity of command (larger Power Distance) as well as by rules (strong Uncertainty Avoidance). The model for the Germans was a well-oiled machine; the exercise of personal command was largely unnecessary because the rules settled everything (strong Uncertainty Avoidance, but smaller Power Distance). The model for the British was a village market; no decisive hierarchy, flexible rules, and a resolution of problems by negotiating (small Power Distance and weak Uncertainty Avoidance). These models left one corner in the diagram of Figure 32.3 unexplained, but a discussion with an Indian colleague led me to believe that the underlying model of an organization for the Indians is the family: undisputed personal authority of the father-leader but few formal rules (large Power Distance and weak Uncertainty Avoidance). This should also apply in the Chinese culture city-states of Hong Kong and Singapore (see Figure 32.3).

The USA is close to the center of Figure 32.3 and so are the Netherlands and Switzerland. This may explain something of the success of US, Dutch, and Swiss multinationals in operating a variety of cultures. In the US literature and practice, all four models of organization – the pyramid, the well-oiled machine, the village market, and the family – can be found, but none of them can be considered dominant.

Motivation

The theories of motivation (what makes people act) and the practices of motivating people can both be related to the Individualism–Collectivism dimension. In the USA, the highest motivation is supposed to stem from individuals' need to fulfill their obligations towards themselves. We find terms like 'self-actualization' and 'self-respect' on top of the list of motivators. In a more Collectivist society, however, people will try primarily to fulfill their obligations towards their ingroup. This may be their family, but their collective loyalty may also be directed towards some larger unit: their enterprise, or their country. Such people do not seek self-actualization or self-respect, but they primarily seek 'face' in their relationships with ingroup members. The importance of face as a motivator does not appear in the US motivation literature at all. The distinction between 'face' cultures and 'self-respect' cultures is similar to the distinction between 'shame' and 'guilt' cultures identified by the anthropologist Ruth Benedict (1974).

Other dimensions relevant to motivation are Uncertainty Avoidance and Masculinity–Femininity. Let us look at Figure 32.4 again. The dominant theme of the US literature of the past twenty years is that people are basically motivated by a desire to achieve something. We should, therefore, allow our people to achieve: give them challenge, and enrich their jobs if they do not contain any challenge. The idea of 'achievement' and 'challenge,' US style, implies two things: a willingness to take some risks (weak Uncertainty Avoidance) and a need to perform, to assert oneself (Masculinity). It is therefore no wonder that in Figure 32.4 we find the USA in the weak Uncertainty Avoidance, Masculine corner. It shares this position with the other Anglo countries. Let us take the case of some other countries, however: Japan or Germany. These are also Masculine countries but with stronger Uncertainty Avoidance. This means that in these countries there is less willingness to take risks: security is a powerful motivator. People are very willing to perform if they are offered security in exchange. Interestingly, these security seeking countries seem to have been doing better economically in the past twenty years than the risk-takers; but the management theories that tell us that risk-taking is a good thing were made in the USA or Great Britain, not in Japan or Germany.

If we go to the other corner of Figure 32.4, we find the Netherlands and the Nordic countries combining weak Uncertainty Avoidance with a more Feminine value system. Here, the maintenance of good interpersonal relations is a strong motivator, and people frown at competition for performance. In these countries we meet a powerful interpersonal motivation which is missing in the US theories. There is a striking difference in the forms of 'humanization of work' proposed in the USA and in Sweden: a stress in the USA on creating possibilities for individual perform-ance, but a stress in Sweden on creating possibilities for inter-personal solidarity. In the fourth corner of Figure 32.4 we find both security and interpersonal motivation; Yugoslav worker self-management contains both elements. We are far away here from the motivation to achieve according to the US style.

Conclusion: the cultural relativity of management and organization practices and theories

Both management practitioners and management theorists over the past eighty years have been blind to the extent to which activities like 'management' and 'organization' are culturally dependent. They are culturally dependent because managing and organizing do not consist of making or moving tangible objects, but of manipulating symbols which have meaning to the people who are managed or organized. Because the meaning which we associate with symbols is heavily affected by what we have learned in our family, in our school, in our work environment, and in our society, management and organization are penetrated with culture from the beginning to the end. Practice is usually wiser than theory, and if we see what effective organizations in different cultures have done, we recognize that their leaders did adapt foreign management ideas to local cultural conditions. This happened extremely effectively in Japan, where mainly US management theories were taken over but in an adapted form. This adaptation led to entirely new forms of practice which in the Japanese case were highly successful. An example is the Quality Control Circle, originally based on US impulses but adapted to the Japanese uncertainty-avoiding, semicollectivist environment. The Quality Control Circle has been so effective in Japan that now the Americans are bringing it back to the USA, but it is doubtful whether most of its present US protagonists realize the role that Japanese educational and social conditions play in the ability of Japanese workers to function effectively in a Quality Control Circle.

Not all other countries have been as fortunate as Japan in that a successful adaptation of American management theories and prac-tices could take place. In Europe, but even more often in Third World countries, foreign management methods and ideas were indiscriminately imported as part of 'technology transfer'. The evident failure of much of the international development assistance of the 1960s and 1970s is at least partly due to this lack of cultural sensitivity in the transfer of management ideas. It has caused enormous economic losses and human suffering. Free market capitalism as practised in the USA, for example, is an idea which is deeply rooted historically and culturally in Individualism. 'Everybody for himself' is supposed to lead to the highest common good, according to Adam Smith (1970). If this idea is forced upon a traditionally Collectivist society, it means that work organizations will be created which do not offer to employees the protection which they expect to get in exchange for their loyalty. The system itself in such a society breeds disloyal, irresponsible employees. Japan has not taken over this aspect of capitalism and has maintained a much higher level of protection of employees by their organization. Many US managers and politicians have great problems with recognizing that their type of capitalism is culturally unsuitable for a more Collectivist society. It is for good cultural reasons that various forms of state capitalism or state socialism are tried in Third World countries.

Most present-day management theories are 'ethnocentric', that is, they take the cultural environment of the theorist for granted. What we need is more cultural sensitivity in management theories; we could call the result 'organizational anthropology' or 'management anthropology'. It is unlikely to be the product of one single country's intellectual effort; it needs by definition a synergy between ideas from different sources. The fact that no single country now enjoys a degree of economic dominance as the USA once did will certainly help: economic power is all too often related to intellectual influence. In a world in which economic power is more widely spread, we can more easily hope to recognize truth coming from many sources. In this process, the contribution of Japanese and Chinese scholars, for example, will be vital, because they represent sources of practical wisdom and ideas which complement practices and ideas born in Europe and the USA.

The convergence of management will never come. What we can bring about is an understanding of how the culture in which we grew up and which is dear to us affects our thinking differently from other peoples' thinking, and what this means for the transfer of management practices and theories. What this can also lead to is a better ability to manage intercultural negotiations and multicultural organizations like the United Nations, which are essential for the common survival of us all.

References

Benedict, Ruth (1974) *The Chrysanthemum and the Sword: Patterns of Japanese Culture* (1946). New York, NY: New American Library. p. 222.

Hofstede, Geert (1980) *Culture's Consequences: International Differences in Work-Related Values*. Beverly Hills, London: Sage.

Hofstede, Geert (1983) 'Dimensions of national cultures in fifty countries and three regions', in J. Deregowski, S. Dziurawiec, and R.C. Annis (eds), *Expiscations in Cross-Cultural Psychology*. Lisse, Netherlands: Swets and Zeitlinger.

Smith, Adam (1970) *The Wealth of Nations* (1776). Harmondsworth, UK: Penguin.

33

Communicating across cultural barriers

Nancy Adler

> If we seek to understand a people, we have to try to put ourselves, as far as we can, in that particular historical and cultural background . . . It is not easy for a person of one country to enter into the background of another country. So there is great irritation, because one fact that seems obvious to us is not immediately accepted by the other party or does not seem obvious to him at all . . . But that extreme irritation will go when we think . . . that he is just differently conditioned and simply can't get out of that condition. One has to recognize that whatever the future may hold, countries and people differ . . . in their approach to life and their ways of living and thinking. In order to understand them, we have to understand their way of life and approach. If we wish to convince them, we have to use their language as far as we can, not language in the narrow sense of the word, but the language of the mind. That is one necessity. Something that goes even much further than that is not the appeal to logic and reason, but some kind of emotional awareness of other people.
>
> Jawaharlal Nehru, *Visit to America*

All international business activity involves communication. Within the international and global business environment, activities such as exchanging information and ideas, decision making, negotiating, motivating, and leading are all based on the ability of managers from one culture to communicate successfully with managers and employees from other cultures. Achieving effective communication is a challenge to managers worldwide even when the workforce is culturally homogeneous, but when one company includes a variety of languages and cultural backgrounds, effective two-way communication becomes even more difficult [. . .].

Cross-cultural communication

Communication is the exchange of meaning: it is my attempt to let you know what I mean. Communication includes any behavior that another human being perceives and interprets: it is your understanding of what I mean. Communication includes sending both verbal messages (words) and nonverbal messages (tone of voice,

---

Abridged from N. Adler, *International Dimensions of Organizational Behavior*, 2nd edn, Belmont, CA: Wadsworth, 1991, pp. 63–91.

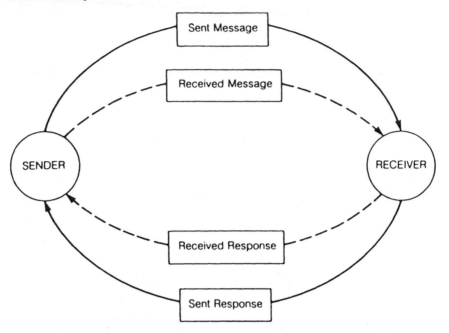

Figure 33.1   *Communication model*

facial expression, behavior, and physical setting). It includes consciously sent messages as well as messages that the sender is totally unaware of sending. Whatever I say and do, I cannot *not* communicate. Communication therefore involves a complex, multi-layered, dynamic process through which we exchange meaning.

Every communication has a message sender and a message receiver. As shown in Figure 33.1, the sent message is never identical to the received message. Why? Communication is indirect; it is a symbolic behavior. Ideas, feelings, and pieces of information cannot be communicated directly but must be externalized or symbolized before being communicated. *Encoding* describes the producing of a symbol message. *Decoding* describes the receiving of a message from a symbol. The message sender must encode his or her meaning into a form that the receiver will recognize – that is, into words and behavior. Receivers must then decode the words and behavior – the symbols – back into messages that have meaning for them.

For example, because the Cantonese word *eight* sounds like *faat*, which means prosperity, a Hong Kong textile manufacturer Mr Lau Ting-pong paid $5 million in 1988 for car registration number 8. A year later, a European millionaire paid $4.8 million at Hong Kong's Lunar New Year auction for vehicle registration number 7, a decision that mystified the Chinese, since the number 7 has little significance in the Chinese calculation of fortune (*South China Morning Post*, 1989).

Similarly, the prestigious members of Hong Kong's Legislative Council refrained from using numbers ending in 4 to identify their newly installed lockers. Some Chinese consider numbers ending with the digit 4 to be jinxed, because the sound of the Cantonese word *sei* is the same for *four* and *death*. The number 24, for instance, sounds like *yee sei* or *death-prone* in Cantonese (Ho, 1988).

Translating meanings into words and behaviors – that is, into symbols – and back again into meanings is based on a person's cultural background and is not the same for each person. The greater the difference in background between senders and receivers, the greater the difference in meanings attached to particular words and behaviors. For example:

> A British boss asked a new, young American employee if he would like to have an early lunch at 11 a.m. each day. The employee answered, 'Yeah, that would be great!' The boss, hearing the word *yeah* instead of the word *yes*, assumed that the employee was rude, ill-mannered, and disrespectful. The boss responded with a curt, 'With that kind of attitude, you may as well forget about lunch!' The employee was bewildered. What had gone wrong? In the process of encoding agreement (the meaning) into *yeah* (a word symbol) and decoding the *yeah* spoken by a new employee to the boss (a word, behavior, and context symbol), the boss received an entirely different message than the employee had meant to send. Unfortunately, as is the case in most miscommunication, neither the sender nor the receiver was fully aware of what had gone wrong and why.

Cross-cultural communication occurs when a person from one culture sends a message to a person from another culture. Cross-cultural miscommunication occurs when the person from the second culture does not receive the sender's intended message. The greater the differences between the sender's and the receiver's cultures, the greater the chance for cross-cultural miscommunication. For example:

> A Japanese businessman wants to tell his Norwegian client that he is uninterested in a particular sale. To be polite, the Japanese says, 'That will be very difficult.' The Norwegian interprets the statement to mean that there are still unresolved problems, not that the deal is off. He responds by asking how his company can help solve the problems. The Japanese, believing he has sent the message that there will be no sale, is mystified by the response.

Communication does not necessarily result in understanding. Cross-cultural communication continually involves misunderstanding caused by misperception, misinterpretation, and misevaluation. When the sender of a message comes from one culture and the receiver from another, the chances of accurately transmitting a message are low. Foreigners see, interpret, and evaluate things differently, and consequently act upon them differently. In approaching cross-cultural situations, one should therefore *assume difference until similarity is proven*. It is also important to recognize that all behavior makes sense through the eyes of the person behaving and that logic and rationale are culturally relative. In cross-cultural situations, labeling behavior as bizarre usually reflects culturally based misperception, misinterpretation, and misevaluation; rarely does it reflect intentional malice or pathologically motivated behavior. [. . .]

Culturally bizarre behavior: only in the eyes of the beholder

While in Thailand a Canadian expatriate's car was hit by a Thai motorist who had crossed over the double line while passing another vehicle. After failing to establish that the fault lay with the Thai driver, the Canadian flagged down a policeman. After several minutes of seemingly futile discussion, the Canadian pointed out the double line in the middle of the road and asked the policemen directly, 'What do these lines signify?' The policeman replied, 'They indicate the center of the road and are there so I can establish just how far the accident is from that point.' The Canadian was silent. It had never occurred to him that the double line might not mean 'no passing allowed.'

Unwritten rules reflect a culture's interpretation of its surroundings. A foreign columnist for the English-language *Bangkok Post* once proclaimed that the unwritten traffic rule in Thailand is: 'When there are more than three cars in front of you at a stop sign or intersection, start your own line!' This contravenes the Western stay-in-line ethic, of course, but it effectively portrays, albeit in slightly exaggerated fashion, a fairly consistent form of behavior at intersections in Thailand. And it drives non-Thais crazy! (Miles, in press)

Cross-cultural misinterpretation

Interpretation occurs when an individual gives meaning to observations and their relationships; it is the process of making sense out of perceptions. Interpretation organizes our experience to guide our behavior. Based on our experience, we make assumptions about our perceptions so we will not have to rediscover meanings each time we encounter similar situations. For example, we make assumptions about how doors work, based on our experience of entering and leaving rooms; thus we do not have to relearn each time we have to open a door. Similarly, when we smell smoke, we generally assume there is a fire. We do not have to stop and wonder if the smoke indicates a fire or a flood. Our consistent patterns of interpretation help us to act appropriately and quickly within our day-to-day world.

Categories

Since we are constantly bombarded with more stimuli than we can absorb and more perceptions than we can keep distinct, we only perceive those images that may be meaningful. We group perceived images into familiar categories that help to simplify our environment, become the basis for our interpretations, and allow us to function in an otherwise overly complex world. For example, as a driver approaching an intersection, I may or may not notice the number of children in the back seat of the car next to me, but I will notice whether the traffic light is red or green (selective perception). If the light is red, I automatically place it in the category of all red traffic signals (categorization). This time, like prior times, I stop (behavior based on interpretation). Although people are capable of distinguishing thousands of different colors, I do not take the time to notice if the red light in Istanbul is brighter or duller than the one in Singapore or more orange or more purple than the one in Nairobi; I just stop. Categorization helps me to distinguish what is most important in my environment and to behave accordingly.

Categories of perceived images become ineffective when we place people and things in the wrong group Cross-cultural miscategorization occurs when I use my home country categories to make sense out of foreign situations. For example, a Korean businessman entered a client's office in Stockholm and encountered a woman behind the desk. Assuming that she was a secretary, he announced that he wanted to see Mr Silferbrand. The woman responded by saying that the secretary would be happy to help him. The Korean became confused. In assuming that most women are secretaries rather than managers, he had misinterpreted the situation and acted inappropriately. His category makes sense because most women in Korean offices are secretaries. But it proved counterproductive since this particular Swedish woman was not a secretary.

Stereotypes

Stereotyping involves a form of categorization that organizes our experience and guides our behavior toward ethnic and national groups. Stereotypes never describe individual behavior; rather, they describe the behavioral norm for members of a particular group. For example, the stereotypes of English and French businesspeople, as analyzed by Intercultural Management Associates in Paris, are described as follows:

We have found that to every set of negative stereotypes distinguishing the British and French there corresponds a particular values divergence that, when recognized, can prove an extraordinary resource. To illustrate: the French, in describing the British as 'perfidious', 'hypocritical', and 'vague', are in fact describing the Englishman's typical lack of a general model or theory and his preference for a more pragmatic, evolutionary approach. This fact is hard for the Frenchman to believe, let alone accept as a viable alternative, until, working alongside one another, the Frenchman comes to see that there is usually no ulterior motive behind the Englishman's vagueness but rather a capacity to think aloud and adapt to circumstances. For his part, the Englishman comes to see that, far from being 'distant', 'superior', or 'out of touch with reality', the Frenchman's concern for a general model or theory is what lends vision, focus, and cohesion to an enterprise or project, as well as leadership and much needed authority. (Gancel and Ratiu, 1984)

Stereotypes, like other forms of categories, can be helpful or harmful depending on how we use them. Effective stereotyping allows people to understand and act appropriately in new situations. A stereotype can be helpful when it is

- *Consciously held*   The person should be aware that he or she is describing a group norm rather than the characteristics of a specific individual.
- *Descriptive* rather than evaluative. The stereotype should describe what people from this group will probably be like and not evaluate those people as good or bad.
- *Accurate*   The stereotype should accurately describe the norm for the group to which the person belongs.
- *The first best guess* about a group prior to having direct information about the specific person or persons involved.
- *Modified,* based on further observation and experience with the actual people and situations.

A subconsciously held stereotype is difficult to modify or discard even after we collect real information about a person, because it is often thought to reflect reality. If a subconscious stereotype also inaccurately evaluates a person or situation, we are likely to maintain an inappropriate, ineffective, and frequently harmful guide to reality. For example, assume that I subconsciously hold the stereotype that Anglophone Quebecois refuse to learn French and that therefore they should have no rights within the province (an inaccurate, evaluative stereotype). I then meet a monolingual Anglophone and say, 'See, I told you that Anglophones aren't willing to speak French! They don't deserve to have rights here.' I next meet a bilingual Anglophone and conclude, 'He must be American because Canadian Anglophones always refuse to learn French.' Instead of questioning, modifying, or discarding my stereotype ('Some Anglophone Canadians speak French'), I alter reality to fit the stereotype ('He must be American').

Stereotypes increase effectiveness only when used as a *first best guess* about a person or situation prior to having direct information. They never help when adhered to rigidly.

Indrei Ratiu (1983), in his work with INSEAD (Institut Européen d'Administration des Affaires – European Institute of Business Administration) and London Business School, found that managers ranked 'most internationally effective' by their colleagues altered their stereotypes to fit the actual people involved, whereas managers ranked 'least internationally effective' continued to maintain their stereotypes even in the face of contradictory information. For example, internationally effective managers, prior to their first visit to Germany, might stereotype Germans as being extremely task oriented. Upon arriving and meeting a very friendly and lazy Herr Schmidt, they would alter their description to say that most Germans appear extremely task oriented, but Herr Schmidt seems friendly and lazy. Months later, the most internationally effective managers would only be able to say that some Germans appear very task oriented, while others seem quite relationship oriented (friendly); it all depends on the person and the situation. In this instance, the stereotype is used as a first best guess about the group's behavior prior to meeting any individuals from the group. As time goes on, it is modified or discarded entirely; information about each individual supersedes the group stereotype. By contrast, the least internationally effective managers maintain their stereotypes. They assume that the contradictory evidence in Herr Schmidt's case represents an exception, and they continue to believe that *all* Germans are highly task oriented. In drawing conclusions too quickly on the basis of insufficient information – premature closure – their stereotypes become self-fulfilling.

Canadian psychologist Donald Taylor (Berry et al. 1976; 1977; Taylor, 1980) found that most people maintain their stereotypes even in the face of contradictory evidence. Taylor asked English and French Canadians to listen to one of three tape recordings of a French Canadian describing himself. In the first version, the French Canadian used the Francophone stereotype and described himself as religious, proud, sensitive, and expressive. In the second version, he used neutral terms to describe himself. In the third version, he used terms to describe himself that contradicted the stereotype, such as not religious, humble, unexpressive, and conservative. After having listened to one of the three versions, the participants were asked to describe the Francophone on the tape (not Francophones in general). Surprisingly, people who listened to each of the three versions used the same stereotypic terms – religious, proud, sensitive, and expressive – even when the voice on the tape had conveyed the opposite information. People evidently maintain stereotypes even in the face of contradictory information.

To be effective, international managers must therefore be aware of cultural stereotypes and learn to set them aside when faced with contradictory evidence. They cannot *pretend* not to stereotype.

If stereotyping is so useful as an initial guide to reality, why do people malign it? Why do parents and teachers constantly admonish children not to stereotype? Why do sophisticated managers rarely admit to stereotyping, even though each of us stereotypes every day? The answer is that we have failed to accept stereotyping as a natural process and have consequently failed to learn to use it to our advantage. For years we have viewed stereotyping as a form of primitive thinking, as an unnecessary simplification of reality. We have also viewed stereotyping as immoral: stereotypes can be inappropriate judgments of individuals based on inaccurate descriptions of groups. It is true that labeling people from a certain ethnic group as 'bad' is immoral, but grouping individuals into categories is neither good nor bad – it simply reduces a complex reality to manageable dimensions. Negative views of stereotyping simply cloud our ability to understand people's actual behavior and impair our awareness of our own stereotypes. *Everyone* stereotypes.

In conclusion, some people stereotype effectively and others do not. Stereotypes become counterproductive when we place people in the wrong groups, when we incorrectly describe the group norm, when we inappropriately evaluate the group or category, when we confuse the stereotype with the description of a particular individual, and when we fail to modify the stereotype based on our actual observations and experience.

Sources of misinterpretation

Misinterpretation can be caused by inaccurate perceptions of a person or situation that arise when what actually exists is not seen. It can be caused by an inaccurate interpretation of what is seen; that is, by using *my* meanings to make sense out of *your* reality. An example of this type of misinterpretation (or misattribution) comes from an encounter with an Austrian businessman.

> I meet my Austrian client for the sixth time in as many months. He greets me as Herr Smith. Categorizing him as a businessman, I interpret his very formal behavior to mean that he does not like me or is uninterested in developing a closer relationship with me. (North American attribution: people who maintain formal behavior after the first few meetings do so because they dislike or distrust the associates so treated.) In fact, I have misinterpreted his behavior. I have used the norms for North American business behavior, which are more informal and demonstrative (I would say 'Good morning, Fritz,' not 'Good morning, Herr Ranschburg'), to interpret the Austrian's more formal behavior ('Good morning, Herr Smith').

Culture strongly influences, and in many cases determines, our interpretations. Both the categories and the meanings we attach to them are based on our cultural background. Sources of cross-cultural misinterpretation include subconscious cultural 'blinders' [or blinkers], a lack of cultural self-awareness, projected similarity, and parochialism.

Subconscious cultural blinders   Because most interpretation goes on at a subconscious level, we lack awareness of the assumptions we make and their cultural basis. Our home culture reality never forces us to examine our assumptions or the extent to which they are culturally based, because we share our cultural assumptions with most other citizens of our country. All we know is that things do not work as smoothly or logically when we work outside our own culture as when we work with people more similar to ourselves. For example:

> A Canadian conducting business in Kuwait is surprised when his meeting with a high ranking official is not held in a closed office and is constantly interrupted. Using the Canadian-based cultural assumptions that (a) important people have large private offices with secretaries to monitor the flow of people into the office, and (b) important business takes precedence over less important business and is therefore not interrupted, the Canadian interprets the Kuwaiti's open office and constant interruptions to mean that the official is neither as high ranking nor as interested in conducting the business at hand as he had previously thought. The Canadian's interpretation of the office environment leads him to lose interest in working with the Kuwaiti.

The problem is that the Canadian's interpretation derives from his own North American norms, not from Middle Eastern cultural norms. The Kuwaiti may well have been a high-ranking official who was very interested in doing business. The Canadian will never know.

Cases of subconscious cross-cultural misinterpretation occur frequently. For example a Soviet poet, after lecturing at American universities for two months, said, 'Attempts to please an American audience are doomed in advance, because out of twenty listeners five may hold one point of view, seven another, and eight may have none at all' (Kanungo, 1980). The Soviet poet confused Americans' freedom of thought and speech with his ability to please them. He assumed that one can only please an audience if all members hold the same opinion. Another example of well-meant misinterpretation comes from the United States Office of Education's (1976) advice to teachers of newly arrived Vietnamese refugee students:

> Students' participation was discouraged in Vietnamese schools by liberal doses of corporal punishment, and students were conditioned to sit rigidly and speak out

only when spoken to. This background . . . makes speaking freely in class hard for a Vietnamese student. Therefore, don't mistake shyness for apathy.

Perhaps the extent to which this is a culturally based interpretation becomes clearer if we imagine the opposite advice the Vietnamese Ministry of Education might give to Vietnamese teachers receiving American children for the first time.

Students' proper respect for teachers was discouraged by a loose order and students were conditioned to chat all the time and to behave in other disorderly ways. This background makes proper and respectful behavior in class hard for an American student. Therefore, do not mistake rudeness for lack of reverence.

Lack of cultural self-awareness   Although we think that the major obstacle in international business is in understanding the foreigner, the greater difficulty involves becoming aware of our own cultural conditioning. As anthropologist Edward Hall (1976) has explained, 'What is known least well, and is therefore in the poorest position to be studied, is what is closest to oneself.' We are generally least aware of our own cultural characteristics and are quite surprised when we hear foreigners' descriptions of us. For example, many Americans are surprised to discover that they are seen by foreigners as hurried, overly law-abiding, very hard working, extremely explicit, and overly inquisitive. Many American businesspeople were equally surprised by a *Newsweek* survey reporting the characteristics most and least frequently associated with Americans (see Table 33.1). Asking a foreign national to describe businesspeople from your country is a powerful way to see yourself as others see you. [. . .]

To the extent that we can begin to see ourselves clearly through the eyes of foreigners, we can begin to modify our behavior, emphasizing our most appropriate and effective characteristics and minimizing those least helpful. To the extent that we are culturally self-aware, we can begin to predict the effect our behavior will have on others.

Projected similarity   Projected similarity refers to the assumption that people are more similar to you than they actually are, or that a situation is more similar to yours when in fact it is not. Projecting similarity reflects both a natural and a common process. American researchers Burger and Bass (1979) worked with groups of managers from fourteen different countries. They asked each manager to describe the work and life goals of a colleague from another country. [. . .] In every case the managers assumed that their foreign colleagues were more like themselves than they actually were. Projected similarity involves assuming, imagining, and actually perceiving similarity when differences exist. Projected similarity particularly handicaps people in cross-cultural situations. As a South African, I

Table 33.1   *How others see Americans*

			Characteristics[1] associated with Americans by the populations of			
	France	Japan	West Germany	Great Britain	Brazil	Mexico
Most often associated						
	Industrious	Nationalistic	Energetic	Friendly	Intelligent	Industrious
	Energetic	Friendly	Inventive	Self-indulgent	Inventive	Intelligent
	Inventive	Decisive	Friendly	Energetic	Energetic	Inventive
	Decisive	Rude	Sophisticated	Industrious	Industrious	Decisive
	Friendly	Self-indulgent	Intelligent	Nationalistic	Greedy	Greedy
Least often associated						
	Lazy	Industrious	Lazy	Lazy	Lazy	Lazy
	Rude	Lazy	Sexy	Sophisticated	Self-indulgent	Honest
	Honest	Honest	Greedy	Sexy	Sexy	Rude
	Sophisticated	Sexy	Rude	Decisive	Sophisticated	Sexy

Source: Newsweek, 11 July 1983, p. 50, copyright © 1981 by Newsweek, Inc. All rights reserved, reprinted by permission.

[1] From a list of fourteen characteristics.

assume that my Greek colleague is more South African than he actually is. As an Egyptian, I assume that my Chilean colleague is more similar to me than she actually is. When I act based on this assumed similarity, I often find that I have acted inappropriately and thus ineffectively.

At the base of projected similarity is a subconscious parochialism. I assume that there is only one way to be: my way. I assume that there is only one way to see the world: my way. I therefore view other people in reference to me and to my way of viewing the world. People may fall into an

> illusion of understanding while being unaware of . . . [their] misunderstandings. 'I understand you perfectly but you don't understand me' is an expression typical of such a situation. Or all communicating parties may fall into a collective illusion of mutual understanding. In such a situation, each party may wonder later why other parties do not live up to the 'agreement' they had reached. (Maruyama, 1974)

Most international managers do not see themselves as parochial. They believe that as world travelers they are able to see the foreigner's point of view. This is not always true.

> When a Danish manager works with a Saudi and the Saudi states that the plant will be completed on time, 'En shah allah' ('If God is willing'), the Dane rarely believes that God's will is really going to influence the construction progress. He continues to see the world from his parochial Danish perspective and assumes that 'En shah allah' is just an excuse for not getting the work done, or is meaningless altogether.
>
> Similarly, when Balinese workers' families refuse to use birth control methods, explaining that it will break the cycle of reincarnation, few Western managers really consider that there is a possibility that they too will be reborn a number of times. Instead, they assume that the Balinese do not understand or are afraid of Western medicine.

While it is important to understand and respect the foreigner's point of view, it is not necessary to accept or adopt it. A rigid adherence to our own belief system is a form of parochialism, and parochialism underlies projected similarity.

One of the best exercises for developing empathy and reducing parochialism and projected similarity is *role reversal*. Imagine that you are a foreign businessperson. Imagine the type of family you come from, the number of brothers and sisters you have, the social and economic conditions you grew up with, the type of education you received, the ways in which you chose your profession and position, the ways in which you were introduced to your spouse, your goals in working for your organization, and your life goals. Asking these questions forces you to see the other person as he or she really is, and not as a mere reflection of yourself. It forces you to see both the similarities and the differences, and not to imagine similarities when differences actually exist. Moreover, role reversal encourages highly task-oriented businesspeople, such as Americans, to see the foreigner as a whole person rather than someone with a position and a set of skills needed to accomplish a particular task.

References

Berry, J., Kalin, R. and Taylor, D. (1976) 'Multiculturalism and ethnic attitudes in Canada', in *Multiculturalism as State Policy*. Ottawa: Government of Canada.

Berry, J., Kalin, R. and Taylor, D. (1977) *Multiculturalism and Ethnic Attitudes in Canada*. Ottawa: Minister of Supply and Services.

Burger, P. and Bass, B. M. (1979) *Assessment of Managers: an International Comparison*. New York: Free Press.

Gancel, C. and Ratiu, I. (1984) Internal document. Paris: Inter Cultural Management Associates.

Hall, E. T. (1976) *Beyond Culture*. Garden City, NY: Anchor Press/Doubleday. Also see E. T. Hall's *The Silent Language*, Doubleday 1959 and Anchor Books 1973; and *The Hidden Dimension*, Doubleday 1966 and Anchor Books 1969.

Ho, A. (1988) 'Unlucky numbers are locked out of the chamber', *South China Morning Post*, 26 December: 1.

Kanungo, R. N. (1980) *Biculturalism and Management*. Ontario: Butterworth.

Maruyama, M. (1974) 'Paradigms and communication', *Technological Forecasting and Social Change*, 6: 3–32.

Miles, M. *Adaptation to a Foreign Environment*. Ottawa: Canadian International Development Agency, in press.

Ratiu, I. (1983) 'Thinking internationally: a comparison of how international executives learn', *International Studies of Management and Organization*, XIII (1–2): 139–50. Reprinted by permission of publisher, M. E. Sharpe, Inc., Armonk, NY.

South China Morning Post (1989), 'Mystery man gives a fortune for lucky "7"', 22 January: 3; and 'Lucky "7" to go on sale', 4 January: 4.

Taylor, D. (1980) 'American tradition', in R. C. Gardner and R. Kalin (eds), *A Canadian Social Psychology of Ethnic Relations*. Toronto: Methuen Press.

US Office of Education (1976), *On Teaching the Vietnamese*. Washington, DC: General Printing Office.

34

Actions speak louder than words

Rosemary Thomson

Imagine that you are interviewing three candidates for a job. All of them have similar technical and educational backgrounds, are about the same age and have two to three years' experience in similar work. All are external candidates and you have never met any of them before.

Candidate A walks through your door, looks you in the eye, smiles and shakes your hand firmly. This person is neatly dressed, shoes are unscuffed, hair is tidy. You notice all these things in the time it takes for you to smile in return. In response to your questions, the candidate explains things clearly and appears to be relaxed.
Candidate B on the other hand appears to be ill at ease with you. He keeps scratching his ear which you find an irritation and you have difficulty in hearing what he is saying because he keeps his head lowered while speaking. He also shifts around in his chair and fiddles with a pen.
Candidate C also worries you but not for the same reasons. She does not meet your eye when she shakes your hand, sits perfectly still and appears to have her gaze permanently fixed on a point slightly to the left of your head. In fact, you glance round to see if there is something holding her attention as you do not feel it is fixed on you and what you have to say.

You have the candidates' application forms in front of you. Candidate A has filled in the form neatly and carefully with the relevant information; the handwriting is clear and easy to read. Candidate B's form is difficult to read and contains much irrelevant detail; his handwriting is almost illegible in places. Candidate C has typed her answers on the form but has left out several important details and offered only the minimum of information; in an accompanying letter, she has only written two lines which you find featureless and uninteresting. You offer the job to candidate A.

You might have had some difficulty, however, in justifying your

Adapted by R. Thomson from R. Thomson, 'Actions speak louder than words', in *Resource Book: Communication*, B784 The Effective Manager, 1992, The Open University.

choice on fair selection criteria such as technical expertise, experience, education and aptitude since all three candidates matched these criteria equally. In all probability, the sense of their answers to your questions would be similar – they may even have used roughly the same words. Yet candidate A seemed such an 'obvious' choice. This person gave out certain positive signals which you received favourably and which had nothing to do with the actual words spoken or written. Appearance, tone of voice, facial expression, eye contact and gesture – all elements of non-verbal communication – had all played a very important part in this hypothetical interview situation and in your final choice.

The American psychologist Albert Mehrabian (1969) attempted to measure the relevant amounts of impact created by the actual words spoken, the tone of the speaker's voice and the accompanying non-verbal signals (facial expression, posture, gesture and so on). He found that the words themselves made less than 10% of the total impact on the listener. The tone of voice made around 40% but the non-verbal signals were, overall, of most importance, creating more than 50% of the total communication impact.

Non-verbal communication (NVC) can be defined as 'all messages (or communications) not coded in words' (Lewis, 1975). Most NVC is unconscious and, normally, accompanies everything we say unless it is deliberately controlled. Try turning down the volume of your television set during a 'chat' show and watch the participants smile, frown, fidget, raise an eyebrow, wave a hand, lean forwards or backwards. Even without the sound of the words, you can usually get a good general idea of how they are reacting to the interviewer – with amusement, nervousness, irritation, bewilderment and so on. Some people may consciously employ NVC to their own advantage because they are aware of its impact. Margaret Thatcher, for example, took voice lessons to help her lower the pitch of her voice and slow down the rate of her speech; her smile was improved by teeth capping and she took expert advice on clothes, hairstyle, jewellery and make-up for television appearances.

The functions of non-verbal communication

As a manager, an awareness of the effect of NVC can help you in two ways. First, you can use it to reveal your feelings and give feedback to other people without the need for words, or to reinforce the spoken words. Secondly, through observation, you can make some reasonable judgements about other people by watching what they are communicating non-verbally and becoming more sensitive to underlying meanings. In most cases, you will need to take into account a whole range of non-verbal signals as well as spoken or written words to get a clear picture of the real message.

At the beginning of this article, I outlined a rather stereotyped interview situation in which NVC played a major part in the selection process. In this kind of situation, NVC can reinforce, contradict or neutralise the spoken word (Delahanty, 1970). In the cases I described, NVC at the interview actually reinforced what the interviewer had already gleaned from the written material submitted by each candidate. But if you are in the position of the interviewer and, in line with fair selection practices, rely on NVC alone when making a decision, you would have great difficulty in justifying such a decision.

This kind of reinforcing, contradictory or neutralising effect can occur in any two-way, face-to-face communication. I once worked for someone who constantly had a slight smile on his face. It was often several moments before I realised that what he was actually *saying* was rather negative or unpleasant. How often have you asked someone if they are feeling alright and received the verbal response, 'Fine, thank you', yet realised that the person is not 'fine' at all? It may be her expression, the way she is sitting, her avoidance of your eyes or some gesture such as tapping her foot or rubbing her nose while speaking to you that makes you sense that all is not well. In this case, NVC is contradicting the spoken words. If, for example, you praise someone's work in a cool and expressionless way, the words themselves lose their impact and the effect is neutralised.

Michael Argyle (1976) subdivides NVC into two categories, tactile and visual, which can be used to describe some of the main features of this aspect of face-to-face communication. The area has been well researched by social psychologists and there are complex notations which have been devised to chart changes in posture and expression. You can learn a great deal about this phenomenon through further reading and observation.

Tactile and visual NVC

Touch and touch-avoidance

Physical contact is the most basic form of NVC. We hug those we love, pat a colleague on the shoulder, put an arm around a friend to offer comfort or sympathy. We touch someone on the arm to get their attention; we may hit out at someone in anger or defence, shake hands in greeting or farewell and pat a child on the head for approval. In different cultures, however, touch is used in a variety of culture-specific ways. In Japan, for example, the formal bow replaces the Western handshake, while some Eskimos greet each other with a gentle blow to the shoulder (Argyle, 1976). Some people avoid touching others at all; some avoid being touched. People from the island of Rhodes, for example, continually touch each other while talking; people from Athens seem to need less physical contact. Inhabitants of Marseilles from similar cultural backgrounds have been observed touching each other eight times or more during a 30 minute discussion. People from the Parisian culture, on the other hand, are only likely to touch each other twice during the same time, and then for the traditional handshake on meeting and parting (Patounas, 1987).

Touch is not, therefore, universal and, in some cases, it can be unproductive as NVC. In fact, it can represent disrespect or create unfavourable reactions which you did not intend. Argyle maintains that the amount and type of physical contact between people depends to a large extent on their age and relationship and on the culture to which they belong.

Physical space

The distance people prefer to keep between them and others also appears to depend on cultural background. Germans, North Americans and Swedes tend to need more personal space than Latin Americans, Greeks, southern Italians and Arabs. Arabs when compared with Americans tend to confront each other more directly, stand closer, touch more often, maintain eye contact and speak louder (Eysenck and Eysenck, 1981).

Most people feel comfortable with a space of between 1.2 metres (personal space) and 3 metres (social space) between themselves and others, depending on relationships. In an experiment carried out by researchers at the University of California, a female experimenter sat down as closely as possible to female college students in a relatively empty university library. Within 30 minutes, 70% of these students left the library. Have you noticed how people who need a comfortable amount of personal physical space will erect barriers between themselves and adjacent or opposite seats by using bags, coats and so on to mark off their 'territory'? And, if you travel in a crowded train or other public vehicle, watch how people avoid eye contact with strangers who are invading their personal space.

Beyond 3 metres is considered to be 'public' space and is also used to indicate status. The more important the individual, the larger the office and, probably, the desk and chair, creating more space between that person and other people. Think of the judge in a courtroom or the politician on the platform, both separated by space and height to reinforce their status.

Posture

The ways in which people sit, stand or move about often reflect both their own culture and the status they feel they have (or want) in relation to other people. The cultural aspect relates to accepted conventions of posture such as standing up when someone important enters the room and kneeling to pray in some churches; others reflect feelings such as pressing one's body against a wall or cowering in a corner when afraid, 'jumping for joy' or hugging one's own body in pain or anguish. Status can also be inferred from body posture; a dominant person tends to tilt the head upwards while submission is indicated by a bowed head.

There are some other generalisations which can be made about posture although they are not always true in every case. Someone who leans forward is usually interested in what the other person is saying, but this position can also denote anxiety or concern or the inability to hear what is being said: you would need to look for other signs of NVC to make the right judgement. Leaning backwards in a relaxed position can indicate detachment, boredom or self-confidence: people who regard themselves as being of higher status than others often adopt a more relaxed posture.

Physical appearance

Non-verbal communication can also be conveyed through dress, grooming and physical appearance. Iles and Robertson (1988) researched this aspect of NVC in their study of physical attractiveness, gender and selection decisions. They suggested, for example, that female candidates for managerial jobs in more 'masculine' dress might have a greater chance of being selected than those wearing 'female' dress, and candidates of both sexes who wore perfume or after-shave might be more likely to be given higher personality ratings by female interviewers, but lower ratings by male interviewers (based on Herriot, 1987). Physical attractiveness appears to have a significant impact on interviewer judgements of candidate suitability because good-looking individuals are often associated with social desirability and success. This is known as the 'beautyism' effect and can even influence marks awarded for performance by students in written essays or lessen the extent of punishment given for civil or moral crimes.

Clothes are a major part of physical appearance since they cover most of the body. Unless a uniform is worn, clothes usually represent the personal choice of the wearer and, thus, are likely to communicate non-verbal signals to the observer. They are also rooted in cultural convention – the 'interview suit', for example, is commonly accepted wear for many men and women in Europe. Unusual or non-conformist clothing tends to communicate messages about the wearer which will interpreted – or misinterpreted – by the observer. So, the wearer may be perceived as a 'rebel', a 'potential troublemaker' or a 'misfit' by some and as 'creative' or 'exciting' by others. Careless dressing seems to be generally off-putting in that it is usually associated with slovenliness, neglect and apathy.

Again, clothing and accessories can represent status: the Gucci bag, the Cartier watch, the pigskin document case all have non-verbal messages attached to them, providing you can recognise them! Would they convey good taste, wealth, vulgarity or extravagance to you? Do you have strong feelings about long or short hair in either men or women? Do you notice – and note – the appearance of people's shoes or fingernails? What non-verbal messages do these convey to you? Do you think it is 'right' to let these factors influence your judgement, or is it unavoidable? Are they relevant to the performance of the individual? How do they relate to current thinking about equal opportunities?

Facial expression

To a considerable extent we can control our physical appearance by choosing what we wear and how we present ourselves. Facial expressions, on the other hand, are much more difficult to control. We tend to smile or frown involuntarily, register surprise or bewilderment unconsciously and have no control over blushing, turning pale or the contraction and dilation of our pupils.

The human face is the most expressive part of the body and plays a major part in NVC. For example, we furrow our brow to indicate puzzlement, raise or lower our eyebrows to denote surprise or irritation, smile when we approve or feel happy, bite our lower lip when we are worried, wink in encouragement, hide a smile with a hand to disguise mirth. As a manager, you can use facial expression to convey a range of emotions such as approval, disapproval and encouragement as effectively as using words. Your expression can often indicate to your staff whether it is worth their while approaching you with a request or a problem. 'I'll wait until she's in a better mood' is often the mental response to an uninviting facial expression.

Eye contact and gaze

'Eye contact is one of the most direct and powerful forms of non-verbal communication' (Tortoriello et al., 1978: Chapter 6). Is the person you are speaking to looking at you or somewhere else, or are you both looking at another object or person? 'Catching someone's eye' – making eye contact – usually signals the desire to communicate either through speech or by other non-verbal signals such as a smile or a frown or a meaningful gesture such as miming the act of drinking from a glass to suggest that you both go for a drink. Does a long, steady look indicate honesty and intimacy or is it some kind of threat? It depends on the situation, obviously. People become uncomfortable if they feel they are being stared at by a stranger but

will gaze into the eyes of a lover almost indefinitely. Short, inter-
mittent bouts of eye contact usually indicate a lack of intimacy or
friendship between two people or that they do not know each other
well. As their knowledge and understanding of each other develop,
eye contact becomes more frequent and prolonged.

Some eye movements convey generally recognised emotions. An
upward gaze can denote remembering, particularly if the eyes are
screwed up. A downward gaze usually means sadness or that the
person is hiding some emotion; it can also denote modesty and
shyness. Wide-eyed expressions are associated with surprise, honesty,
wonder or fear.

In the interview situation described at the start of this article, the
interviewer was disturbed by one candidate's inability to make eye
contact. Avoidance of eye contact often means the person is emotionally uncomfortable for some reason: it may be from fear, shyness,
reluctance to reveal something or unwillingness to communicate.

Gesture

Gestures can be as meaningful as words. In mime, for example,
gestures and expression are raised to an art form in which the actor
carefully exaggerates them so that we can understand what is going
on: gripping the hands tightly together to signify grief, clenching a
fist for anger, outstretched hands with palms uppermost in suppli-
cation and many, more subtle, combinations of NVC. Again, watch
out for cultural differences: in the West we nod our heads to signify
agreement while in Sri Lanka people shake their heads slowly from
side to side to make the same non-verbal point.

We use gestures every day instead of, or to accompany, words:
'Come here', 'I agree', 'Stop', 'Go away' and many more. People
with hearing impairment have a complete sign language of their own
to replace oral speech. Combine all the tactile and visual signs
discussed so far and you can see why the actual words we use are
relatively unimportant.

Visual imagery

The final non-verbal signals I want to identify in this article are
related to the written and printed word rather than to speech. What
does the written word convey to you and what images accompany it?
We can all recognise 'good' English, if we are English-speaking, as
distinct from badly punctuated prose or limited use of vocabulary
and poor grammatical structure. In the latter case, we usually
assume that the person does not speak English as their first language
or is poorly educated – but which is it? The structure of what is
written also signals whether the person is a clear thinker, able to put

thoughts down in a logical sequence. Sometimes, great stress is laid on handwriting. In the USA and in France in particular, some employers rely on graphologists to analyse the handwriting of potential employees at the pre-interview stage.

We also pick up signals from the type of notepaper used, the graphics which head a commercial communication, the layout and clarity of the printing and so on. Marketers are very conscious of the non-verbal signals put out by poor quality written communication: it 'says' something unfavourable about the organisation.

Non-verbal aspects of speech

So far we have been looking at NVC which can be seen or felt. In this part of the article we will concentrate on the way in which the speaker can vary the meaning of words depending on several factors such as tone, timing, silence, speech errors and accent.

Tone and pitch

It is often difficult to separate the tone and pitch of a voice from the actual words themselves, but spend a moment or so saying 'hello' when you want to express different emotions such as warmth, surprise, fear, questioning and puzzlement. How often do people say the word 'no' but you can tell from the tone of their voice that they actually mean something else?

The tone of someone's voice can range across several emotions; it can be sarcastic or sincere, warm or cold, rich and expressive or dull and flat. Apart from their bizarre appearance, why do many robots in films appear menacing? It could be because we can hear no emotion in their voices, which is as alien to us as their shape.

Experiments have been done which show that, when listening to the voice of someone unknown and unseen, the listener tends to judge the content of the message by the speaker's tone rather than by the words themselves. A colleague might *say*, for example, 'That is really great', but from the sarcastic tone of her voice you can tell that she means quite the opposite. In some non-European countries, meaning is conveyed by varying the pitch rather than the tone of the voice. In some remote parts of the world, words are not used at all: instead, a complex whistling language has been developed which carries over long distances.

Actors are trained to vary tone and pitch to enable them to express a wide range of emotions. They are often set the task of reading the same passage of relatively innocuous prose in as many ways as possible to express different emotions such as fear, joy, resentment, surprise, anger and so on. People who are skilled at manipulating their own vocal tone and pitch are usually equally skilled at recognising variances in others. For most of us, this can be rather a hit-and-miss process.

Tone and pitch can affect your impression of a person quite radically. A high-pitched, strident voice can be intensely irritating and is often associated with nervousness: look for other forms of NVC to confirm this. The low-pitched mumble is equally annoying. You need to be sensitive to the judicious use of both the tone and the pitch of your own voice as well as to its volume.

Timing

Time is an important factor in a manager's working life. Often the job can seem to be composed of impossible deadlines or unexpected events which disrupt a carefully planned schedule. Timing in speech is also important. The person who speaks too fast is likely to be misunderstood; the slow, ponderous speaker risks boring the listener. Jerky speech is difficult to listen to, and abrupt speaking gives out messages that the person is angry or uninterested in you.

Time is often related to status. The more important the speaker, the greater the length of time that is accorded to him or her. Other people defer in terms of time to the leader of the group. You may find yourself with an allocated time in which to make a presentation about the work of your department in a bid for resources. The way in which you time your presentation may be a more crucial factor in whether or not you are successful than its content.

You can also use timing to control communication. If you ask open-ended questions, for example, you encourage your listener to spend more time on the answer than if you ask questions which require short, factual answers.

Silence

Used well, silence can be a very powerful form of NVC for both the speaker and the listener. You can use it to emphasise a point, letting it sink into the listener's consciousness. The pregnant pause before an important announcement is an effective way of building up anticipation in your listener. As a listener, you can buy time through silence and, in some cases, encourage the speaker to say more than he or she intended. However, silence can also create tension and unease if it is misunderstood or goes on for too long.

Speech errors

By 'speech errors' I do not mean speech defects: the latter usually result from physical abnormalities of the throat and mouth or from other causes (for example, stuttering). Common speech errors include the over-use of hesitancies such as '. . .er' or '. . .umm', repetition of part of what has already been said, slips of the tongue, leaving words out or sentences unfinished. Some of these errors are caused by, or increase as a result of, nervousness and anxiety, but often they serve as momentary pauses while the speaker thinks about what to say next. If you find yourself listening to someone whose speech is full of errors, he or she has probably not thought much about what is being said to you.

Accent

In the UK, accents are related to different parts of the country and to social class. The UK is becoming more 'classless' and boundaries are shifting; regional accents are actively encouraged in public broadcasting. In the USA, accent is not related to class, only to geographical region. However, accent still affects communication: if it is very broad and the listener is unfamiliar with it, the intended message may not be received.

Conclusion

The study of non-verbal communication is both complex and fascinating. Its importance in conveying messages should never be underestimated. However, you need to watch for a combination of NVC signals to make an accurate judgement; you can all too easily misinterpret NVC if you treat it superficially.

Perhaps I can illustrate this from my own experience. For the past 12 years, I have been partially deaf. The modern wizardry of electronic miniaturisation means that few people realise this: often people with hearing impairment are the 'hidden disabled'. I am told by specialists that I lip-read 75% of the time during verbal communication. As a result, I rely much more heavily than most people on visual NVC and find telephone conversations, especially with people whose voice patterns I don't know, and listening to heavily bearded men, difficult as I cannot see their lips clearly. Facial expression, gestures and posture are all of considerable importance to me in reinforcing the imperfectly heard words.

This has its drawbacks. I tend to react to NVC rather than to the spoken word; where these are contradictory, the speaker can be taken aback by my 'perception' or feel puzzled at my reaction. I have been known to disagree with colleagues over what has been 'said' since I rely on NVC not words. How many of your colleagues, staff or superiors have this problem to a greater or lesser degree? Do you mumble when you speak, necessitating greater reliance from your listeners on NVC? Do you make assumptions about other people's reactions which are unfounded or inaccurate?

References

Argyle, M. (1976) *Social Interaction*. Harmondsworth: Penguin.

Delahanty, D (1970) 'Three aspects of non-verbal communication in the interview', *Professional Journal*, 49 (September): 757–9.

Herriot, P. (1987) 'The selection interview', in P. Warr (ed.), *Psychology at Work*, 3rd edn. Harmondsworth: Penguin.

Eysenck, H. and Eysenck, M. (1981) *Mindwatching*. Michael Joseph.

Iles, P.A. and Robertson, I.T. (1988) *Getting In, Getting On and Looking Good: Physical Attractiveness, Gender and Selection Decisions*. London: British Psychological Society.

Lewis, P.V. (1975) *Organizational Communications: the Essence of Effective Management*. Columbus, OH: Grid. p. 156.

Mehrabian, A. (1969) 'Communication without words', *Psychology Today*, December.

Patounas, G. (1987) 'Body language', *Training Officer*, April: 112–13.

Tottoriello, S.J., Blatt, S.J. and Dewine, S. (1978) *Communication in the Organization: an Applied Approach*. London: McGraw-Hill.

35

Diversity: more than just an empty slogan

Rajvinder Kandola and Johanna Fullerton

We are all aware of management fashions: those ideas that represent a new way forward, the actions that every organisation must take to ensure their survival, and the buzz-words that every self-respecting HR professional must have as part of their personal armoury. Equal opportunities is one area which has been slow to develop any fads (apart from the 'demographic time bomb', which became extremely fashionable but which ultimately fizzled out before the explosion).

However, a new phenomenon that originated in America – 'managing diversity' – could give equal opportunity its greatest chance yet of creating a management trend, of establishing a bandwagon and of being in the limelight. Unfortunately, as with many other fashionable management theories, the phrase itself will be used more often than it is understood.

It is certainly a term that has more immediate positive associations than equal opportunities, but with this comes a danger that is noticeable already, namely that managing diversity will be used only as a convenient and more readily accessible replacement term for equal opportunities. If managing diversity is to be seen as a new concept, the set of ideas that has come to represent the body of conventional wisdom within the equal opportunities field must be fundamentally re-examined and, where necessary, changed.

In our book, *Managing the Mosaic*,[1] we take a critical look at diversity based on the first comprehensive review of the diversity literature, a survey of diversity policy and practices in nearly 300 UK organisations, and our own experience. We believe that diversity, properly understood and implemented, represents a significant step forward in the evolution of equal opportunities.

In this article, we give our definition of diversity; state how we believe it differs from equal opportunity; examine two of the more contentious areas – positive action and targets – and explain why

Abridged from R. Kandola and J. Fullerton, 'Diversity: more than just an empty slogan', *Personnel Management*, November 1994, pp. 46–50.

they do not fit easily within a managing diversity framework; and outline MOSAIC, our vision of the diversity-orientated organisation.

Many definitions of diversity have been produced.[2] The definitions share certain key beliefs:

- Diversity and differences between people can, and should, if managed effectively, add value to the organisation.
- Diversity includes virtually all ways in which people differ, not just the more obvious ones of gender, ethnicity, disability.
- Diversity has as its primary concern issues of organisational culture and the working environment.

Our definition of diversity is:

> The basic concept of managing diversity accepts that the work-force consists of a diverse population of people. The diversity consists of visible and non-visible differences which will include factors such as sex, age, background, race, disability, personality, work style. It is founded on the premise that harnessing these differences will create a productive environment in which everybody feels valued, where their talents are being fully utilised and in which organisational goals are met.

This definition can be contrasted with the melting-pot or assimilation theories of the 1960s and 1970s. Our overriding image of diversity is a mosaic. The differences come together to create a whole organisation in the same way that single pieces of a mosaic come together to create a pattern. Each piece is acknowledged, is accepted and has a place in the whole structure.

Diversity, therefore, represents an evolutionary step in the implementation of equal opportunities, and differs from it in a number of ways (Table 35.1).

Managing diversity is about the realisation of the potential of all employees: no-one is excluded, even white middle-class males. Some equal opportunity practitioners would no doubt say that their work is inclusive, but their words are belied by their actions. In our survey of 285 organisations, we found many examples of actions that were specifically aimed only at women, minorities or disabled people.

Diversity takes individuals as the primary focus of concern, not groups. Such an approach, however, will mean that certain group-based equal opportunity actions need to be seriously questioned, in particular positive action and targets.

There has been a lot of debate recently, particularly in the United States, about the effectiveness of positive action, or affirmative action as it is sometimes known. This is where organisations take special initiatives to redress perceived gender or ethnic imbalances in the workforce, for example by providing special training for women and minorities.

Table 35.1 *How managing diversity is different*

Managing diversity	Equal opportunities
• Ensures all employees maximise their potential and their contribution to the organisation	• Concentration on issues of discrimination
• Embraces a broad range of people; no-one is excluded	• Perceived as an issue for women, ethnic minorities and people with disabilities
• Concentrates on issues of movement within an organisation, the culture of the organisation, and meeting business objectives	• Less of an emphasis on culture change and the meeting of business objectives
• Is the concern of all employees, especially managers	• Seen as an issue to do with personnel and human resource practitioners
• Does not rely on positive action/ affirmative action	• Relies on positive action

The argument often put forward in support of positive action is that it helps those who are disadvantaged get to the 'starting line', or that it helps to create a 'level playing field'. However, if managing diversity is truly about creating an environment where everyone feels valued and their talents are being fully utilised, then actions ought to be targeted on any individual who has a particular development need and not restricted to those who are members of a particular group.

Paul Burstein[3] states that there are possibly three competing views of positive action: a 'remedial action' view, i.e. such policies are needed to counteract the effects of past discrimination; a 'delicate balance' view, i.e. helping minorities without adopting actions which harm the majority; and a 'no preferential treatment' view, i.e. that individuals should not be given preference based on group membership.

In the US there has been a shift away from 'remedial action' towards 'no preferential treatment', and managing diversity is part of this trend.

It is ironic to find that, just as the Americans are reviewing their approach to affirmative action, more and more British organisations particularly in the public sector, are moving towards 'remedial action'.

In a recent survey in the UK produced by the Local Government Management Board (1993), 61 per cent of local authorities had provided assertiveness training for women. If one had to define the issue being addressed here, it would be along the lines of 'lack of assertiveness is a problem for women.' As the problem has been defined in this way, the solution obviously has to be applied to women. It also pre-supposes that whereas women lack assertiveness, men do not. Another way of approaching this would be to ask, firstly, is it right that we value assertiveness as a characteristic? If the answer to this is yes, then the alternative way of describing the issue would be to say that 'lack of assertiveness is a problem.' In this case, the solution would be to provide assertiveness training to anybody felt to be lacking in it, regardless of their sex or ethnicity.

The conventional approach to positive action means that whereas some people are benefiting by virtue of their group membership, other individuals are excluded, even though their developmental need may be as great, if not greater. As Gary Powell, Professor of Management at the University of Connecticut, says: 'Women and men should be recommended for training and development according to their individual needs rather than their sex.'[4]

American psychologist Madeline Heilman not only reviewed the positive action literature, but also conducted several carefully designed studies. She concluded affirmative action helped neither organisations nor individuals.[5]

Those people who were perceived to have gained some form of advantage through affirmative action were more likely to have negative evaluations made of them by others. Heilman calls this 'the stigma of incompetence'. The reason for this is that if someone is good enough to begin with, then they will not need extra assistance. Heilman's conclusions are critical of what affirmative action can achieve: 'Our research suggests that, as currently construed, affirmative action policies can thwart rather than promote workplace equality. The stigma associated with affirmative action can fuel rather than debunk stereotypical thinking and prejudiced attitudes.'

Gender and ethnic targets are a form of positive action and, as such, can be criticised for the same reasons. In our survey, targets were the least successful of initiatives undertaken by organisations. Targets are problematic not only in the ways they are currently established (which often seems to be a combination of wishful thinking and maximum PR coverage), but also in the basic thinking and philosophy behind them.

That some groups have experienced discrimination and prejudice in the past is undeniable, but to counteract this by singling out people for attention because of one particular factor (such as their colour or gender) will invariably mean that members of these groups will receive special attention. The impression given is that the overriding concern is not about fairness or equal opportunity, but improving the numbers. This may be fine if you are a member of the targeted groups, but unfortunate if you are not.

There are other problems with targets. First, the preoccupation with numbers can lead to a neglect of the processes that organisations use to make decisions about people and the skills of the managers in using those processes. The assumption seems to be that as long as the numbers turn out right, everything is fine. However, unless you have confidence in both your systems and your managers, this is a big presumption to make. Of course, if you did have confidence in these two aspects, then you would not need targets anyway.

Another problem is tokenism. This is the assumption, as British sociologist Stephen Small points out, that once organisations 'had got an acceptable number of black recruits – usually in single figures – they need look no further'.[6]

Targets can also prevent minorities from achieving their potential. Sociologist Deborah Woo cites examples from American universities which are concerned about the numbers of certain minorities who are succeeding in gaining university places.[7] Some university presidents feel that in the interests of 'diversity', the number of such people entering university needs to be controlled. Therefore, targets can be a double-edged sword: it may lead to short-term improvements in numbers, but in the long term may be used against the previously under-represented groups.

What can organisations do to manage diversity effectively? This can be summed up in one word, MOSAIC: Mission and values; Objective and fair processes; Skilled workforce, aware and fair; Active flexibility; Individual focus; Culture that empowers.

Mission and values A strong, positive mission and core values are needed which make managing diversity a necessary long-term business objective of the organisation and a responsibility for all employees. The values must reflect the personal and work needs of all employees. The values also describe the behaviours which are held to be important within the organisation, and managing diversity must be incorporated here if it is to be regarded as a central issue. The mission and values also provide a focus for all work, not just diversity. Without this there is a danger that diversity can lead to fragmentation of individuals into cliques with tension and conflict between them.

Objective and fair processes All the key processes and systems, including recruitment, selection, induction, and appraisals, must be regularly audited to ensure objectivity and fairness. The tools and techniques for assessment must be regularly examined to ensure that no other techniques are available that are more objective or fair.

Skilled workforce, aware and fair This involves having a workforce which is aware of and guided by the principles of diversity. Employees understand why it is important and how to make it a reality. It also requires people with the skills to manage: the emphasis here is on the managing, not the diversity. Managers will actively develop themselves and their employees. They will develop and acquire new skills where appropriate. They will listen and solicit feedback on their performance and act upon it. They will make people feel valued and not leave development of their staff to chance.

Active flexibility   This means increased flexibility, not just in terms of working patterns, but also in policies, practices and benefits. Flexibility would encompass all employees, not just those with families (this is the assumption behind the 'family-friendly organisation' initiative). For example, many organisations provide assistance with childcare, a benefit for those with families. In our view, a fairer approach would be to provide a 'cafeteria' of benefits from which employees select those most suitable for their needs. In this way, it is the work/life needs of an employee that are being addressed rather than only the work/family needs.

Individual focus   This is the overarching principle of all actions in a diversity-orientated organisation and was discussed earlier in relation to positive action and targets. It is worth noting that for several American organisations, for example Digital, the 'individual' approach has evolved from the more traditional group approach. As Linda Gottfredson, professor of educational studies at the University of Delaware, recognises: 'The broadening of focus to include all employees often results from the limitations or side effects of the narrower focus.'[8]

Culture that empowers   The basic assumptions underlying all activity in an organisation are incorporated in its culture. The diversity-orientated organisation must ensure that this culture is consistent with, and complementary to, managing diversity. The organisation will understand the importance of its culture and how this impacts on individuals within it. It will ensure that all employees have an understanding of how the organisation operates, what it values and how it expects employees to behave. Other features of the empowering culture include: decision making is devolved to the lowest point possible; participation and consultation will be encouraged and management will listen to and act on what employees are saying; the need for experimentation is valued and encouraged, and people are allowed to fail; there will be an open, trusting environment in which there is an absence of prejudice and discrimination.

Managing diversity offers a real chance to re-evaluate, review and, where necessary, revise what has been done in the name of equal opportunities. In order for this to be done effectively, we are required to have a good grasp of what managing diversity means and how it differs from equal opportunities. Unless this is done and we have the courage to change, managing diversity will be seen as an empty slogan and the latest short-lived management fad.

Celebrating differences at International Distillers and Vintners

Phil Wills, director of compensation and employment policy with International Distillers and Vintners, argues that diversity, in comparison with equal opportunities, is a more progressive and positive way of addressing the needs of the economically disadvantaged, whoever they are.

It looks positively at the diverse contributions which people can make and celebrates their differences: 'It creates an environment in which people learn to work comfortably with colleagues who are varied in outlook, style and background,' he says.

Diversity at IDV has involved 'a more holistic approach' than previous equal opportunities policies. 'Equal opportunities tended to be about specific initiatives or programmes and diversity is about changing a company's culture,' says Wills.

IDV is part of GrandMet, whose former group employment policy director, Malcolm Greenslade, described in the December 1991 issue of *Personnel Management* how the group approach to diversity was being stimulated by its American businesses.

Since then, group policy has progressed from identifying employee attitudes via focus groups and discussing how to approach diversity, through an education and awareness programme for senior managers which took place last year, to a broader spectrum of activities to keep the issue to the forefront.

'For instance, we are now talking in IDV about how we ensure that diversity is integrated into performance management. Our aim is to make sure that valuing and managing diversity are recognised as essential leadership qualities without which you cannot progress as a manager in the company,' says Wills.

In addition, IDV and Pearn Kandola are reviewing ratings of both performance and potential in the annual appraisal to ensure consistency and that appraisals are fair and are conducted with maximum objectivity. IDV is also reviewing all communications, internal and external, to ensure they do not conflict with the diversity message.

Finally, Wills and his colleagues are developing separate

modules on gender, ethnic and national differences and reviewing the content of all training programmes, including professional and technical training.

Although IDV does not like numerical targets, it does watch the numbers carefully. 'We are monitoring our position all the time and if a business showed no improvement in, say, the promotion of women to management positions over a three-year period, we would want to know why.'

'Monitoring is positive and enables you to know where you are. But we don't set targets because it gives the wrong emphasis. Suppose you set a target that 15 per cent of executives will be women. Who says 15 per cent is the right proportion? And what happens to them after they have got there? Can you be sure that the 15 per cent feel valued in their work and that they themselves value diversity?'

Notes

1 Rajvinder Kandola and Johanna Fullerton, *Managing the Mosaic* (IPD, 1995).

2 T.R. Hammond and B.H. Kleiner, 'Managing multicultural work environments', *Equal Opportunities International*, 11, 2 (1992); M. Greenslade, 'Managing diversity: lessons from the United States', *Personnel Management*, December (1991).

3 P. Burstein, 'Affirmative action, jobs and American democracy: what has happened to the quest for equal opportunity?', *Law and Society Review*, 26, 4 (1992).

4 G.N. Powell, 'One more time: do female and male managers differ?', *Academy of Management Executive*, August (1990).

5 M.E. Heilman, 'Affirmative action: some unintended consequences for working women', *Research in Organisational Behaviour*, 16 (1994).

6 S. Small, 'Attaining racial parity in the United States and England: we got to go where the greener grass grows!', *Sage Race Relations Abstracts*, 16, 2 (1991).

7 D. Woo, 'The "over-representation" of Asian Americans: red herrings and yellow perils', *Sage Race Relations Abstracts*, 15, 2 (1990).

8 L.S. Gottfredson 'Dilemmas in developing diversity programs', in S.E. Jackson and associates (eds), *Diversity in the Workplace: Human Resource Initiatives* (Guildford Press, New York, 1992).

36

Sex

*David Sims, Stephen Fineman and
Yiannis Gabriel*

'Well, I'll sit here to look at Vanessa's legs', announced the ageing
director of a manufacturing firm as he sat opposite the student
trainee at the start of a meeting. Vanessa was not impressed. 'Before
I worked at Powertech', she said later, 'I did not have much
sympathy with women who complained about sexism in the workplace as I really did think it was a thing of the past. I was absolutely
unprepared to deal with all the comments and attitudes I encountered on placement. Many of these attitudes are very subtle.
Many of the offenders do not understand that they are being sexist,
they just feel they are "having a laugh", or being friendly.'

The issue of sexual harassment has lately placed sexuality in the
centre of discussions about organizations. For a long time, sexuality
in organizations has been a non-topic. Try looking at the index of
any organizational behaviour text. It is as if people lock up their
sexual thoughts and desires the minute they walk into their
workplaces. After all, workplaces are not places for pleasure,
romance or sensuousness, let alone sex. Most people see sex as a
private matter, not as public business.

Sex talk

Looking at organizations purely as places of work is almost as naive
as looking at sex purely as sexual intercourse. Men and women are
sexual beings. Our sexuality is a central part of our personality. We
all have sexual desires, anxieties and fantasies and we spend some of
our working time talking, joking and thinking about sex. The graffiti
in toilets and lifts, the pin-ups in lockers and workshops, the sex
gossip and casual conversations, provide ample evidence that sex is
very much on people's minds during their time at work.

In some organizations, sex talk goes on incessantly. Its variety is
enormous, ranging from the subtle to the explicit, from the friendly

From D. Sims, S. Fineman and Y. Gabriel, *Organizing and Organizations: An
Introduction*, 1993, London: Sage, pp. 145–57.

to the hostile to the downright nasty. Consider the following two examples:

> I had been doing consultancy for the launch of a US software product called Soft-tool. With a name like this you don't stand a chance, I told the manufacturers, you have to change the brand-name. No luck, it was company policy to use the same name in all its geographic divisions. My job was to come up with a logo for this product, imagine now 'Buy Soft-tool to increase your performance.' When they realized their gaffe, they changed the name to . . . Hard-tool! (Computer executive)

> I think it's mainly me really they tease, about the postboy. Because he's so sweet, you know, I say he is my toy boy, and the others ask me 'Have you seen your toy boy today?' Silly things like that, it just lightens the day up . . . Or the gentleman across the corridor, I notice him because he is always working, he's such a nice gentleman, such a nice character, and I always say 'I just met him on the first floor, I think he's madly in love with me!' Silly things. We just laugh about them. (Office worker)

It may come as no surprise that the first story was told by a man and the second by a woman. Men and women do not often see the world the same way. They do not think in identical ways about sex, nor do they talk about it in the same way. The explicit sarcasm of the first quote contrasts with the delicate innuendo of the latter. Yet, in their distinct ways, both narratives reveal sexual anxieties – the man's worry about masculinity and the woman's concern about being loved. They both suggest fantasies, the first a fantasy about sexually inadequate men, the second about an innocent postboy and a romantically inclined 'gentleman'. Both stories court embarrassment as they shake some taboos and use potentially risky words. Told in the wrong way to the wrong audience, they could lead to stony silence and embarrassed glances. Told in the right way to the right audience, they generate a unique kind of pleasure, strengthen the sense of intimacy among those present and bring femininity and masculinity into the heart of organizational life.

Wholly male and wholly female work environments spawn distinct brands of sex talk. Yet, sex talk is not confined to groups of the same gender. In some mixed offices continuous sex teasing goes on between men and women. Men may tease women about their appearance while women may tease men about their virility. In two district offices of a privatized utility, sexual banter and obscene jokes were traded endlessly across the genders in apparently good humour. Not one of the 47 people interviewed by one of us admitted to being upset about them. For Andrew, fresh from university, the office had been a culture shock.

> *Andrew*: When I first came here, I just couldn't believe the language people used. Gossip about who's going out with whom, who fancies whom, it's just like

school. The jokes! Not down to the level of whistling, but about how people look.

Interviewer: Do the women mind about it?

Andrew: I'd say they enjoy it. I've got to be honest, the difference between here and college is huge, people could no way get away with some of the jokes. The attitude here is totally different. It's horrible saying this but most of the women seem to enjoy it. Totally sexist thing to say. But it goes on and on and on. Like the story about two people who are having an intimate situation, this is how it started, and people just constantly crack jokes about them. It's become like a serial. Probably none of it is true.

Nicky, a 21-year-old clerk who had joined the company as a trainee four years previously, said:

I don't mind sexist jokes, I make them myself. Men tease me about the size of my backside but it's all in good spirit. Mind you, I have taken down the nude calendars. I wouldn't like nude men on the walls either, in fact, I'd rather have the women!

Office romances

Much of the sexual behaviour at work takes place at the level of talk and fantasy. Nevertheless, physical display and contact are not entirely absent. Touching, hugging or kissing may not be much in evidence in most workshops or offices, but many have apocryphal tales, such as what went on at the Christmas party, or during the residential conference, or behind the closed doors of the office. In the organization above, in the interest of better understanding between clerical and technical staff, once a year each clerical worker accompanies a service engineer on house calls. On a different day, each engineer sits in the office paired with a clerical worker. The joint house calls fed a constant stream of innuendoes. Eventually, one of the women in the office married 'her' engineer, providing a happy ending to another local soap opera.

This type of sexual chatter is generally thought of positively by men and women in the workplace. Sexual fantasies are an escape from the ordinariness of work. Sex talk breaks the monotony, introduces a playful element in a highly controlled environment. Sex talk also reminds people that their bodies are not just labouring instruments hiding inside uniforms and suits, but are also sources and objects of pleasure and desire.

This is half the story; the other half is less agreeable. Sex in organizations goes far deeper than being a mere diversion from the monotony of work. Discrimination, AIDS and harassment point to some darker aspects. The rest of this chapter explores some of the way in which sex cuts across and strengthens the power relations in organizations.

Sexual harassment

Increasing awareness of the dark side of sexuality within organizations has coincided with an explosion of concern about sexual harassment in the United States, and to a lesser extent in Britain. Sensitivities, attitudes and feelings are changing. On the one hand, there is an increasing recognition that sexual harassment is not an exceptional occurrence but a routine phenomenon in many workplaces and that large numbers of women (and to a lesser extent men, especially gay men) suffer in silence. On the other hand, there is a sense that forms of behaviour which used to pass as 'innocent' and 'well-intentioned' involve a covert attempt to humiliate women, to bolster negative stereotypes and to preserve organizational forms in which men generally occupy superior positions to women.

The norms of permissible and abusive sexual behaviour are changing. What used to pass as 'innocent banter' is rapidly being reclassified as offensive behaviour. 'Friendly' compliments are frequently resented, either because they are perceived as implied propositions or because they are seen as devaluing other qualities. Many women now feel that they tolerated such forms of behaviour in the past, pretended not to notice or felt ashamed about it, instead of recognizing the hurt that it caused and fighting back.

Sexual harassment comes in many forms. At its worst it amounts to nothing less than rape, or the demand for what some call 'sexual favours' in return for promotion or other material benefits. This is sexual bullying, the abuse of power to exploit, humiliate or hurt and the pleasure of doing so. Sexual harassment may, equally, assume more subtle forms. Persistent compliments can be irritating as can excessive familiarity, exaggerated intimacy or physical closeness. One of the commonest forms of harassment, however, lies in sexist remarks which either reduce women to sex objects or re-affirm unpleasant stereotypes. These put women in a rather invidious position; if they express disgust or disapproval this tends to reinforce the stereotype ('women lack a sense of humour', 'they are emotional' and so forth), while if they bottle up their feelings they offer tacit encouragement for their aggressor.

One of our students reported three incidents that took place in quick succession between her and her manager in a bank:

> I came to work in a smart trouser suit and Paul greeted me with 'Did you forget to take your pyjamas off, Suzie?' (he knows I hate being called Suzie). A little later I was trying to print some documents and said 'This printer is so temperamental!' and Paul quipped 'It's obviously female.' Eventually, the fault was found to be in the computer and he said 'Have you broken it already?' Me: 'No.' Paul: 'Ah! that's what happens when you let women near machines.'

Susan tolerated this type of put-down for several days. The worst thing, she explained, was not knowing whether these comments were meant as friendly teasing or as serious criticism. She put on a brave face, hid her feelings and tried to 'rise' above this baiting. One day, however, she felt especially annoyed and when Paul told her that he planned to take a three-week holiday, she quipped: 'Why, visiting your Spanish sweetheart again?' before she had time to check herself. 'Don't be cheeky!', said Paul. 'I can remember experiencing mixed feelings about what had happened. Perhaps I overstepped the mark, the fine line between what an employee can and cannot say to a manager. As a result I told myself off for not checking myself, I blamed myself. But I also felt that it didn't seem fair that I had to take his jokes in good humour, no matter how bad they were, while his position meant that I couldn't give as good as I got.'

The ambiguities of harassment

When does a well-meant joke or compliment become sexual harassment? This is a thorny issue. A joke which in one organization may cause amusement may cause offence in a different one. During a workshop run by one of our colleagues, a participant told of his plans to tour the Far East, 'just three men, without women to complicate the party or disapprove'. Challenged to say what they intended to do, he casually remarked 'Oh, a little bit of rape and pillage!' The comment outraged many of the others and led to a heated debate in which men and women were sharply polarized. What seemed like an innocent joke to some of the men was felt to be a vicious sexist and racist comment to the women. Whether or not the teller of the joke had meant it as an abusive comment to the women present, this is exactly how they experienced it.

In normal circumstances we rely on social norms to guide us through what is acceptable and what is unacceptable social behaviour. Tact and sensitivity alert us to the needs and feelings of others. In the area of sex, however, norms vary enormously from place to place and leave a lot of ambiguity. What is more, this is an area where many men have not had to think about or do not realize what issues are involved for women. All the same, the excuse 'I didn't mean to hurt you' sounds highly unconvincing in most cases. Nor does the word 'innocent' stick to the many sexist jokes one hears. The obscenities of the graffiti in male lavatories or many all-male conversations in bars suggest that hate and scorn are as much part of men's feelings towards women as attraction and love.

Men's emotions towards women are often ambivalent. Their feelings are often in conflict with each other. They frequently stereotype the women they meet in one of a few basic categories, like mother figure, iron maiden, witch, whore, or defenceless 'pet'. Men idealize 'the virgin' while denying that the 'mother figure' has any sexuality at all. Women with independent sexual desires are often typecast as 'tarts' or 'whores', against whom large amounts of both male lust and aggression are directed. Unless perceived as virgins or mothers, women are often said to be bringing male violence upon themselves through provocative or flirtatious behaviour. 'She asked for it' becomes the stock defence of perpetrators of male violence against women. Instead of the wrongdoer, it is the victim who gets the blame.

Sex and organizational politics

Blaming the victim by turning women into rightful targets for male violence, presents sexual harassment as a purely personal matter. But sexual harassment would not have become a major issue if it amounted to nothing more than the actions of a few male chauvinists, let alone the experience of a few oversensitive females. One of the reasons it has become a central political and management issue is, as feminist theorists have pointed out, that sexual politics is enmeshed in organizational politics and conflicts.

Sex is a feature of many organizational games. As Susan noted in the earlier story, men and women rarely enter these games as equals. In competing for jobs in the labour market, women have faced many visible and invisible barriers, prejudice or discrimination. If direct discrimination is rare these days (women being paid less for doing the same jobs as men), many more or less subtle forms of discrimination make it harder for women to rise to positions of great power or influence.

In most organizations, women tend to occupy subordinate positions, either directly 'servicing' male managers and bosses or coming into direct contact with the organization's customers as sales staff, telephonists, air stewardesses, waitresses and the like. Feminists have pointed out that women's sexuality is far from peripheral in most of these jobs. On the contrary, it is harnessed either to lure the customer, or to boost their boss's ego/image or to project a glamorous image for a company or an industry. Femininity and sex appeal are virtual prerequisites for employment in many such jobs. In many organizations, a 'sexy' secretary is still seen as indicative of the status of her boss, while glamour is part of the image cultivated by industries such as cosmetics, airlines, advertising and the mass media.

But women's sexuality is also harnessed by organizations in subtler ways. In jobs involving direct contact with customers, consumers or employees, the 'feminine touch' is deployed to defuse awkward or dangerous situations and to maintain a discreet form of social control. Telephonists, sales staff, receptionists, cashiers, nurses, teachers and police officers are all expected to exercise their delicate interpersonal skills on behalf of their organizations, preventing things from getting out of hand. A feminine presence in most organizations is seen as a civilizing influence and a balancing counterpart to male aggression.

In some organizations, management maintains a low-level sexual 'simmer', placing great emphasis on women's appearance and demeanour, encouraging smart dressing, make-up and so on. One of our students worked for a pizza restaurant which placed high emphasis on the appearance of the waitresses; it also paid minimal wages. Result:

> Some of the waitresses would do anything to earn a tip. Some of the younger ones wore black bras which were clearly visible underneath their pink blouses. Some deliberately shortened their skirts. Some compared this to prostitution, selling yourself in order to make money. I have to agree with them.
>
> Other waitresses adopted their own tip-making strategies. For example, Elaine in her spare moments would go over to the customers and start up a conversation. She would often tell customers about any personal problems that she had. It appeared as though she was begging for a tip.
>
> I swore I would not sink to this level. However, I did and developed my own strategies. One of these was to ask customers with relatively young children whether they would like a bowl and a spoon for the children to use. This was actually quite successful and I believe that it encouraged customers to leave tips.

Using sex

This astute account illustrates sharply the linkage between sexuality and power in organizations. The waitresses were forced because of their inferior positions to adopt sexual and emotional tactics, which could then be used against them (and women in general) to stereotype them and disparage them. It also illustrates some of the distress that having to adopt such demeaning forms of behaviour causes women.

Femininity, encompassing physical allure, warmth, tenderness and subtle interpersonal skills, is part and parcel of how some of women's work in organizations gets done. In as much as women's sexuality serves organizational goals it is taken for granted and often encouraged. When the self-same feminine qualities are seen as serving women's own interests, they are frequently turned against women. Women are then placed in a 'double-bind' or no-win situation. The same work environment which encourages femininity and even seductiveness chastises women for using their 'feminine charms' to gain personal advantage and influence. On the other hand, women who suppress their sexuality and seek to confront men as equals are often branded 'iron maidens', lesbians and so forth.

Women frequently feel that they are treading a dangerous ground of permissible and non-permissible displays of femininity, between being 'too sexy' and 'not sexy enough'.

There is little evidence that women gain personal advantage against male colleagues by using their sexuality, although they are often accused of doing so. If anything, there is some evidence of the opposite. To the extent that certain jobs emphasize attractiveness, they are seen as requiring little in the way of intellectual abilities, qualifications and motivation. Attractive women in positions of genuine power are automatically suspected of having risen on the basis of their physical attributes, and become the commonest target of male hostility and sexual harassment.

Male sexuality

While sexual harassment and discrimination have forced us to look at female sexuality in organizations, it would be wrong to imply that male sexuality is excluded from them. To be sure, the stereotypes of men in organizations tend to underplay sexuality, in the same measure as those of women emphasize it. Think of grey-suited businessmen, rational, tough, analytic, and you would be forgiven for imagining that they are pure brain and will, detached from bodies and desires. As we saw earlier, however, sexual fantasies and wishes are rarely far from men's minds and frequently feed organizational sex talk.

Physical appearance is a central ingredient of male sexuality as it is of female. A computer analyst in a large firm prided himself on his bulging muscles, the product of long sessions spent in the gymnasium. 'I had an office', he recounted not without self-irony, 'next to the girls in the legal department, and they were talking about the sexiest man in the building, and they were coming up with all these men I'd never heard of before. So I went into their office and said "Sorry about this ladies, I thought that I was the real myostar, the hulk." They cracked up laughing and said "We had a vote and you were voted the most boring old fart in this place."'

Sex teasing in organizations can be good-humoured and benign, but relations between men and women are unsymmetrical and unequal. A woman entering an all-male office saying 'Sorry about this lads, but I thought that I was the sex sensation here', would doubtless elicit a very different response from the witticism of the earlier story. A man who prides himself on his sexual exploits may attract a well-deserved taunt but may be secretly admired as a 'stud' or a 'ladies' man'. A woman doing likewise would probably be derided as fast, promiscuous or worse.

While women have to tread a precarious line between 'not sexy enough' and 'too sexy', displays of masculinity come under laxer controls. Even when it assumes the distasteful shape of sexual harassment it often goes unpunished. There is, nevertheless, a taboo in most workplaces against homosexuality and, more generally, against men's displays of physical closeness or affection. Hugging and kissing among Mediterranean men scandalize many Anglo-Saxons, who regard them as a possible blot on their masculinity.

One of us was attending a conference in Italy, in the company of two close colleagues from our university department, and remembers vividly the following incident:

> There was Roberto, an old associate, who I met about once a year. He threw his arms around me and gave me an affectionate hug. I was pleased to respond to his warmth. My two British colleagues gave me 'knowing' glances. I was a little embarrassed and they teased me. I laughed it off. Throughout the day, the teasing continued – jokes, quips and innuendo about my 'relationship' with Roberto. I still smiled. After all, I could take a joke, couldn't I?
>
> The teasing, as I recall, resumed the next day. They seemed to be having great fun at my expense, while I felt increasingly uncomfortable. It was now beyond a joke. It seemed curiously childish behaviour, insensitive, silly. Then it was one remark too many. 'I am not enjoying these remarks, could you please stop?' I snapped at Chris. He seemed surprised. Chris communicated my comment to Geoffrey. There was a slightly uncomfortable feeling between us, and then it stopped. A couple of years later, Chris and I discussed the incident. We both agreed about the 'facts'. As for the meaning of the incident, there seemed to be a gulf dividing us.

With few exceptions, Western organizations are neither kind nor permissive towards gays and lesbians, who often become victims of vicious sexual harassment. Gays and lesbians find themselves in especially invidious situations, looking for strategies of survival while constantly suppressing their sexuality. Denial, overcompensation, avoidance or straight lying are strategies which take their toll emotionally. Having to laugh at your colleagues' anti-gay jokes (or even initiating them yourself), not disclosing the gender of your living companion, keeping constant vigilance over what others know of your desires and fantasies, 'splitting' your sexual self from your work self; these are all psychological ways of coping, which exact their price in anxiety, stress and guilt.

But male sexuality at the workplace is not limited to displays of masculinity and bravado. Throughout the 1980s a style of management attracted attention which is widely referred to as 'macho management'. Confrontation, ostentatious use of force and intransigence, contempt for compromise and compassion became the trademarks of this style of management. Its champions included 'hard men' like Michael Edwardes and Ian MacGregor in Britain and Lee Iacocca and John Akers in the United States, who introduced new tough regimes in their companies and, in the cases of the first two, broke the power of trade unions. Talking tough and acting tough became a matter of masculine pride for those who saw it as their mission to restore 'managers' right to manage'. Many macho managers seemed inspired by the confrontational rhetoric of political leaders like Ronald Reagan and Margaret Thatcher. Ironically, the latter debunks the notion that macho leadership is restricted to men and suggests that a woman can provide a role model for ultra-masculine behaviour.

Whether macho management has become the norm or not is debatable, as is its success in restoring order and peace in many organizations. What it does highlight is the fact that aggression, competitiveness, rigidity and hardness are all qualities which are not only accepted but encouraged by organizations which find them as useful as they find the feminine qualities we discussed earlier. The essential difference lies in the fact that while masculine qualities enhance career prospects, feminine ones, though indispensable for many organizations, are frequently an impediment to personal success.

Summary

Sexuality plays a large part in how men and women relate to each other. Whether they meet as colleagues or as rivals, as superiors or as subordinated, as friends or as lovers, gender is ever present. Our ways of looking at things and relating to others are shaped by our identities and our identities are sexual identities. It is not surprising, therefore, to find sexuality in many episodes of organizational life. In this chapter, we have argued that sexuality is not just incidental to organization, but of the very essence.

Organizations harness the sexuality of both men and women, mould it and frame it. The women's and gay movements must claim the credit for demonstrating how sexuality becomes entangled in organizational politics, revealing its ugly side in incidents of sexual harassment and intimidation. Women's femininity is more severely manipulated and controlled than masculinity, with stereotypes from wider culture conveniently invoked as excuses for discriminatory and unequal treatment.

At the same time, we have argued against the view that automatically equates sex in organizations with oppression and exploitation. We have suggested that sexual joking, banter and innuendo are welcomed by the majority as a break from the impersonal routines of organizations and as a reminder that inside every overall, suit or uniform there is a human body, which is not just an instrument of labour, but also the source and object of pleasure and desire.

37

Professional and openly gay: a narrative study of the experience

David Shallenberger

In recent years, debate about the roles of gay men and lesbian women in our society has increased. Although there has been much attention given to many aspects of their lives, until recently, little has focused on the workplace. Over the past few years, however, this area is drawing some notice, both in the popular media and in the academic press. Feature articles in business and other periodicals (e.g., Stewart, 1991) and two recent books on gay people in corporations (McNaught, 1993; Woods and Lucas, 1993) are examples of work that reflects an increasing social controversy: how should we relate to gay and lesbian people in our workplaces, as our ministers and rabbis, soldiers, doctors, and managers? Should they be condoned, condemned, or appreciated? Is homosexuality a private matter to be kept quiet or a life orientation that demands openness and discussion?

This article explores the life narratives of one group of gay workers, 12 openly gay male professionals. The overriding focus of the study is to uncover issues and concerns that are significant to them, and then use the data to address broader social issues. [. . .] The description that follows attempts to reflect the story of the men who shared their lives with me, and to focus especially on the impact of being gay in the workplace. [. . .]

Statement of procedures

The core investigation of this study was done through intense interviews. A group of 12 volunteers was found through personal contacts and notices in the gay media. Each person was told the interviews would take approximately 6 hours over several months, that they were confidential, and that they would have an opportunity to comment on the findings (indeed, that their comments were essential). Given these conditions, 16 gay men volunteered to

Abridged from D. Shallenberger, 'Professional and openly gay: a narrative study of the experience', *Journal of Management Inquiry*, 3, 2 (1994), pp. 119–42.

participate. I chose the final group of 12 because they represented a variety of professional positions, a range of openness in their workplaces, and a division between three very different geographical areas (San Diego/Los Angeles, Chicago, and San Francisco), all of which were easily accessible to a graduate student on a limited budget. Twelve was a large enough number to give some diversity in experience, yet small enough to permit in-depth study.

Each individual was formally interviewed three times with a semistructured design, and the sessions were recorded. The goal of the first session was to learn broadly of the major movements and events in the participant's life. We began by discussing his personal history (including family background, school, work, and major life turning points), and coming-out story. In subsequent sessions, we turned to his work environment (including the context of his professional coming-out experiences and the differences in relationships with others before and after self-disclosure) and current life situation. Although these were the general areas covered, the situation and the individual participant dictated exactly how we did it, in what order, and what additional points were pursued. This flexibility to work within the perspective of the interviewee, rather than to direct inquiry in a heavy-handed fashion, was of significant value in understanding the interpretation and meaning each participant gave to his own life. [. . .]

Although the interviews and journal were the heart of my research, I followed several ancillary avenues to corroborate and enrich my research:

1   *Secondary interviews*   Shorter interviews, both transcribed and not, were done with other men who were willing to participate; these included two bankers, a college department head, and two mental health administrators.
2   *Correspondence*   I received letters from men who responded to my notice in the gay press, among them a consultant, an entrepreneur, a teacher, and a television producer.
3   *Gay work group*   One of the richest sources of background material for me has been a gay work group in which I participated for several months. This group of seven gay male professionals gave me the opportunity to bounce ideas and findings around among several people simultaneously, much like informal focus group interviews.
4   *Workshops*   I have run workshops on 'Coming out as a gay professional' and 'The career experience of gay men' for both heterosexuals and homosexuals. Again, my insights are all the richer, by virtue of their development in an interactive setting.
5   *Significant others*   I have had the opportunity to speak with the lovers and friends of several of the primary participants, allowing

me to confirm and expand my understanding of their experiences.

Each of these has been a valuable addition to the process. Formal interviews – even when done in someone's home in a fairly unstructured manner – can be somewhat stilted and artificial. By taking as many avenues as possible to understand the experience of the openly gay male professional, I have been able to effectively round out my findings.

Participants in the study

Each person who participated in this study is, of course, unique and needs to be understood within his context, although there were, by virtue of the study's purpose and design, some similarities. All are medium- or high-status professionals, dealing more with human interaction than with the manipulation of technical information. They range in age from 26 to 36, averaging 33. And, as was stated above, all live in major urban areas of either the West Coast or the Midwest. These common historical, developmental, and geographic facts undoubtedly have some impact on the findings. The respondents' lives, one could argue, are certainly different than gay men born 10 years earlier and raised in a generation which tended to ignore homosexuality publicly; in the lives of the present study's participants, it was more likely that being gay was a topic of open argument and discussion. Similarly, those born substantially later than these men will probably have a significantly different experience of being professional and openly gay. It also should be noted that living in major urban centers also colors their experience; even those respondents in this study who were raised outside of the city made conscious decisions to move to environments more accepting of their lifestyle. Gay men in more rural areas can be expected to have somewhat different experiences, as can those in different socio-economic circumstances.

As significant as their similarities are, some aspects of the participants' lives are clearly different. Some work in very small organizations, others in very large ones. Some are out to everyone in their lives, whereas others are not out to their parents (even though they are open in the workplace). One of the 12 has been married and several used to date women, whereas others have always been both behaviorally and psychically homosexual. Here again, a different mix of experience might lead to different summary findings.

Table 37.1 provides a demographic introduction to the 12 men in this study. Please understand that this summary chart [. . . does] not come close to providing the richness that emerged out of the many hours of conversation I had with participants in the study. I hope,

Table 37.1   *Demographic summary*

Name	Age	Position	Home
Andrew	36	Senior art director, professional association	Chicago
Broderick	32	Vice president, high tech firm	Silicon Valley
Chris	32	Manager (corporate), bank	San Francisco
Ed	29	Manager, graphic arts company	Chicago
Felix	36	Manager, performing arts organization	Chicago
Forrest	35	Regional sales manager, specialty wholesaler	Los Angeles
Mark	33	Entrepreneur, real estate brokerage and development	San Diego
Marshall	34	Manager, marketing research firm	Los Angeles
Rob	33	Design director, service corporation	Chicago
Roger	36	Administrator/manager, holistic health center	San Diego
Ron	36	Senior editor, publishing firm	San Francisco
Wilson	26	Senior research consultant, 'Big 8' accounting firm	Chicago

however, that [it] will give the reader some useful information and a context in which to better understand the findings outlined below. [. . .]

Group findings: similarities and differences

Overlaying their historical contexts, these men are all facing similar development tasks. Although there is a span of 10 years between the oldest and the youngest, their salient concerns tend to gravitate around these large issues associated with their age, largely the forging of their careers and the establishment of significant relationships (Gould, 1978; Levinson, 1978; Vaillant, 1977; and others). For some there is an indication of a midlife questioning and a search for the meaning of life and career. As an example, Roger stands out for his introspection and reflectivity on his personal development and values, on where he is now, and how he got there. He has invested himself in his self-discovery process, and is committed to his growth and the values which he holds dear, such as honesty ('telling your truth'), maintaining high self-esteem, and being 'open to as much diversity as I can'. One of the older men in the study, Roger is less certain about his professional future:

> My professional life is probably my greatest area of dilemma at this point . . . I don't have a good sense of my purpose. About 10 minutes ahead of me my purpose gets real cloudy. It's a coming to grips with . . . purpose, and ambiguity is still something I'm struggling with . . . Probably the essence of who I am is a spirit who has come to experience and express myself, and that probably is what you're about, and what a wonderful thing for us to come together to do that, so let's enjoy it.

Edward, who at 29 is managing the night shift of a graphic arts company as he prepares to open his own business, also admits to some uncertainty: 'My goals are kind of like I don't know right now. Things are kind of up in the air right now.' Wilson's life is changing, too; he is about to leave his work as a research consultant to go to law school:

> I'm going into law to do some good. And I wouldn't work in an area in which I couldn't be open . . . [I'll] do work in regard to gay people or AIDS-related things, although I hope by then it won't be necessary.

Others are more settled in their work. Ron, for example, is very happy with his career, and feels his present position and opportunities are ideally suited for where he is in his life:

> [The job] aligns with all the things we've talked about. Finally, at 36, I feel a desire to settle here . . . I've reached that level of peace . . . I've decided to stay here, set down roots, become part of the chorus, live with someone, commit to a house, or a home, and the level of relationship that that brings. A lot of pieces are coming together.

Whether in a relationship or not, the presence or absence of lovers is a second weighty theme in these lives. Many seem to be in a constant state of flux: Ron and Rob would like to have life partners, although now they are single; Mark and Andrew are in new relationships, whereas Chris still lives with his former lover, Jim; Andrew has just met someone who he feels is 'promising'. Partners, for others, are an ongoing source of stability: Edward and his lover, Henry, have been together for 8 years, and Marshall and Frank, for more than 10.

In addition to these two major life issues, other common experiences are more directly related to being an openly gay professional. The following discussion presents the most important findings in this area and discusses their contribution to the present state of knowledge about being both professional and openly gay.

There is a strong commitment to both gay and professional identities among the participants in this study

Contrary to the findings of other researchers working with men in earlier time periods (Gagnon and Simon, 1973; Harry and DeVall, 1978; Weinberg and Williams, 1974), the identification with and commitment to being gay and the gay community is very strong in these men. Seven (Wilson, Ron, Andrew, Chris, Mark, Felix and Broderick) participate heavily in gay organizations, five in leadership positions. [. . .]

All 12 would refuse a pill to make them heterosexual, although they acknowledge the struggle it took them to get to this point of comfort. The following three responses are typical:

> *Wilson*: When I first started realizing not just that I was gay, because that was a realization that was made long ago at certain levels, but when I started connecting with other gay people it was a big adventure, more so then than it might be now. It was an adventure of meeting people at different social levels that I would never have met. Some different lives and lifestyles that I would never have seen. At some point back there – this is all just to tell you where at some point I made some sort of realization – it just dawned on me that at that point I was never really happier before. I guess I made the decision that it's because I'm finally accepting of being gay. Again, I'm not saying being gay is a preferable life to being straight, but I think that [is] an irrelevant comparison, because if you're gay it's like trying to envision what it's like to be another race; if you could take a pill, would you be White? No, because I'm not White, I wouldn't be me. That's the same feeling I have.
>
> *Andrew*: I like my lifestyle an awful lot, even at its worst I like it, and when it's best you can't touch it, when it's best, it's phenomenal. I wouldn't change for anything. Certainly I wouldn't have to for my family's sake because they've totally accepted it. I wouldn't have to for my career and I wouldn't have to for my own happiness.
>
> *Roger*: Immediately I say no and that's in the context of my life right now. It took me 36 years to get comfortable with this (chuckle), I don't want to have a whole new set of things now. No, although I try to be flexible there's a certain amount of me that's kind of happy that I've come to grips with who I am, and changing that expression of who I am would take a lot of work and I'm not sure I want to go through that.

Taken together, these two findings (a strong identification with the gay community and comfort with their sexual orientation) and the conclusions of earlier studies suggest that the experience of a gay male professional who has chosen to come out at work may be different than that of nondisclosing high-status gay professionals. It seems logical to suspect that the difference is related, at least in part, to how one sees oneself in the context of the community and being gay. Given that an individual is committed to the gay community and values his sense of self as a gay person, he probably finds it more compelling to come out. Were he less committed or self-affirming, he might not be so open.

This observation appears to be supported, at a microlevel, by the range of commitment and openness of the men in this study. Those who are most open are, by and large, highly involved in their (gay) communities. The two least out men, at work and elsewhere, Forrest and Rob, are also relatively uncommitted to gay organizations (although their support networks are largely gay). This does not mean that Forrest and Rob are not committed to gay people on a one-to-one level, but rather that they are not openly committed to the community; similarly, it does not necessarily mean that they are any less accepting of their own gay identities.

The point is that the way in which these men define themselves has an impact on their openness. Most participants in this study have found a need to express themselves fully as gay men, at least in certain parts of their work lives. Ten of the 12 said they could not anticipate anything that might push them back into the closet, but that in extreme circumstances, they might reconsider or move someplace safer. [. . .]

At the extreme, two (Andrew and Broderick) said that they would definitely 'go down fighting'. Andrew puts it this way:

> As I said, I'm lucky enough to be in a profession. If the [professional association] disbanded, I'd simply get another job as a graphics artist some way or another. Again, I wouldn't flaunt it. But I certainly wouldn't [hide] . . . I'm gay and that's it. I can't imagine going in the closet for any reason.

It also is interesting that these men are as invested in their careers as the typical male in American society. The literature on the meaning of work indicates that work has a great deal of salience in the lives of most men. Veroff et al. (1981) reported that 84% of the men in a national sample would continue working, even if they did not need the money; when looking specifically at those who had some college or had graduated from college, the figures were 83% and 91%, respectively. Ten out of 12 men in this study (or 83%, all but Marshall and Broderick) also said they would keep working (although perhaps in different jobs), so they fall into the same range of work salience. Yet even Marshall expresses a strong identification with his work:

> I'm real committed to this industry of marketing research. I would like to do something in the long run that's different [from] what I'm doing, maybe more generally understood research, instead of a very special niche. But I definitely want to stay in an environment where I'm managing people that are producing research, and that I'm dealing with clients, probably in a selling environment.

When speaking on work in general in his life, Marshall also said:

It's real important because I spend so much time at it. That's something else that I think I resent about working, is that it is so much of my time and my energy. I consider myself a person that doesn't have a extraordinary amount of energy, and probably a lot of it is associated with being an allergic person. So that I'm very single-minded in terms of devoting the primary energies towards work. And yet, a conflict within me is that I don't want it to become too important.

Veroff et al. (1981) looked at attachment to the specific work men do (through the question, 'Is there any other kind of work you'd rather be doing?'). Among professionals, they found an overall job commitment level of 56%, but among managers, commitment was 72%. In this study, six men, or 50%, said they would stay with the same job, even if they were free to change.[1] [. . .]

The coming-out literature (such as Cass, 1979; Coleman, 1982; deMonteflores and Schultz, 1978; Lee, 1977; and Troiden, 1979) helps inform our understanding of these reports on commitment to the gay community and commitment to profession. Although using different terms and emphasizing distinct aspects of the journey, the literature generally posits a progression that begins with a sense that one is different, passes through self-acknowledgement as gay and sharing that information with others (including the establishment of relationships), to a final stage called *integration* by Coleman:

Here individuals incorporate their public and private identities into one self-image. New feelings about self will continue to emerge, new labels and concepts will be discovered, new social networks will be identified and explored, and new relationships and intimacies will be enjoyed. (1982: 39)

In my judgment the sense that the men in this research have of themselves as gay and professional indicates a fairly advanced stage of personal identity formation as described by these theories. Clearly, for most at least, they have reached a point of synthesis or integration, in which being gay has been incorporated into their lives as a legitimate and full, but not exclusive, element of their self-definition. In other words, they have by and large accepted their gayness totally, but they have also accepted other parts of their self-concept – including their professional identification.

Participants in this study handled the self-disclosure process very differently, at different times in their lives, with different people

Each self-disclosure decision includes considerations as to how, to whom, and why one would disclose. Regarding the persons to whom they disclose, one (Forrest) is out to his two bosses and one other person; another (Rob) to two gay men and two straight women; four (Edward, Chris, Wilson and Felix) assume they are out to most of the people in their offices; and six (Andrew, Ron, Roger, Marshall, Mark, and Broderick) are completely out at work.

As for how they tell others, three of the men in this study (Forrest, Rob, and Broderick) generally self-disclose by sitting people down and telling them proactively, nine (Chris, Wilson, Roger, Felix, Marshall, Ron, Mark, Edward, and Andrew) by not hiding it (e.g., letting it out in casual conversations and letting people draw their own conclusions), and some passively, that is, by having the other person discover it by walking into a gay bar (Forrest), or reading a letter of theirs addressed to someone else (Wilson), or having someone else 'come out for them' or ask about it (e.g., 'Are you married?' or 'Are you gay?'). All have experienced a combination of methods, although they tend to favor one category. [. . .]

Andrew responded this way to a question about telling people in the workplace he was gay.

> *David*: Was there a point when you made any sort of decision at the [professional association] to be out to certain people or were you just sort of your natural self?
>
> *Andrew*: Day one. It was inconceivable of me to lie and say, 'My girl friend and I last night . . .' At the very beginning I think my own shyness and my own reticence to talk about my own personal life just asserted itself and I just didn't talk, period. Or if I did I would say we went out last night or something, I could always say Felix and I did this, and you would assume Felix was a brother, or a neighbor, or friend, whatever you wanted to.

[. . .] Perhaps most interesting is why the men in this study chose to self-disclose. Some (Roger, Chris, and Ron) come out because they want people to know them as they are (a 'statement of being', as an investment in a meaningful relationship); some (Roger, Mark, Felix, Marshall, Edward, and Andrew) to improve a relationship or avoid potentially uncomfortable situations in the future ('I can't bear the lying', 'I'm lost and schizo', 'It's easier to deal with people when I'm out', 'I want to have control'); some (Broderick and Wilson) to make a political statement out of a sense of responsibility to the community; and some (Forrest, Wilson, and Rob) by accident (someone found his gay magazines, his lover was killed, he ran into someone in a bar). Again, most respondents come out for a combination of reasons, but may favor one. Chris and Roger, for example, describe their reasoning:

> *Chris*: I always felt that the alternative to not be open could eventually lead to being even less respected and being not only less respected because you were gay, but also because you're not going to be open to other people. I always told myself that wasn't one of the reasons that I wanted to get out of the Air Force, that I wanted to do it under my control rather than putting a lot of

energy into a career that at any moment could be ended by somebody else telling somebody that I was gay.

My tendency [as an MBA student], and I think everyone's, was that all of their activities in business school went on their résumés. I didn't see any reason to edit that one out. I also wanted it to be there because I thought it would prevent me from not being open and out when I started the job. The longer you go without being out the harder it gets to come out. I figured this was one way of having to deal with it up front so that I couldn't get into, 'I'll just stay. It's nice and comfortable and not mention it,' or tell myself that it hasn't been an appropriate occasion to mention it yet. And soon, I'd have been there a year or two and . . . then I start wondering will it make a difference now if I'm out and then have it be detrimental?

Roger: I just want people to be open and honest, communicative with me. I feel to get what I want I need to give it first. That's a very conscious decision. I think I'm reasonably successful with it. There are times that I'm not. I still have elements of covertness that I'm working on rooting out, but I think for the most part it's successful.

As in other studies (such as Feo, 1986), openness for Chris, Roger, and for some others in this study was found to be important in and of itself. Honesty was a cherished value, and negative feedback from the self-disclosure, although it might be important, did not seem to deter these men from their commitment to be open; they were willing to pay the costs. Broderick says: 'I got to the point where I felt I'm damned if I'm gonna live a second-class life because of other people's ignorance.' Self-disclosure did serve to convert their stigma from discreditable to discredited (Goffman, 1963). Although the differences reported by the participants between being hidden (discreditable) and open (discredited) are somewhat ambiguous, there is nothing unclear about the value they place on being open. There is some indication that most no longer were focused so intently on managing information with people to whom they had self-disclosed and were much less concerned about who found out. To manage the tension of their new visibility, they set up their lives to support them as openly gay by participating in organizations which accepted and embraced them as gay men, and by being friends with people who affirmed their gay selves as well as the other parts of their self-concepts.

Participants find support among both gay and heterosexual (particularly female) individuals

The support systems of the men interviewed appear to be very significant aspects in their lives. Nine of the 12 men in this study spoke of having close gay and nongay friends and indicated they were crucial for their happiness. For example:

Mark: I have a lot of good friends. I say I'm lucky. I probably have 10 or 12 people that I can call good friends, that I can call for anything, any time and they'd drop anything, 'cause they know I would do the same. And that's a lot – to have that many that I feel that close to.

David: A strong investment with a lot of people.

Mark: Yeah, I have that and it's mutual and it's real nice, but that leads to a lot of social interaction with those people, dinners . . . my life revolves around dinner.

The participants in this study developed, by and large, new support groups after accepting their homosexuality, which have subsequently evolved as they have progressed in their personal development. Typically, right after coming out, their friends were almost exclusively gay, and as they progressed toward integration (as defined by Coleman, 1982), their friendship circles also became more mixed:

David: You mentioned that your support group is changing as you go through this. Does it tend to be mixed in terms of gay and straight?

Roger: Yeah, I would say the majority of my – people I would consider my support group – are gay, but there are straight people, and the nice thing is that I have some straight men that I'm friendly with and who know me and know Steve and me and feel comfortable in socializing with us, being active parts of our world.

[. . .] Roger and Andrew offer examples of this comfort and companionship:

Roger: I would say probably throughout my life straight women have always been my easiest friends, the people that up until the time I came out and had some really close gay friends, they were my support.

Andrew: If something goes wrong at work, I turn to Joann or Laurie or Pat, three straight women, who are my three closest friends at the [professional association]. I'm closer to those three women than to any gay men at work. I'm not exactly sure why, it's just the way it's worked out. And Liz and Janice, there's this circle of straight women at the [professional association] that are terribly supportive, and of my personal life too. They know what's going on in my personal life and they can be real supportive of that. I love to go out and talk and I love to gossip about what's going on in the office. We talk about our personal lives. One of the things I'm trying to do is free up my privacy thing. I don't have any problems talking with these women, which I find kind of surprising. Maybe that is factored in, and maybe it's because I just enjoy their company. The other thing is that for some of these women, they are in a unique position to understand what's going on with me professionally.

Many of the men in this study also indicate that they perceive that these relationships with women at work are deeper than women's relationships with their heterosexual male colleagues. Wilson, for example, says:

To the men at work . . . women are something to either date or to ignore. They don't treat them as professional equals. I think they try to, but somehow it just doesn't happen. They will go to a man to talk over a business situation instead of going to a woman if they have a choice. They will even choose a man for a project over a woman without realizing they're being discriminatory. I think I do have different relationships with women, and people have noticed it. People have said – actually a couple of guys at work wondered why I was so close to this one woman, who is real attractive and everything and we were real friendly and worked on our project together – so it was natural that we were close. But these guys somehow thought this is really weird. Why would she be interested in Wilson? Why also are they so friendly, and all of this? The reason obviously was because there weren't any pretensions between us. We were able to become friends.

Participants report feelings of being an outsider in adult relationships with male heterosexuals and in relationship to other gay people who are less out

All of the men in this study have experienced themselves as marginal in the societies in which they lived. Even as children, when they were not clearly different, 11 of the 12 felt apart. As professionals they have to deal with heterosexual men in the workplace, and obviously – by virtue of their positions – they do so successfully. Five reported occasional discomfort with these contacts, however. Even Ron, whose integrated support circle includes nongay men, feels like 'the macho thing' gets in the way at times, in this case with clients:

I've only felt it as an issue with a couple of clients, who I felt were really overly macho, for whatever reason. I just found it offensive, I would find it offensive if I were an androgynous heterosexual man, I'm sure. I was uncomfortable because I had to spend 3 or 4 hours with them over dinner, and didn't enjoy it. But I had to do it to get a book. And they're one of the top authors in the field or something. But I don't know that it was specifically my gayness that was at stake. I think it was the issue of macho . . . certain values, and the way they talked about people and things. The objectifying of other humans was more distasteful.

As gay men – who, in many cases, are very active in the gay community – they must often relate to other, closeted, gay people, but these contacts are less frequently the individuals they call on for support. Broderick, for example, speaks of how important it is to him that his gay friends are open:

I identify with strongly out gay people. I'm very uncomfortable with people who are halfway. And I think a lot of the people at the meeting yesterday are halfway, and you probably noticed that too. Maybe I'm giving you values, assuming values. That's a little bit uncomfortable for me. I would much prefer to be in a group which is completely out. Also, I enjoy – that's a little unfair – I also like to spend time with people struggling with what they're going through. There was one young kid there, who was a guest, about 24 or 25 and I think that was a real big deal for him to go to that party. He worked in San José, he was a technician, everybody else was out of his league. It was interesting to watch him interact. My social circle of gay friends is all very much out.

[. . .] This is not to say, of course, that the feeling of difference is a uniquely gay experience. As a man in the gay work group said, 'I feel very different from the rest of those men who are wearing the same three piece "uniform" that I am wearing – but I don't know that they don't feel the same way.' Feeling different as a child and as an adult are common human experiences. Feeling different from other gay people who are closeted might be unique to those who are out, but even that may be parallel, for example, to the situation of women who work outside of the home, when interacting with those who do not seek outside employment. What we are learning here is how human the experience of being a gay professional is. [. . .]

Several themes were identified in relation to the career impact of being gay

There is a strong belief in (and practice of) competence as a defense against potential discrimination   The perceived need to overachieve is frequently discussed in relation to women and other minority groups (see, e.g. Davis and Watson, 1982; Kanter, 1977; Moore, 1985), but typically has not been connected to gay professionals. The findings of this study extend the validity of competence as a defense mechanism because they suggest that some of the experiences of workplace minorities may indeed apply to a group who appears to occupy a favored status in the workplace, that is, White men, when they identify themselves as members of a disfavored group.

Eight people (Felix, Forrest, Rob, Broderick, Chris, Marshall, Ron, and Edward) said they had developed a high degree of competence in their fields because they wanted to be sure they would be invaluable to their employers and couldn't be fired. Forrest and Felix, for example, shared the following views.

> *Forrest:* We had a sales contest which I just won. It's supposed to last all month. It started Monday and by noon I had won it. I told my friend it takes two straights to keep up with this one queer [chuckle]. Waving this incentive in front of me, especially money. It took two of them to sell as much as I did. In other words, there is another case where I thought I had to overachieve. I felt like I absolutely had to overachieve to compensate, so just in case back at the head office they say, 'Yeah, he's gay, but look what he does.'
> *Felix:* I think one of the reasons there has never been any problem is because I'm good at my job. There is no reason to question anything, because I do my job well.
> *David:* I assume that if you didn't do your job well then . . .

Felix: Then all sorts of things would be called into question. You don't do your job . . . well because – not because you're dumb or stupid or don't know what you're doing, because you're a faggot.

It is important to note that the participants did not indicate that the drive for competence arose after they came out. Indeed, it was more a product of their fears of being discovered when they were closeted. Ron said this most clearly:

Actually, I've always said that one of the reasons that I'm so successful professionally is . . . because I'm gay. Initially in my work, it was like I had this dark side of me, and I didn't want anyone to discover it. And if they did, I had to be so good at what I did that it didn't matter. So good, that if ever I were fired, I would know that it was because of bias, rather than just conflicts. It drove me to be exceptionally competent. Whereas with some people, it would probably paralyze them, but for me it drove me.

Once out, there is a continuing need to protect oneself from homophobia. Changing from a discreditable to a discredited status does not erase the fear; it just changes its nature. [. . .] Those who know one is gay, may now judge one because of that information. The interesting point is that a gay person is never completely out, for the quality of gayness is itself invisible, and there are always new people to come out to. In a sense, then, all of these men are both discreditable and discredited.

Some participants felt they had been exposed to opportunities that they would not have encountered, had they not been gay Being gay may mean that one is introduced to people and situations that might not have been encountered otherwise. Seven of the men in the study (Andrew, Forrest, Wilson, Felix, Ron, Rob, and Broderick) indicated some significant awareness of and/or participation in a gay version of the 'old boy network', enabling them to meet and/or develop relationships with (influential) people they might otherwise not have met. In the following statements, Wilson and Felix both speak succinctly of how this has worked in their lives:

Wilson: At work I talk to managers and things like that and I did from the time I started . . . because they were gay. Somebody introduced them to me and we became friends. Whereas, other staff people starting the job thought it was real impressive to get a phone call from a manager, it's like 'so what!' Because of the little gay network and that sort of thing you make contacts with people and that can translate into opportunities. I'm not convinced that it does as much as it could. I have a friend who is a tax manager at work and he has made contacts with other gay business people, in fact people in positions with power that could direct work his way, but there is always reluctance to use that, take advantage of that acquaintanceship or whatever. In my case I'm not sure I'd take advantage of any extra opportunities. There may have been some, but somehow I just wouldn't take advantage of them.

> *Felix*: I suppose if I were not gay there would not be contact with some people that there are. The fact that I can call up [music critic] and invite him to my fifth anniversary party, I was not doing that because he was a music critic and I'm in the arts, it's because I know he's gay and he knows that I am, even though we've never talked about it.

[. . .] Of related interest, Schneider (1981) found that networks were very active among lesbian workers. Evan's (1963) research shows that the peer group can uniquely perform the function of reducing strains and alleviating tensions for other groups, as well, and Kram and Isabella found peer relationships to be important in 'supporting psychosocial and career development at every career stage' (1985: 110).

Participants are aware of homophobia in the workplace and have a strong sense that they would not work in a situation where they would have to be hidden The men in this study have clear values about their openness, which they are unwilling to compromise, even in the midst of a society that devalues their lifestyle. They have made some clear choices to support their decision to self-disclose, most notably that of working in largely gay-affirmative organizations. Typically, they believe they have risked a loss of income by (a) coming out and (b) choosing an organization based on its lack of homophobia, but this is a decision about which most of these men [. . .] feel settled. Although there is some range in the degree of acceptance of the participants' organizations, all but one seemed somewhat gay affirmative. Considering that there is a substantial incidence of antigay discrimination in the workplace, it is notable that these men have experienced relatively little overt bias. Although there are significant exceptions – Forrest's car was vandalized, Wilson lost a contract, Rob feels he has suffered in invisible ways – by and large, the overall level of homophobia has been low. (Naturally, any is too much.)

The question that follows from this finding is, of course, whether these men have purposefully chosen their positions – indeed, their professions – to be supportive of what they consider an essential part of their makeup. Again, the evidence is mixed. None of the three artists in the study felt that he had chosen art as a career because he was gay; all said that their acceptance of their gayness came after they were well on the path to their careers. On the other hand, the choice of specific positions appears to have been substantially determined by the freedom to express who they are; of the 12, 11 said they would not work where they could not be out or would make (or had made) other choices in their careers because of being gay. Five people either had to, or chose to, change earlier career plans to accommodate their gayness: occupations shelved as a result of their coming out included the military (Chris), college president (Ron), and mayor (Forrest). Edward suffered psychosomatic afflictions because of the sexual harassment of a former (male) boss and said that his health is now a major determinant in choosing employment. Wilson, on the other hand, chose to change careers because of his gayness, but not because of avoiding a job or situation which is homophobic, but to become a public advocate, dealing with gay-related legal issues.

That they are more professionally satisfied now that they have self-disclosed confirms the findings of Blumstein and Schwartz (1983) and Schneider (1981). In their study of American couples, the former researchers found that 'gay men [who are part of same-sex relationships] seem happier with their work if they are open about their sexual preference' (Blumstein and Schwartz, 1983: 158). Although this conclusion seemed to be less true for lesbians in the American couples study, Schneider found in her research that 'coming out at work makes lesbians feel better, more able to integrate into the life of the workplace, and less anxious about who they are and how they are perceived' (1981: 8).

There is some evidence of stereotyping, as seen in the reactions of both the participants and the people with whom they interact in the workplace Being gay is a major issue at work for these men and, in spite of the fact that their homosexuality is physically invisible, they attracted attention because they were open about it. Most of the men sensed that their openness had repercussions for them, and ascribed behaviors of co-workers to stereotypes co-workers had of homosexuality and gay people. Stereotyping suggests that these gay male professionals may be perceived as tokens, although the evidence here is mixed. [. . .]

There is a strong belief that the experiences of growing up as a gay person develop certain personal qualities that are professionally useful. This finding – that certain personal qualities (sensitivity, creativity, 'being a stronger swimmer', and so on) developed out of the experience of coming out and relating to the world as a gay person – radically changes the stereotypical picture of the gay male as sick, unstable, and an immoral drain on society. Here we have evidence, as it arises in the minds of at least seven of the participants (Ron, Wilson, Forrest, Marshall, Edward, Andrew, and Felix), that they may be more valuable members of an organization (and society, in general) because of their gayness. Among the positive qualities cited in their reflections were a tolerance of ambiguity (Ron), sensitivity (Wilson and Ron), understanding of oppression and minorities (Edward, Andrew, and Ron), inner strength (Roger), creativity (Wilson), courage or willingness to take risks (Ron and

Wilson), intuition (Ron), collaborativeness (Ron), humility (Ron), ability to come at an issue from a different angle (Ron and Wilson), maturity (Wilson and Forrest), a professional attitude (Forrest), a sense of drama (Marshall), and an appreciation of the finer things in life (Felix). Ron is perhaps the most expressive about these qualities:

> There're certainly attributes that, it's hard to generalize, but there are certain attributes – in fact we were talking about it at lunch. A friend's mother was here and we took her to lunch, and she was describing how wonderful it was to be with gay men, Chuck and all of his friends, because she felt in general all the gays that she had met had a greater sensitivity to other people's needs and issues, how grateful she was to be with us . . . I think there's some truth to that.

These attributes are particularly relevant to the new managerial attributes now being demanded in the global workplace. As Ron goes on to say:

> There's [also] a certain level of sensitivity that goes with the typical androgyny of a gay male, that is not as apparent. I think I'm maybe more collaborative in my style. I mean I have an ego, but the whole issue of macho pride and some of those male issues that I've seen other very successful men get wrapped up by and get into, they just haven't affected me as much . . . I think there's a level of humility I have, because I know what it's like to be oppressed, a minority. It's made me a much better manager, I know that . . . Knowing what it's like to be oppressed, knowing what a hierarchy works like, what subordination means. Knowing what it means to question values, plus the more positive side, the sensitivity, the listening, the empathy, it's been helpful.

He continues by discussing how being gay has taught him to deal with complex situations in which things are not always as simple or straightforward as they appear, and where openness and flexibility are needed:

> Getting into the new literature about managers, the need for flexibility, tolerance of ambiguity, I mean those are things that I've had to grapple with as a gay man. I've had to learn to be more flexible. I don't fit into certain norms. I've had to learn to deal with ambiguity, I mean I ride the train of ambiguity every day. That's my life: it's not black, it's not white, it's gray. And that's alright. So I think that translates to how I manage people, how I handle business situations, how I can handle what's going on at [my company] at this time, in relative calm, yet get all my other work done.

Summing up his comments, he says:

> I'm not speaking as stereotypically gay, but [about] what I think my sexuality has contributed to me: capabilities. In a way it's defying the stereotype, which I've had to do to learn who I was and succeed and be me. But it also works in business, because the way you start in a business is to defy stereotypes. There are certain . . . things I've brought on line [at my company] that people have said won't work. But it's really coming at life from a different angle, a book idea or something from a different angle, and it works . . . Out of darkness comes light, or . . . as the Indians say, [out of] your shadow side. My analyst . . . used to say

the richness of your own personality, your own distinctiveness will come out of your shadow side, those things you would like to cut off and throw away, those are the unique pieces. I began to understand what he meant. To me that was my differentiation, that was my uniqueness, it was those things that at one point drove me to excel. [Then] it just all came together as a blend, so now I just excel because it's a part of my fabric, not because I'm gay.

This sense of having developed valuable qualities through one's life experience is reminiscent of the work of Bellah et al. (1985). In *Habits of the Heart*, they speculated about the special contributions that a marginal person (the 'mythic individualist') might make by virtue of his or her separation from mainstream society. Describing the cowboy and hard-boiled detective as fictional reflections of this value, these authors say:

> The cowboy, like the detective, can be valuable to society only because he is a completely autonomous individual who stands outside it. To serve society, one must be able to stand alone, not needing others, not depending on their judgment, and not submitting to their wishes . . . One accepts the necessity of being alone in order to serve the values of the group. (1985: 146)

The men in this research are not completely outside society. Indeed, they are part of it as professionals in the workplace. Yet they are also on the margin and may have developed a certain insight because of that experience of living in the borderlands (Rosaldo, 1993). As Rosaldo argues, the borderlands where marginal groups within a society live (metaphorically speaking) are places of significant culture that are unavailable to those who are part of the dominant group. [. . .]

A common experience of participants in this study is the questioning of values they had been given by their families and communities. However, many feel they had come full circle, to a point where they are either embracing or modifying family values

[. . .] In this study, 11 men said they had looked at and rejected during their coming out many of the values they had been given as children. As they matured, the values they questioned came back into focus. All men face this process as they take on career and family. Gay men, however, have different career considerations (as this study and others indicate) and their families include lovers and friends, so the values they were given at an early age may continue to feel inappropriate. A surprising finding of this study, given the adoption of a lifestyle that many of their parents find disgusting and the confrontation of many issues most men never encounter, is that 8 of the 12 gay men interviewed ended up adopting significant values from their families. For example:

> *Rob*: Yes [I questioned my parents' values], and what's real funny is even after I reassessed them most of them are still there.
>
> *David*: But there was a questioning point?
>
> *Rob*: There was, sure. I questioned a lot of them because first I thought I was doing something immoral. When I took that title off of it, I saw nothing immoral about wanting to love someone and wanting to share life with someone. And then it brought back some of the other stuff like not just having sex to have sex, but being able to express a feeling that you have towards someone. So all, yeah, all the good stuff that I was taught is still there.

Perhaps this group is different from most gay men, in that they (a) are working in neutral, if not supportive, organizations, (b) have entered high-status professions, and (c) in general have encountered little homophobia among their families and friends. These differences may make traditional values more appropriate for their relationships with their families and in their workplaces. Those for whom the workplace, their families, and society in general are not so accepting, who live in rural or more conservative parts of the country, or who work in more traditional organizations, may find that they are not as comfortable returning to the values they learned from their parents, and so remain distant from them.

Conclusion

In this study, I looked at a group of 12 professional men who were gay and open about their sexual orientation, and asked them to tell about their experiences. The men were candid and eloquent; their stories have striking differences and similarities. In closing, it is important that I thank them for making this research possible, and for sharing their lives with me. From them, I have learned a great deal both about myself and about the experience that they have so richly described. I hope that others appreciate the gift of these participants as well; the lessons are there for social scientists, managers, and helping professionals, both gay and straight.

The key message of this study to heterosexual men and women in the workforce, particularly those in management, is that it is possible to be gay and a successful professional. There are very few examples of openly gay managers and executives, probably because of the fears of most gay men and women that they will suffer severe repercussions, personally and professionally, in the workplace if they choose to come out. [. . .]

Perhaps these circumstances are changing with workshops on embracing diversity, organizational statements of nondiscrimination, and the promoting of openly gay personnel (who are effective in their jobs). Managers can do even more to make the workplace more supportive for gay people by instituting efforts to decrease personal and organizational homophobia. For example, they can demonstrate they will not tolerate antigay/lesbian bias in the work setting by confronting it as it occurs. Similarly, they can institute gay-inclusive benefit policies (such as those relating to insurance and bereavement leave).

Helping professionals – therapists, social workers, and teachers, for example – can also learn from the men in this study. On the one hand, it is important for them to understand the complexity and salience of career decisions made by gay men; on the other hand, they need to know that it is possible, under the right circumstances, for gay male professionals to be open about who they are. There are clearly costs and complications, such as stereotyping and homophobia, but the participants in this study indicate they can be handled successfully.

Scholars and students of human behavior may find something of value here as well. To the extent that the lives of one group help us understand more fully the experience of others, they provide us with metaphors that reflect a broader human reality. The expression 'coming out' represents one of these concepts. Not only do gay men and lesbian women come out, so do all people exploring feelings or experiences that previously were hidden to themselves and/or others. One can come out as a born-again Christian, a recovering alcoholic, an ex-priest, or a survivor of incest. As members of these groups come to an awareness of their stigmatized characteristics, how do they come to own this identity? What are the dynamics that come into play in the workplace around these issues? We can frame broader questions with respect to the coming-out experience, as well: the contributions that emerge from internal and external struggles; the pattern of relationships that evolves as one comes to accept and affirm previously repudiated aspects of oneself; the balance, tension, and contradictions among and between one's multiple and alternative identities; the ways in which one's expectations of another's reactions may drive one's actions; and so on. Understanding more about what it means to be openly gay in the workplace can teach us something about these larger questions of lived experience.

Openness, as Jourard (1971) and others have suggested, can be a sign of health and maturity. The experiences of the men in this study – highly functioning and openly gay – have not always been positive, but there is a strong indication that it is possible to be happy, self-fulfilled, and openly gay. Certainly, there are struggles, many of them painful. By being open, one has to deal directly and on a personal level with stereotypes and rejection. Coming out is an iterative and drawn-out process, repeated with each new person. Although the experience of these men in these organizations is not universally translatable to other people and to other organizations, it suggests that coming out may be less formidable and less dangerous than many expect.

Many life choices involve revealing what is not physically apparent. The study thus offers encouragement for other types of openness in the workplace. If these men are typical, being honest about who we are can be scary, challenging, and empowering. Moving beyond the fear – when we are ready – can bring us to a place of strength in which we are more fully ourselves.

Notes

The research discussed in this article was done for a dissertation at the Fielding Institute, Santa Barbara, California.

1 The questions Veroff et al. (1981) asked were not exactly the same as those I posed, so it would be unfair to make any sweeping comparisons, although it does appear that these gay men are somewhat less committed to their current jobs. On the surface, this conflicts with Bell and Weinberg's (1978) finding that the gay men in their study were more satisfied with their jobs than their heterosexual counterparts. In addition to the unreliability of small sample statistics, these differences could relate to different levels of education, professional identification, historical and societal changes in the 10 years between the two studies, the presence and absence of support systems, and so on. Indeed, it is consistent with new paradigm methodology to see the interrelationship between these factors as arising out of the individual context of the participants. The juxtaposition of the two studies does, however, raise interesting questions.

References

Bell, A.P. and Weinberg, M.S. (1978) *Homosexualities: a Study of Diversity among Men and Women*. New York: Simon & Schuster.

Bellah, R.N., Madsen, R., Sullivan, W.M., Swidler, A. and Tipton, S.M. (1985) *Habits of the Heart: Individualism and Commitment in American Life*. Berkeley: University of California Press.

Blumstein, P. and Schwartz, P. (1983) *American Couples*. New York: William Morrow.

Cass, V.C. (1979) 'Homosexual identity formation: a theoretical model', *Journal of Homosexuality*, 4(3): 219–35.

Coleman, E. (1982) 'Developmental stages of the coming out process', *Journal of Homosexuality*, 7(2/3): 31–43.

Davis, G., and Watson, G. (1982) *Black Life in Corporate America: Swimming in the Mainstream*. New York: Doubleday.

deMonteflores, C. and Schultz, S.J. (1978) 'Coming out: similarities and differences for lesbians and gay men', *Journal of Social Issues*, 34(3): 54–72.

Evan, W.M. (1963) 'Peer-group interaction and organizational socialization', *American Sociological Review*, 28: 436–40.

Feo, A. (1986) 'Homosexual professional identity formation'. Unpublished doctoral dissertation, Fielding Institute, Santa Barbara, CA.

Gagnon, J.H. and Simon, W. (1973) *Sexual Conduct*. Chicago: Aldine.

Goffman, E. (1963) *Stigma: Notes on the Management of Spoiled Identity.* Englewood Cliffs, NJ: Prentice-Hall.

Gould, R.L. (1978) *Transformations: Growth and Change in Adult Life.* New York: Simon & Schuster.

Harry, J. and DeVall, W.B. (1978) *The Social Organization of Gay Males.* New York: Praeger.

Jourard, S.M. (1971) *The Transparent Self*, rev. edn. New York: Van Nostrand Reinhold.

Kanter, R.M. (1977) *Men and Women of the Corporation.* New York: Basic Books.

Kram, K.E. and Isabella, L.A. (1985) 'Mentoring alternatives: the role of peer relationships in career development', *Academy of Management Journal*, 28(1): 110–32.

Lee, J.A. (1977) 'Going public: a study in the sociology of homosexual liberation', *Journal of Homosexuality*, 3: 49–78.

Levinson, D.J. (1978) *The Seasons of a Man's Life.* New York: Ballantine.

McNaught, B. (1993) *Gay Issues in the Workplace.* New York: St Martin.

Moore, L. (1985) 'Issues for women in organizations', In A.G. Sargent (ed.), *Beyond Sex Roles.* St Paul, MN: West. pp. 215–25.

Rosaldo, R. (1993) *Culture and Truth: the Remaking of Social Analysis*, rev. edn. Boston: Beacon.

Schneider, B. (1981) 'Coming out at work: determinants and consequences of lesbians' openness at their workplace'. Paper presented at the Society for the Study of Social Problems annual meeting, August.

Stewart, T. (1991) 'Gay in corporate America', *Fortune*, 124 (16 December): 42–6.

Troiden, R.R. (1979) 'Becoming homosexual: a model of gay identity acquisition', *Psychiatry*, 42: 363–73.

Vaillant, G.E. (1977) *Adaptation to Life: How the Best and Brightest Came of Age.* Boston: Little, Brown.

Veroff, J., Douvan, E. and Kulka, R.A. (1981) *The Inner American.* New York: Basic Books.

Weinberg, M.S. and Williams, C.J. (1974) *Male Homosexuals: their Problems and Adaptations.* New York: Oxford University Press.

Woods, J.D. and Lucas, J. (1993) *The Corporate Closet: the Professional Lives of Gay Men in America.* New York: Free Press.

38

Taking action on harassment

Kerry Hawkins

Japan's labour ministry, after years of disbelief, has recently introduced a new word – *sekuhara*, or sexual harassment – and produced an official definition.

The Japanese no longer regard sexual harassment as a problem unique to foreigners. A government survey has shown that 26 per cent of Japanese women have experienced harassment at work.

The US Navy has issued a colour-coded guide to avoiding sexual harassment, denoting green for socially acceptable behaviour, amber for 'slow down to stop', and red for acts of harassment which should be stopped. This follows the Tailhook scandal, where naval aviators went on a drunken sexual rampage at their annual party.

Closer to home, the EC recommendation and subsequent code of practice on the 'Protection of the dignity of women and men at work' (1991) drew attention to the prevalence of sexual harassment at work and provided a framework for dealing with it. The IPM's 'Statement on harassment' (1992) offers advice on developing a policy and drew attention to the many grounds, other than sex, on which harassment can occur and the forms it can take.

In the UK, some progressive organisations have introduced harassment policies and many more are contemplating doing so. All the research into harassment demonstrates its prevalence and the serious consequences it can have for those who suffer it. The level and type of press interest, coupled with the removal of the upper limit for compensation at tribunal for discrimination cases, also create serious consequences for organisations that fail to deal with harassment effectively.

The main factor making the development of an effective harassment policy particularly challenging is the reluctance of victims to complain. To counter this, organisations need to create a climate in which people are sufficiently confident to raise problems [and] have access to effective procedures and appropriate support for resolving them, and where there is commitment to eliminating harassment in all its forms.

Abridged from K. Hawkins, 'Taking action on harassment', *Personnel Management*, March 1994, pp. 26–9.

The first task is to gain management acceptance that harassment is a problem in their organisation. Senior management may not understand what harassment is, or they may believe that their employees are above such things. Equally common is trivialising and legitimising harassment as 'just harmless fun'.

A simple 'litmus test' on sexual harassment (*see box*) has concentrated many minds on what is acceptable workplace behaviour and demonstrated that standards of acceptable behaviour have changed.

Litmus test for sexual harassment

Corning, an American company famous for its kitchenware, has found that a commonsense approach works. Its employees are told to apply four tests in deciding whether their behaviour constitutes sexual harassment:

- Would you say or do this in front of your spouse or parents?
- Would you say or do this in front of a colleague of the same sex?
- Would you like your behavior reported in a local newspaper?
- Does it need to be said or done at all?

Experience suggests that management will recognise that harassment is an issue when presented with: specific research evidence revealing its prevalence and impact; similar findings, often through chance, from their employee opinion surveys; competitors introducing harassment policies; the cost consequences of failing to address the problem effectively; trade union pressure; and incidents in the organisation – particularly involving a senior person.

The creation of a climate to challenge harassment begins with the policy. A firm, unequivocal statement from the top that harassment is totally unacceptable sends a clear message throughout the organisation.

There is a wealth of good quality advice available from publications like the IPM 'Statement' on what should be included in a harassment policy statement, and numerous networks and organisations are willing to share experiences, including the EOC's Equality Exchange and the National Harassment Network, University of Central Lancashire.

Scope of policy

One of the key decisions for policy makers is the scope of the policy. Many early initiatives focused on sexual harassment in isolation. As general awareness of harassment has increased, policies have had to be broadened to include such issues as race, religion, disability, and sexual orientation.

The fact that many staff are now being urged to improve performance and efficiency raises the question of whether undue pressure to perform should also be covered by the harassment policy. Unreasonable pressure to perform directed at individuals on grounds covered by law, including sex and race, is clearly harassment, and the policy should cover it. Other forms of undue pressure to perform may be better covered by existing grievance procedures.

The translation of the policy statement into detailed, effective procedures presents a challenge. The provision of effective routes for complainants to challenge harassment is a critical factor in overcoming reluctance to complain and providing a means to resolve problems.

Most complainants simply want the behaviour to stop: employers want to correct unacceptable behaviour and prevent it recurring. Other than in serious cases, there is likely to be a shared objective to resolve problems quickly and at a low-key level. Resolving problems in this way is likely to be less disruptive to work, maintain confidentiality and avoid unnecessary litigation and conflict.

Informal routes will be most effective if there are as many options as possible available, they are straightforward, and the complainant is supported throughout them.

Among the common options for the complainant at the informal stage are to: make a direct approach to the harasser alone; make an approach to the harasser accompanied by a colleague; make a written approach to the harasser; have access to a help-line or counsellor.

A higher level of support to the complainant is potentially more effective. Less common, informal options are to: make a direct approach to the harasser accompanied by a counsellor; ask a colleague to make the approach; ask a counsellor/adviser to make the approach; ask a supervisor, manager or the personnel department to deal with the problem on an informal basis.

A single harassment policy is unlikely to include all of these procedural routes, but they all feature in some. Whatever routes are included, they should be clearly explained during the communication process so that employees are aware of them.

Nor should more traditional options be forgotten. Eliminating harassment is high on the agenda of a number of trade unions who offer support and representation to their members.

The existence of counselling support for complainants throughout the procedures provides tangible evidence of organisational commitment and is the cornerstone of an effective harassment policy.

Where counsellors are included as a feature of the harassment policy, the role needs to be clear to the counsellors themselves, to supervisors and managers, and to employees. The key decision is whether the role should be restricted to a pure counselling one, or whether it should allow more representation and intervention. This decision is inextricably linked to what procedural routes for resolving complaints have been included in the policy, and to the amount of support the organisation wishes to provide to complainants.

Where the policy requires the complainant to take full responsibility for the complaint, the role may be restricted to one of pure counselling comprising an empathetic ear, an explanation of the procedural options, and, perhaps, behind-the-scenes support through assisting in the preparation of any written complaint or statement. Where the policy provides a higher level of support, the role may extend to accompanying the complainant at meetings with the alleged harasser or, less commonly, taking up the complaint on their behalf informally.

It is equally important to be clear that the role should not be to investigate complaints, or to encourage or discourage a course of action. Unless the limits of the counsellor role are clearly spelled out, there is likely to be widespread misunderstanding of it.

Who should take on the counsellor role? In practice, it is commonly assigned to personnel staff – they have counselling responsibility in their day-to-day jobs and harassment is seen as a personnel issue. Yet personnel staff may feel uneasy about the conflict between their management responsibility in investigation and grievance and the non-managerial counselling role. They may recognise they lack the level of skill needed for it. They may also be tempted to encourage complainants to use the informal routes because of a wish to protect the firm's interests, or they may want to resolve problems outside the confines of the counsellor role.

Any involvement of personnel staff as counsellors will preclude their participation in the investigation or discipline of the same case. Crucially, evidence suggests that many victims of harassment are reluctant to approach personnel staff because they are perceived as management. These factors suggest that the counselling role is better assigned elsewhere.

Employee volunteers avoid these problems. They often bring counselling skills from outside the organisation through prior work experience or voluntary work and are likely to be interested in the subject and committed to justice. The essential requirements are that they are volunteers who possess, or can acquire, the necessary skills through training. They should reflect the employee population they will serve – a mix of women and men, of ethnic groups and of grades. They should be sufficient in number and location to provide a speedy, effective response to victims of harassment.

Large, multi-site organisations may be reluctant to establish and train the number of counsellors necessary to provide adequate employee support. However, this can be done cost-effectively. British Gas introduced its harassment policy in 1991 as part of a well-established equal opportunities programme. It covers all its 70,000 staff.

Julie Mellor, equal opportunities director, says:

> We decided that for our harassment policy to be effective it was essential that counselling support was provided to any staff who requested it. Recognising the scale of the exercise, we employed external consultancy expertise to train our own training staff and to provide them with a comprehensive package which they were able to use to train the network of counsellors across the organisation. In this way, 295 counsellors were put in place quickly and cost-effectively. The research we have recently completed into the effectiveness of the harassment policy confirms their important role in reassuring staff of our commitment to eliminate harassment and giving them the confidence to resolve problems.

Training for counsellors is essential and is likely to include the fundamentals of what constitutes harassment, the routes for resolving problems within the policy, and practical exercises in counselling skills. Written guidelines on how to perform the role will reinforce the training. Top-up training and networks enable the counsellors to learn from each other's experiences in a confidential environment.

Supporting counsellors

Practical support needs to be given by the organisation to allow counsellors time away from work and facilities to undertake the role. Easy access to counsellors and the quality of the initial response is critical. The counsellor's role is unlikely to be time-consuming. British Gas has found that the typical time spent on counselling was 1.5 hours a month, though a number of counsellors were not called on at all.

Formal procedures for pursuing complaints will need to be included in the policy so that complainants have clear access to them if they choose. Existing grievance procedures are unlikely to be adequate for dealing with harassment for two reasons. First, they require complaints to be directed to the immediate boss, who may be the subject of the complaint. Secondly, they require the boss to carry out the investigation of the complaint – and experience indicates that they are unlikely to have the skills to do so to a sufficient standard.

Numerous tribunal cases point to the central importance of a prompt, thorough, impartial investigation of harassment complaints. The investigative role can be assigned either to management or to specially appointed investigators. Requiring line managers to take on the role reinforces their day-to-day managerial responsibility for eliminating harassment, but those involved would need extra skills.

One of the additional challenges when line managers are assigned responsibility for investigating harassment is that they are often men, dealing with complaints about male colleagues. They may find it difficult to consider complaints sufficiently seriously through embarrassment or scepticism, or because they do not understand what constitutes harassment, or because they underestimate its impact. Allowing line managers to investigate complaints of harassment unassisted, particularly in the early stages of a policy, is likely to be very risky.

Communications

These factors, coupled with the costs of equipping all line managers with the level of skill required, have led some organisations to conclude that a team of investigators should be appointed to undertake the investigative role in support of line managers. An alternative is to assign the role to personnel staff, or to ensure that personnel is involved in all investigations with line management as a matter of policy. Even where the investigation role is assigned to personnel staff, the findings of a review by British Gas of its harassment policy suggest that they are likely to request specific training in harassment investigations.

Properly designed and introduced, policies and procedures provide a framework for challenging harassment, but to be successful they must also be well communicated. Even among organisations with deserved reputations as 'equal opportunities employers', apprehension about the issue of harassment is so strong that a number have developed sound harassment policies which gather dust in their personnel manuals: all but the authors are oblivious to their existence.

An effective policy requires everyone to be aware of it, to believe their problems will be taken seriously, to understand the routes available to seek redress, and to know how to get access to counsellors or advisers.

Whitbread Inns introduced a harassment policy in 1993 as the first of its equal opportunities initiatives. Dick Pearson, personnel director, says:

The creation of a work environment free of harassment in our 1,600 outlets was an essential step to achieving equal opportunities. We were determined that all our staff would be fully aware of the harassment policy. An extensive process of communication took place, based on an established team briefing procedure. Our commitment to eliminating harassment and details of our policy and procedures were cascaded through the company. A leaflet was distributed to all staff specifying the names and telephone numbers of confidential counsellors, backed by a poster campaign. Harassment is a subject for induction of both staff and new manager appointments. In this way, everyone in the company should understand the policy and our commitment to it – but we will be reinforcing the message this year.

It is essential to ensure that managers and supervisors understand the policy and their role within it. Short workshops, typically of a half-day's duration, backed up by integration of harassment into general management training, can help achieve this. Where scale is a problem, workplace briefing and guidelines on the manager's role may be the most practical approach.

Firm central advice and co-ordination from personnel can ensure consistency and proper operation of the harassment policy. In the early stages it is likely that mistakes will occur. Typical problems include pressure on complainants for issues to be progressed informally, refusal to act on complaints, inadequate investigations, lenient or inconsistent disciplinary sanctions and misunderstanding of the counsellor role. Many of these problems result from a lack of training or asking too much of line managers.

It is only after the introduction of a harassment policy that managers will begin to appreciate the difficulties of their role within it. Calls from them for more training are then common.

Numbers of complaints

The common fear of a flood of complaints is not justified. Certainly there will be an increase in the number – it would be an indication of an unsuccessful initiative if there were not – but the incidence is likely to be low.

Experience with organisations employing many thousands of staff in a range of sectors is that annual complaints are counted in tens rather than hundreds, though many others are being resolved at the informal stage after counselling. Malicious complaints, another common concern, are exceptionally rare.

All the indications are that harassment will be an issue of increasing importance for employers. Developing an effective harassment policy presents significant challenges to the personnel function, but the experience of organisations who have done so provides valuable pointers to how those challenges can be met.

Dos and don'ts for managers

Do

- Set a good example by treating all staff and customers with dignity and respect.
- Be alert to, and correct, unacceptable behaviour.
- Ensure staff know how to raise harassment problems.
- Deal with any complaints fairly, thoroughly and confidentially, respecting the rights of all the parties.
- Remember the impact of the behaviour determines harassment, not the intent.

Don't

- Assume that no complaints means no problems.
- Try to dissuade people from making complaints.
- Assume that complainants are over-sensitive or trouble-makers.
- Accept 'I didn't mean any harm' as an excuse for harassment.
- Allow retaliation or victimisation.

POSTSCRIPT

39

A new deal for middle managers

Peter Herriot and Carole Pemberton

> My organisation has destroyed motivation, loyalty and trust, and has a long way
> to go to restore staff relationships – if it cares.
>
> Only when the economic climate becomes less oppressive will the pendulum
> swing from my organisation's attitude of 'do it or else' to one of worrying about
> staff turnover and nurturing loyalty instead of abusing it.

We don't often hear sentiments like these expressed out loud. They
don't make palatable reading for HR professionals trying to work in
the new business environment. But they are what many employees
are actually feeling, and we ignore them at our peril.

Those who feel this way are scared because they fear for their jobs,
or else what they have to say is drowned out by rhetoric which seeks
to persuade them that reality is the opposite of what they know from
their own experience to be true. Many are not only aware of the
structural changes in organisations, they can also explain why these
had to happen for them to survive. But few outside the HR department have recognised the huge impact these changes have had on
managers' motivation and morale.

Only now is it being recognised that all may not be well among
middle managers and professionals. We are hearing whispers of
'change weariness' and 'survivor syndrome'. The recent prize-winning
rechristening of HR in the magazine *Management Consultancy* was
'human remains'.

Many middle managers and professionals are feeling angry and
deceived. This is understandable – they thought they had a deal with
their organisation. To empathise with them, ask yourself: what was
the deal you had with your organisation in 1985 (or 1975 if you can
remember that far back)? For most people in larger organisations,
the psychological contract ran something like this: 'I gave them

From P. Herriot and C. Pemberton, 'A new deal for middle managers', *People
Management*, 15 June 1995, pp. 32–4.

loyalty, compliance and functional expertise, and they gave me security, regular promotions, salary increases and care in times of trouble.'

Not a bad deal for those who aren't too worried about excitement. Many of today's managers in their forties more than fulfilled their side of this bargain; they were the solid organisational citizens who were always willing to go the extra mile.

Yet by downsizing, outsourcing and delayering, many organisations have appeared to renege on their side of the old deal. Security is a thing of the past, and prospects of promotion are much reduced; the new plateau is often reached in one's thirties. In place of the old deal, organisations now offer constant challenge, and they reward those employees who are eager to meet it. In exchange they expect flexibility, responsibility, accountability, and the longest hours in Europe.

So people are angry, because the organisation broke the old deal unilaterally, although they are perfectly willing to concede that it couldn't continue as it was. They also feel aggrieved by the inequity of it all. The present deal seems considerably less favourable than the old one, and comparisons with top managers' salary increases and share options rub salt into the wounds. The final straw is to see their colleagues paid off at minimum expense, while those they hold responsible walk away with golden handshakes.

The following example was quoted in a Birkbeck College PhD thesis:

> There was a guy who had master-minded and written a brilliant client proposal and won a large contract in a very difficult competitive situation. At that time he was the best thing since sliced bread and earned a very fat bonus. Within four months he was made redundant. It reverberated round the corridors, because it was so unjust. There were no hidden reasons, they were thinning out his division and just picked on him. They left behind people who were nowhere near his calibre.[1]

So it's not just the contents of the new deal that have upset middle managers' sense of fairness; nor is it only the odious comparisons with those at the top. It's also the process. How old deals are broken and new ones imposed matters just as much as the balance of the deals themselves. If you're ending a relationship, they feel, at least do it decently to show that it mattered. Some redundancy procedures have treated people like cattle. Those who remain may believe they are next in line for the treatment; they clearly aren't valued either.

Another example from the Birkbeck thesis:

> Jim worked his guts out to fit three lots of staff together and to merge the client list. He had been highly commended, and hints had been dropped that he was in line for a big promotion. This particular day in question, Jim was called into the director's office. He straightened his tie, dusted his shoulders, wiped his shoes up

the back of his trouser legs, and in he went. He thought this is it – and it was! When he came back he looked terrible. He phoned his wife and she was crying, his secretary was crying, and in the end we were all crying. It was like receiving news of a sudden death in the family.

Yet those who are angry about unfairness at least feel they have a deal, albeit an unfair one. Others have lost all sense of agency and power. As they see it, the old deal was reneged upon, and the new deal, together with a biennial series of management fads, was imposed. Their advice was either not asked for or ignored. All they were allowed was the implementation, on top of all their other tasks. The organisation has been able to do what it likes, they feel. Instead of a deal – in which, by implication, each party needs what the other has to offer – the employment relationship feels as though it is one of ownership.

What we are seeing, though, isn't just feelings of anger and powerlessness. It's action, too; action which expresses these feelings in ways which are actively hostile to business needs. The strategic dilemma facing organisations is how to combine the cost competitiveness acquired so painfully over the past 10 years with the innovation needed to beat the competition into new niche markets. We can discern at least four forms of response:

- *Get ahead* seems appropriate to meet the new challenges, as long as it doesn't imply constant promotions.
- *Get safe* is a frequent one – taking risks is dangerous, so keep your head down below the parapet. Few innovative sparks fly there.
- *Get even* - the company has reduced what it is offering, so I'll put less into my side of the bargain.
- *Get out* - the ultimate hope for many; financial independence, or over to the other side of the fence where the grass is greener.

Middle managers are not, in general, unreasonable people. Our research revealed that they were still willing to be committed, despite the marked reduction in promotion prospects. What they want is more variety, more responsibility and the resources to help them meet these new demands. But job redesign and sideways postings are not enough. A whole range of new deals will have to be struck with individuals and honoured if mutual trust and commitment are to be restored; and more organisations will have to make the kinds of deals that we now look at.

While the imbalance in the psychological contract we have outlined above may be sustainable in the short term, as recovery returns, and as individuals learn to tolerate increased job insecurity, the issue of whether organisations can afford to leave individuals' careers up in the air will start to reassert itself. The issue is as much a business imperative, linked to the strategic possibilities of human resourcing, as it is one of employee satisfaction.

So what sort of contracts will HR professionals be managing in 2005? Our conclusion is that the changing balance of core and peripheral workers will have an impact not just on written contracts, which will increasingly differentiate between key and 'just in time' employees; it will equally influence the process of psychological contracting. As much as organisations will want flexibility, individuals will seek different forms of contract to meet their changing needs (Table 39.1).

The focus on core and peripheral workers has been based on organisational agendas, but it is also possible to consider work contracts in terms of their match with both individual and organisational needs. For example:

- Core working can meet individual and organisational needs for development.
- Project working can meet the individual and organisational need for an autonomous source of expertise.
- Part-time working can meet the individual and organisational need for flexibility through matching with lifestyle requirements.

Each of these 'contracts' carries both the potential for meeting individual and organisational needs and the threat of exploitation (see table). An employee who seeks to remain in the core, accepting demands for flexibility, a pay system contingent on their contribution, and total commitment, is visibly signalling the weight they give to security. If the organisation does not create a sense of security through ensuring their future employability, the contract will be seen as exploitative.

If a contractor who is hired for their technical expertise finds their contribution constrained by poor internal management, their expectations of challenge and autonomy will be undermined. Part-timers who offer flexibility may find the lifestyle benefits they expected to gain being threatened by demands that they are available at the employer's whim and price.

In a future defined by transactional contracting, do these risks matter? Has the stripping away of the relational model given both side *carte blanche* simply to protect their own interests? We believe it does matter, both to individuals and to human resource professionals.

Careers are becoming more complex sequences of actions, based on choices and constraints, which can take an individual from the core to the periphery and back again. HR staff will be involved not just in managing different contracts, but in brokering them for the same individual at different times in their career. An explicit role is emerging for HR as broker of the psychological contract.

Table 39.1 *The deals of 2005*

Contract	Individual offers	Organisation offers	Risks
Development (core)	Flexibility Continuous added value Commitment, not dependence Innovation	Security Employability Use of skills core to the organisation's purpose Continuous development	Exploitation of security needs Life imbalance Insufficient security to allow for risk-taking Generality of skills will reduce their external market value
Autonomy (project)	Ready access to specific skills Experience gained in a wide range of organisations High performance with low management	Autonomy to exercise skills Freedom in how individuals work Challenge Experience that increases employability	Performance delivery undermined by: inadequate resources, poor management or organisational politics/culture Constraints on how they work
Lifestyle (part-time)	Flexibility in matching demand and resourcing Performance levels to match customer expectations Performance levels of full-time employees	Willingness to balance work and other role demands	Pay and conditions exploitation Lack of career development

Figure 39.1   *The four stages of psychological contracting*

Personnel professionals must be capable of working with increasingly individualised needs, while simultaneously retaining a strategic perspective. It is the process management skills of HR that will be key to making that dialogue workable.

Figure 39.1 illustrates the much talked about, but frequently misunderstood, concept of the psychological contract. It also shows that contracting has to be based on a recognition of the interdependence between individuals and their organisation, through incorporating them into each of the four stages. Some UK organisations are already skilled in managing one or more of these stages. The challenge for the next 10 years is to integrate that process.

Stage 1: inform

Consider your own organisation: do employees know what is expected of them now and in the future? How do they learn about how the business is going? How confident are you that senior managers are well informed about what employees are thinking?

When we asked these questions, Hewlett-Packard (HP) seemed to have found some of the answers. It is perhaps not surprising that an information technology company should regard information-seeking and giving as of crucial importance. Feedback from the company's employee satisfaction survey, which highlighted staff concerns over decreased promotion prospects and increasing life imbalance, has led HP's chief executive in the UK, John Golding, to make career management the 1995 'breakthrough' issue – the one issue to which extraordinary attention will be given in the next year.

Hewlett-Packard already has multiple information systems, and now it also has a top-down commitment to finding out more. Its strategies for supporting effective career management include an employee feedback system, 360-degree appraisal, and framework profiling for devising individual skills from key result areas.

Stage 2: negotiate

Does your organisation engage in career negotiations that try to accord with employees' changing wants and needs? Does it provide explicit opportunities and occasions for career negotiations? Or does it negotiate only with those who are in a sellers' market?

It is salutary to be reminded that sometimes negotiating power does not lie in the employer's hand. Geraldine Bown of the Domino Consultancy recognises that her past negotiations with staff were based on universal concepts of fairness that she now believes are untenable. By using the principles she applied to the running of her business in the negotiating process, she found herself trapped by a growing spiral of employee demands. An offer made to meet an individual need quickly became a universal expectation. The balance of psychological contracting lay in the hands of those people she managed.

However, the recession forced the organisation to restructure, and this provided an opportunity to define new negotiating principles. Those principles are ones based on making offers which allow self-employed associates to deliver confidently to clients, while ensuring that Domino's quality expectations are not undermined. For Bown, the shift has been in redefining the meaning of an offer of employer loyalty and responsibility so it does not challenge business delivery.

Stage 3: monitor

Does the organisation check whether it is in the process of developing skills and knowledge to meet likely future needs? Does it monitor labour market trends to discover the likely availability of skills and knowledge? Or does it only monitor the concerns of those who are on the 'fast track'?

In all the attention given to the impact of Rover's 'New Deal' for shopfloor workers, it was not immediately apparent that it would have implications for those staff who managed them. As the benefits of an end to compulsory redundancies and the death of clocking on were being felt by one group of employees, middle managers were simultaneously feeling that they had lost important levers of control.

Senior management recognised that the value of the managerial deal was seen to have diminished, and have consciously sought to rebalance it. Managerial autonomy has been increased, coaching [has been] offered to support a new leadership role, and performance self-assessment and development reviews [have been] introduced. This new deal is not made explicit, but its norms have quickly become embedded in the managerial culture of Rover.

Stage 4: renegotiate or exit

Does the organisation know the career points at which people are most likely to leave voluntarily and look to renegotiate with them before they leave, or does it see a request for a change of contract as a reduction of commitment?

The nature of accountancy training and career progression has made KPMG Peat Marwick skilled in managing renegotiation and exit at key career transition points. Its ability to retain many of those staff who do not achieve partner status is testimony to those renegotiation skills. Accountants it does not wish to retain after they complete their articles are 'counselled out'. They are given advance warning of the decision, not held to departure by a set date, and given help in their job search.

The process is managed sensitively, according to KPMG personnel partner David Westcott, because 'it's important that people leave feeling good about us. One day they could be our clients.' Leavers are treated as alumni, sent professional information and invited back to events. It is enlightened self-interest to manage exit with the same care as entry, and to look for scope for renegotiation rather than risk experience loss.

We have looked at each of these stages from the organisation's perspective, but equal attention must also be given to the employee in this process. As the model shows, for individual employees to be able to enter psychological contracting as equal partners, they need to be equally skilled in looking at each of the four processes, both from their own perspective and that of the organisation. They need assistance in identifying where opportunities are increasing or decreasing in the organisation; how their career objectives can be broken down into time frames for negotiation; how well they monitor changes in themselves as well as the environment; and how to judge the right time to look to renegotiate.

Human resource professionals are well positioned to help individuals construct more satisfactory 'deals', and to increase the organisation's awareness of the need for creating post-transactional contracts. HR as broker of the psychological contract – could this be a new role for the next decade?

Notes

1 W.E.G. Manning, 'The content of the psychological contract between employees and organisations in Great Britain in the early 1990s', PhD thesis, Birkbeck College, University of London, 1992.

Index

risk-taking, 259
rituals: in macho cultures, 91–2; in
    process cultures, 99–100; in work-
    hard/play-hard cultures, 94
Robbins, S.P., 22, 115
Robertson, T., 280
role reversal, 274–5
roles, and processes, in teamwork,
    199–201
Rosaldo, R., 322
Rostow, W.W., 170
Rover, 341–2
Rusk, Dean, 174

sales organisations, 89, 93, 94
satisficing, 157–9
Schein, E.H., 113, 115
Schlesinger, Arthur, 171, 172, 173, 174
Schneider, B., 319, 320
Schwartz, P., 320
security, 25, 253, 259, 336, 339
selection, 131–8, 151, 153, 291; and
    person-organisation fit, 139–49
self-appraisal, 236
self-awareness, 37–8; lack of, 272
self-censorship, 173
self-disclosure, of professional gay men,
    312–14
self-fulfilling prophecy, 246
self-interest, 41
self-perception inventory, 183–7
self-respect, 259
'Seven Ages of Team' myth, 193
sex talk, 295–7
sexual harassment, 298–300; action on,
    327–34
sexuality, 24, 295–7, 304; and
    harassment, 298–300 and
    organisational politics, 300–1
silence, 284
Simon, Herbert, 157–8
skills, 143, 291–2; low use of, 63, 78
Small, Stephen, 291
'smart macho culture', 108–9, 110
Smircich, L., 113
social sex role division, 255
socialisation, 29, 153–4
speech: errors in, 284–5; non-verbal
    aspects of, 283–5

stability of employment, 30, 53–4, 55–6,
    57
staff development, 20–1; *see also*
    management development
Steffy, B.D., 85
stereotypes, 23, 162, 230, 267–70;
    groupthink and, 171–2; and
    homosexuality, 320; of women,
    223, 225–6
Stevens, James, 258
stress, 14–15, 77, 147; coping with, *see*
    stress management; groupthink
    and, 168–9; job characteristics
    influencing, 62–6, 78–80;
    organisational change and, 128–9;
    reduction of, 66–7; research on
    causes of, 61–2
stress management, 70–1, 74–5, 80–3,
    82–5; case studies in, 71–4
subconscious cultural blinders, 271–2
Sun Microsystems, 140, 144
support systems, for gay professionals,
    314–16
sympathy, 41

targets, ethnic and gender, 290–1
tasks: processes and, 196–7; for
    teamwork, 195
Taylor, Donald, 269
team roles, amd self-perception,
    182–9
teams, 19–20, 124, 126, 179–81; failures
    of, 206–8; myths about, 192–3;
    new model of, 194–203; norms of,
    167, 168; using knowledge
    through, 190–2
technological gatekeeping, 125
technology transfer, 260
Thatcher, Margaret, 223, 224, 277
theory, 1–5, 9–10
Thompson, J.C., 170
timing, in speech, 284
tokenism, 291
tone of voice, 283–4
total quality management, 10, 234
touch/touch avoidance, 278–9
tough-guy, macho culture, 89–93
Toyota, 10, 140, 144, 206
trade unions, 57, 67, 208
traditionalists, 200, 201

Printed in the United Kingdom
by Lightning Source UK Ltd.
129074UK00001B/67-87/P